# Modernity and Independence

## Essays on the Hispanic Revolutions

François-Xavier Guerra

Translated by **Patricia Simonson, Mariana Ortega-Breña** and **Victoria Furio**

Foreword by **Geneviève Verdo**

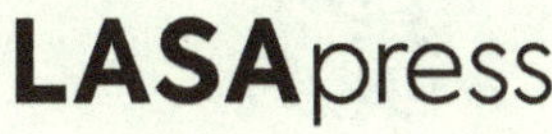

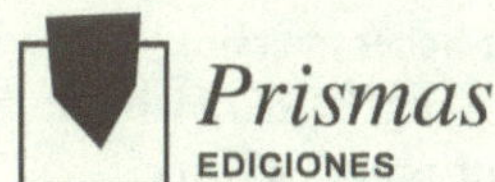

Latin American Intellectual History Series
LASA Press and Prismas Ediciones
www.lasapress.org / www.historiaintelectual.com.ar
lasa@lasaweb.org / centrohistoriaintelectual@gmail.com



*Modernidad e independencias. Ensayos sobre las revoluciones hispánicas* was originally published in Spanish by Editorial MAPFRE, 1992.

Centro de Historia Intelectual has received support for this initiative from the Open Society Foundations.

Cover design: Estudio Entre
Cover image: ©MALI
Print version typesetting: Lara Melamet
Digital versions typesetting: Estudio Ebook
Copy editor: Melina Kervandjian
Index: Florencia Osuna

ISBN (Paperback b&w version): 978-1-951634-62-9
ISBN (PDF): 978-1-951634-63-6
ISBN (EPUB): 978-1-951634-64-3
ISBN (Kindle): 978-1-951634-65-0
DOI: https://doi.org/10.25154/book18



Suggested citation:
Guerra, François-Xavier. 2026. *Modernity and Independence: Essays on the Hispanic Revolutions.* Pittsburgh/Buenos Aires: LASA Press and Prismas Ediciones. DOI: https://doi.org/10.25154/book18. License: CC BY-NC 4.0.

To read the free, open-access version of this book online, visit https://doi.org/10.25154/book18 or scan this QR code with your mobile device:

# About the Latin American Intellectual History Series

The Latin American Intellectual History Series is a joint initiative of LASA Press and Prismas Ediciones (Centro de Historia Intelectual, Universidad Nacional de Quilmes). The series is part of the existing LASA Press collection, In Translation: Key Books in Latin American Studies, with a more specific objective: the translation into English of works that are significant to the field of Latin American intellectual history.

In alignment with the long-standing tradition of the Centro de Historia Intelectual, the series defines this field in a very broad way, as the historical study of the symbolic dimension of social life. This is an inclusive definition of various traditions, welcoming diverse perspectives, from conceptual history to the history of ideas, from the sociology of intellectuals to cultural history, among many others. The scope includes ideas viewed as acts of discourse, ideological languages, and works of thought and of artistic expression, examining how these elements are woven into the social fabric, tracking the trajectories of intellectuals and the institutions they both inhabit and create. The approach balances the intrinsic meaning of a work with its materiality—the textual or physical formats through which ideas are produced and circulated. It may also include the study of more diffuse cultural dimensions, such as social imaginaries, collective representations, and urban cultures.

The series selects books already regarded as foundational for their contributions to understanding the cultural life of the continent, alongside innovative new works that challenge and renew the methodologies of intellectual history.

Denis Auguste Marie Raffet (French,1804–1860), *Memorable y decisiva batalla de Ayacucho (en el Perú), el 9 de diciembre del año 1824 (Memorable and Decisive Battle of Ayacucho [in Peru], on December 9, 1824)*, 1826, lithograph on paper, 33.4 × 44.5 cm. © Lima Art Museum, Collections Development Committee 2013, gift of Ana María Guiulfo.

# Note on the translation

The introduction and Chapters 1-4 were translated by Patricia Simonson; chapters 5-7 were translated by Mariana Ortega-Breña, and chapters 8-10 were translated by Victoria Furio. Chapters 5-10 were revised by Patricia Simonson, Natalia Maljuf and Cristina Soriano.

# Table of Contents

# Foreword to the English Edition

Geneviève Verdo[1]

Exceptional in many respects, the book the reader has opened was considered a classic even shortly after its release. Few works have had such an impact on the field of Spanish American studies, and many commentators have identified a "before" and an "after" *Modernidad e independencias. Ensayos sobre las revoluciones hispánicas* in the historiography of nineteenth-century Latin America. In this collection of ten essays, French historian François-Xavier Guerra offers a comprehensive interpretation of the revolutions in the Hispanic world from 1808 to 1825, as well as, more broadly, of the political and cultural mutation brought about by the advent of modernity. In so doing, he lays the foundations for a new paradigm for rethinking the political and social history of Spain and Spanish America in the nineteenth century and beyond.

In 1992, when the book was published in Madrid, François-Xavier Guerra was at the peak of a career that would come to an abrupt end with his premature death ten years later. Of Spanish origin, but educated in Paris and Grenoble, this specialist in the French labor movement joined the Sorbonne in 1970 as *maître-assistant.* Under the supervision of François Chevalier, a historian of large landholdings in Mexico, he undertook a thesis on the origins of the Mexican Revolution. This work,

1 Geneviève Verdo is professor of contemporary Latin American history at Université de Paris 1 Panthéon-Sorbonne, and director, CRALMI (Centre de Recherches sur l'histoire de l'Amérique Latine et du Monde Ibérique).

defended in 1983 and published in 1985 under the title *Le Mexique: De l'ancien régime à la révolution*, was recognized both for the originality of its approach and the importance of its contributions. In it, François-Xavier Guerra inaugurates a method that would henceforth become his trademark, paying particular attention to individual and collective actors, as documented by an impressive prosopographical survey. He was thus able to highlight the gap that existed at the end of the Porfirian era between the modernity of watchwords and the traditional character of social relations, structured by networks and clienteles.

Having replaced François Chevalier as chair of Latin American history in 1985, he turned his attention to the revolutions of independence. By his own admission, "these first revolutions seem far more important [than the others], in that they brought about a profound change in mental structures [and] cultural references."[2] This passion for the revolutionary processes of the early nineteenth century, this determination to decipher them and restore their intelligibility, is at the root of a prolific body of work, of which *Modernidad e independencias* is the quintessence.

These were propitious times for such questioning. In France, the 1980s saw the revival of political history, a history that opened up to other social sciences and turned its back on structuralist analyses, rehabilitating the individual, the short term, and the weight of events. At that time, Guerra was drawing inspiration from the anthropologist Louis Dumont[3] for thinking about holistic societies, rediscovering Augustin Cochin[4] and the importance of sociability, and reading sociologists of collective action and methodological individualism. He was also in passionate discussion with his Sorbonne colleagues, notably Alain Corbin

---

2 Alicia Salmeron and Elisa Speckman, "Entrevista a François-Xavier Guerra," *Históricas: Boletín del Instituto de Investigaciones Históricas* 50 (1997): 32.

3 Author, among others, of *Homo Hierarchicus: Essai sur le système des castes* (Paris: Gallimard, 1966) and *Essais sur l'individualisme: Une perspective anthropologique sur l'idéologie moderne* (Paris: Le Seuil, 1983).

4 French historian and sociologist (1876–1918), famous for his work on the French Revolution and the "societies of thought" that, according to him, were at its origin. François Furet praised his work in *Penser la Révolution française* (Paris: Gallimard, 1978).

and Roger Chartier, whose interest in the history of cultural sensibilities and practices he shared. At the time of the bicentenary of the French Revolution,[5] he was close to François Furet and his intellectual premises. To paraphrase Furet, Guerra set out to "think the Hispanic revolutions." His initial findings point to the existence of a "rupture" model common to these revolutions and the French Revolution, a comparison that opens *Modernidad e independencias.*

If this book is presented as a collection of essays, focusing on historiographical and conceptual issues, it is precisely because the author intends to "think" the Hispanic revolutions, rather than simply provide an account of them.[6] The book's central theme is the transformation of social and political imaginaries engendered by the revolutions triggered by Napoleon's invasion of Spain in 1808.

The first point on which Guerra's interpretation breaks new ground is his choice of the Spanish monarchy[7] as the framework for his study. Now that imperial and global history have become established categories of analysis, it is worth emphasizing what was, at the time, a fundamental turning point in the approach to Spanish American independence. Until then, Spain and America had turned their backs on each other: American patriotic history (*historia patria*) focused on national variants of the phenomenon (Chilean, Colombian, Mexican independence, etc.), while in Spain, hardly anyone worked on this subject. By highlighting the simultaneity and similarity of Spanish and American reactions to the 1808 invasion, Guerra demonstrates the validity of considering the Spanish empire as a framework for intelligibility. Far from being a sui

5 In 1989, the fall of the Berlin Wall had a profound influence on François-Xavier Guerra's thinking. The dismantling of the Soviet bloc, conceived as an empire, inspired him enormously in his conceptualization of the process affecting the Hispanic world at the beginning of the nineteenth century.

6 In his view, "history cannot remain a mere description of phenomena or partial knowledge, but must have the ambition to propose global explanations." Verónica Zárate Toscano, "Entrevista con François-Xavier Guerra," in *Una docena de visiones de la historia: Entrevistas con historiadores americanistas* (Mexico: Instituto Mora, 2004).

7 "Monarchy" is used here in the territorial sense, referring to the whole of peninsular Spain and the territories of the Crown of Castile.

generis phenomenon, Spanish American independence had its origins in the crisis that shook the metropolis: born in Spain in response to the absence of the king, the liberal revolution reached the American territories, which declared independence after several years of war. This observation leads to an essential conclusion: it is from the dismantling of the Spanish empire that today's nations emerged; they are the outcome, not the starting point, of the Hispanic revolutions. Guerra's interpretation thus contributes to the denationalization of the history of American independence.

This choice of the "Hispanic world" as a framework for analysis implies a constant back-and-forth between Spain and the American territories. In the essays, the focus is sometimes on the Peninsula (chapter VII), sometimes on empire (chapters VI and VIII), and most often on the whole. Far from ignoring or minimizing the variety of these contexts, Guerra demonstrates that what unifies them is the coherence of cultural references and practices (reading habits, sociability) and political and social imaginaries (the Catholic religion, but also the "pactist" imaginary, characteristic of the Spanish "composite monarchy").

The essays devoted to the legal, political, and sociocultural structures of the monarchy are interspersed with "focuses" on a particular moment, hitherto neglected by historiography: that of the "two crucial years" (1808–1809) when everything turned upside down. This choice reflects the methodological attention paid by Guerra and the proponents of political history to the role of the event and its disruptive character: "Revolutionary periods," he asserted, "can be defined as periods in which the event is king, in which short time is essential [...] in which events radically and irreversibly alter the situation [...] in which the real players come to light, along with the actual workings of the political system, the premises on which it rests."[8]

This decisive shift in 1808–1809, during which the figure of the king was supplanted by the implementation of political representation, was accompanied by a no less decisive cultural mutation, driven by the "political pedagogy" of the liberal press. Herein lies one of the book's

8 Marcela Ferrari, Julio C. Melon, and Elisa Pastoriza, "Entrevista a François-Xavier Guerra," *Secuencia* 37 (1997): 137–52.

fundamental theses: the rapidity with which modernity took root in the Hispanic world was the result of cultural practices—literacy, reading, elite sociabilities—that prepared and preceded the "reign of opinion." In addition to the essential political upheaval represented by the transfer of sovereignty from the king to the people, the great revolution was one of the imaginary, which took place in the space of just a few years and took a lasting hold on the public sphere. This explains the rapid and irreversible triumph of the most preeminent "figures of modernity," the nation and the sovereign people (alongside the citizen, the public space, or the republic...), which are the subjects of the last two chapters.

In evoking this complex process, Guerra once again places the emphasis on actors, leading him to question the concept of the "bourgeois revolution" so dear to his contemporaries. These include collective actors—local elites, town councils (*ayuntamientos*), members of the militias, kinship groups, clienteles, village communities—as well as a new breed of actors, now dedicated to conquering and exercising power. According to Guerra, during this process, "modern" principles were grafted onto societies that remained "holistic" (today, we would rather say "corporate") and structured by "tradition." This hybridization of "tradition and modernity" is regarded as characteristic of the Hispanic revolutions and, more broadly, of the Spanish American variant of liberalism.[9] Guerra was not the first to put forward this specificity, but the coherence of his demonstration and its systemic character have transformed this interpretation into a genuine paradigm. Historians now read the period of revolutions and independence in the light of *Modernidad e independencias*, adopting these interpretations and analytical tools as a new "grammar" for revisiting the Spanish and Latin American nineteenth century.

From this point of view, the impact of *Modernidad e independencias*—written in Spanish and distributed very rapidly in Latin America—was massive and incredibly fruitful. The book strongly accompanied—indeed, even sparked—a renewed interest in the "era of revolutions." It has to be said that the context was particularly propitious, with the structuralist paradigm running out of steam, the reestablishment of

9 Annick Lempérière, "Avant propos," in *Penser l'histoire de l'Amérique latine: Hommage à François-Xavier Guerra* (Paris: Éditions de la Sorbonne, 2020), 12.

democratic regimes and the interest of Latin American historians in issues addressed by the new political history such as citizenship, elections, political mobilization, public spaces, or democratization processes. By highlighting Latin America's full participation in the Atlantic revolutions and its early liberal and democratic experiences, *Modernidad e independencias* made these experiences appear as political laboratories. Rediscovered in this way, the revolutions of independence gave substance to another myth of origins, no longer that of nations, so dear to the *historia patria*, but that of Latin American democracies.

Like all great works, especially those in the essay form, *Modernidad e independencias* has also provoked passionate debates. Among other issues, the binomial "tradition and modernity" has been the subject of criticism. While some authors have highlighted the teleological nature of Guerra's equation of modernity with individualism and progress,[10] others have criticized the "all-purpose" nature of the category, which can be used to interpret extremely diverse situations, and have stressed Guerra's lack of attention to other aspects of modernity, such as equality of conditions or secularization.[11]

The vigor of these criticisms in itself testifies to the importance of the work and the questions it raised, which Guerra himself took up in his later work[12] and which other historians have subsequently developed. Some of the book's themes, such as the question of sociability and the public sphere, or the existence of a Euro-American cultural space, have

10 Elías Palti, *El tiempo de la política: El siglo XIX reconsiderado* (Buenos Aires: Siglo XXI), 2007.

11 Medófilo Medina Pineda, "En el Bicentenario: Consideraciones en torno al paradigma de François-Xavier Guerra sobre las 'revoluciones hispánicas'," *Anuario Colombiano de Historia Social y de la Cultura* 37, no. 1 (2010): 149–88; Roberto Breña, "Diferendos y coincidencias en torno a la obra de François-Xavier Guerra (una réplica a Medófilo Medina Pineda)," *Anuario Colombiano de Historia Social y de la Cultura* 38, no. 1 (2011): 281–300.

12 These have been the subject of an exhaustive publication: François-Xavier Guerra, *Figuras de la modernidad: Hispanoamérica siglos XIX–XX*, Annick Lempérière and Georges Lomné, eds. (Bogotá: Taurus-Universidad Externado de Colombia, 2012).

inspired numerous historians.[13] Among them are the doctoral students Guerra trained, many of whom now hold university positions in France and Latin America. Beyond the themes, his methodological proposals have also won support: the refusal of methodological nationalism, the option for comparative and conceptual history, discourse analysis, and attention to the actors (notably through the use of prosopography) have been benchmarks that have changed the way we work with sources.

Nearly thirty years—the span of a generation—have passed since *Modernidad e independencias* was first published. What conclusions can we draw? First of all, the bicentenary of Spanish American independence and of the liberal revolution in Spain has led to a proliferation of works on this period, definitively inscribing Hispanic and Luso-American cases in the repertoire of Atlantic revolutions. Compared with Guerra's work, these new contributions have of course innovated: the periodization has evolved, with many studies now taking as their starting point the Bourbon reforms, at the end of the eighteenth century, and going right up to the symbolic date of 1830, which saw the breakup of Bolivarian Colombia. The focus shifted to other actors, less present in Guerra's research agenda: men-at-arms and the phenomenon of warfare, popular sectors in general, and Amerindians, free people of color (*castas*), and slaves in particular. Hispanic liberalism, captured through the variations of the Cádiz Constitution in America, had its moment of glory.[14] The question of religion, clergy, and secularization was raised,

---

13 Pilar González Bernaldo de Quiroz, *Civilité et politique aux origines de la nation argentine: Les sociabilités à Buenos Aires, 1829–1862* (Paris: Publications de la Sorbonne, 1999); Olivier Compagnon, *Jacques Maritain et l'Amérique du Sud: Le modèle malgré lui* (Villeneuve-d'Ascq: Presses Universitaires du Septentrion, 2003); Marco Morel, *As transformações dos espaços públicos: Imprensa, atores políticos e sociabilidades na cidade imperial* (São Paulo: Hucitec, 2005).

14 Examples include Manuel Chust and Ivana Frasquet, *La transcendencia del liberalismo doceañista en España y en América* (Valencia: Generalitat Valenciana, 2004); Jaime E. Rodríguez, ed., *The Divine Charter: Constitucionalism and Liberalism in Nineteenth-Century Mexico* (Lanham: Rowman & Littlefield, 2005); Roberto Breña, *El primer liberalismo español y los procesos de emancipación de América, 1808–1824: Una revisión historiográfica del*

as was the fate of counter-revolutionaries. Important methodological innovations, introduced by the critical history of law[15] and the history of concepts,[16] deepened some of the fundamental intuitions present in *Modernidad e independencias*. The predominance of jurisdictional culture, for example, now makes it possible to understand how the old conception of law was constitutionalized at the time of independence, shedding new light on the articulation between "tradition" and "modernity." These results have been extended to the entire history of the nineteenth century, which has been profoundly renewed by the revaluation of republican, democratic, and even socialist cultures.[17] Nevertheless, while these works, in their richness and variety, have refined or complemented Guerra's analyses, none of them has brought out a new paradigm enabling us to interpret differently, as he himself did at the time,

---

*liberalismo hispánico* (Mexico City: Colegio de México, 2006); Javier Fernández Sebastián, ed., *La aurora de la libertad: Los primeros liberalismos en el mundo iberoamericano* (Madrid: Marcial Pons, 2012).

15 This is mainly the work of the Historia Cultural e Institucional del Constitucionalismo en España (y América) (HICOES) group, founded in Madrid in 1996. Among its most representative titles, Carlos Garriga and Marta Lorente, *Cádiz, 1812: La Constitución jurisdiccional* (Madrid: Centro de Estudios Políticos y Constitucionales, 2007); Marta Lorente and José María Portillo, *El momento gaditano: La Constitución en el orbe hispánico (1808–1826)* (Madrid: Congreso de los Diputados, 2012).

16 Javier Fernández Sebastián, dir., *Diccionario político y social del mundo iberoamericano*, vol. 1, *La era de las revoluciones 1750–1850* (Madrid: Fundación Carolina-Sociedad Estatal de Conmemoraciones Culturales-Centro de Estudios Políticos y Constitucionales, 2009); vol. 2, *Conceptos políticos fundamentales, 1770–1870* (Madrid: Universidad del País Vasco, Centro de Estudios Políticos y Constitucionales, 2014).

17 James Sanders, *The Vanguard of the Atlantic World: Creating Modernity, Nation, and Democracy in Nineteenth-Century Latin America* (Durham and London: Duke University Press, 2014); Hilda Sabato, *Republics of the New World: The Revolutionary Political Experiment in Nineteenth-Century Latin America* (Princeton and Oxford: Princeton University Press, 2018); Clément Thibaud and Eugenia Palieraki, *L'Amérique Latine embrasée: Deux siècles de révolutions et de contre-révolutions* (Paris: Armand Colin, 2023).

the fundamental mutation taking place at the dawn of the nineteenth century in Latin America.

Sociable, insatiably curious, and attentive to the events of his time, François-Xavier Guerra was characterized by his openness to the world, and enjoyed practicing as much as theorizing about intellectual circulations, encounters, and exchanges. Although he was linked, by friendship or polemic, to many British and American historians, the dissemination of his work in the English-speaking world remained limited, which is why we particularly welcome the publication of this translation, which we hope preserves intact, beyond the years, the book's power to invite discussion and generate new dialogues.

Paris, October 2024

# INTRODUCTION

## A Unique Revolutionary Process

In 1808, a period of profound transformations began throughout the Hispanic world. In Spain, this date marks the onset of the liberal revolution; in Spanish America, the first stages of the process that would lead to independence. These phenomena are of crucial importance, and they pose several problems of interpretation.

The first is their mutual relationship. Most studies have approached these radical upheavals as if they were two independent phenomena, perhaps because we still see them through the eyes of the nineteenth-century historians, whether American or Spanish, for whom the frame of reference was the nation-state. The former sought to use the independence "revolutions" to give legitimacy to the emancipation of the new Spanish American "nations" and the creation of modern political regimes. For the latter, the liberal revolution was the central and self-sufficient theme for a Spain torn apart by its traumatic passage to modernity. They all quickly forgot the political structure that had preceded their existence as separate states: the ancien régime structure formed by the Spanish monarchy, with its two pillars, as they called them at the time—Spain and Spanish America.

Studies on Spanish America would certainly include references to peninsular events, and Spanish ones would mention American issues; but in both cases the references were contextual elements, with no real interpretive weight. Of course, it was important to understand Spain's policy toward America, since it partly determined the struggle for emancipation; in Spain it was also important, though less so, to remember the existence of the Spanish American insurgents, in order to contextualize military and financial issues. But in both cases, these obligatory references pointed to external causes. We find this perspective too limited, since both phenomena—the Spanish liberal revolution and the Spanish American wars of independence—are constantly intertwined in all the sources. As we will try to show in the following pages, they form, in fact, a single process, beginning with the abrupt intrusion of modernity into an ancien régime monarchy and leading to the breakup of this political whole into many sovereign states, one of which would become present-day Spain.

The global character of this process can be better understood now than it could a few years ago, since we have just witnessed how the crisis experienced by another great political conglomerate (though of a different kind)—the USSR—ended up giving rise to a multitude of new states.

The second problem has to do with the nature of the process. For its protagonists, and for a long historiographical tradition, it was undoubtedly a revolutionary process. For the Spanish Americans, from the outset, it was *the* revolutionary age par excellence. For the Spaniards, also from the start, there could be no doubt about its revolutionary character. However, this terminological consensus conceals considerable differences, depending on what is meant, or has been meant, by *revolution*. Though clear to its protagonists, our period's revolutionary character tends to become blurred, if not downright questionable, when revolution is seen primarily as a radical transformation of social and economic structures, or as the access to power for a new social class.

Since in Spanish America independence involved few substantial changes in the deeper economic or social structures, in recent years there has been a tendency to downplay its revolutionary nature. Many authors have come to see the revolution of independence as a "purely political" phenomenon, whose importance is therefore relatively minor compared to the structural continuities. "Purely political" refers here both to the break with the metropolis and to the fact that the Creoles replaced the peninsulars in power.

In Spain, the revolutionary character of the process that began in 1808 continues to be broadly accepted, but often the adjective "liberal" is used to diminish to some extent the force of the word "revolution," as if indicating a limited variety: the transition from the ancien régime to a bourgeois society, both of which are defined primarily by their institutional, social, and economic features. In both cases, in Spain and in America, scholars use criteria taken from classical interpretations of the French Revolution to speak, at the most, of a bourgeois revolution, carried out in Spain by a revolutionary bourgeoisie, or in Spanish America by a Creole one.

But such interpretations are becoming more and more difficult to uphold. To limit these revolutions to a series of institutional, social, or economic changes leaves out the most visible feature of the period: the actors' own awareness, reflected in all the sources, that they were entering a new era, founding a new man, a new society, and a new kind of politics. This new man was an individual, sundered from the bonds of the old society of estates and corporate bodies; the new society was one based on contracts and born out of a new social pact; the new politics were the expression of a new sovereign—the people—through competition between those who sought to embody or represent it. To consider only the concrete measures of institutional, social, or economic reform leads us to downplay the novelty as well as the effectiveness of the process. In this area, we find precedents for almost all these measures in the Enlightenment period: as Tocqueville already pointed out with respect to the French Revolution, it brought to completion many processes begun under the ancien régime.

Nor did the radical innovation lie in the existence of a new global system of references combining the ideas, social constructs, values, and behaviors which were to shape the new man and the new society. To a great extent, all these innovations had begun to emerge throughout the eighteenth century among limited groups of men gathering in new forms of sociability. What was radically new was the creation of a public sphere of action, when this new system of references left the private circles in which till then it had been cloistered and burst into the open. We see then the triumph of a new legitimacy—that of the nation or the sovereign people—and a new kind of politics with actors belonging to a new class, who can, for the first time, be called *political*, insofar as they came into being precisely in order to conquer this new legitimacy.

The victory of all these transformations, which we sum up under the single term "modernity," is what caused this radical break of which the actors themselves have left a record. However profound the concrete measures of reform may or may not have been, however serious the vicissitudes of the struggle between the revolutionaries and their opponents, the break was manifest and irreversible. Subsequent attempts might occur to restore the ancien régime, but they could no longer be mere returns to the past; instead, they would have to be new regimes aiming, for a time, to set limits on the new politics and the new underlying system of references.

Now we can examine the question of who the actors were. Can we affirm that the new frame of reference and the concrete measures it inspired were conceived and imposed by a specific social group, and that this group was bourgeois? To a great extent, we already know the answer. If we look closely at the circles in which the new standards made progress, and at the main actors of the revolutionary process, we will certainly find some members of the bourgeoisie, along with a much greater number of nobles and patricians, members of the clergy, professors and students, public employees, and so forth: a whole group of men whose common feature was not a single socioeconomic status, but their belonging to the same cultural universe. The triumphant bourgeoisie is *introuvable*—nonexistent. As the present example of the countries of Eastern Europe and the USSR clearly shows, the progression toward a social system centered on the individual and toward representative democracy is not linked to a hypothetical bourgeoisie, but to cultural and political transformations acting on the groups in power and on society.

That is why we have chosen a deliberately political and cultural viewpoint. *Political* in the strongest sense of the word: that of the relations of alliance and opposition, authority and subordination between social actors. It is obvious that there is also an economic component to such relations. It follows that a "political" point of view does not ignore economic or socioeconomic aspects but seeks rather to achieve a more complete analysis. This approach necessarily includes the socioeconomic dimension in the study as one of the variables which constitute the actor and his relations to other actors. Given the preliminary nature of these essays, we will deal with these aspects, and therefore with socioeconomic topics, only in passing.

But the relation between the actors was not governed merely by a mechanical interaction of forces, but also, and above all, by the cultural codes prevailing at a given moment among a social group or a series of groups. Any social relationship includes a fundamental cultural component: How is society conceived or imagined? What constitutes the social bond? What kind of authority is considered legitimate? What are its functions? What powers are usually attributed to it? What are the mutual rights and duties of those who govern and those who are governed? Every social unit, from the smallest to the largest, has its own answers to this sort of question.

Every social organization also contains, albeit only implicitly, its own model of the ideal society, which can just as easily be located in the past or in the future: it can as easily be a nostalgic vision or a project, or both at the same time, since the return to the Golden Age has often been a major driving force of revolutions. This is the terrain where we find models or projects of societies in close connection to the principles of legitimacy and to values: a key field of study in which our period holds a privileged place, since it was precisely the time when the radical changes took place that made it the revolutionary age par excellence in the Hispanic world. We have here a vast field of study: that of the social and political imagination, of values and behaviors, which will provide the main topics for these essays.

Finally, there remains a third problem: the relationship between the Hispanic Revolution and the French Revolution, only twenty years apart. To speak of the possible filiation or kinship between these two revolutions is unavoidable, since the French Revolution not only disrupted the European political balance, but presented a social, political, and cultural phenomenon so new that it dominated—as something to be emulated or rejected—the entire European political debate of the day.

Curiously, what at first sight might seem a topic for academic analysis has given rise to passionate debate and controversy in political discussions on both sides of the Atlantic. The forms and timing of the debate have differed, though the terms, in fact, are the same. In both cases, the central issue has been the opposition between the French element, identified with modernity, and the Spanish one, identified with tradition.

In Spain, though the origins of this dualism go back to the eighteenth or even the seventeenth century, the topic became controversial precisely during the revolutionary period, because those who were following in the footsteps of the French Revolution were the same people who were, at the same time, fighting its heir, Napoleon Bonaparte. However much they planned to transform the French revolutionary model, the model itself was unspeakable, since it provided their opponents with a very effective counterargument, given the national character of the war. Hence the ritual invocation of Spanish precedents, and the emphasis on the idiosyncrasy—also real and visible—of the Hispanic

Revolution. The original trauma has persisted up to the present day, giving this topic the status of a veritable historiographical taboo.

In Spanish America, the debate occurred later, and in some ways took the opposite form. Whereas in Spain, the antiliberals were the ones accusing their opponents of being "Frenchified," in America, the liberals in the second half of the nineteenth century were the ones openly affirming their debt to revolutionary France. This gave rise to an interpretation of Hispano-American independence which remains vigorous even today: Spanish American independence was a daughter of the French Revolution and a result of the spreading of its principles throughout Spanish America. In the face of this late-nineteenth-century liberal narrative, a revisionist school would gradually emerge, and insist, instead, on the "Hispanic"—therefore, traditional—nature of the independence revolutions.

Let us state at once that whatever position we adopt, whether favorable or unfavorable to the French Revolution or the Hispanic one, it is conceptually impossible to identify any ideological position with a supposed national "spirit": not everything French is modern, nor is everything Spanish traditional, or vice versa. No country is culturally homogeneous, and the task of the historian is precisely to attempt, for any given period, to grasp and assess—geographically and socially—this inevitable cultural heterogeneity. Only after this stage is over may we venture to define what might be, at a particular moment, *l'air du temps*, the spirit of the age: the intangible, fleeting combination of ideas, images, passions, and value judgments pertaining to a country's many actors during a specific period.

However, setting aside the endless argument about "influences," it is certainly possible to attempt a comparison between revolutionary processes, not in order to produce a moral judgment or a claim to primacy, but rather for the sake of better understanding. Comparative history, by bringing similarities and differences to light, makes it possible to weigh the different interpretive variables: for example, in our case, the relation between the social body and government, the political and territorial structure of society, the strength of community or "national" allegiances, the makeup and size of the elites, the characteristics of popular culture, or the role of religion.

The comparative perspective can thus attempt to explain, within the broadest possible typology of a series of similar phenomena, the reasons for any particular case. In ours, for example, why did the passage to modernity follow different routes in the Latin and the English-speaking world? And what were the consequences?

Finally, let us add explicitly that the present essays are also a first attempt at a different reading of the Spanish American independence movements. The multiplication in recent years of studies on this topic, which had been largely neglected for several decades, is a sign that there is a new awareness of all that we still do not know about this key period, and of the inadequacy of classical interpretations. Many studies carried out from the standpoint of social and economic history, whether regional or more global, have contributed many elements for a better understanding of the strategies of the period's many actors. Others are providing a very relevant analysis, from a more anthropological point of view, of popular movements and local cases.

But we cannot neglect the global view, because neither the socioeconomic aspect nor the local perspective can provide a satisfactory explanation of the essential feature of the independence movements: their simultaneous nature and the similarity of the processes, despite the diversity we find among the American economies and societies. Plurality and diversity cannot account for the unity of a phenomenon, nor can structures account for sudden upheavals. What all the regions of Spanish America had in common, then, was their belonging to a single political and cultural whole. It is therefore in the political and cultural field—without neglecting the others—that we must seek first causes. This is also the reason for the fundamental importance of chronology, which cannot be overlooked in any political history, especially in revolutionary times. If studying the "long duration" suits the analysis of structures, of whatever kind—economic, social, mental—upheavals require the "short duration." At such times, priority must be given to the singular event—like the fall of the Berlin Wall, to cite a present-day example—which, by its uniqueness, irrevocably transforms political situations.

The period we will study is full of such events, beginning with the royal abdications of Bayonne, which initiated the crisis of the Spanish monarchy. Many more would follow, but this book will focus mainly on this key period, the years 1808 to 1810, when these singular events were particularly numerous and were all the more important because in 1810 they caused a break which, in our view, though not yet completed, was already potentially irrevocable.[18]

Paris, May 1992

---

18 Different versions of some of these essays have appeared in various publications. For this reason, chapters I and IV must be read as global analyses, and the rest as specific approaches to some of the main topics of the book.

I

# The French Revolution and the Hispanic Revolutions: A Complex Relationship

The connections between the French Revolution and Spanish America are among the truisms of historiography. For a long time, it was believed that the principles proclaimed by revolutionary France, in crossing the Atlantic, had caused the independence of Spanish America, thus making her a daughter of the French Revolution.

This position, widely publicized by the historians of the early twentieth century—though not by the generations writing immediately after the event[19]—is impossible to sustain today in its original form. The "French ideas" are far from being the only ideas underlying independence, and a great number of historians have brought to light the role played in these events by classical Spanish political thought. Moreover, independence cannot be explained solely on the basis of ideological factors, as can be seen in the many studies of the social and economic causes which contributed to the process.

We need, then, to separate two phenomena which took place at the same time and were closely interconnected, but which should not be confused with one another, as the example of Brazil demonstrates very clearly: on the one hand, the independence from the metropolises, and on

19 See, for example, Nikita Harwich Vallenilla, "La Révolution française chez les premiers historiens vénézueliens"; Andrés Lira González, "La recepción de la Revolución francesa en México, 1821–1848: José María Luis Mora y Lucas Alamán"; and Charles A. Hale, "El renacimiento de la Historia política y la Revolución francesa en México," in Guerra 1989, vol. II.

the other, the revolution—that is, the sudden adoption of a system of new political and social references which attempted a historical tabula rasa.

To analyze independence, we would need to give a picture of the tensions which may have existed between the Iberian Peninsula and its American territories, something we do not plan to do here; but above all, we must analyze independence for what it basically is: a political crisis disrupting a political whole which until then had been extraordinarily coherent.

If we wish to explain the revolution, we must take both a cultural approach, allowing us to grasp the peculiarities of the Iberian Enlightenment, and a social and political approach, which examines, over the "long duration," the relations between state and society in the Iberian world. This second approach, we believe, is all the more important because the Enlightenment—modernity—did not necessarily imply revolution.

Whether we are referring to independence or to revolution, we need to adopt a global perspective which does not separate the Iberian Peninsula from Spanish America, since the characteristic feature of both processes—independence and revolution—was precisely their simultaneous nature and their similarity. To explain them, we cannot limit ourselves to local causes; from the local point of view, Spanish America is completely diverse. We need to start out from what the different regions had in common: that is, their inclusion within a single cultural and political whole. To consider this whole means also to study peninsular Spain, not as an external factor, but as a necessary and, in some periods, a central component of these processes.

There is still a great deal to do in this field, even though in recent years specialists in Spanish history have begun to study the Americans in the Spanish revolution,[20] while specialists in America have begun to analyze Spanish events.[21] However, a great many obstacles connected to nationalist feelings still need to be overcome.

---

20 See, for example, Varela Suanzes-Carpegna 1983, which studies the American delegates as one more group within the Cortes; Berruezo 1986 and Rieu-Millán 1990.

21 See, for example, Rodríguez 1984; Anna 1986; and Hamnet 1985.

On the Spanish side, an impartial study of the relation between the French Revolution and the Spanish liberal revolution is needed. The latter's filial connection to the former is quite clear, although its originality and idiosyncrasy are also undeniable. The shadow of the War of Independence and the implicit accusation of Frenchification still define many studies, and account for some strange silences.[22]

As for the Spanish Americans, they must assume their past inclusion in the political and cultural whole from which they broke away, and avoid overemphasizing direct filial debts to France, which, though real, were minor.

Returning to the question of revolution, we need to ask ourselves why the passage to modernity, in the Hispanic world as well as in France, adopted revolutionary rather than evolutionary forms, like those we find in other countries, among which England may be considered the prototype. Although these two forms of modernity have produced relatively similar results in the present, it is clear that the countries of both regions still have different political cultures as a consequence of profoundly diverse histories in the nineteenth and twentieth centuries.

Reflecting on the French Revolution, far from being merely an erudite commemoration of the past, amounts to reflecting on the origins of modernity in a whole cultural area: it means analyzing the particular rationale which has governed, and still governs, this area's history.

---

22 Curiously, all the Spanish papers presented on Spain and the French Revolution during the World Congress for the bicentenary of the French Revolution, held in Paris in July 1989, limit themselves to the beginning of the nineteenth century. *Not a single one* discusses the most important consequence of the French Revolution in Spain: the Spanish liberal revolution. See Vovelle 1989. All of these papers stop at 1808. The same thing occurs with the works published in Spain on the occasion of the bicentenary of the revolution; see, for example, Aymes 1989 or Moral Sandoval 1989.

## The Transformations of the Eighteenth Century

To understand why the European countries followed such different routes in their progression toward modernity, we need an overview of the relations between political regimes, society, and culture during the eighteenth century. Both in France and in Spain, the changes were manifest in these three areas; the problem we face, then, is the mutual compatibility of the different transformations.

The victory of absolutism and its consequences was undoubtedly the key phenomenon of the French and Iberian eighteenth century. This victory was one of the possible outcomes of an old struggle rooted in medieval Europe, that of the emerging modern state with the representative institutions of society: the Cortes in the Iberian kingdoms, the Estates General in France, Parliament in Britain. This struggle had given rise to diverse political traditions. In some, the power of the king and the modern state was limited by that of the old representative institutions, as in Britain and the Crown of Aragon. In France, Castile, and Portugal, the crown had succeeded in slowing down this institutional development.

The pressure of the state on society and its representative institutions would everywhere increase in the sixteenth and seventeenth centuries. As a result, the middle of the seventeenth century would witness serious and spectacularly synchronized political crises in all the great monarchies: in Britain, the first English Civil War; in the Hispanic monarchy, the rebellions of Catalonia and Portugal and the resistance of the Castilian Cortes; in France, the Fronde. By the end of these crises, the relations between the crown and the realm's representative institutions took three different forms: in France, the victory of royal power; in Britain, after the second Civil War, the final victory of Parliament; and in the Hispanic Habsburg monarchy, a temporary draw preserving the status quo.

At the beginning of the eighteenth century, with the arrival of the Bourbons to the throne of Spain, these three forms would be reduced to two. The Cortes of the kingdoms of the Crown of Aragon—precisely where the power of the king had been most restricted—were suppressed. The new unified Cortes of the Hispanic monarchy, comprising a small number of privileged cities and convening only occasionally—1789 would be their last session—had neither the representative character nor the functions which might have allowed them to slow the growth of royal power. As for the crown, it would take pains to impose the theory and spread the mindset of absolutism, forbidding the teaching of Spanish neo-Thomism and its pactist conceptions. The Hispanic monarchy began more and more to resemble the French political model. From then on, the two political areas of the eighteenth century were clearly established: the first was the English one, where the realm's representative institutions had triumphed over royal power; in the second one, formed by France, Spain, and Portugal, royal absolutism largely prevailed.[23]

Absolutism would determine to a great extent the revolutionary break at the end of the century. In effect, the growth of the state began increasingly to displace the functions and attributes of the bodies which made up the structure of society. The state tended to conceive its relation to society, not as a relation with necessarily heterogeneous corporate bodies, but as the binary, more abstract relationship between sovereign and subjects. The struggle against any rival power would lead the state to an assault on the privileges of the corporate bodies, and thereby to an attempt to homogenize society.

Simultaneously with the advance of absolutism, the eighteenth century also witnessed the great cultural sea change that we describe by the handy name of Enlightenment. Actually, it consisted of a series of multiple transformations in the field of ideas, social constructs, values, and behaviors. We cannot discuss its extraordinary complexity here; we will only stress what can be considered the center of the new frame of reference: the victory of the individual, considered as the supreme value and the touchstone against which both institutions and behaviors were to be measured.

This triumph of the individual, clearly visible in philosophy with Descartes, in politics with Hobbes, Locke, and Rousseau, and in economics with Adam Smith, was inseparable from the spread of new forms of sociability. These modern forms of sociability, characterized by the association of individuals from different backgrounds for the purpose of discussing topics of common interest, presented very different features

---

23 For a more detailed study of this question, see "The King and His Kingdoms" in chapter II.

from the old corporate bodies and associations. In the "salons," *tertulias* (salons or social gatherings), academies, Masonic lodges, economic societies, and so forth, modern public opinion was born as a result of debate and consensus among members. These societies, created for the purpose of a simple discussion in which only reason counted, were egalitarian. Authority arose out of the will of the associates, something which would lead to modern-style electoral practices. For all these reasons, they have been called "democratic."[24]

Of course, these transformations in mindsets and forms of sociability could be found throughout Europe, but their consequences varied, as Tocqueville has shown,[25] according to their relation to the prevailing political regime. In Britain, which had gone further even than France in this direction, the cultural elites affected by these changes—which were also the social elites—participated in government by means of the old representative institutions. Here, the ongoing process of individualization would give rise to a gradual modernization of these old institutions, along with the spread of cultural modernity. At the same time, the new ideas and social imaginaries—inevitably tempted by an ideal model—were always counterbalanced by actual political participation, which made constant compromise with reality necessary. As a result, in the English-speaking world, the evolution toward modern democratic institutions—the vote, for example—was in the end slower than in the Latin world; at the same time, it happened gradually, empirically, thus avoiding the break with a past many aspects of which were preserved.

In France and Spain the situation was completely different. The elites, excluded from participation in government by the disappearance or decay of the old representative institutions, had no proper title to political participation. Some were admitted to it as servants of the state, but in a subordinate position which could only be tolerated while the new society was still young. Its new forms of sociability and new culture took shape on the margins of the exercise of power. As a result, they

---

24 For these topics, see "The Individual and Society" in chapter III.

25 His classical explanation can be found in Tocqueville, *L'Ancien Régime et la Révolution* [1856] 1985.

gave rise to a model of the human being, of society, and of politics which was ideal, pure, and disengaged from actual reality. This ideal model appeared, in a way, as a projection on the scale of the whole society of the structure and workings of the new forms of sociability. This created the image of a contractual and egalitarian society, a homogeneous nation formed by a free association of individuals, whose power arose out of itself and was at all times subject to the opinion or will of the associates.[26]

Compared with this ideal, the existing society seemed like a bundle of absurdities: corporate bodies and estates instead of individuals; hierarchies, instead of equality; heterogeneous political communities created by history, not association; powers based on tradition or Providence, and not the will of the citizens... The contrast between ideal and reality was so great that reforms appeared inadequate. Only an upheaval, a new foundation, a new social pact seemed fitted for the building of this new world.[27]

## Absolutism, Enlightenment, and Revolution

This explanatory model, though on the whole correct, needs to be somewhat qualified, however. To radically oppose Enlightenment and absolutism, and to posit this opposition as a constant of the whole eighteenth century, is too simple. On the contrary, in many areas there was a kinship

---

26 Not every new form of sociability was necessarily revolutionary in practice, but they all shared a "utopian, transactional mode of thought." Roche 1988.

27 In a way, the United States was situated halfway between the two cultural areas we are describing. On the one hand, the ideal of the founding of a new society was clearly stated in the preamble to the Declaration of Independence. On the other hand, the text of the Declaration itself appears much more in line with the traditional liberties: as a "pact" between thirteen colonies, each one with its own laws. This is effectively what Edmund Burke was saying when he defended the American rebels in the British Parliament: he was not defending their abstract ideas, but the old British liberties.

between the mindset of absolutism and that of the modern elites. Both shared the same hostility toward the corporate bodies and their privileges, a unitary conception of sovereignty, and the ideal of a binary, unmediated relationship between government and individuals. These shared elements explain the alliance which did in fact exist between the modern elites and "enlightened despotism" during much of the eighteenth century. What united them was greater than what divided them. Most of all, both faced two common enemies: society's traditionalism and inertia, with its old-fashioned pactist mindset,[28] and, frequently, its violent rejection of new fashions and ideas. The modern elites, still in the minority and unsure of their strength, preferred for much of the eighteenth century to undertake their projected reforms under the shelter of the king's authority.[29]

Hence a visible continuity, in the social field, between the reformism of the absolute monarchy and that of postrevolutionary liberalism. Both wanted to "enlighten" a society rife with "ignorance" and traditions which opposed "reason"; to subordinate the church to the state, disentail property, put an end to the privileges of the nobles and the various corporate bodies—universities, guilds—establish free trade and freedom of economic initiative, reduce the autonomy of municipalities, replace education with the teaching of useful sciences, develop primary schools...

The objectives were sometimes so clear and the language so modern, even in the political sphere, that the Enlightenment seems like a veritable pre-liberalism. In 1766, for example, the crown imposed on the most important municipalities, which were controlled by hereditary oligarchies, the election by all *vecinos* (householders) of *diputados* (delegates) and *síndicos personeros* (administrators) for the common people, the *común*. All *vecinos* were eligible, since none of these positions required any distinction of estates: they "could all be occupied indifferently by nobles or plebeians, being entirely dependent on public opinion."[30]

---

28 See "The Political Frame of Reference: Pactism Reborn" in chapter V.

29 For this topic in Spain, see Sánchez Agesta's classic book published in 1953.

30 NRLE, vol. III, book VII, title XVIII, file II, no. 9.

As a result, it would be useless to seek, as some occasionally do, the harbingers of revolution in the modernity of the ideas or measures of social reform that marked the period of the Enlightenment. A large sector of the modern elites at the end of the eighteenth century were simultaneously enlightened and deeply addicted to an absolutism which they saw as the essential instrument of reform. This explains why high-ranking royal officials were often, in the Hispanic—and Portuguese—world the main agents, not only of administrative modernization, but also of the new ideas.[31] This fact was even more notorious in Spanish America, even on the eve of the revolutionary era; the distance between the region and the main centers of European modernity, and the greater traditionalism of its society, made the gap between the standards of the administrative elite and those of the majority of the population more visible.

But as the Enlightenment spread, the modern elites grew, and the power of the state was strengthened, cracks began to appear in this alliance. The absolutist state could not go to the final extremes of reform that the new imaginary demanded because a considerable part of its legitimacy—perhaps the greatest part—belonged to the traditional frame of reference. The monarch was still, for himself and for many of his subjects, *le premier seigneur du royaume*, the first or "natural lord" of the realm, placed at the summit of a pyramid of dignities and honors. The bonds that tied him to his subjects, rather than being the abstract connection between subject and sovereign, were conceived as something more personal and traditional: the relationship between the vassal and his lord, or between the father of the family and his children. The "organicist" view of society as a body, with its head and its several limbs, was still omnipresent even at the end of the eighteenth century.[32] The metaphor of the "mystical body of the monarchy," also very widespread, referred in a similar way to a hierarchical and religious

---

31 See for example, in the case of Mexico, the ideas and practice of the high-ranking officials connected to the Gálvez family in Horst Pietschmann, "Revolución y Contrarrevolución en el México de las reformas borbónicas (1780–1794)," in Guerra 1989, vol. I.

32 For a portrayal of this mental construct openly at work in 1808, see "Images of the King and Duties of the Vassals" in chapter V.

perspective that was hardly in consonance with the egalitarianism of the new imaginary. The resistance of the privileged corporate bodies was not that of an external enemy: it found undeniable support within the monarchical mindset itself.

At a stage which varied from one country to another, and which in the case of the Spanish monarchy can be definitively identified with Charles IV's ascension to the throne and Godoy's period of royal favor, the monarchy, in the eyes of the modern elites, ceased to be "enlightened," that is, to be the moving force for the construction of a new society.[33] Gradually, the all-encompassing power of the king and his ministers, previously considered the ideal means for reform, began to be seen as "arbitrary power." Although at first the king himself was not questioned, "ministerial despotism" was. The example of Britain and its representative institutions added to this discontent a nearby model that could, it seemed, be emulated. The aspirations of the modern elites and those of the privileged groups coincided temporarily in their common desire to set limits to the powers of the king and the modern state. They also coincided, in this early phase, concerning the means for attaining this end: the convening of the traditional representative bodies of the realm, that is, the Estates General in France,[34] and later, the Cortes in Spain.

This is how "historical constitutionalism" developed, with the aspiration to a "free government" resorting to a vindication of the old liberties and the old representation of the realm.[35] In 1780, in Spain, Jovellanos's speech on his admission to the Royal Academy of History already contained a celebration of the old representative institutions.[36]

---

33 In France, this change may be dated to 1776, with the failure of Necker's reforms. For an overall interpretation of the French Revolution, see the synthesis in Furet 1988 and Furet and Ozouf 1988.

34 The first act of the French Revolution took place in 1788, when the provincial estates of the Dauphiné called for the convening of the Estates General.

35 It is impossible to discuss here all the different varieties of French "historical constitutionalism," which could just as easily be aristocratic, as in the case of Boulanvilliers, or popular, as in the case of Mably or Antraigues. On these topics, see Furet 1978, 52, and the following pages.

36 See "The Political Frame of Reference: Pactism Reborn" in chapter V.

This trend would continue to increase in the Hispanic world until it became a stock reference in any political speech. The most radical revolutionaries of the Cortes of Cádiz would still have to disguise their support for the French revolutionary model under the vocabulary and the frame of reference of "the fundamental laws of the realm."

## Two Different Rationales

Thus, on the eve of the beginning of the revolutionary process—1789 in France, 1808 in the Hispanic world—the aspiration to "free government" took the shape of nostalgia for the old representative institutions. For some, this nostalgia was a mask designed to legitimize the conquest of a new kind of freedom. For others, it took on a utopian dimension: it meant the return to a Golden Age in which harmony prevailed between king and realm.

The convergence between the two groups was largely based on the ambiguity of a common political language which in fact referred to different mental constructs. When speaking of liberty, one group understood it as that of individuals equal under the same laws; the other group saw it as the liberties/privileges of the old corporate bodies. For the first, "nation" meant the people, a homogeneous entity: all the individuals united by a social pact. For the second, it meant the realm, a heterogeneous reality born of history: the peoples. When speaking of a constitution, the first group had in mind a new text: something like the pact which would found a new society based on reason. The second group was thinking of "the fundamental laws of the realm" as they had accrued over centuries of political practice.

What both groups did agree on, if we are going to use a modern terminology, was the need for society to be represented before the state; what they disagreed on was how they pictured the society that was to be represented. For some, it was a modern nation made up of individuals; for others, an ancient society, or realm, made up of corporate bodies. As a result, the differences stood out clearly when the question of the composition and the vote of the realm or nation's representation arose: Should there be representation of all the estates, or only of the "Tiers," or Third Estate, in France, or the "Común" in Spain? Should the estates meet and vote separately, or should there be a single assembly with an individual vote? This was no technical debate, but the practical expression of two different imaginaries.

These problems would become very important once the revolutionary process was underway. In the meantime, both groups shared the same desire to see the representative institutions restored. However, there were other possibilities of alliance and conflict, in so far as there were still supporters of royal absolutism. The different political positions can be visualized in the form of a triangle, with each apex occupied respectively by the moderns, the absolutists, and the historical constitutionalists. Each one of these groups shared with the other two a certain number of views, concepts, and aspirations. The moderns and the absolutists had in common their view of power as a binary relation between state and individuals, their struggle against the privileges of the corporate bodies, and their attempts to make society more homogeneous. The absolutists coincided with the historical constitutionalists on the historical foundations of society and on their view of it as consisting of estates. And finally, the moderns and the historical constitutionalists concurred in rejecting absolute power and believing that society needed to be represented. This tripolarity of the various political positions might explain many of the different types of political regimes operating during the revolutionary and postrevolutionary period.

In any case, the alliance between the moderns and the historical constitutionalists, which was crucial for the beginnings of the revolution, was not destined to last. The defense of the old representative institutions could not take the form of a restoration. In France, the Estates General had not met since 1614, and the Spanish Cortes of the eighteenth century were very unrepresentative bodies, subject to strict control. The return to the Golden Age could not restore; it could only invent. The constitution that everyone was demanding for the safeguard of civil liberties, though it appeared at first as a restoration of the "fundamental laws," would have to be a new creation, the work of reason.

That is why "French liberty" was a new, abstract kind which had to be constructed according to an ideal model, whereas "English liberty" was an ancient practice which had to be preserved and perfected. The battle between the rationale of representation and the rationale of the construction of an ideal model is at the very center of the French type of modernity and explains both its universal influence and the kind of problems it raised.[37]

In France, this battle lasted for a very short time. Almost immediately the ideal model of man and society burst onto the public stage. Man was conceived primarily as an individual and a citizen; the nation, as a voluntary pact between these men, in which there was no room either for corporate bodies or for special statutes. The only possible source of legitimacy was that which arose out of this nation, and national sovereignty replaced that of the monarch. The sovereign nation was free to make for itself a new code of laws, the constitution, which did not spring from the restoration of the "fundamental laws," but from a new social pact, able to cure all social evils and to create *ex nihilo* a new man and a new society.

The French Revolution, rather than introducing new actors onto the social and political stage, was a cultural revolution which made possible the creation of politics and the appearance of these actors.[38] Modern politics arose out of the need to elicit the opinion or the will of the new sovereign: the nation. The social practices that were creating public opinion and driving the modern forms of sociability spread to the whole social body and became a struggle to produce—actually or symbolically—the new legitimacy. The rivalry for power among groups, which had previously been restricted to the private sphere, broke out into the streets and created public space, the stage on which the new actors would compete.

The revolution was a radical cultural transformation: in ideas, mindsets, values, behaviors, political practices, but also in the languages which expressed all these things: in the universalist discourse of reason, in political rhetoric, in symbolism, iconography, and ritual,[39] and even

---

37 Gauchet 1988 offers an acute study of the paradox embodied by a revolution that laid the foundation of democracy while at the same time making it impossible.

38 In this I am following Furet 1977.

39 Ozouf 1976 has become a classic for this sort of analysis.

in aesthetics and fashion. These new languages revealed a new view of man and society; but they also had a pedagogical dimension.

The revolution was pedagogical because society was not yet the ideal people. Instead of a modern people, made up of free and autonomous individuals, unanimous in manifesting their will, there was a society made up, like all societies, of a ragbag of groups, most of them still corporative and traditional, and too complex to be reduced to any imagined unity.

The sudden intrusion of the ideal model into this society made the construction of a representative political system a secondary consideration because any real representation implies recognizing society's heterogeneous character, and, at that period, the traditionalism of many of its members. In the face of this reality, the groups that embraced the new standards—the only ones who felt themselves to be citizens and conceived of themselves as a people—quickly became radicalized.[40]

This radicalization appears as a result of the new system. It arose, on the one hand, from the struggle within the modern elites: if the construction of the ideal model was possible and desirable, then logically enough, those who proclaimed themselves closest to the purity of the principles would gradually prevail. On the other hand, the process also resulted from the spread of the new standards to groups ever lower on the social scale. The abstract, indeterminate nature of the new language had considerable mobilizing power. In some cases, this language was able to express the grievances and complaints of the old corporative actors, such as, for example, the masses that participated in the "Great Fear" (the "Grande Peur"), the great peasant revolt of 1789.[41] In others, it opened a space for social utopias and egalitarian revolts. In all these cases, since the possibilities of this ideal world were unlimited and its benefits obvious to reason, any inertia, or worse, any social resistance could only come from the enemies of liberty, who, by definition, could not be the people. The people which fit the model—the minorities who

40 On the difficulty of accepting a heterogeneous society, see Baczko 1989.

41 In Lefevre's classic work from 1932, we find a number of elements that support this explanation.

identified with it—were an ever-narrower group, until finally we come to the period of the Committee of Public Safety: by then, any representative rationale or safeguard for a "free government" had disappeared. As Augustin Cochin said ironically:

> In the political order, we have the government of the people by itself, direct democracy [...] and, since [the People] governs on its own account, it suppresses the public liberties which were merely safeguards for itself against its rulers: if the vote has been suspended, it is because it governs; if the right to a defense has been suppressed, it is because it judges; if the freedom of the press is gone, it is because it writes; if freedom of opinion has disappeared, it is because it speaks.[42]

The situation, of course, had reached such extremes that the process had to be stopped. Thermidor represented both a compromise with society and the laying down, within the revolutionary group itself, of certain rules that had to be respected in order to ensure their own physical survival. However, this model did not imply the return to a logic of representation, but the setting up of hybrid systems—the Directory, the Consulate, the Empire—whereby the revolutionary group could stay in power by preserving the new frame of reference while moderating its application in order to make it viable. In an unforeseen and yet quite logical combination, the Empire intermixed the legacy of the absolutist state[43] with the new principles. Although the foundations were different, there was a return to the reformist strategy of the enlightened elites: that of relying on the state's all-encompassing authority in order to transform society gradually. The revolutionary sovereignty of the people, the new mental construct of the citizen-individual, and the

---

42 "Les actes du gouvernement révolutionnaire," in Cochin 1979, I. The term "Jacobinism" will be used later in the Latin world to describe any radical political movement, and more especially those that, based on forms of modern sociability in which we find a strong popular element—whether real or rhetorical—aim to take or exercise power independently of representative practices.

43 Tocqueville has made this continuity between the modern absolutist state and the state of the revolutionary period admirably clear.

key terms of the new political language were all preserved, but realizing these ideals was left to other means and to the action of time. And yet the model of the ideal society persisted, if only as a latent possibility: this would allow its reactivation at other moments or in other places.

The establishment of a "free government" would also have to wait, for the time being. As François Furet has aptly shown, it was not until the final establishment of the Third Republic, in the last third of the nineteenth century, that the logic of representation would be fully restored.[44]

## France and the Hispanic World: Similarities and Differences

This somewhat lengthy reflection on the origins and rationales of revolution in the absolutist area, and more particularly in France, was no mere display of erudition: it aims to show the kinship between the two revolutions and the reasons that explain it. However, kinship is not identity, and the differences between France and the Hispanic world are as obvious as their resemblances.

The resemblances, which were the result of a similar Roman and German heritage, consistently fostered by very intense human[45] and cultural exchanges, showed themselves in similar institutions, an analogous cultural universe, and a similar political evolution, though along different timelines.[46]

---

44 Furet 1988.

45 From this perspective, the Pyrenees were more a connection than an obstacle. The number of Frenchmen emigrating to Spain at the end of the eighteenth century was still considerable.

46 In 1792, Condorcet, in his "Avis aux Espagnols sur les avantages que l'Espagne doit retirer de la Révolution française," starts out from the common "despotism" established by the House of Bourbon on both sides of the Pyrenees; aware of the Spaniards' stronger traditionalism, he proposes to them a more modest kind of liberty than the French one, along the lines of historical

The main difference had to do with religion. From the seventeenth century onward, no significant religious minorities remained in the Hispanic world. Catholicism was from then on an essential feature of Hispanic identity, which explains why, unlike France, there should have been no religious conflict during the first revolutionary period, and why the new principles should have coexisted peacefully in the constitutions with the exclusive status granted to Catholicism.[47]

Another important difference was the composite structure of the monarchy. Until early in the eighteenth century, it continued to consist of different kingdoms, each with its own institutions, united only in the person of the king. Hence a very strong pactist tradition, related both to political theory and to the memory of still recent institutional practice. A great number of the inhabitants of the monarchy—especially those of faraway America, where the effects of the Bourbons' centralizing reforms would be felt later—still conceived the Spanish "nation," even by the early nineteenth century, as a group of kingdoms. The sovereignty of the people during the revolutionary period would very often be conceived and experienced not as the sovereignty of a unified nation, but as that of the "peoples": communities of an older kind made up of kingdoms, provinces, or municipalities.[48]

A series of factors which made the French Revolution more socially radical were also lacking in Spain. We do not find here to the same extent as in France, except in certain regions, many "feudal rights," or a significant reaction among the nobility on the eve of the crisis; hostile feeling against the nobility was also much more limited, perhaps because of the diversity of this class in Spain due to the high percentage of *hidalgos* in the total population and the prestige this status still commanded among large segments of society. What was also lacking was a

---

constitutionalism. See Eduardo Muñoz, "Deux thèmes de l'époque de l'Indépendance: Pacte social et constitution historique au Chili," in Guerra 1989, vol. II.

47 Both the constitution of the Spanish monarchy, enacted in Cádiz in 1812, and the first Spanish American constitutions, recognized only "the Catholic religion, exclusive of all others."

48 See "Victory of the Modern Nation" in chapter IX.

numerous urban lower class already partly affected by modern culture, like the people of Paris.[49]

The political circumstances also differed: while the French Revolution clashed with the king and in the end turned against him, the Hispanic Revolution was carried out to a great extent in the king's absence and in his name. The fact that the first stages of the Revolutions should have taken place at the very time when a war against an external enemy was underway contributed powerfully to preventing social tensions from becoming exacerbated.

And finally, the different timelines, related both to the degree of modernity achieved in each state and to the earlier dates of the French Revolution, produced further differences between the two revolutions. Though their evolution was similar in terms of the transformation of ideas—imaginaries and forms of sociability that we call modernity—Spanish and even more so Spanish American society was more corporative and traditional and included fewer modern elites than French society. The fact that the French Revolution had taken place twenty years before the Hispanic ones implies additional differences. The most significant is that there were no precedents for the French Revolution, and therefore its capacity for invention was incomparably greater than that of its successors. The Hispanic revolutions, on the contrary, would have at their disposal a wealth of new references—ideas, imaginary constructs, symbols, and constitutional experience—which they would be able to use, sometimes in different ways or combined with other material, but which they would not necessarily have to create.

The French Revolution modified later revolutions because the actors knew ahead of time just where the logic of revolution could lead. That is why, though the tension between the logic of representation and that of the construction of an ideal society existed in the Hispanic revolutions, the transition from 1789 to the Terror and later to empire was also a known quantity, as well as the debate these events gave rise to, from Edmund Burke to Benjamin Constant. As a result, the Hispanic

---

49 For these comparisons, see Antonio Domínguez Ortiz, "La Corona, el gobierno y las instituciones ante el fenómeno revolucionario," in Moral Sandoval 1989, 1–16.

revolutionaries, obsessed by a possible Terror, would cut short any revolutionary form of sociability or discourse which might lead to "Jacobinism," would show caution when mobilizing the urban masses in their internal quarrels,[50] and would use the language of liberty very sparingly, in order to avoid a new Haiti.

This absence of a modern mass mobilization and of Jacobin-style phenomena was undoubtedly the main peculiarity of the Hispanic revolutions. One of the most hotly debated topics in France in the year of the bicentenary of the Revolution was whether 1789 led inexorably to 1793, that is, to the Terror; perhaps the Hispanic experience might contribute some elements toward resolving the debate. There is no doubt that the France of 1789 led to that of 1793, but this may have been because the revolutionary phenomenon was completely new; at the same time, the French revolutionary experience would make this evolution unlikely to repeat itself, whether in France or in other countries.[51]

## Echoes of the French Revolution in the Hispanic World

Let us now attempt a quick analysis combining the direct impact of the French Revolution with the preliminaries and beginning of the Hispanic revolutions. In peninsular Spain the impact was immediate and very great. Geographical proximity, the very intense commercial exchanges

50 The urban masses were very rarely mobilized, and when they were, the revolutionaries preferred to appeal to traditional bonds or military forms of sociability, instead of revolutionary societies. See, for example, Pilar González Bernaldo, "Producción de una nueva legitimidad: Ejército y sociedades patrióticas en Buenos Aires entre 1810 y 1813," in Guerra 1989, vol. II.

51 During the second Spanish liberal revolution, in 1820, the moderates gained control of the patriotic societies, which had a great deal in common with the French revolutionary clubs. See Gil Novales 1975. This is when the Spanish Revolution, in its conflict with the king, began to follow in the footsteps of the French Revolution. See the excellent comparative study of Carlos Seco Serrano, in the introduction to Artola 1983.

between the two countries, the existence of continuous French emigration to Spain and the presence of considerable French colonies in the main Spanish cities—there were several thousand French residents at the time in Cádiz, for example[52]—favored the swift spread of news and propaganda.[53] The same thing was true of America. The regions which experienced the greatest influence were the ones that were best connected: the ports and capitals and the coasts near the revolutionary focal point in the French Antilles.[54]

The social circles most interested in the events in France were, first of all, the cultural elites: the top-ranking public administrators, the upper clergy, the professors and students of the seminaries and universities, the professionals, the Spanish nobility, and the Creole aristocracy.[55] In these milieus, which had witnessed the development of historical constitutionalism, 1789 was seen with sympathetic eyes.[56] The convening of the Estates General undoubtedly appeared to a part of the elites as a restoration of the old liberties to which they themselves

---

52 There were certainly more than a thousand people: from the great merchants to the temporary immigrants from the Limousin who did all sorts of menial work. See Didier Freva, "Le Consulat général de France à Cadix à la fin du XVIIIe siècle" (graduate thesis, Université de Paris I, 1989), and Solís 1987.

53 See Luis Miguel Enciso Recio, "Actividades de los franceses en Cádiz (1789–1790)," *Hispania: Revista española de historia* XIX, no. LXXIV (Madrid, 1959): 251–86.

54 On these topics, see, for example, Anne Perontin-Dumon, "Révolutionnaires français et royalistes espagnols dans les Antilles" and Carlos Vidales, "Corsarios y piratas de la Revolución francesa en las aguas de la emancipación americana," in Guerra 1989, vol. I.

55 This social makeup can be seen both in the biographies of the future Spanish and American revolutionaries and in a report of the places and people being investigated by the government and the Inquisition, based on Domergue 1984.

56 The links between historical constitutionalism and academic circles had increased thanks to the reforms introducing not only natural law but also the study of the legislation of the realm into legal studies; this explains the extraordinary knowledge of medieval law that we find among the men of the revolutionary period.

aspired. The poet Manuel Quintana would later describe a feeling that was very widespread at the time: "When twenty years ago the voice of liberty was heard to ring out on the banks of the Seine, the hearts of good people throbbed with joy on hearing these beneficent echoes."[57]

The French revolutionaries, who were aware of the analogies between the two situations, encouraged the Spaniards to follow in their footsteps. In 1792, Condorcet concluded his "Avis aux Espagnols..." with an appeal that seemed to be in the spirit of historical constitutionalism: "Spaniards, summon your Cortes."[58] These revolutionary Cortes which French propaganda called for would take twenty years to convene: the early sympathy for the French Revolution would soon become, first, distrust, then hostility.

The execution of Louis XVI and religious persecution played a key role in this transformation. An atmosphere of religious respect enveloped the person of the king, who was seen as the bond uniting the various political communities of the monarchy. Religious persecution struck even more strongly at the supreme values of society. The war on the Convention was experienced by many as a crusade, all the more so because the invasion of the Basque country by the French revolutionary troops had closed churches and persecuted the clergy.[59] The public opinion campaign against the revolution[60] did not only express the official ideology, it also met with very broad popular support, reinforced by the direct experience and the presence in Spain of many French bishops

---

57 *Discurso de un español a los Diputados de Cortes* (Mallorca: Royal Printers, 1810), quoted by Hans Juretschke, "Concepto de Cortes a comienzos de la Guerra de la Independencia. Carácter y actualización," in *Revista de la Universidad de Madrid* IV, no. 14 (1955).

58 Quoted by Muñoz, loc. cit.

59 See Antonio Elorza, "L'invasion des provinces basques: La guerre de la Convention en Espagne," in Vovelle 1989, II, 700 and the following pages.

60 For its themes, see Jean René Aymes, "L'Espagne et le refus de la Révolution, 1789–1795: Les thèmes de la campagne d'opinion," ibidem, 660 and the following pages.

and priests who had emigrated.[61] Reactions were the same in Spanish America. An analysis of the American press reveals themes identical to those of the Peninsula, with one specific feature: a special emphasis on anarchy and social dissolution, which can be explained, no doubt, by the vicinity of Santo Domingo and the fear of native revolts.[62]

The subsequent alliance between revolutionary and imperial France and the Spanish crown would lessen this profound hostility, but without entirely erasing a hostile imaginary, more deeply rooted in the masses than in the elites, which identified the French Revolution with impiety. In the propaganda war between royalists and insurgents which would take place later in Spanish America, the opposing factions would each accuse the other of being supporters of the French Revolution and its impiety.[63]

When, later, Napoleon was to give a more "respectable" image of France, the Hispanic elites would be divided between admiration for his administrative and military efficiency and disappointment at his suppression of liberties, which identified his government as a new form of despotism.[64]

---

61 Almost eight thousand French priests took refuge in Spain. Despite the crown's instructions to isolate them, these clerics exerted great influence in many Spanish regions. See for Galicia, which was closely connected to the dioceses of western France, Jesús de Juana, "L'influence de la Révolution en Galice," ibidem, 707 and the following pages.

62 See Jean-Pierre Clément, "La Révolution française dans le 'Mercurio Peruano,'" and Renán Silva, "La Revolución Francesa en el 'Papel periódico de Santa Fe de Bogotá,'" in Guerra 1989, vol. I.

63 This argument was used more especially in Mexico in 1810–11. In Quito, on the eve of independence, an analysis of the Creole elites' mindset reveals an opposition between Jerusalem—pious America—and Babylon—Europe with its taint of revolutionary ideas. See Demélas and Saint-Geours 1989.

64 This admiration, discouragement with the traditionalism of society, and the absolutist practice of reform from above, explain why in 1808 part of the enlightened elites collaborated with the invader: this position is called "Frenchification."

In all these reactions, there was also a difference between generations. The older, enlightened generation had set its hopes on the monarch's absolute power as a means to carry out reforms. In their view, political reform, for which the country was not yet ready, would come after social reform.[65] The younger generation, which had been educated during the revolutionary age, had opposite priorities: first, political, then social reform. The members of this generation were those who would later carry out the revolution in Spain and America.[66] But even for them, excepting a few individuals, the goals of the French Revolution were to be pursued without falling into its excesses. As Quintana, the key man in the first stage of the Hispanic Revolution, stated very clearly in 1808, at the beginning of the Spanish crisis:

> And so, because a frivolous, frenetic, and changeable nation was incapable of benefiting from their revolution [...] the rest must be condemned to suffer all the evils of a bad government? [...] Let the French Revolution be to us as the wreckage of ships broken up in the shallows, which teaches the navigator to steer clear of dangerous reefs, but does not distract him from his journey.[67]

Even taking these distinctions into account, for twenty years the sympathizers of revolution in the Hispanic world were very few. The register of known cases so far[68] allows us to infer that they represented an absolute minority. Most of the conspiracies that the authorities spoke of then, or the historians do now, are difficult to assess: were they conversations, tertulias, or genuine preliminaries to political action? In Spain there were some unusual cases of fervent support for the Revolution, like that

---

65 See Sánchez Agesta 1953 for a description of the order of priorities of the enlightened generation.

66 On this generation and the difference between it and the enlightened generation, see Martínez Quinteiro 1977, IV and V.

67 *Semanario patriótico*, no. IX, October 27, 1808, 149–50.

68 In some countries, like Spain or Mexico, the sources that have been studied are sufficiently numerous by now to give us a fairly accurate idea.

of Marchena, which led to his exile in France and his participation in the French Revolution and its propaganda.[69] We find the same situation in Spanish America; but the well-known case of Miranda, a general of the Convention, is both a mythical example and an exception.[70]

When we read accounts of the investigations carried out by the authorities and of the trials held against these sympathizers of the Revolution, the main accusations are licentiousness, imprudent comments on French events,[71] or social gatherings in which French books or newspapers were read and discussed.[72] Only very rarely do we find any genuine active propaganda,[73] direct connections to revolutionary France or attempted plots.[74] Many of these activities, moreover, were connected to the presence of French subjects, who aroused the distrust of the authorities.[75] The Spanish state's "cordon sanitaire" policy and the traditional-

---

69 See Fuentes 1989.

70 See the classic book Parra Pérez 1989. Miranda was a very unusual case, being both an exile and an early supporter of independence.

71 In Mexico and Peru, the individuals accused of revolutionary sympathies seem to have been persecuted mainly because they were Freemasons or were accused of licentiousness. See *La vida colonial: Los precursores ideológicos...*, 1929 and 1932; also José Antonio Ferrer Benimelli, "Masonería e Inquisición en Latinoamérica en el siglo XVIII," in *Montalbán*, no. 2, Universidad Católica Andrés Bello, Caracas, 1973.

72 These are the most frequent examples in Spain, where gatherings of professors and students, clerics, and some professionals have been documented (see Domergue 1984); but also in America, in Mexico, Caracas, Bogotá, Lima, Santiago de Chile, Chuquisaca, Buenos Aires, Rio de Janeiro, etc.

73 Even the case of Nariño, who translated the Declaration of the Rights of Man in Bogotá and had it printed, appears as an isolated act of enthusiasm.

74 The best-known cases are the republican conspiracy of San Blas Day in Madrid, whose participants were deported to America, where they joined with Venezuelan Creoles to organize another conspiracy, that of Gual and España in 1797. See Grases 1978.

75 See, among others, Frédérique Langue, "Les Français en Nouvelle-Espagne à la fin du XVIIIe siècle: médiateurs de la Révolution ou 'nouveaux créoles'?"; Georges Baudot and María Águeda Méndez, "La Revolución francesa y la

ism of society were effective obstacles to the massive propagation of the new standards.[76]

The only significant exceptions to the minority and elitist character of the support for the French Revolution can be found in slave-holding societies, with the conspiracies or uprisings involving Black and Brown people. The "liberty of the French" served as a banner to rally the slave revolts; the equal common denominator was the watchword of the revolts involving free Blacks and Browns, and sometimes poor whites.[77] These movements, nevertheless, involved only minorities, since these societies were not made up primarily of Blacks, nor were the social differences as marked as in Santo Domingo. Their main consequence would be the great caution exercised by local elites in applying the new principles.

A final assessment of the revolution's direct impact can only be a very mixed one. Among the elites, sympathy for the new frame of reference made progress in so far as these standards could largely be understood as a continuation of the enlightened project. However, the French revolutionary process itself aroused more distrust than outright support, and this led the elites not only to exercise caution, but also to a reflection along constitutionalist lines in which we may perceive, explicitly or not, the influence of Benjamin Constant.

---

Inquisición mexicana: Textos y pretextos"; Carmen Castañeda, "El impacto de la Ilustración y de la Revolución Francesa en la vida de México. Finales del siglo XVIII," in Guerra 1989, vol. I.

76 They were effective, at least, against mass propaganda, but much less so among the elites, who easily evaded such prohibitions. On these topics, see also Anes 1969, "La Revolución Francesa y España, algunos datos y documentos."

77 The best-known cases are those of Coro in 1795 and Maracaibo in 1799, in Venezuela, and that of Salvador, in Brazil, in 1798. In the Venezuelan events, there is evidence of the influence of propaganda from the French Antilles, and even of the participation of enslaved people brought from these islands. See Federico Brito Figueroa, "Venezuela colonial: Las rebeliones de esclavos y la Revolución francesa," and Matthias Röhrig Assunção, "L'adhésion populaire aux projets révolutionnaires dans les sociétés esclavagistes: Le cas du Venezuela et du Brésil (1780–1840)," ibidem, 1989, vol. I.

These attitudes were already less evident among the younger members of the elites, among whom the desire for change began to prevail.[78] The new forms of sociability in which they congregated multiplied in the late eighteenth century and the early nineteenth, and with them, as in prerevolutionary France, the new imaginary and the new political practices spread. Godoy's period as favorite and the financial crisis made "ministerial despotism" increasingly intolerable, and a "free government" more and more desirable. However, revolution would not begin in the Hispanic world as the result of internal growth, but as a consequence of the crisis of the monarchy caused by Napoleon's invasion of Spain.

## Spanish Revolution and Spanish American Revolutions

Then everything changed, and very quickly. The forced abdication of Ferdinand VII at Bayonne was only truly accepted by a part of the elites, those for whom the new regime would make a reform of the monarchy possible along revolutionary lines, but from above, without a revolution. The rest of the elites, and above all, society, unanimously rejected the new dynasty. May and June of 1808 would see multiple uprisings against the French and the creation of insurrectional juntas throughout Spain.[79] The massive nature of the Spanish rebellion and the unanimous support it received from Spanish America clearly show the political unity of the two pillars of the monarchy. Patriotism undoubtedly played an important role, but the rejection of revolutionary France, with its contempt for the historical legitimacy of the king and its anticlericalism, also carried considerable significance.

---

78 For a case study of this evolution, see Carlos Herrejón Peredo, "México: Las Luces de Hidalgo y de Abad y Queipo," ibidem.

79 We only sum up these events here. See the classic books by Artola 1968, chapter IV, Lovett 1975, and Aymes 1973.

However, the resistance to Napoleon, which had begun largely within a very traditional frame of reference, would eventually sow the seeds of revolution in the Hispanic world. What explains this strange phenomenon, whereby the patriots who opposed the heir of revolutionary France were precisely the ones who would carry out a revolution inspired by the French one?

The answer points to the problem of representation. In effect, with the disappearance of royal legitimacy and the rejection of the intruders, Spanish resistance and American loyalty had no choice but to justify their actions by appealing to the sovereignty of the realm, the people or the nation. The terms used were fluctuating and extremely diverse, as was the nature of the reversion of sovereignty.

The creation of juntas in Spain from the first moments of the rebellion was an improvised form of representation of society, the affirmation of a legitimacy opposed to that of the invader and of the authorities who had recognized him. In Spanish America we find an identical reflex, and, as soon as the abdications became public, similar attempts to confer on the authorities an indisputable legitimacy.[80] But these first juntas, because of their imperfect representativity, could not grant definitive legitimacy to the provisional powers of the resistance. As a result, in the very first weeks of the rebellion, the demand for general juntas, a Congress, or Cortes was universal. Some provinces even convened old representative institutions which had disappeared or had never existed separately.[81]

These partial attempts, however, could not endow the whole monarchy with a unified and indisputable power. Nor was the problem resolved with the creation in Aranjuez, in September 1808, of the Junta Suprema Central. Although this body's legitimacy was acknowledged by Spaniards and Spanish Americans alike, it remained precarious because it arose out of the delegation of powers of the Spanish insurrectional juntas. As a result, a few days after its creation, these juntas were already debating the question of the Cortes and the election of

80 See "American Reactions" in chapter IV.

81 See "Constituting a Legitimate Government" in chapter IV.

the American deputies who would represent America before the Junta Central.[82] A few months later, in May 1809, the Junta Central decided to convene the Cortes while at the same time holding a general deliberation as to the mode and objectives of their meeting. The public debate about representation, which had begun at the very moment of the rebellion, was intensifying and becoming official.

It is this public debate on representation that would bring about the great transformation of the Hispanic elites' frame of reference. In effect, debating on representation meant discussing the two key questions that would open the door to the Spanish revolution and Spanish American independence: What is the nation? And within the nation, what is the relationship between peninsular Spain and America?

The first question held center stage in the new political imaginary and was also the key issue in the French Revolution. Is the nation made up of ancient political communities, with their estates and privileged corporate bodies, or of equal individuals? Is it a product of history or the result of voluntary association? Is it already established, or still to be created? Does sovereignty reside in it? And what kind of sovereignty? According to the answers given to these questions, the Cortes would be a restoration of the old institutions, in which the kingdoms and estates were represented, or a single national assembly of representatives of the nation. The French debate around the convening of the Estates General and its first sessions up to the creation of the National Assembly happened all over again between 1808 and 1810 in the Hispanic world.

As in France, we also see first of all a coalition between the historical constitutionalists—the most famous of whom was Jovellanos—and the revolutionaries—headed by Quintana—in order to obtain the convening of the Cortes. Then a struggle took place between them over who should be represented—whether the estates or merely the "plain state"— and over the forms of assembly and voting—whether by estate or not. As in France, the victory of the revolutionaries sprung from the impossibility of restoring, unchanged, the old Cortes. The fact that

82 The electoral regulations were published on January 22, 1809, in Seville. The elections of deputies were carried out in America in 1809 and 1810. Concerning these elections, see chapter VI.

Jovellanos should propose equipping them, in the English style, with two houses—something for which there was no precedent in traditional Hispanic institutions[83]—clearly showed the weakness of the argument for tradition and the ambiguities in the historical constitutionalists' position. If circumstances were forcing a transformation of tradition, this meant that nothing stood in the way of the nation providing itself with whatever institutions best suited its needs.[84]

The second question—What place should be granted to peninsular Spain and Spanish America in the national representation?—posed, openly and decisively, the dangerous problem of equality between Spaniards and Americans. This problem had its origins in the period of the Conquest, had frequently come into the open in quarrels over public posts and was now acquiring crucial importance. It concerned the very identity of the Indies. What were they? Kingdoms in their own right, subordinate kingdoms, or colonies? It was also, at the same time, a very practical and urgent problem, since it would determine both the existence in Spanish America of juntas similar to those of the Peninsula, and whether the new representative institutions—first the Junta Central, and later the Cortes—would give these bodies a numerically proportional representation. The peninsulars' rejection in practice of the proclaimed equality would be the essential cause of the independence of America.[85]

---

83 More difficulties for this party lay in the question of which Cortes they should take as a model, whether the unitary Cortes of the eighteenth century or those of the old kingdoms, and in that case, which ones?

84 It is significant that no one should have considered restoring the eighteenth-century Cortes, which had convened for the last time in 1789.

85 The declarations of equality were made solemnly and repeatedly: for example, in the decree of January 22, 1809, which called the elections to the Junta Central; in the decree of January 14, 1810, which called the elections to the Cortes; or in the proclamation voted by the Cortes of Cádiz, on October 15, 1810. The denial of equality in practice was just as continual, as shown both in the refusal to allow or recognize the American juntas and in the field of representation, with the ridiculous number of deputies America was to elect for the Junta Central, the system of voting, and the limited number of deputies to

Thus, beginning in 1808, the Hispanic world would in its turn embark on a revolutionary process which presented extraordinary similarities to that of the French Revolution. This is when the new references that the French process had constructed would spread massively, first in Spain and then in Spanish America. In the Peninsula, in fact, with the collapse of the absolutist state in 1808, the limitations on the freedom of the press also disappeared in the political field. A veritable avalanche of printed material of all kinds, including a multitude of newspapers, would spread throughout the Peninsula.[86] They were patriotic publications designed to fire people's spirits in the struggle against the invader; but they were also full of all sorts of opinions, from the most traditionalist to the most modern, about the political solutions to be used in reforming the monarchy.

In America, such a freedom of the press did not yet exist and censorship continued to operate; yet the peninsular debate crossed the Atlantic, thanks to the handbills and gazettes arriving from the Peninsula and against which the authorities, even those most hostile to the new opinions, were powerless. Indeed, how could they prevent the arrival and reprinting in America of these patriotic publications that, moreover, were often produced by the Spanish authorities themselves?[87] Much of the Spanish American editorial activity consisted of the reprinting of these publications. Books, handbills, proclamations, and the main newspapers were reprinted as soon as they reached America or were published again in the press. The new standards no longer needed to take such devious routes as smuggling and clandestinity:[88] they arrived openly by way of peninsular publications.

From afar, but with an ardor just as great and fanned by the fear of being left out in the reform of the monarchy, Spanish America joined in the peninsular debates; this is when revolutionary France's cultural

---

be elected for the Extraordinary Cortes of Cádiz, as well as the denial of the right to vote for Blacks and African castes in the Constitution of 1812.

86 The Colección del Frayle in Madrid holds a large collection of these materials.

87 See chapter VIII.

88 See chapter VII.

transformation came flooding into the region, but in Spanish and publicly, via the Peninsula. The number—scarce at the beginning—of those who had come out in support of the new frame of reference would increase constantly throughout this period, as well as the modern forms of sociability in which they met. Although they continued to be a minority within an extremely traditional society, these groups already included most of the younger members of the cultural elites; they would be the moving force behind the revolution. We speak of groups, for the spread of the new standards was inseparable from that of the new forms of sociability: the members of the revolutionary elite were educated and came together in social gatherings of all kinds, in the groups formed around a newspaper, in the cafés, in the literary societies, and in various other types of society.[89]

The revolution itself would follow, along strangely similar lines, in the footsteps of the French Revolution, not only because of the analogy we have already mentioned between the two political systems, but also because the elites were well-acquainted with the French version; in fact, it served as a model and a counter-model to their reflections.[90] For the more radical, it was a hidden model, since they could hardly appeal openly to what many saw as the embodiment of impiety and the invader's ideology. The French Revolution was still a prohibited topic. Mexía Lequerica, from Quito, one of the most brilliant and influential deputies of the liberal majority in the Cortes of Cádiz, found this out for himself in 1810:

89 Among these spaces, Manuel Quintana's tertulia and his newspapers—two driving forces of the Hispanic Revolution until early 1810—played a central role. See chapter VII, and also Moreno Alonso 1989.

90 For a more detailed analysis of the ambiguities of the references to the French Revolution among the more radical, see "An Original Political Moment" in chapter VII. These references were not only doctrinal; they were also useful in practical discussions about what measures to take. See, for example, Palafox's words in the Junta Central on November 20, 1809, concerning the concentration of power in the government, which were closely connected to the experience of the Directory, AHN, Secretaría de Estado records, Papeles de la Junta Central, file 7C.

> People talk about Revolution and say that it must be avoided. Sir, my regret is not that there should be need for a revolution, but that it should not yet have taken place. The words revolution, philosophy, liberty, and independence are all of the same nature, words which those who are not acquainted with them look upon as birds of ill omen; but those who have eyes, judge; and I, in judging, say that it is a grief that there should be no revolution in Spain. Revolution is reduced [He tried to define it, there was an uproar, and he sat down][91]

The Spanish liberals would have to advance covertly, under the garb of historical constitutionalism, but with close attention to the French example.[92] As a result, the declaration of national sovereignty—to which the Cortes of Cádiz opened the way on the very day of its convening, on September 24, 1810—was followed by the writing up of constitutions and laws designed to destroy the ancien régime in the social sphere. The French model prevailed: these projects embraced the new social imaginary—that viewed the nation as made up of citizen-individuals—and broke with the old "fundamental laws"; the constitution was seen as a compact founding a new society, educational projects were proposed for the purpose of creating the new man, etc.

In this great cultural transformation, the Spanish American elites began by following the evolution of the elites in Spain, where the central government and the ideological center of the revolution were still located. Later, older and more recent tensions, sparked by the debate on equality between Spain and America, would lead to the first insurrections and to civil war. In Spanish America, the process leading to the break with the Peninsula sometimes preceded revolution and sometimes came later.

The loyal regions—New Spain, Central America, Peru—evolved in step with the different stages of Spanish liberalism.[93] Political modernity

---

91 DSCGE, December 20, 1810.

92 The constitution of the Spanish monarchy enacted in Cádiz in 1812 was inspired by the French Constitution of 1791. See Díaz Lois 1976, for the way in which the Rights of Man and the Citizen were expressed in the text.

93 For Central America, see, for example, Rodríguez 1984.

in this area mostly arrived from the Peninsula via the constitution, the laws, and political practices. As Vicente Rocafuerte, the Equatorian liberal who was living at the time in Mexico, would say in 1822: "America, enlightened not only by the doctrine of all the books which have circulated here since the Spanish Constitution was established, but, more important, by the example the Peninsula gave her in the struggle against the sycophant.[94]"[95]

In the insurgent regions, the break was justified first of all by a pactist discourse containing many of the features of historical constitutionalism. This system would serve as the basis both for American autonomy and for the project of founding a new society; but very soon, the inspiration for setting it up would be sought in the French revolutionary standards.[96] Thus, the insurgent elites in Spanish America went further than the Spanish liberals. In their search for principles and symbols that would help them to highlight their own particularities, they adopted more straightforwardly the new system of reference, since the traditionalist element, which the king represented in Spain and in royalist America, was no longer present. With the aim of founding a new identity as soon as possible, and at paces that varied for each region, they quickly adopted the language,[97] the symbols and

---

94 In Spanish, "el servil," a term used in the early years of the nineteenth century for the supporters of royal absolutism. *Diccionario de la Real Academia*.—Trans.

95 Rocafuerte 1822.

96 Although sometimes the constitutions of the new Spanish American countries were formally inspired by the English or North American model, the underlying rationale was different and conceived along French lines: they did not propose an improvement on the old liberties, but an *ex-nihilo* construction founded on reason.

97 See, for example, Anne-Marie Brenot and David Chacón Rodríguez, "Du sans-culotte français au sans-chemise vénézuélien: Étude d'un itinéraire de la Carmagnole," in Guerra 1989, vol. II. See also Noemi Goldman, "El discurso político de Mariano Moreno," in *El discurso como objeto de la historia* (Buenos Aires: 1989).

iconography,[98] the festivals and ceremonies,[99] the forms of sociability,[100] and the institutions[101] of revolutionary France.

It still remains to be seen to what extent all these innovations, which were embraced by a part of the elites, were accepted by the rest of society. For example, the propaganda of the delegate to the Junta of Buenos Aires, José Castelli, undoubtedly mobilized considerable indigenous groups by means of a Jacobin discourse, but his message was understood in the society's much more traditional terms, and his prestige depended on elements that refer us to an older frame of reference.[102]

One way or another, the need to create unprecedented political units reinforced the desire, typical of modernity as rupture, to create a new society and made the age of independence a period of great creativity in all these areas.[103] Revolutionary features intermingled with the

---

98 See, for example, José Emilio Burucua and others, "Influencia de los tipos iconográficos de la Revolución Francesa en los países del Plata," in Guerra 1989, vol. I.

99 On the civic festivals of Buenos Aires, see the works of Henry Ph. Vogel, and for the hybridization of French revolutionary symbols and rituals with Hispanic and American traditions, see Georges Lomné, "La Révolution française et le symbolisme des rituels bolivariens," ibidem, vol. II.

100 For the period of independence, see, for example, Pilar González Bernaldo, "Phénomènes révolutionnaires et formes d'organisation politique: Sociabilité et modernité au Río de la Plata (1810 et 1815)," in Vovelle 1989; and for the liberal period, Fabio Zambrano, "Las sociabilidades modernas en la Nueva Granada, 1820–1848," in Guerra 1989, vol. II.

101 Institutions that were both political—see, for example, O. Carlos Stoetzer, "Le modèle français dans les régimes politiques et dans les documents constitutionnels des nouvelles républiques du Río de la Plata, 1811–1848," ibidem, vol. II—and educational, see Sol Serrano, "La Revolución francesa y la formación del sistema nacional de educación en Chile," ibidem.

102 See Joëlle Chastin, "Comment rallier les foules à la Révolution? Les discours de Juan José Castelli dans l'expédition libératrice du Haut Pérou (1810–1811)," ibidem, vol. I.

103 See Pons 1990. On the founding of ideal societies, see, for example, for Venezuela, Luis Castro Leiva, "El arte de hacer una revolución feliz," and for Brazil,

Hispanic base and native roots, producing very diverse combinations, which still remain to be studied, along with the paces, the regional peculiarities, and the French models that were used in each case.[104] In effect, the spread of French models, which took place in the early days by Spanish means—often by way of Blanco White's London newspaper *El Español*—would adopt other, more direct routes after independence. Journeys to France,[105] the emigration of military men, intellectuals, or politicians to America after the fall of the Empire,[106] and the publication of a great many French books[107] would lead at that time to Spanish America's cultural incorporation into France.

## American Particularities and Problems

Unlike what occurred in Europe, the adoption of the French mode of access to modernity would never again be contested in Spanish America. In fact, both in Spain and in France itself, the restoration of the monarchy was still possible. In Spain, the return of the king in 1814 and the popular support he received, which proved that the liberals were

---

Estevão de Rezende Martins, "La Révolution au Brésil: L'idée du nouveau et du définitif," in Guerra 1989, vol. II.

104 The political experiments of revolutionary and postrevolutionary France were numerous enough to inspire very diverse political regimes: from the constitutional regimes to the Empire.

105 This is when the continuous flow of Latin American students and intellectuals traveling to Europe, and more especially to France, began; it would become a constant of the contemporary period. On this topic, see our article "La Lumière et ses reflets: Paris et la politique latino-américaine," in *Le Paris des étrangers* (Paris: Imprimerie Nationale, 1989).

106 For Brazil, see François Chevalier and Jean Chazelas, "Le Brésil différent: un héritage original de la Révolution française," in Guerra 1989, vol. II.

107 Dozens of French plays were being staged at the time in Mexico. See María Poumier, "José María de Heredia (Cuba 1803–Mexico 1839) et la Révolution française," ibidem, vol. II.

still in the minority, allowed him to abolish the constitution and restore absolute monarchy. In France, the reign of Louis XVIII, though it witnessed a reestablishment of the old legitimacy, preserved many of the revolutionary principles and measures, for the changes that had come about were too considerable for any return to a previous status quo. Even in Spain, the transformation of the elites was so great that soon a new liberal revolution, that of 1820, would set the revolutionary process in motion again. Though another restoration, carried out with the help of the Holy Alliance in 1823, would subsequently interrupt the process, all of contemporary Spain would be marked by the coexistence, or competition, between these rival principles: the sovereignty of the king or of the nation.[108]

Spanish America occupies a singular and, in a way, a paradoxical position in the Latin zone. When all of Europe had returned to monarchical, sometimes even absolutist, regimes, only the Spanish American countries remained republics, with modern constitutions and liberties. The explanation for this should be sought in the very fact of independence. By breaking their bond with the Peninsula, they also broke their bond with the king, that is, with historical legitimacy. No other means was then left to legitimize power than the modern sovereignty of the people. That is why all attempts to establish a monarchy would fail in America, even though at certain periods a considerable sector of the elites found this solution tempting. For what legitimacy could there be for a king who was not the "*señor natural*," the natural lord, of the kingdom? There was no solution to the problem, however traditionalist the society, and the case of Brazil, with an empire lasting until 1889, is the perfect counterexample to what happened in Spanish America.

It was a singular situation, then, but also a paradoxical one, in the sense that this legal modernity in Spanish America coexisted with a social traditionalism incomparably greater than that of Latin Europe, heightened, no doubt, by the aftermath of the wars of independence. This contrast between the modernity of the elites' and the state's theoretical frame of reference, on the one hand, and social archaism, on the other, would long characterize the whole contemporary history of

---

108 Sánchez Agesta 1978 gives a magnificent description of this clash.

Spanish America. This gap between the elites and society was not a feature of this region alone, but of all the countries that have followed the path of modernity as rupture; but we find it here on a much greater scale. This situation would give rise to a series of unsolved problems that would exert enormous influence during the entire contemporary period, and more especially during the nineteenth century. Let us mention them briefly by way of conclusion.

The first, which is specific to Hispanic America, is territorial disintegration. Independence was certainly founded on national sovereignty, but what was to be done when the modern nation did not exist yet? What did exist were political communities on the old model, similar to those of Europe under the ancien régime, whose main mutual bond was their common allegiance to the same crown and their union with the sovereign. Their modern elites had translated an old form of cohesion into the modern nation, but there was nothing to prevent other elites from repeating the same transposition and setting up their community as the new "nation." The Brazilian case once more provides a counterexample, since here independence coexisted with the preservation of royal legitimacy.

The other problems are similar to those of Latin Europe. The new legitimacy was based on the sovereignty of the people, but the society's imaginary, values, mutual bonds, and behaviors remained traditional. There was no people, in the modern sense of the word, beyond the men who had experienced the cultural upheaval we call modernity: that part of the elites who had embraced the modern frame of reference and who met in the new forms of sociability. Under such conditions, how could a genuine representative regime based on the vote of citizen-individuals be constructed, when these individuals constituted a minority?[109] What could be done, in case there were genuine representation, to prevent the society's traditionalism from prevailing? To resolve this contradiction,

109 This statement does not amount to affirming the political incapacity of ancient societies, but only their unfitness for individual representation on modern lines. An indigenous tribe may be represented as such in a negotiation with the state or with another tribe, but not by an individual vote, which denies its very existence.

the modern elites fabricated various kinds of "democratic fictions." These fictions might consist of redefining the people and limiting the vote.[110] They might also take the form of one man being endowed with the sovereignty of the people,[111] or of parties belonging to the world of the elites taking turns in power.[112] In both cases, either the elections were a fiction or they were rigged.

Under such conditions, given that the legitimacy of any government could always be contested, how could a stable political regime be constructed? In these political systems, military uprisings, coups d'état, or revolts fulfilled the function which elections could not: the change of governments. Moreover, since the elites had faith in constitutions as a means to construct the perfect society,[113] quarrels over the constitution contributed an additional factor of political instability.

And finally, how to bridge the cultural rift between the elites and the rest of society? The means adopted were various: laws designed to eliminate any trace of the old corporate bodies still in existence, the use of history, symbols, and iconography in order to create the modern nation, educational projects to form the citizen... When this "pedagogical" enterprise took a radical turn and disrupted factors that traditional society considered fundamental, not infrequently popular insurrections would break out.[114] The modern elites' impatience with social tradition-

---

110 This solution would be used several times in France, especially during the July Monarchy, and in Spain and America during the period of the doctrinaires.

111 This man could be a president for life—a dictator—or an emperor like Napoleon I or Napoleon III in France.

112 This was the case of the "*turno*" in Spain at the end of the nineteenth century, or of various Hispanic countries during the "oligarchical" period.

113 This "constitutional faith" would last in most countries until the final third of the nineteenth century, when positivism, among other factors, would stress governmental stability and the fitness of institutions to society.

114 The classic example of such uprisings was, of course, the Vendée in France, but other examples would be the Carlist wars in Spain and many agrarian and religious revolts in America.

alism often led to accelerated attempts to construct the ideal model, which in their turn would provoke the corresponding social resistance.

None of these problems was specific to Latin America: they could also be found in France and the other Latin countries whose institutional tradition and whose culture led them to the kind of passage to modernity that France had adopted first. This precedence on the part of France explains why the French model and its political and cultural circumstances should have been predominant in the Latin world, and more especially, in Latin America during the entire nineteenth century. This influence was not, then, a mere trend, but the result of a common rationale, a specific form of modernity which implied both benefits and particular problems.

The most serious of these, as we have already shown, was the coexistence between the logic of representation and that of building an ideal world. The first prevailed once and for all in France with the Third Republic, almost a hundred years after the French Revolution. Perhaps this is a problem that remains to be solved in much of Latin America.

II

# Absolutist Modernity

The history of the revolution in France and in the Spanish monarchy is inseparable from absolutism. This regime, described at the time as despotic, tyrannical, or arbitrary, is what the revolutionaries rose up against. True, they did not limit their goals to a mere change of political regimes; instead, they aimed at a radical reform of society and even man himself. Nonetheless, for all of them, this second, ambitious goal depended on a prior condition: the disappearance of the king's solitary power, whether by means of the restoration of the old representative institutions or by the new and radical proclamation of the sovereignty of the nation, counterweight or alter ego of the monarch.

The expression "ancien régime," a negative, reverse type of all the values of modernity, emerged as the counterpoint to the new regime that the revolutionaries were attempting to establish. And yet, despite this polarization, befitting an age of combat, the continuities between the old and the new regimes were also manifest. The revolutionaries themselves often admitted their filial debts to the men of the Enlightenment, and on many occasions they pursued and even completed the reforms which the latter had tried to carry out. Yet these men had usually been servants of the "despotic" state and had carried out their reforms in the shadow of the king's absolute power.

The relationship between the modern elites and the absolutist state may, of course, be analyzed in strategic terms: alliances determined by common goals and enemies subsequently became antagonism, for reasons which we will examine below. However, we should perhaps also ask ourselves whether absolutism did not implicitly include a conception of society and of the relations between men and government which was already a form of modernity. Whether, in the long run, the absolutist political regime was compatible with the modern society that it was itself attempting to construct is, precisely, the central problem of the late eighteenth century. To address this question, let us try to examine the main features of the innovations brought about by the victory of absolutism in the Spanish monarchy.

## The King and His Kingdoms

The first innovation was undoubtedly the disappearance of what had been until then the fundamental political feature of the Spanish monarchy: its pactist nature. In its two dimensions, theoretical and practical, pactism meant the contractual relationship between king and kingdom, consisting of mutual rights and duties; and the respect for the specific characteristics—*fueros* (municipal charters), privileges, and liberties—of the different political communities the sum of which, precisely, made up the monarchy.

This does not mean that pactism, until then, had been an unchanging, harmonious reality. On the contrary, the growth of the sovereign's power, his attempts to diminish the autonomy of the various kingdoms, and the emergence of a political literature devoted to unrestrained glorification of the royal dignity, had raised, here as in other modern European monarchies, a conflict fundamental to the birth of political modernity: that of the relationship between royal power—and its instrument, the modern state—and the representative institutions of society, that is, the Cortes in the Iberian kingdoms, the Estates General in France, and Parliament in Britain.

This long-standing problem, rooted in medieval Europe and inseparable from the formation of the modern state, had given rise during the seventeenth century to a variety of political situations. In some countries—Britain and the kingdoms of the Crown of Aragon—the power of the king found itself limited by a very strong constitutional tradition, in which the representative institutions played a crucial role. In others, like France, Castile, and Portugal, royal power had succeeded in slowing this institutional development, though early in the seventeenth century it was still impossible to foresee what forms it would take in the future. The men of the seventeenth century were aware of these different lines of development. As the Cardinal de Retz explained at the time:

> The authority [of the kings of France] was never regulated, like that of the kings of England and Aragon, by written laws. It was merely tempered by custom, transmitted and kept in trust, so to speak, first by the Estates General and later by the Parliaments.[115]

The great crisis of the 1640s—in Britain, the first English Civil War; in the Hispanic monarchy, the rebellions of Catalonia and Portugal and the resistance of the Castilian Cortes; in France, the Fronde—was the first great clash between society and the modern state. During the final years of the century it gave rise to three kinds of political situation: in France, the king's absolute power prevailed completely; in Britain, with the second Civil War, Parliament carried the day once and for all; and finally, in Spain, the precarious stalemate between the two forces was more the result of general exhaustion than a third option. It was a stalemate with respect to the composite structure of the monarchy, since, once the crisis was past, Philip IV returned to the previous status quo; but also with respect to the relations between the king and the most powerful of his kingdoms, Castile. The Castilian Cortes of 1660–64 would be the last until the change of dynasties, not because the monarch had prevailed, but as the result of mutual paralysis: neither the king nor the Cortes were able to bend the other to their will.[116]

That is why, by the end of the seventeenth century, the Spanish monarchy still preserved its traditional political configuration. The monarchy was still composite:[117] that is, it was the union in the person of the king of different kingdoms endowed with a few shared institutions, each of which preserved most of their specific public institutions and laws. The Spanish monarchy presented, simultaneously, examples of the two political regimes embodied abroad by Britain and France. The political regime of the states of the Crown of Aragon resembled the English system, insofar as the king's powers were circumscribed by the

---

115 Cardinal de Retz, *Mémoires* (Paris: Bibliothèque de la Pléiade), 1956, 66.

116 I. A. A. Thompson, "El reinado de Felipe IV," in Andrés-Gallego 1986, 443–92.

117 The term that is sometimes used—"federal" (*federativa*)—carries overly modern connotations.

laws and by customary practice and limited by Cortes endowed with ample powers. The regime of the Crown of Castile was more like the French system, in that the limits of royal power were much vaguer: the king, in fact, could dispense with the Cortes.

This hybrid situation would not survive the change of dynasties, nor the War of Succession, which was in fact a civil war. The evolution toward an ever-stronger royal power, suspended by the mid-seventeenth-century crisis, resumed, under two forms: on the one hand, the uniformity imposed on the institutions of the different kingdoms to form a unitary monarchy; on the other, the assertion of a royal power that had cast off the counterweights of representative institutions. From then on, of the three political models extant at the end of the seventeenth century, only two would remain: the British parliamentary regime and the French-style absolutist regime with its Spanish variety.

Chronologically, though not conceptually, the first change struck at the composite structure of the monarchy. Though the measures taken by Philip V against the kingdoms of the Crown of Aragon that had supported his rival may be considered punishment, they also explicitly expressed the "desire to reduce all my realms of Spain to the uniformity of identical laws, usages, customs, and courts of law."[118]

Uniformity was patterned on the Castilian institutional model. The various *Nueva Planta* decrees—1707 for Aragon and Valencia, 1716 for Catalonia—imposed the Castilian public institutions on the kingdoms of the Crown of Aragon.[119] The specific Cortes of each kingdom were eliminated, and with them the constitutional limits on the king's power. Only a few of their cities would be incorporated into the Castilian Cortes, thus forming the monarchy's new unitary Cortes. The Council of Aragon disappeared, to be replaced by the Council of Castile; Castilian-style audiencias were set up in the different kingdoms, and municipalities were reorganized along the same lines. As a logical consequence of this assimilation, customs barriers between the two crowns were abolished, and it was proclaimed that the inhabitants of

118 Quoted in Domínguez Ortiz 1976, 85.

119 Valencia did not even keep its own civil legislation.

both kingdoms had the same rights as Castilians. Rather than merging the different kingdoms into a single new one—a synthesis of them all—these political reforms, in fact, incorporated the Crown of Aragon into the Crown of Castile. The only autonomous political entities which remained in the new monarchy were the kingdom of Navarre and the Basque provinces, the so-called exempted provinces, which were separated from the common regime by customs barriers and *fueros* which set institutional bounds to the power of the sovereign.

The Spanish monarchy was gradually becoming a unitary state governed by a single system of laws within a unified territorial organization. At least it was tending in this direction, since uniformity was far from being complete, even within the political space that was structured on the Castilian model. For the former kingdoms of the Crown of Aragon, the *Nueva Planta* decrees did not mean mere incorporation into Castile, but rather a laboratory for more radical innovations, which the Crown of Castile would adopt later, in some cases—the system of *intendentes*, for example—or never, in other cases: for example, the modern system of taxation.[120] Moreover, the old kingdoms, each preserving—in part—their own personality and laws, continued to exist within the Crown of Castile. As we shall see below, the most peculiar among these were the kingdoms of the Indies, American extensions of the Crown of Castile: their status and human reality, and the way in which they were perceived, both in the Indies and in Spain, would gradually become a central issue for the monarchy.

A second area in which the sovereign's power manifested itself was that of his relations with the kingdom, the "extended" Castile which was Spain in the making. The monarch's victory over the representative institutions of the realm was overwhelming. Although the role of the newborn unitary Cortes was not as minor as most scholars claim,[121] neither their nature nor their powers made them able to counterbalance

---

120 Called "catastro" in Catalonia, "única contribución" in Aragon, "talla" in Mallorca, or "equivalente" in Valencia. See Domínguez Ortiz 1976, 87, and the failure in Castile of Ensenada's "catastro," in ibidem.

121 The role of the "millones" delegation, an offshoot of the Cortes and in charge of the tax bearing the same name, continued to be important. In 1789, the

the power of the sovereign. For one thing, like the old Castilian Cortes of which they were a continuation, their convening depended on the king's will; and in fact, they met very rarely during the eighteenth century, mostly for the sole purpose of swearing in the new king or the prince of Asturias or modifying the law of succession, even though these meetings were used to carry out other reforms.[122]

As a result, the Cortes had neither the periodicity nor the powers that would enable them to maintain a permanent dialogue with the crown, let alone limit its powers. A further obstacle to their claiming a more important role was their limited geographical and social representativity.

Poor geographical representation was more especially a problem for Spanish America. The kingdoms of the Indies did not participate in the peninsular Cortes, nor had they ever had their own Cortes, even though old laws established that they could be convened should the king see fit.[123] The absence of institutions to represent the kingdoms was, in this case, complete.[124] The evolution toward concentration of power in the sole person of the king and toward the modern state took place earlier and was more radical in Spanish America than in the Peninsula.

---

Cortes also managed to block various measures of disentailment that were being proposed at the time.

122 The Cortes convened in 1712–13 and 1714, 1724, 1760, and 1789. In the first meetings, Salic law was adopted, and in the last, in 1789, the traditional rules of succession were reestablished. Corona 1957, 34.

123 These laws envisage the preeminence to be given in such Cortes to Mexico and Cuzco, the centers of power for the kingdoms of New Spain and New Castile. RLRI, vol. II, book III, title VIII, laws II and IV.

124 In some cases, town juntas did exist for the purpose of addressing appeals to the crown on important issues. This was the case in 1561, when a general junta of city *procuradores* was convened in Peru, endowed with powers resembling those of the Cortes of the realm. See L. Pereña, introduction to Las Casas, *De regia potestate o derecho de autodeterminación* (Madrid: CSIC, 1969), CLVII, 316. We also find in eighteenth-century Venezuela juntas of the cabildos, whose role remains to be studied.

In peninsular Spain, the lack of representativity was not so much a function of the low number of cities convened, as of the limited social representativity of the *procuradores*. It is true that the number of cities represented was limited[125] (a total of 37 in 1789: 22 for the Crown of Castile; 6 for Aragon; 2 for Valencia; 1 for Mallorca; and 6 for Catalonia); but with a very few exceptions[126] all the main cities—the ones which in the nineteenth century would be provincial capitals—were included. The cities convened were, in fact, the capitals of each kingdom, in addition to a few others. This system was not in itself an obstacle to a genuine representation of society, since it really did correspond to the traditional imaginary of representation, in which each body was naturally represented by its head.

The most serious failure in representativity, both in the Peninsula and in America, followed rather from the oligarchical nature of municipal governments, the bodies in charge of appointing *procuradores*. Despite the crown's attempts during the eighteenth century to revert the alienation of appointments to municipal councils,[127] most of these positions continued to belong to a small number of privileged, often noble, families. The municipal reform of 1766, which created the positions of *diputados* and *síndicos personeros del común*, elected by all householders (*vecinos*),[128] did not materially change the oligarchical nature of municipal government: it remained in the hands of narrow local oligarchies belonging to a very exclusive and almost always hereditary patrician class. This framework made it very difficult for the century's social changes—the appearance of new groups of prominent citizens—to find any practical expression; this meant a further obstacle to any possible transformation of the old representative institutions of the realm. As a result, the election of municipal authorities by all *vecinos* that would be

---

125 Proceedings of the Cortes of 1789, in Salvá and Sainz de Baranda, 30–31.

126 Besides the Basque provinces and Navarre, which had its own representative institutions, Cádiz was undoubtedly the most spectacular exception, considering its commercial and financial importance.

127 See Domínguez Ortiz 1976, chapter 24.

128 NRLE, book VII, title XVIII, laws I and II.

decreed during the revolution, though its terms were modern, in fact responded to a growing demand on the part of the new urban dignitaries on the eve of the revolution.[129]

Thus, with the exceptions of Navarre and the Basque provinces, there remained no institution that could stand up to the crown and claim any kind of representation of the realm. In this sense, Spanish absolutism was more advanced than the French version: in the Hispanic monarchy there were neither parliaments nor provincial estates that could attempt to assume representation of the nation, as the parliaments did in France. Neither the central councils of the monarchy nor the most important among them, that of Castile, nor the audiencias, composed of removeable magistrates who were entirely dependent on the king, ever forgot the delegated nature of their power as a continuation of the king's authority, not that of the realm. The crown also suspended the "congregations of the Clergy" and did not show itself particularly in favor of the convening of provincial synods: that is, it avoided any assembly that could represent any branch whatsoever of the social estates, let alone the whole kingdom.

All that remained as a counterweight to the crown was the inertia of society, and the particular resistance of the various social actors, that is, the various corporate bodies that made up the organization of ancien régime society.

## Unusual Kingdoms: The Indies of Castile

Within the group of kingdoms that formed the Hispanic monarchy, Spanish America constitutes a particular case, though not fundamentally different from that of the other kingdoms. Its status would not change materially during the eighteenth century; what did change was how the governments and inhabitants of peninsular Spain perceived it. Legally, it continued to be what it had always been: the group of overseas

129 See for example the petition filed by the *vecinos* of Mérida (Yucatán) in 1810 and 1811, in ACE, general series file 4.

kingdoms of the Crown of Castile. These kingdoms were certainly singular by virtue of their remoteness, the ethnic and cultural complexity of their population, their products and trade, etc. Singular, but not radically different from the realms incorporated into the crown during the final period of the Reconquista: hardly more than a decade separates the incorporation of the realm of Granada and the creation of the American kingdoms. In this area too, the Conquest was a continuation of the Reconquista.

However, the region's peculiar problems very quickly gave rise both to specific legislation and jurisprudence[130] and to a specialized government body—the Council of the Indies—which would last until independence. These particular characteristics did not indicate a "colonial" status: instead, they responded to the very nature of ancien régime political communities, which were in themselves heterogeneous. The identity of laws, rights, and duties as a standard for defining "colonial" status belongs to the imaginary of modernity, which would appear, precisely, during the revolutionary period. Until then, Spanish American demands had belonged entirely to the ancien régime imaginary.

The Creoles, who felt they were being held back in favor of peninsulars or by the crown's policy of uniformity, demanded the "distinctions, privileges, and prerogatives"[131] pertaining to them as the descendants of these kingdoms' founding fathers. In this sense, the kingdoms of the Indies are the last and strongest bastion of pactism and the old composite structure of the monarchy, to such an extent that the main distinction between the "Spains" at the end of the eighteenth century will be that between peninsular and American Spain.

We should perhaps ask ourselves, however, whether the American kingdoms presented the same consistency as the peninsular ones. This question points to a crucial issue of the revolutionary period: Which groups of people achieved independence?

---

130 See, for example, the *Recopilación de Leyes de los Reinos de Indias, mandadas a imprimir y publicar por la Majestad Católica del rey Carlos II*, Madrid, 1681, 4 vols., and Juan de Solórzano Pereira, *Política indiana*, Madrid, 1647, 5 vols.

131 As late as 1809, this is one of the leitmotifs of the famous *Memorial de agravios* drawn up by Camilo Torres, of New Granada (1809) 1960, 9.

In the pyramid of communities making up ancien régime society, the realm appears as a territorial community of a higher order, enclosing, in specific combinations, the manifold local communities and the different corporate bodies that made up the structure of society. The kingdom was a human community tending to completeness by virtue of its territory, its government, and its inhabitants' sense of common belonging as well as common difference from other, similar communities. From this point of view, though institutional aspects were important, they clearly counted less than the specific combinations of social groups in a space ruled by the same authorities, as well as the cultural construction of an identity on which the sense of belonging was founded.

In the Peninsula, the kingdoms, though not all endowed with the complete range of organs by means of which the king exercised his authority, were undeniable realities, true communities of belonging, resulting from a centuries-long existence which in fact made them indivisible. In Spanish America, most of the kingdoms were more uncertain, still shifting entities, as we can see in the eighteenth century from the many changes in administrative circumscriptions,[132] and most of all, from the creation of new viceroyalties—New Granada in 1739 and Río de la Plata in 1776—which break up the former, single viceroyalty of Peru.

The crown's action aimed at administrative rationalization, no doubt, but these changes could only have taken place because the unity of the viceroyalty of Peru was more a bureaucratic than a human reality.[133] Within it, other, smaller communities existed and were quite distinct in the minds of their inhabitants: the kingdoms of Chile and Quito

132 Among the most important of these changes in the region were those affecting Venezuela, which in 1742 received its own governor and in 1786 its own audiencia.

133 Nonetheless, there are signs that its long existence had created a certain sense of belonging. Even by the end of the century, Miranda defined himself as "Peruvian." And along the same lines, the legacy of the Incas would be mythically claimed by the revolutionaries of Caracas and Buenos Aires.

and the New Kingdom of Granada,[134] and specific peripheral areas such as Venezuela and Río de la Plata.

As in the creation of any ancien régime political community, the formation of the American kingdoms was a result of their history: that is, a multiplicity of factors, some of which went back to the period of the Conquest, and others to more recent periods. Among the first, we must consider the density and level of native settlements, the existence of pre-Columbian political units, the areas of action of a given group of conquistadores, the intensity of Spanish settlement and the network of towns the settlers occupied. According to these factors, the crown, and with it the church, organized the territory and gradually installed their representatives. That is why during the first stage, which lasted for two centuries, only two viceroyalties existed, New Spain and Peru, even though within these regions other kingdoms—Guatemala, Quito, New Granada, Chile—inheriting pre-Columbian political or ethnic units and autonomous projects of conquest were believed to exist.

Among the cultural factors involved we should mention more especially the degree to which each of these kingdoms had constructed an identity of its own. This was a long and complex process, during which, as in medieval and modern Europe,[135] the Creole intellectual elites used very diverse means to glorify their homeland. Belatedly, and thanks to the eighteenth century's interest in science, they would invoke nature and geography;[136] but before and after that, they always had recourse to history, whether religious or secular.

Religious history emphasized God's special providence toward each community: in particular, the special protection of the Virgin under her various regional or local names, or that of the saints. Secular history, too, was written and staged in the form of feast days and ceremonies,

---

134 In the work of Huamán Poma de Ayala, *Nueva Coronica y buen gobierno*, references to "this realm" and "these realms" are numerous and mutually equivalent.

135 See for example, for France, Beaune 1985.

136 As in peninsular Spain, the newspapers and various scholarly societies assigned an important role to these regional geographical descriptions. See "The New Forms of Sociability" in chapter III.

which had to include the pre-Columbian civilizations, both to dignify the realm by virtue of its ancient past and to incorporate in the same whole the two "republics," that of the Spaniards and that of the indigenous peoples. Pactism, in this case, provided the necessary conceptual and symbolic tools, by making the Conquest into a founding pact by means of which the indigenous realms were incorporated, like the Islamic kingdoms in their day, into the Crown of Castile. In this sense, the king of Spain was a descendant of the Inca.[137]

It was an uphill undertaking, all the same, which could give priority to the glory of the winners or the dignity of the defeated.[138] In various and complex ways, most of which yet remain to be studied, each kingdom took its own road. Religious New Spain in particular chose for its heroes the evangelizers rather than the conquistadores and united around the Virgin of Guadalupe.[139] The viceroyalty of Peru simultaneously embraced the continuation of the Inca empire[140] and the protection of Saint Rosa of Lima.[141]

By the end of the century, the task of forging each kingdom's peculiar imaginary had not progressed equally everywhere: while it had made considerable headway in New Spain and Peru proper, in New Granada, Venezuela, or Río de la Plata it was barely beginning. Thus, only two American kingdoms, Chile and New Spain, could compare with the peninsular realms in terms of all these factors. The first, by virtue of its geographical isolation and the cohesion of a small and

137 For this reason, on the feast days of colonial Peru, the role of the Inca was always represented by the Spanish authorities. Carlos R. Espinosa Fernández de Córdoba, "La Mascarada del Inca: Una investigación sobre el Teatro Político de la Colonia," *Miscelánea Histórica Ecuatoriana*, Quito, no. 2, 1989, and for the iconography, Gisbert 1980.

138 In Chile, the glorification of the defeated, with Alonso de Ercilla's *La Araucana*, provided the Creoles with an essential element of their identity.

139 See Brading 1988.

140 Hence the importance of Spanish-Inca genealogies and utopias. See on these topics, Demélas 1990, 34 and the following pages, and Gisbert 1980.

141 See for example, for her role in Quito, Demélas and Saint-Geours 1989.

homogeneous population. In the second, the main factors were the existence of a political space already partly structured by the Aztec empire, along with the early occurrence of Conquest and administrative and ecclesiastical organization, the density of the indigenous population, of Spanish settlement and racial intermingling, the intense evangelization and shared worship of the Virgin of Guadalupe, a relatively unified economic space, and the progress made by the kingdom's elites in the creation of a cultural identity of their own.

The other Spanish American regions, though presenting some of the traits characteristic of kingdoms, were mainly administrative divisions of the state[142] superimposed on a series of social units belonging to a lesser territorial area of a different type. These social units consisted in the territory ruled over by a principal city, whether a capital or the administrative center of a whole region with its *villas* and "vassal" towns. This was the American version of one of the most original aspects of the Castilian political and territorial organization: the great municipalities, genuine collective manors ruling over a very broad group of dependent *villas*, villages, and hamlets.

## The American City as the Basic Political Unit

The conquistadores carried with them to the New World the forms of political organization of sixteenth-century Castile, whether municipal or manorial, as well as values and ideals of social organization that were to some extent contradictory. On the one hand, they took the Mediterranean imaginary of the city as the ideal setting for human sociability—a city whose government would be elected by all its *vecinos*, something that was disappearing at the time in Castile. On the other hand, they also took the aristocratic ideal of men who aspired to become lords of vassals. These aspirations were only in part contradictory because the city, for many Castilian nobles—especially those who came from the

142 See for example, for the complexity of Spanish American jurisdictions, Pietschmann, "Las Indias de Castilla," in Hermann 1989.

south, like many of the conquistadores—was the setting par excellence of social existence. The aspiration to municipal government was not incompatible with the desire for noble status.

Of the two known forms of social and political organization—landed estates and municipalities—that the conquistadores had attempted to establish in Spanish America, the first eventually failed after the New Laws of 1542 and the great crises that they unleashed: rebellion in Peru, attempts to transform the encomiendas into genuine hereditary feudal estates, etc.[143] The emerging modern monarchy prevented the creation in America of the landed estates it had to put up with in the Peninsula until the revolution.[144] In this institutional sense, Spanish America seems more modern than the Peninsula, as if it were a field for experimenting with the modern state. This does not mean that it really was more modern: the seigneurial aspiration to "live like nobles" on the part of the conquistadores and their descendants would take shape later in the haciendas, which were hybrid, quasi-seigneurial social forms.

The only legally recognized political units remaining were the villages, *villas*, and towns which, as in Castile, organized the space around the main cities according to a hierarchy of dignity and powers—even more so than in Castile, because of the lack of landed estates and a royal authority made weaker by distance. This was the basic territorial structure of all Spanish America: the main cities with their dependent territories and towns. These were human communities, and therefore undeniable and permanent political units, integrated, in the previously mentioned examples, into the higher unit of the kingdom, and in other cases—the majority—grouped by the modern state, more or less convincingly, in extremely diverse administrative divisions. This variability of the higher political units can be explained not only by the

143 Only a handful of landed estates remained, like that of the Cortés family in Mexico, or a few jurisdictions delegated to nobles in the border regions of northern Mexico. In the latter case, the nobles added military and jurisdictional powers to their mining interests and *latifundia*, Langue 1987.

144 In the America of the peripheral missions, we also have the *reducciones*, or Indian settlements, which, speaking comparatively, were similar to ecclesiastical landed estates.

immensity of the territory and the advance of settlement, but also by the homogeneity of the basic units and their municipal governments. Hence, as well, the strength of what has been inaccurately called Spanish American localism or regionalism[145] and the relative inconsistency of the higher political units; these phenomena would become manifest during the independence period.

The resemblance of this kind of territorial structure to that of Castile was great, but there were also some important differences. Among the resemblances we find the government's speedy alienation of town council offices and the oligarchical nature of municipal governments in major cities. In these cities, as in Castile and most of the Peninsula during the eighteenth century, elections had disappeared, and municipal offices were the property of a few great families, whose struggles within the cabildo made up most of local political life. However, unlike many local governments in the Peninsula, in Spanish America the struggle between nobles and plebeians over the distribution of council offices does not seem to have been significant. First, because the titled nobility was scarce, except in the capitals of the kingdoms and a handful of other cities, such as the prosperous mining cities of northern Mexico: Guanajuato or Zacatecas, for example. Second, because in America every dignitary, every principal citizen, tended to consider himself a hidalgo, even when his title to the name was far from proven. And third, because whatever his real status, by the end of the eighteenth century the "patrician" was defined, precisely, by his belonging to these urban oligarchies. To these men, the first "citizens"—real or imaginary descendants of the founders and first inhabitants of the city—pertained by dignity and birth the government of their "fatherland."

Another particularly Spanish American characteristic was the special relationship which these urban oligarchies maintained with the rural areas. Though their peninsular counterparts also exercised a de facto control over the countryside by means of manifold municipal regulations, obtaining from it perhaps the better part of their income

145 Insofar as these are not particularities arising within a preexisting higher unit, but human communities which predate the formation of this higher unit: first the kingdom, and subsequently the modern nation.

and even holding jurisdictional rights on their estates,[146] the American situation displays a much more complete dominance. More complete because the elites controlled the distribution of labor owed by the dependent indigenous peoples; moreover, they often owned haciendas, on which the peons' condition as freemen before the law was counterbalanced by a variety of customs and usages which bound them to the owner of the hacienda. By virtue of the seigneurial mindset and practices which persisted on these haciendas, though without any legal foundation, the members of these oligarchies were "patricians" in the city and lords of vassals in the country. And finally, their dominance was more absolute because of the reduced presence of the royal administration in these remote regions and the frequent corruption of public employees—*corregidores*, *alcaldes mayores*, and later subdelegates—who were connected by bonds of kinship or patronage to the urban patricians.[147] Though by the end of the eighteenth century the economic prosperity of many regions increased the number of local dignitaries who were excluded from these municipal offices, their desire was not so much to eliminate the gap between "patricians" and the people as it was to gain access for themselves to the offices that were among the most powerful symbols of social status.

So far, we have discussed, on the one hand, the kingdoms, and on the other the cities and towns. This leaves out a term which was being used increasingly during the eighteenth century: the province. The term is ambiguous since it can mean just as easily the structure of society or its government by the state. In the first sense, it is often understood as if there were intermediary human communities between the higher level—the kingdom—and another, local level, that of the *patria chica*, the "small homeland." But as we have pointed out a number of times, until the eighteenth century there was no such thing, whether in the Peninsula or in America, as an intermediary territorial district of civil government between the kingdom, on the one hand, and the towns

146 See Artola 1979.

147 See for example Brenot 1989.

and cities on the other.[148] Until then, in the Peninsula, the meaning of the term "provinces" had been mainly fiscal and referred to territories depending in this respect on towns that had a vote in the Cortes.

The province really emerged with a precise meaning, but referring to the government of society by the state, with the creation of the intendencias as a result of the absolute monarchy's ideal of uniformity and centralization. This was an attempt to bridge the gap between the central administration of the state—the crown or the kingdoms—and the municipal government of the towns, *villas*, and cities. It was also an attempt to create in all the realms a unified territorial division, entrusted to a representative of the state who would unite previously fragmented powers in a single person, so as to intervene more energetically and efficiently in local governments, thus in fact diminishing their powers. In America, this reform went hand in hand with the creation of subdelegates, who replaced the *corregidores* and the *alcaldes mayores* who were in charge of governing the indigenous peoples.

The task of implementing this reform—an important step in the creation of the modern state—was difficult and slow, due to resistance, on the one hand, from the organs and representatives of the state, whose powers were being curtailed, and on the other, from the social actors whose prerogatives it sought to reduce. The reform, first established in the Crown of Aragon during the War of Succession, and once and for all in the whole of Castile in 1749, did not fully reach America until the 1780s.[149]

True, the establishing of the *intendentes* drastically modified, everywhere, the balance of power between the various authorities of the state and the multitude of social actors; but their existence was still too recent for them to generate human communities different from the

148 The *corregimiento*, as an intermediary level of government, was not a genuine territorial division. See Artola 1978, 152n5, and for the previously mentioned situation as well, Domínguez Ortiz 1985, 11 and the following pages.

149 In 1782, in the Río de la Plata; in 1784 in Peru; and in 1786 in New Spain. It was not implemented in New Granada, which was still traumatized by the revolt of the Comuneros.

existing ones.[150] The provinces, when the term did not refer explicitly to public administration, meant, in fact, the spaces of power of the main cities and their governing oligarchies.

These city-provinces, to give them a simplified name, were small "republics,"[151] autonomous actors of social and political life, and could even become city-states should the authority of the state disappear. They were political actors of the first importance, and inescapable in political life; but they were also dominant actors, against whom other rival cities and many subject peoples had fought and would continue to fight. The judicial equality of peoples proclaimed by the revolution would find here its precedents and foundation.[152]

At the height of the revolutionary period, when the weakening of the state would bring to light the deeper social and political structures, the persistence of the old organization in city-provinces and its consequences would be manifest on both sides of the Atlantic. Spain, said the marquis of Palafox in 1809, "has as many Sovereign Corporate Bodies as there are provinces making up the Realm, and as many populous cities and villas as have shown pride enough to [...] exercise a power that does not belong to them."[153]

And shortly after, in America:

> It is necessary, [most Excellent Sir,] to keep in mind that the Cabildos of the provincial capitals command all its other towns, just as a Captain-General might do in his district, even when there are towns of greater importance than that in which the Cabildo holds

---

150 It is true that the boundaries of many intendencias coincided, precisely, with those of the major cities, but this was not always the case: there were more major cities than intendencias.

151 In Spain the *regidores* were often called "republicans."

152 For this movement in the Peninsula, see Domínguez Ortiz 1976, 461 and the following pages.

153 Palafox to the Junta Central, Seville, October 20, 1809, AHN, Secretaría de Estado records, Junta Central, file 7 C.

> its sessions. Thus, they are not a municipal body for one town, but rather a government for an entire district or Province.[154]

In America, many of the civil conflicts of the revolutionary period and the difficulties encountered in the making of the "nation" were a direct result of this centuries-old political configuration.

## The All-Encompassing Power of the King

Although the discarding of the composite political structure of the monarchy, the uniformity imposed on institutions, and the marginalizing of the Cortes were indeed novelties introduced by the Bourbon era, these novelties, nevertheless, were relative, since there already existed numerous precedents for them. The most radical innovation was the ideological construct invoked to justify them, which granted the monarchy a power which was all-encompassing: that is, absolute—no one could set limits to it—and universal, that is, exercised in all areas. Thus, the absolutist conception worked out in Louis XIV's France prevailed, breaking with the political theory previously accepted in the Spanish monarchy—pactism—though each of these conceptions presented diverse premises and manifestations around a common core.

The common core in the various versions of pactism included above all the belief that the relationship between king and kingdom was a bilateral one, implying mutual rights and duties which both parties had to respect. As a result, the king's power was not considered to be absolute, but limited, not only by the law of God, as absolutism would argue, but by the fundamental laws of the realm and the rights proper to each group of vassals: liberties or privileges, considered as compensation for the faith sworn to the king. Another result was that the monarch's ignoring such rights in serious matters could free vassals from their bonds of loyalty, as several rebellions proclaimed: those of Peru

154 Pablo Morillo to the minister of war, 1816, in Laureano Vallenilla Lanz, *Obras completas*, vol. II, Caracas, 1984, 171.

and Aragon in the sixteenth century, for example, or those of Catalonia and Portugal in 1640.

Although more modern conceptions of the king's power also existed, extolling it as the supreme political authority, different in nature from all other powers, it was not until the eighteenth century that these doctrines managed to prevail over pactism. The latter conception rested not only on a political practice that was still in use, but also on a diffuse and deep-rooted social imaginary, dating back to the Middle Ages: that of the lord-and-vassal relationship. It was also supported by a whole team of prestigious writers, the Golden Age's Spanish neo-scholastics: Vitoria, Las Casas, Suárez, Mariana, and others. The fact that these authors, whose political theories directly confronted the monarchs' claim to absolute power,[155] not only were published freely but in fact represented the dominant viewpoint in the universities, was one more indication of the strength of pactism in the Spanish monarchy.

In the common core of absolutist theories we find the insistence on royal sovereignty, now considered as a supreme and absolute authority controlling society while existing outside of it and above its laws. Hence the tenacious upholding of "royalties," the rights of the crown, considered now from a different point of view, which pactism would have called one-sided. The privileges or "liberties" of corporate bodies or individuals were no longer seen as part of a bilateral relationship between the king and his vassals, but as rights wrested from the monarch by force in difficult times, and which he must now win back. This "defense" of the crown's royalties would manifest itself more especially in the struggle to subject the church to the king, but also in the broader but less successful effort to curtail or suppress the privileges of the different estates and corporate bodies making up society.

The sovereignty of the king sought to embrace not only the church and the privileged corporate bodies, but the family, private property,

155 *El Defensor Fidei*, by Suárez, was written in 1613 against James I of England and his aspiration to an absolute power based on the direct divine origin of royal authority. Suárez's book was publicly burned in London and Paris in 1614 because it upheld the legitimacy of rebellion and tyrannicide against the despotism of governments, whether it lay in their origins or their practice.

and even the very fact of belonging to civil society: "The ability to acquire and own land in the realm, and the right to continue belonging to civil society within it, all of this depends on royal authority."[156]

Hence, also, the refusal to admit any appeal against abuse of power on the part of the monarch. This included not only rejecting the right to rebellion and tyrannicide, but even that of mere admonishment, something that Bossuet had expressed in religious terms: "the king's word is all-powerful, and none can say to him: Why do you act thus? [...] the only defense of private individuals against the public power must be their innocence."[157]

All of these aspects developed gradually, from the first piece of advice given by Louis XIV to the future Philip V—"kings are absolute lords"—via highly judicial expositions on the king's royalties by Macanaz or Campomanes, for example, to later theological constructions, very much inspired by Bossuet, as we shall see below.

But under the surface of the explicit political theory of absolutism, a very new imaginary began to prevail concerning the constitution of society and the nature of authority. Classical political theories were all rooted in the Aristotelian conception of man as a naturally social being, that is, a being necessarily belonging to a group. From this point of view, and starting with the family, the existence of the various human groups and therefore of society as a whole did not present particular difficulties. Nor did the existence of authorities in society: in modern terms, since a group is a unit structured by a specific "code" that governs its internal organization and its workings, authority is merely one of the constituent elements of this "code."

What political philosophy did debate, traditionally, were the characteristics and comparative advantages of the various political regimes, that is, the various structures a human group could adopt. In this area Christianity had not fundamentally changed the Aristotelian model when it stated, in Saint Paul's words—which subsequently became a

156 Campomanes, "Expediente del obispo de Cuenca," quoted in Sánchez Agesta 1953, 97.

157 Bossuet (1679) 1967, 92–93.

much-repeated truism of philosophers and theologians—that "all authority comes from God." What this actually meant was that since the world and man had been created by God and were governed by his providence, so were the social nature of man and the existence of authorities in society, whatever the political regime any particular society might adopt: whether democratic, aristocratic or monarchic.

In these classical conceptions, the power of the authorities came undoubtedly from God, but *per populum*: via society. Nor was this power unlimited: under various forms, all of these conceptions affirmed a relationship between rulers and the ruled consisting in mutual rights and duties. Nor did the law depend on the mere will of the prince, since human laws were also bound both to the nature of creation—natural law—and to divine positive law. In general, these conceptions all rested on an imaginary that considered society to be made up of groups, something which was quite coherent with the social structure—a society of estates—and even the political structure—the composite monarchy—existing at the time.

The first novelty in this area was the gradual invention of the individual and his manifestations in the field of political ideas. Although the first signs of this transformation may be sought as far back as the period of nominalism,[158] the fundamental break took place around the mid-seventeenth century. Hobbes's philosophical atomism also appeared in his political theory, under the form of that state previous to society in which individuals, unconnected by any social bond, experienced a constant struggle "of all against all." Hence the compact into which they entered to construct political power: the collective man, the Leviathan in which they would delegate completely and irrevocably all their rights, and which from then on would be the absolute source of all laws. Here, the individualist social imaginary, social "artificialism," law as the creation of power, all made a spectacular stage entrance in the form of a pessimistic version of man, which justified the all-embracing power of the state. Later, different versions of the new modern social

158 Insofar as universals were considered mere names, political communities lost their real existence; this required the existence of an external authority in order to preserve the cohesion of the group.

imaginary would appear, which, while they all preserved the primal individualism, the social artificialism and the view of law as an autonomous creation of society brought together by a founding compact, would differ as to the consequences they deduced from their various judgments on man. Some of them—the optimists like Locke—would see the social compact as the means to ensure man's freedom; others, like Rousseau, who were optimistic about the state of nature and pessimistic about society, would attempt to construct, via the government of the general will, a novel society, reconciled with the primal liberty.

Monarchic absolutism was certainly in conflict with the traditional social imaginary and political doctrines, and in league with the modern conceptions, especially in Hobbes's version; not explicitly, but via the Christianized version provided by Bossuet, the best theoretician of French absolutism, whose reception in the Spanish monarchy was belated but very powerful. Curiously enough, the pious bishop of Meaux, who was firmly convinced of the created nature of the world and man and of its government by divine providence, shared with Hobbes the materialist—whose complete works he owned—the same vision of a pre-social state of man in which the struggle of all against all prevailed.[159] Although he added that this state was not man's primal state, but the result of original sin, this clarification did not fundamentally change the situation that needed to be remedied. The solution, as in Hobbes, was to invest the sovereign with an absolute authority destined to preserve social cohesion from outside and above. In the final analysis, the social bond depended on authority; hence Bossuet's obsessive fear of social dissolution when that authority was questioned, something which would explain his popularity after 1789.

To provide a theological foundation for this all-embracing power of the king, he transformed the maxim "all authority comes from God" into a direct divine origin for the monarch's power,[160] besides granting it biblical dignity by appealing to the monarchy of David. The power

159 Both, moreover, were witness to two periods of weakness of the state and political dissolution: the first English Civil War and the Fronde in France.

160 Bossuet never clearly formulated this theory, so much at odds with the traditional doctrine.

of the sovereign was that of God's representative; like divine power, it brooked no limitations, admitted no appeals. The glorification of the sovereign's all-encompassing power went hand in hand with that of the monarchy as an ideal regime, and of the immeasurable dignity of the king's person. One of Bossuet's Spanish disciples, the bishop of Tarragona, would express the same view in almost identical words: "You all know, [...] that Kings reign through God; that they are true ministers, lieutenants on earth, and living images of the Divinity."[161]

The revolutionaries' subsequent attack on the king's absolute power should not conceal, despite differences as to the identity of the sovereign—whether the king or the people—the kinship existing between the absolutist and the revolutionary imaginaries. Both shared a common hostility toward the corporate bodies and their privileges, a unitary conception of sovereignty and the ideal of an unmediated binary relationship between government and individuals, to such an extent that absolutism may be seen as a version of modernity.

The paradox of the Spanish—and French—situation during the eighteenth century was that the absolutist theory, so much at odds with the traditional pactist conceptions that were common theological doctrine, should have become in the course of the century the official teaching of very broad segments of the church: so much so that for most nineteenth-century liberals the union of Throne and Altar, from the absolutist point of view, ended up being naturalized.

The explanation for this must undoubtedly be sought in the victory of regalism, which, in gradual stages, finally subjected most of the clergy to the monarch's authority. The Concordat of 1753, which increased to an extraordinary extent the bureaucratization of the Spanish church and its dependence on the state, was an important stage in this process. Docility to the crown and adherence to its conception of power became requisite conditions for nomination to the higher ecclesiastical offices. A second key stage was the expelling of the Jesuits in 1767 and the banning of many of the works written by the classical Spanish political authors,

---

161 Pastoral letter of April 15, 1793, quoted by Lluis Raura, "Cataluña y la Francia de la Revolución," in Aymes 1989.

labeled "Jesuitical writings."[162] Yet traditional doctrines concerning the indirect divine origin of royal power, and even concerning the legitimacy of resisting tyrants, could not be entirely eliminated, since, in fact, they appeared in most handbooks for training the clergy.[163]

Despite this, and despite much resistance, the "Bossuet-style" defense of absolutism gradually became a commonplace both in the so-called Jansenist literature and in sermons, pastorals, civil catechisms and other apologetic literature. Bossuet's works were translated and published several times throughout the eighteenth century: *La politique tirée de l'Ecriture Sainte* was reedited in 1743, 1768, and 1789; and there were six new editions of the *Discours sur l'histoire universelle*.[164] But it was mostly during the 1780s that his influence seems to have reached the widest audience. During these years his doctrine appeared in a number of works as a weapon against events that seemed to endanger social cohesion and the monarch's authority. Some of these works were American, and were responding to a traditional uprising against absolutism, like that of the Capuchin friar Finestrad,[165] written after the revolt of the Comuneros in Socorro in 1781, or to internal tensions in colonial society, like that of the bishop of La Plata, José Antonio de San

---

162 Works by Mariana, Molina, and Suárez were banned, and university professors had to take an oath not to teach them. These bans were renewed after 1789, and even by 1801 instructions to this effect were being sent to university censors, stressing the absolute respect owed to royal authority and repeatedly rejecting the right of insurrection and tyrannicide. Sánchez Agesta 1953, 109–13.

163 See, for example, the modern handbooks of theology, which were permitted by the crown, that Miguel Hidalgo used for his training and teaching in Valladolid de Michoacán; those used by the Dominican Gonet, the Augustinian Berti, and another Dominican, Cardinal Goti. Carlos Herrejón Peredo, "Hidalgo: La justificación de la insurgencia," *Cuadernos Americanos*, Mexico, XLII, no. 1 (1983): 162 and the following pages.

164 See C. E. Corona, "La doctrina del Poder absoluto en España en las crisis del siglo XVIII al XIX," in *Cuadernos de la Cátedra Feijoo*, no. 13, Universidad de Oviedo, 1962, and Eduardo Muñoz, "Deux thèmes de l'Indépendance: Pacte social et constitution historique au Chili," in Guerra 1989, vol. II.

165 J. de Finestrad, *El Vasallo instruido en el estado del Nuevo Reino de Granada y sus respectivas obligaciones.*

Alberto.[166] Most of these works were peninsular, like those of Antonio Vila y Camps,[167] Joaquín Lorenzo de Villanueva,[168] Clemente Peñalosa y Zúñiga,[169] and were written and reedited to fight the French Revolution and its assault on the king's absolute power.[170]

Spanish absolutism had begun by giving priority to civil arguments in support of royal powers, in the line of a well-established Hispanic tradition of not granting too much importance to religious discourse;[171] by the eighteenth century, it had become an official ideology in which the religious and the profane were inextricably intermingled. This was precisely what the revolutionaries would fight against.

## American Grievances

When it comes to the progress of absolutism, Spanish America holds a special place within the general framework of the monarchy. In the Peninsula, absolutism progressed until the end of the eighteenth century without encountering much opposition. The same cannot be said for Spanish America, where more traditional pactist conceptions were very widespread and came to the fore as a great force of reaction to the surge of great Bourbon reforms.

Most of these reforms were not, in their content, radically different from the ones that had been carried out in peninsular Spain. The administrative reforms—new territorial divisions, the establishment of

---

166 *Catecismo real*, Madrid, 1793. See Demélas 1990, I, 151 and the following pages.

167 *El vasallo instruido en las principales obligaciones que debe a su legítimo monarca...*, Madrid, 1792.

168 *Catecismo del Estado, según los principios de la religión*, Madrid, 1793.

169 *La monarquía*, Madrid, 1793.

170 See also Antonio Elorza, "El temido árbol de la Libertad," in Aymes 1989 and Herrero 1988.

171 See Maravall 1972.

the system of *intendentes*, the reorganizing of public finances, and so forth—were part of a strategy aiming to rationalize public administration and give the state greater control over society. This strategy had already been displayed under various forms in the Peninsula.

What made Spanish America different was undoubtedly the fact that this onslaught of the modern state was directed at societies which in fact enjoyed much greater autonomy than the Peninsula. A variety of factors, among which physical distance was crucial, had contributed to an informal but very effective distribution of powers between royal civil servants and the various groups that made up Spanish American society. By means of very diverse mechanisms, among which family alliances, patronage, and corruption played a key role, American society had succeeded in integrating most of the royal officials into its complex power strategies. Actual political practices were even more remote from what the laws established than they were in the Peninsula; this neutralized in fact the great theoretical power the state wielded in Spanish America. Thus, the modernizing onslaught of absolutism must inevitably cause greater trauma there, all the more so because the conception of America underlying it was quite new, and, for the Spanish Americans, quite disturbing.

The attempt to impose greater subjection of the church to the crown, as well as to achieve greater efficiency in public administration and higher tax returns did not in itself manifest a change in the status of Spanish America within the monarchy, but rather an attempt to recover or broaden royal prerogatives which was typical of the absolutist period. What was new were the drastic methods adopted to seek these goals, and the language used to justify them, as in the words chosen by the viceroy of Mexico to silence complaints about the expelling of the Jesuits: "Once and for all, the subjects of the great monarch who sits on the throne of Spain must henceforward know that they were born to be silent and to obey, not to argue or to express opinions on high matters of government."[172]

---

172 Proclamation of the Viceroy Marqués de Croix, June 25, 1767, in Miranda 1952, 159.

In a similar sense, the main watchword of the 1780 uprisings in Peru and those of New Granada the following year—"Long live the king, death to bad government!"—refers us to the pactist standards of a society traumatized by tax and customs measures brutally imposed from above and maintained against opposition from the society.[173]

Newer, and to some extent more traumatic for the Spanish Americans—especially the elites—was the novel conception of the role that America was to play within the monarchy. In the higher spheres of the state there had always been an awareness of the Indies' vital importance to the crown's finances; from this point of view, the reforms aimed at making them yield the highest possible tax returns did not deviate from traditional policy. But to this traditional financial conception was now added a view that gave the Indies a more economic role: that of providing the products that the Peninsula lacked and offering a market for peninsular products. The Spanish administrative elite was beginning to consider the kingdoms of the Indies as colonies: that is, territories existing primarily for the use of a metropolis, in this case peninsular Spain.

It is clear, in fact, that part of the Spanish American economy did answer to this kind of asymmetrical relations; it is equally clear that the greater part of the Spanish American economy and society did not conform either to this rationale or to the discourse of the peninsular elites. With the exception of the tropical agricultural regions, most of the economic sectors and social groups in Spanish America were not primarily oriented outward.

And yet, this new conception would make constant progress throughout the eighteenth century. The traditional, legal way of considering Spanish America as a group of realms belonging to the Crown of Castile, with their own institutions and authorities, gradually changed. Little by little, infected by the possessions of other European powers in the Caribbean, the kingdoms of the Indies would begin to be seen as colonies.[174] The word is in itself ambiguous, since it can be interpreted in var-

---

173 See for example, for New Granada, Leddy Phelan 1978, and for Peru O'Phelan Godoy 1988, and Demélas 1990, vol. I.

174 The example of the Count of Aranda illustrates this evolution: starting out from a traditional conception of the monarchy as made up both of peninsular

ious ways, not all of which necessarily indicate unequal status. The word "colony" can refer to antiquity, if we understand it as the establishing of a city or mother community overseas, something which may—but does not have to—imply political inequality with the metropolis.[175] But "colonies" can also mean, in a much more modern sense, factories created for purely economic ends and deprived of any political rights of their own.

The fact that this vocabulary almost never appeared in official documents, which continued to use the old terminology of realms and provinces, was no obstacle to the term "colonies" being used frequently in the press, in books, and even in the private correspondence of royal officials.

Whatever the meaning given to the word, its use smacked of inequality between the two parts of the monarchy. This was something the Spanish Americans were especially sensitive to, since it brought into question something they considered essential: their status within the monarchy. From their point of view, they remained kingdoms, like the peninsular realms, as Fray Servando de Teresa y Mier would state with strength and conviction as late as 1813:

> Thus the Kings, ever calling the Indies these our kingdoms, from which they take their titles as from the others, did not establish there a government of Consulates or Factories, but of Viceroys,

---

Spain and Spanish America, he moved subsequently to considering the latter as colonies, which could even be treated as exchangeable commodities in the relations between powers. See on this point Jesús Varela Marcos, "Aranda y su sueño de la independencia americana," *Anuario de Estudios Americanos*, Seville, no. XXXVII (1980): 351 and the following pages. There was some reason for the protests the Spanish Americans expressed so frequently during our period, about being integral parts of the monarchy and therefore unalienable.

175 The reference to the English colonies in North America also illustrates this. This is the meaning Spanish Americans gave to the term when they themselves occasionally used the words "metropolis" or "colony." See, for example, Fray Melchor de Talamantes, "Representación de las colonias, discurso filosófico," summer of 1808, in De la Torre Villar 1964, 132 and the following pages. Fray Servando de Teresa y Mier also begins his *Historia de la Revolución en Nueva España...* with a quote from Thucydides in which Corcyra presents its grievances to its metropolis, Athens, about the inequality in rights between them.

> Chancelleries, Audiencias and a Supreme Council of the Indies, invested with the same honors and distinctions as that of Castile; equal establishments of Cabildos, Courts, Universities, Mitres; a particular Code of laws which are replaced little by little by those of Castile, in the points in which they differ [...].[176]

The inequality was not shocking in itself, since the entire judicial structure of the ancien régime was based, precisely, on the diversity of laws and statutes; what was shocking was that this inequality did not stem from a respect for the "*fueros*, franchises, and privileges" repeatedly granted to the Spanish Americans by the crown; on the contrary, it arose from a supposedly subordinate relationship between a metropolis—Spain proper—and colonies whose rights were presented as inferior.

As a result, by the end of the eighteenth century there was considerable touchiness among Spanish Americans concerning any measure that could be interpreted as expressing this unequal conception of the monarchy. American complaints to the peninsulars about their occupying the best public offices displayed from the beginning a pactist component—that of the rights pertaining to natural-born subjects of the realm with respect to those who had not been born there—thus acquiring new weight.[177] The crown's strategy of designating more and more peninsulars to these offices during the final third of the eighteenth century[178] could of course be explained by a desire to make the public administration more independent of local power networks; but this policy enormously increased the Americans' feeling that the pact binding them to the crown was being modified and that their rights—both individual and collective—were being infringed upon.

---

176 Mier 1813, 1990, Book V, 138.

177 See, for example, the petition to this effect presented by the City of Mexico to Charles III in 1771, in Hernández y Dávalos 1877, 427 and the following pages.

178 For these changes and their regional specificities, see Burkholder and Chandler 1977.

# III

# Another Kind of Modernity

Side by side with the progress of absolutism, the eighteenth century would also witness the great cultural transformation that we call the Enlightenment, but that we could just as easily refer to by the broader term of modernity. This process consisted of a series of multiple transformations—some of them identical with those that absolutism had brought about, and others new—in the field of ideas, imaginaries, values, and behaviors.

Modernity is primarily the "invention" of the individual. The concrete individual, the "empirical agent, present in every society," would now become the "normative subject of institutions"[179] and values. This process went back a long way; but it culminated in the late eighteenth century. By way of a whole series of changes gradually affecting the various fields of human activity, the individual and individualistic values began to predominate. Gradually, the individual would occupy the center of the entire frame of reference, reconfiguring values, imaginaries, and institutions despite social inertia and manifold resistance.

The progress of individualism cannot be separated from the triumph of a view of society that conceived it as a juxtaposition of equal, homogeneous, and in fact interchangeable individuals. This view would later be expressed in the modern constitutions; we already find it, however, in the structure and workings of the modern forms of sociability. It is here, in this new world of societies of all kinds, in the "republic of

---

179 Dumont 1966, 22. This author has also analyzed in other works the extraordinary novelty that this birth of the individual represented in relation to traditional societies. See also Dumont 1977 and 1983.

letters,"[180] that the new system of cultural references came into being and spread, and a new model of society began to take shape: public opinion and modern politics,[181] precisely what would burst into the open during the revolutionary period.

All these transformations were common to the European cultural area, and therefore also to the Hispanic monarchy. Yet in any transformation, at the beginning the changes only affect a limited number of individuals. That is why we need to examine where, when, and in what circles and areas the transformations took place: that is, we need to establish a geography and a chronology of modernity in the Hispanic world, and an outline of its specific features. Among these, the most important were undoubtedly those that had to do with the modern groups' relationship to the absolutist state and the traditional society that both were attempting to transform.

## The Individual and Society

One may address the phenomenon of the Enlightenment from very diverse angles; in this case we will limit ourselves to considering the aspects which most directly serve to explain the appearance of modern politics. Politics as we conceive it in the nineteenth and twentieth centuries—and the revolutionaries perceived this clearly—was a novelty in the history of our civilization. The sovereignty of the people, that new and irreversible principle of any legitimacy, was a novelty; so was the existence of written constitutions, those acts of foundation of societies

---

180 To use Augustin Cochin's terms. See, for example, "Les philosophes," 1912, in Cochin 1979, vol. I.

181 What Habermas calls "literary public space." See, for his various concepts, Habermas (1961) 1978. The cultural aspect of the explanatory model continues to be convincing, much less so its economic and psychological premises. As in other books on the same topics, the absence of any mention of the Hispanic world is one more indication of how far the Hispanic revolutions have been forgotten.

that perceived themselves as unprecedented; the appearance of systems, whether electoral or otherwise, for transferring the sovereignty of the people to those who exercised authority in its name was quite new, as well as the emergence of men and groups specializing in political action, and the birth of an abstract political language charged with moral connotations.[182]

This modern politics, and the social imaginary underlying it, is what would prevail in incipient form with the American Revolution, later more radically with the French Revolution, and finally, in our area, with the Hispanic Revolution. Although the originality of the phenomenon is clear, the explanation for it is less so. For example, it is not enough to invoke the people bursting onto the public stage: there had been countless previous examples of riots, rebellions, uprisings, and *jacqueries* of a notoriously popular nature and involving distinctly popular demands; and yet, not only do we find in them none of the distinctive traits of modern politics, but on the contrary, they express a deeply traditional mental world. The people we perceive in such events is not the abstract sovereign people of modern politics, but the very concrete and complex people of traditional society: the many social groups that did not belong to the world of the privileged.[183]

To explain all these innovations we may also invoke the progress of ideas and make long lists of works and authors in which these ideas appear as a way of tracing the "progress of Enlightenment." But though we cannot do without the history of ideas, in the end it always comes up against a two-fold problem: not only the question of how widespread the writings were, but also of how many people really embraced the ideas that these writings contained. Reading a text is one thing; sharing or assimilating its ideas is another.

Another more promising method is undoubtedly to analyze the places and modes in which people socialized. In this area the rediscovery of the insights formulated by Augustin Cochin early in the twentieth

182 See Furet 1977, a seminal study in this new interpretive approach.

183 For the multiple meanings of the word "people," see chapter X.

century[184] has opened the way for more satisfying interpretations by revealing the correlation to be found everywhere between the appearance of new forms of sociability and the construction and spread of modernity. This approach makes it possible, and not only for the modern forms of sociability, to reveal the constant interconnection existing between the ideas, imaginary, and values of a certain group—a social actor—and that group's internal structure and workings. This allows us to grasp the profound transformation taking place in these areas, and the distance separating the actors in traditional societies from those that take center stage in modern societies.

The social actors on the old model were characterized by mutual bonds that did not depend on the actual will of the men of whom they were made up. These bonds were not usually the product of personal choice, but of the individual's birth within a specific group: they were kinship ties (in the broadest sense of the word, including both political connections and the relation with godfathers), ties to a village, an estate, a hacienda, or an ethnic group. In other cases, the bonds did arise out of a personal decision; but the individual who willingly became a member of a group or corporate body in the ancien régime was not free to establish the rules or modalities of his membership.

All these groups were governed by custom, law, or the rules of the corporate body. A man could join a family clan or the clientele of a powerful patron; he could establish bonds of friendship or begin to practice this or that trade which would make him a member of this or that corporation or guild. But ties of kinship, patronage, or friendship depend in any given period on a content determined by custom; the same was true of the membership of a trade or guild, which was established by rules. The choice of such bonds could be more or less free, but once it was made, they were usually unbreakable, unless the person joined a different group or became a social outcast.

In all these cases, the bonds were decidedly personal, man to man, with reciprocal rights and duties of a pactist kind, generally unequal

184 This rediscovery is due to Furet 1977. Most of Cochin's works were published after his death during the First World War. See, for example, Cochin 1925, 1978, and 1979.

and hierarchical. In the imaginaries of these old actors, the highest value was given to custom, tradition, precedents, since these were the sources that legitimized the existence of the bonds. The same was true for values like fidelity, loyalty, honor: all these elements contributed to preserve the identity and cohesion of the group over time. For it was the group, whatever its structure, that stood at the center in traditional societies. The group—a village or family clan, for example—preceded and survived the individuals it was composed of at a given moment in its history. Men passed and the group remained, renewing itself endlessly in its individual components without change in the overall structure; or if there were changes, they were very slow. The old actors had a life expectancy and an inertia far superior to that of their members.

Because they were societies made up of social actors on the old model, the European societies of the ancien régime, to which the Hispanic societies belonged,[185] naturally saw themselves as a great body with diverse organs and functions: a whole composed of diverse estates, corporations, and political communities. They saw themselves as what they were: a whole made up of groups that were juxtaposed, superimposed, and intertwined, each of them with its own specific rights and duties, its "privileges"—its specific laws—defining its situation with respect to the other groups and to the state. The solitary individual, independent of his or her ties of belonging, was almost unthinkable.

The actors we find in modern societies present a very different aspect. Here, instead of the ties we have just been describing, we find bonds of association, but of a very particular kind. These are associations which derived their legitimacy, not from custom or law, but from the association itself: from the members' will. The intensity and shape of these ties were the result of the very act of constituting the association.

---

185 The Spanish American societies were also part of the European ancien régime, though this does not mean that they were identical to the European societies. To the differences already mentioned when we discussed the realms of the Indies we may add, with respect to the social actors, the existence of extremely coherent ethnic groups—African or indigenous, or castes—that had very few counterparts in Europe; we can also mention the extreme cohesion of many local communities.

Members defined it themselves, and they could—at least in theory—redefine it at any time.

At the root of this kind of bonds we find not only the growth of an imaginary founded on the individual, but also the emergence of the new forms of sociability that were spreading in Europe at the end of the seventeenth century: salons in France, tertulias in the Hispanic world, academies, literary societies, Masonic lodges, economic societies, and so forth. The expression used for them later in France, *sociétés de pensée*—literally, "societies of thought"— expresses very well their primary purpose: thinking and conversing together, reaching a common opinion. In this world of opinion, governed solely by the laws of "clear and distinct" ideas, all individuals were necessarily equal since they were seen solely as associated "wills" and/or as thinking "reasons." As a result, from the outset men came together in these forms of sociability independently of their belonging to the various corporate bodies and estates. These bonds were therefore seen as egalitarian, devoid of any personal character, and revocable: that is, radically different from the traditional kind of bonds.

The difference also lay in the systems of authority: if the very existence of the group depended on agreement among members, so did its authorities. The legitimacy of authorities, whose foundation presented no special difficulty in the traditional systems, would in the modern world become a central problem and a prize that men would compete for. A problem, because how could a group even be conceived, when the individual will had become an absolute origin? A prize to be fought over, since the associates would seek to set themselves up as the representation or embodiment of the group's will. It has rightly been said that these societies constitute the roots of democratic sociability.[186] Once this model was adopted by the society as a whole, the new legitimacy would emerge: the sovereignty of the people.

In the new imaginary that went hand in hand with the spread of the new forms of sociability, the emphasis, as we mentioned, was on the individual. The main thing was not the group that someone joined, but the individual who did the joining. Rousseau clearly expressed both

186 The expression is taken from Halévy 1980.

the individual's primacy and the advantage of his position. The individual, who is "in himself a perfect and solitary being," that is, free from any inherited bond, may nonetheless achieve solidarity by virtue of the bonds he himself chooses to assume. These bonds, of course, are voluntary and of the modern type: otherwise, they would be in contradiction with what man was and must be.

Little by little, as these forms of sociability and their corresponding imaginary spread, the entire society began to be conceived in the same terms as the new sociability: as one vast association of individuals willingly united, the sum of whom made up the nation or people. The groups that conformed to the traditional model—with its extremely different bonds and values—then came to be considered as unworthy of man and contrary to his freedom. We find here the basis for one of the governing trends in the evolution toward modern societies: the struggle to eliminate the social actors of the ancien régime, those highly coherent communities and corporate bodies that were so foreign to the mental universe of modernity.[187]

Only the expansion of the modern social actors, the spread of the new forms of sociability and the imaginaries they carried would provide the conditions for the emergence of modern politics. A kind of politics that would demand a continuous effort to transform the social actors' heterogeneity into the unity of general opinion, interest, or will. It would also require a kind of personnel specially trained for the job—politicians—and a competition for control of the legitimacy arising out of the new sovereign: the people. In this competition, speech would play a crucial role, since the expression "the people" refers here to an abstract, homogeneous entity, whereas society, in contrast, is nothing if not sheer diversity. This process of transmuting society into the people is what explains the key role played in modern politics by the men who wielded the word or the pen: they were the only ones capable of saying what the people or the nation wanted or thought.

---

187 Only in certain cases—in the political or cultural spheres—could these groups be replaced immediately by actors of a modern type. In other cases—in the social and religious spheres—it would be necessary to wait longer before attempting such a replacement.

The march toward a new way of conceiving man as an individual and society as a voluntary association was thus inseparable from the emergence of the new forms of sociability and their corresponding social practices. Though clearly we must give up here any rigorously deterministic approach or attempt to establish some impossible first cause, the new forms of sociability were certainly the social space in which modernity took root, and its main means of dissemination.

## The New Forms of Sociability

The Hispanic world shared with the rest of the European cultural area most of the features of this general evolution, though it also presented some peculiar traits. Among the shared features, we should mention first of all that these transformations began among the intellectual elites, and very limited ones at first; and second, that these kinds of sociability assumed increasingly diverse forms in the course of the century.

The most significant trait specific to the Hispanic world was the lesser diversity of forms taken by these modern kinds of sociability. Though almost all the ones that occurred in the rest of Europe did exist, two of them seem to have been predominant: the tertulias, on the one hand, and the Economic Societies of Friends of the Country, or patriotic societies, on the other.

The tertulia was the first known form of modern sociability in Spain, as the salon was in France. In both cases, it was at the outset an elite form of sociability, operating in very narrow circles and with origins going back to the seventeenth century.[188] The salon and the tertulia were to some extent the primary forms of a "society of thought," insofar as nobles, clerics, public servants, or affluent citizens, united in their common belonging to the cultural elite and with no statutory

188 The first meetings of this kind, the French salons, were already well-established by the second half of the seventeenth century. Their origins certainly date further back, and in the 1640s, we already find Hobbes in Paris attending Mersenne's salon, where scientific topics were discussed.

distinctions between them, would discuss various topics: literary, worldly, scientific, or religious. Even though these were still informal meetings, without definite statutes or members, they were already the seeds of genuine societies since they usually brought together the same people at each meeting and presented a specific periodicity and shared habits. In a way, the forms that came later were officialized versions of the salon and the tertulia. In the eighteenth century the scientific and literary societies[189] and the academies,[190] the patriotic societies—or Societies of Friends of the Country—gave the group an institutional character with official membership statutes and sometimes specialized topics of discussion.

But though the tertulia was in a way the original model for all the modern forms of sociability, this does not mean that later societies made it disappear. On the contrary, on the eve of 1808, tertulias of all sorts continued to be the most common form of sociability. There are various reasons for this phenomenon. The first is that even though the tertulia can be seen as the earliest and still informal mode of the new sociability, it was more than that: it was also the space which brought together people whom other powerful bonds, not only cultural but also bonds of kinship and affection, impelled to meet regularly. Thus, even by the nineteenth century and later, many tertulias continued to be family gatherings of men and women, often extending to friends and acquaintances.

The importance of kinship and friendship bonds in the Hispanic world—and more generally in the entire Mediterranean world—contributes then to explain the extraordinary persistence and scope of the tertulias.[191] It also explains the somewhat hybrid character—intermingling traditional and modern behaviors—that we find in every form of

189 The first scientific tertulias appeared in Spain at the end of the seventeenth century in Valencia, Seville, and Barcelona.

190 The academies were usually private societies, though endowed with formal statutes.

191 See for example, on the importance of friendship in the Sociedad Vascongada de Amigos del País, José M. Portillo Valdés, "El País Vasco: el Antiguo Régimen y la Revolución," in Aymes 1989, 239 and the following pages.

sociability in the Hispanic world. The individualistic rationale of the new modes of sociability, whereby relations between members were supposed to be exempt from passion and governed exclusively by the laws of reason, often clashed with the internal solidarities of informal groups structured by kinship or friendship. This gave rise to oppositions that had little to do with differences of opinion and can be explained by rivalries inherited from the past or springing from a variety of personal factors. Here we have one reason for the extremely personal nature of modern political life in the Hispanic world.

The second reason for the predominance of the tertulias was the lack of legal freedom of association. Though, as we shall see below, a number of societies were in fact institutionalized, and even promoted by the crown, most of the groups formed during the eighteenth century had no legal status. In all of Europe, the growth of modern forms of sociability went hand in hand with the growth of the private sphere. Social life tended to a great extent to take place privately, in the intimacy of the home, the monk's cell, the lodgings of students or seminarians.[192] This is where people with mutual affinities born of friendship or culture would meet, seeking in this intimacy a freedom of interaction and speech not to be found in public spaces. The term "tertulia" used to describe these meetings might have been a protection against state intervention,[193] or a sign of the still incipient nature of the society or of its elite character. Some would achieve public status and recognition, like the tertulia of the Count of Peñaflorida, which became in 1764 the Basque Society of Friends of the Country; others would never achieve this status, like the group that published *El Telégrafo mercantil* in Buenos Aires early in the eighteenth century: their request, made in 1802, was never accepted.[194] Still others, like the one founded by a few clerics

---

192 See Habermas (1961) 1978.

193 At the time of the French Revolution, many of those on trial for collusion with the revolutionaries claimed as an excuse that their meetings were mere tertulias. See several examples in *La vida colonial: Los precursores ideológicos...*, 1929 and 1932.

194 See Robert J. Shafer, "Ideas and Work of the Colonial Economic Societies, 1781–1820," *Journal of American History*, American Institute of Geography

and intellectuals in Seville in 1793, the Academy of Human Letters, would choose to remain in the private sphere, in order to continue discussing controversial issues.[195]

Thus, the term "tertulia" had a great many meanings and referred to very diverse realities that need to be specified in each case, just as people did at the time when they would add to the word a more precise adjective: literary, scientific, political, and so forth. For despite their shared features, each one involved different social practices and relations to the rest of society. In this sense, the venue where the tertulia took place and whether women were present or not were very important factors. If the tertulias took place in the homes of prominent families and in the room used for social activities, it was normal that women should attend and be the organizers of the event. The range of topics discussed in this type of tertulias, since they included courtly themes, was inevitably broader than it would have been in a meeting with only male participants, which does not mean, however, that the first kind excluded discussions about ideas or politics. In Cádiz, in fact, during the period of the Cortes, the most important political groups seem to have been the ones defined by attendance at the tertulias of Doña Francisquita Larrea or Doña Margarita de Morla.[196] But usually ideological or political topics would be more freely discussed when the tertulias were exclusively masculine. The group's meeting would be more private, which made it easier to approach such themes, especially when the authorities disapproved of them. We should add that when these tertulias moved out of private homes and into cafés, inns, and taverns, as began to occur in certain cities by the late eighteenth century, their function changed. Something that had begun as a private conversation between people of the same social circle inevitably extended to other, less select, social groups. Even when the meeting took place in a reserved room, physical proximity easily led the other clients to become a first audience for the tertulia's members, which made it easier for ideas and passions to spread

---

and History, no. 44 (December 1957): 331–68.

195 Pons 1990, vol. I, 43 and the following pages.

196 On these tertulias see Martínez Quintero 1977, 31–32.

to more lower-class groups. Hence the surveillance exercised on such places during the period of the French Revolution in Cádiz, Madrid, San Sebastián, Barcelona, and others; hence also, later on, during the revolutionary crisis, the measures taken in certain places, like Mexico, to close the cafés or keep watch on the local stores (or *pulperías*).[197]

Another specifically Hispanic feature was the central role played by the Societies of Friends of the Country, which have already given rise to very numerous studies. Here we merely wish to stress some of their features in relation to the emergence of this other version of modernity that we have been discussing. One of their most peculiar traits was that they were located at the meeting point between two different trends: on the one hand, society's spontaneous move toward new forms of sociability, shown by the flourishing tertulias; on the other, the policies of the enlightened state elites that were seeking to enlighten society. In peninsular Spain, at the outset, the initiative came from society, as we have seen with respect to the very first of these associations, the Basque one, and shortly afterward with that of Madrid. But in the spread of the phenomenon throughout the rest of the Peninsula a crucial role must be assigned to the policies of Campomanes, who from 1774 onward sought to use these societies as a means for disseminating the Enlightenment, beginning with that piece of pedagogical writing, the *Discurso sobre el fomento de la industria popular.*

In the following years the Council of Castile would promote the multiplication of these societies, which were obliged to adopt statutes and regulations on the model of the Economic Society of Madrid. A whole combination of motives explains why these societies flourished: in many cases, it had to do with society's aspiration to cultural renewal; in others, there were also motives of another kind, such as a public servant's zeal to comply with official policy, some high-ranking person's desire to display his concern for the progress of the Enlightenment, or in more practical terms, someone's wish to improve their *curriculum vitae*, since membership of the societies was considered meritorious. In most of these cases, the state's role was primary, and provides a good

197 This was one of the first measures taken after the "peninsular" party's coup d'état in September 1808.

illustration of the role played by the modern elites in the absolutist state. Modernity almost always spread from above, in a pedagogical effort to disseminate the Enlightenment.

But despite the state's promotional policy and its control, the economic societies undoubtedly contributed to the progress of social modernity, not so much because of the work they carried out, the publication of proceedings, or the founding of educational establishments, though some of them were very active in these fields, but most of all because of their social practices. The equality between members, whether or not they belonged to a corporate body or estate, which in the tertulias was informal and the result of bonds of friendship or belonging to the same cultural or family circle, in the societies was established by statute. This equality displayed itself even physically, in such concrete provisions as banning of precedence and stipulating that members should be seated by order of arrival. Within the societies, members were "citizens pure and simple," in the terms used by the Guatemalan society.[198] When you know that the order of precedence was a symbolic reflection of the social order and its hierarchies, and consider just how fierce the quarrels could be on this point in ancien régime society—especially in Spanish America[199]—you can see to what extent these new practices represented a silent revolution.

Thus, we find emerging, in a way, a forerunner of a new society made up of individuals disburdened of the preoccupations of their social status and associating freely in the search for the general interest of their country and the common good. This new image of social affairs found itself reinforced by other egalitarian practices as well, such as the election of the society's authorities by the vote of all its associates, or the rules that regulated debates on the society's concerns and the writing up of conclusions and proceedings. A whole series of practices began thus to predominate which we might very well call "democratic," and which were a kind of apprenticeship for those that would later carry the day in modern politics.

---

198 Quoted by Shafer, loc. cit., 338n32.

199 See for example Leal Curiel 1990.

Another feature that was shared among all the modern forms of sociability, but which the economic societies institutionalized to such an extent that many of them took their name from it, was the concern for the improvement of their homeland, of their country. Solutions were to arise out of the common reflection and debates of their members. That many of these debates should indeed have been "academic" and not based on a technical knowledge of the topic at hand was from this perspective largely irrelevant. What really counted was that, since light—the Enlightenment—was supposed to illuminate everything per se, any topic could become a possible object of reflection, and that people should believe that the solution depended solely on the use of reason properly applied. The argument of authority and the legitimating force of tradition, so crucial in ancien régime society, thus gradually lost their value, and an active and critical attitude began to make headway, acting first in the social and economic sphere, and later in other areas. All these elements favored the questioning of the status quo, the search for new solutions, and the development of utopias.

The emphasis on country and homeland took on particular importance in Spanish America, because it produced a great many geographical studies, reports on flora and fauna, accounts of resources and economic statistics which contributed to reinforcing local identities and their correlative patriotism, since these elements were appealed to as a way of contradicting the frequently unflattering opinions of the Europeans.[200]

Finally, another particularly Hispanic trait which distinguishes the area from most European countries is the almost total absence of Freemasonry up until the first years of the nineteenth century. We must wait until 1808, and more especially until 1814, with the restoration of absolutism, before Masonry can be considered an important social phenomenon.[201] Up until then, the only significant Masonic network was the one Miranda founded in London in 1797 or 1798 under the name of

---

200 See for example, for New Granada, Silva 1988, and for the controversy with Europe, Gerbi 1960.

201 As always when it comes to the study of Masonry, these statements depend on the sources known and explored to date. This is the position defended by Ferrer Benimelli in various works, 1974 and 1980, or in "Masonería e Inquisición

Gran Logia Americana, which would give rise later, with the revolutionary period in full swing, to the Lautaro societies or lodges. These were crucial in Cádiz and various parts of America as meeting places for the partisans of independence. But their Masonic character was not in fact very clear, and they could be better defined as a political society that used secrecy to achieve its ends in a hostile environment.[202]

## The Modern Elites

On the eve of the Hispanic Revolution, the most important modern societies could be found primarily in the world of the elites. In Spain, the tertulias of students and professors in Salamanca and Zaragoza, of enlightened clerics in Seville, of nobles and clerics in Azcoitia and Vergara, of professors, students, and members of the professions in Murcia all belonged to this milieu, as did the various academies and literary and political tertulias in Madrid and elsewhere. In Spanish America, the same thing was true for the tertulias of students and clerics in Mexico, Guadalajara, and Chuiquisaca; of clerics, officers, and "patricians" in Valladolidad de Michoacán, Dolores, and Querétaro; the patriotic societies of Guatemala and Lima; the patrician tertulias in Caracas, Quito, or Santiago de Chile; the one formed by the members of the Bogotá scientific expedition; and the embryonic patriotic societies that published some of the new American newspapers, such as *Mercurio peruano, La Gazeta de Guatemala, Las Primicias de la Cultura de Quito, El Papel periódico de Bogotá*, or *El Telégrafo mercantil* in Buenos Aires.

By these means, the new forms of sociability and the new cultural frames of reference would gradually spread to other groups lower down on the social scale. But compared to other European countries, especially France—the center of the Enlightenment during the eighteenth

---

en Latinoamerica durante el siglo XVIII," *Montalbán*, no. 2, Universidad Católica Andrés Bello, Caracas (1973).

202 See Berruezo 1986, 92 and the following pages, and Pons 1990, vol. I, 301 and the following pages.

century—this social dissemination was much weaker. Though the topic has not yet been sufficiently studied, it seems clear that even by the end of the century, all these innovations were still reserved for a tiny intellectual elite, mostly composed of members of the nobility and the urban patrician classes, and of the clergy, as well as royal civil servants, professors and students of the universities, and some merchants.

Only a few Spanish American societies had a significant number of merchants among their members, perhaps because these societies played to some extent the role of consulates in cities which had none. We only find hints of modern forms of sociability of a more popular character at the time of the French Revolution, whether in the Peninsula or in Spanish America. Among those accused of being "assemblyists," that is, supporters of the French Revolution, we occasionally find, along with members of the cultural elites, a few middle-class tradespeople and higher-level artisans. But even then, these groups were very much in the minority, except in the Spanish regions near the French border, and they often gathered around French residents.[203]

Not until well into the revolutionary period would the new forms of sociability begin to spread toward lower-class social circles. The meetings would then abandon the private sphere and move into public and semi-public spaces: cafés, inns, taverns, and *pulperías*. In this way, they would become one of the main connections between the world of the elites and that of the people, by way of conversations or public readings of writings and newspapers. A contemporary description of the atmosphere in Seville during the period of the French Revolution gives a flamboyant but explicit portrayal of this trend:

> being politicians is all the rage now: no one talks of anything but news, reforms, judgments, and so forth. Even the street porters buy the *Gazeta* and in the taverns, the courts of law, next to Mariblanca, in the cafés, there is talk of nothing but battles, revolution, the Convention, national representation, freedom, equality. Even the

---

203 See, for example, Domergue 1984, or *Los precursores ideológicos…*, 1929 and 1932.

> whores ask you about Robespierre and Barrère [*sic*] and you need to equip yourself with a good quantity of *Gazeta* tall tales if you want to please the girl you're courting.[204]

What was still at the time merely a nascent development, whose progress would be reined in by a state fearful of contagion, later would gradually become something more general. A knowledge of these public spaces where the new sociability took place and their connections with the world of the elites is undoubtedly crucial to understanding many of these periods' movements, of which many sources were already giving a glimpse and which are described in excessively simplified terms as "popular." Important examples could be the role played by the cafés in mobilizing the people of Cádiz during the Cortes,[205] to put pressure on the deputies, or the Madrid cafés during the second liberal revolution.[206]

For the time being, on the eve of the revolutionary crisis, the modern forms of sociability continued to present a very elitist makeup. Rather than emerging from a nascent bourgeoisie, these elites came from the most cultivated sector of ancien régime society. Very often, the members' families and fortunes placed them at the summit of society; in any case, all of them belonged to the intellectual elite. Very rarely did they belong to the middle class in the modern sense of the term. It is significant, as Domínguez Ortiz has pointed out, that in the Peninsula the most active cities and those presenting the most markedly bourgeois character, like Cádiz, Barcelona, or La Coruña, had no Societies of Friends of the Country.[207] The makeup of these societies, in any case, does not point to specific social origins; rather, it reflects the "urban models" of the cities where they were created.[208]

---

204 Letter from Estala to Forner, quoted by Javier Varela Tortajada, in Moral Sandoval 1989, 93.

205 For information on this point, see Solís 1987.

206 Alamán 1972, vol. V, 27, gives an excellent description of the Madrid cafés and the patriotic societies that met there. See also Gil Novales 1977.

207 Domínguez Ortiz 1976, 395.

208 Barrio, in Enciso 1991, 332.

What all these modern forms of sociability do point to is a cultural milieu held together by dense networks of epistolary and human exchanges.[209] It was a social milieu that shared the same sensitivity, the same sense of the useful, the same belief in progress; it read the same books, shared the same social practices promoting free suffrage, the equality of all associates and the reign of opinion. The "republic of letters" was indeed a constellation of diverse societies united by these common elements more than by their belonging to a group determined by socioeconomic criteria or even by their embracing the doctrines of the "philosophes."[210] As Alexis de Tocqueville incisively said, speaking of eighteenth-century France: "At the bottom, all the men who stood higher on the social scale than the people resembled each other; they had the same tastes, sought the same pleasures, read the same books, spoke the same language."[211]

Even though this group in the Hispanic world was far from being as widespread as Tocqueville indicates for France, the portrait he gives of it is relevant. The main actors, first of the French and later of the Hispanic Revolution, belonged more to a "cultural class" than to a social one.

If we examine the social makeup of the revolutionary assembly par excellence in the Hispanic world—the Cortes assembled in Cádiz from 1810 onward—we see that the features of this social category are very distinct. The most numerous group was made up of the clergy (30 percent); then there were members of the public administration (21 percent), the military (9 percent) and the professions (9 percent), and members of the municipal oligarchies (7 percent), categories which all included a great many nobles. Merchants occupy the very last rung of this scale, with only 1 percent.[212] The revolutionary group mirrored the

---

209 On this cultural milieu in France, see Roche 1988.

210 Augustin Cochin's article, "Les philosophes," written in 1912 and recently reedited in Cochin 1978, already presents a very brilliant conceptualization of the "republic of letters," which subsequent studies have only confirmed.

211 Alexis de Tocqueville, *L'Ancien Régime et la Révolution*.

212 These calculations were made based on the DSCGE of ACE, Credenciales, I, 6, Chávarri Sidera 1988, and Berruezo 1986.

elites of an ancien régime society. What truly defined it were not its material characteristics but its belonging to the intellectual elite, and its youth. Clerics and nobles, academics and lawyers, royal and military functionaries, members of the municipal oligarchies, students and sons of great families, the occasional merchant, artist or artisan: this was the modern group par excellence on both continents.

## Geography and Circumstances of a Cultural Area

Within this general march of the Hispanic world toward the new forms of modernity, we still need to examine the respective timelines of the process and its regional differences; above all, we need to compare peninsular Spain and Spanish America. One way of approaching the problem, as we mentioned, is to try and compare the progression of the elements that function as signs of the ongoing transformations: the forms of sociability, the press, and the condition for its dissemination, that is, the spread of literacy.

It is difficult to quantify the growth of the new forms of sociability, insofar as the most numerous among them were precisely the tertulias, which by virtue of their informal nature left few written traces. Only the memoirs of their members, and in some cases the police files, allow us to guess at their importance in configuring the modern elite. It is more feasible to compare societies that received the authorities' approval, more especially the economic, also known as patriotic, societies.

The figures available for these societies are very significant: about a hundred in peninsular Spain and a dozen in Spanish America. Even adding to the American figure a few other societies which did not officially possess this status but in fact functioned as such, the imbalance continues to be considerable, if we consider the similarity in population numbers between the two regions at the time. How can we explain this phenomenon? One important factor, undoubtedly, was royal policy. It is well known that the creation of many of the peninsular economic societies was closely linked to the will of the crown. They came into being with its backing and survived while this backing persisted. By the end of the 1780s, many of them had only a listless and rather theoretical existence. In Spanish America, this driving role of the state seems to have been lacking. Judging from the known cases, it would seem that the societies created in America arose despite the state rather than with its support, as if the enlightened elites in America had needed to demonstrate with irrefutable facts—newspapers and publications[213]—that they were worthy of royal approval. It is possible then that the existing ones responded primarily to social initiatives and that if the peninsular societies had had to be born under the same conditions, there would have been fewer of them. We still need to explain, however, why some of the most important cities in Spanish America, especially Mexico City, did not possess this kind of societies. Perhaps this is because the existence in such cities of a great many educational institutions and professional corporations already provided the cultural and social elites with enough spaces for sociability.

In any case, these limited numbers had an impact on the spread of modernity in America by reducing the number of places where modern social behaviors could be learned in practical ways. Many of the modern groups existing in Spanish America never moved on from being tertulias or informal literary societies, with all the corresponding implications: that is, the essentially private character of the group and the mingling of modern practices with behaviors and attachments that came directly from the older forms of sociability. In the final analysis, the absence of official support was understood by many Americans as the sign that the crown was not interested in them, or worse, that it was holding them back and deliberately keeping them in ignorance.

Another significant difference is the time lag between the two continents that we find in the foundation dates of the patriotic societies. The great wave of foundations in the Peninsula took place in the period between 1775 and 1784. In Spanish America, though some societies were founded during the 1780s, most of them appeared in the following decade: for Santiago de Cuba, in 1783, for Lima, in 1790, Havana in 1792, Quito and Guatemala in 1794, and so forth. This time lag tells us

213 For Lima, for example, see Jean-Pierre Clément, "El surgimiento de la prensa periódica en América española: El caso del *Mercurio Peruano*," in *La América española en la Época*..., 1988; and for Bogotá, Silva 1988.

clearly where the center of gravity of the Enlightenment was at the time; another indication is the fact that many of the founders of the Spanish American societies—for example, the American Jacobo de Villaurrutia, the heart and soul of the Guatemala society—were men who had discovered this kind of sociability in the Peninsula. We have here a repetition of what had already happened in peninsular Spain with respect to the other European countries, especially France. When the count of Peñaflorida founded the first of them all, the Basque society, he found his inspiration in the provincial academies and various scholarly institutions that he had discovered during his stay in France, as well as other similar institutions existing in Italy.[214] In this area as in others, it is easy to see that the time lags were the logical consequence of models being transmitted from the center to the periphery of a single cultural area.

Other important points of comparison that we need to consider in order to understand the discrepancies between the two continents and their various regions are literacy and the press. Neither of these factors was by itself a sign of ideological modernity: who reads, what they read and how, can refer us to a very traditional world. It is true, nonetheless, that the press and levels of literacy are two necessary conditions for the appearance of a "public" of readers, a constitutive element of "literary public space" or the "republic of letters."

We will not discuss literacy at length: though there have been more and more studies on the topic, a great deal remains to be done if we are to have a complete view of the question. It is clear, however, that during the eighteenth century, and especially during its last three decades, a considerable effort was made to increase the number of primary schools. In the Peninsula, a law of 1781 made primary school free and mandatory and made the municipal authorities responsible for it.[215] No doubt this was more a matter of good intentions than immediate achievement, but the number of people who knew how to read did undoubtedly grow. In Spanish America, the case of Mexico and several others suggest that

---

214 See Herr 1973, 129 and the following pages.

215 Barrio, in Enciso 1991, 338.

the number of literate people also increased noticeably in the region.[216] Though it is impossible to give precise figures, there are indications that much of the urban population and a lesser proportion of the rural population were literate: the figures would seem to be significant, and much higher than was believed until now.[217] This spread of literacy explains the role played in the revolutionary process by written documents: newspapers, letters, cheap satirical publications, proclamations, poems, and so forth, addressed, as their contents indicated, to very diverse and sometimes very lower-class audiences.[218]

The Hispanic societies by the end of the ancien régime were already societies in which written material had ceased to be scarce, and the products of the printing press were multiplying. Of course, most of this printed material did not propagate the values of modernity. In the Peninsula as well as in Spanish America a considerable proportion of it—whether made up of *pliegos de cordel*[219] or of other kinds of publications—was clearly directed at a lower-class audience. Even the very high percentage of religious themes to be found in more "noble" publications shows how crucial traditional themes and values continued to be in written culture. A comparison between France, the Peninsula, and Spanish America in terms of the proportional amount of space these topics occupied gives us an idea of the geography of modernity. In France, religious titles represented 40 percent of published material at the beginning of the eighteenth century, 30 percent by mid-century, and 15 percent between

---

216 For Mexico, see chapter VIII. In some rural areas of Guatemala, the number of people who knew how to sign their name by the end of the eighteenth century had risen to 55 percent of mestizos and 20 percent of Indians. See Michel Bertrand, *Terre et société coloniale: Les communautés Maya-Quiché de la région de Rabinal du XVIe au XIXe siècle*, Mexico, 1987, 146.

217 The region about which there is least information from this point of view is undoubtedly the Andes, not because this effort to increase literacy did not take place there, but because the sources are much less abundant, or less well-known.

218 See chapter VIII.

219 Popular works printed on loose sheets and sold cheaply in the streets.—Trans.

1784 and 1788.[220] In peninsular Spain, the approximate percentages were 50 percent by mid-century, and 19 percent by the end.[221] In New Spain, the region of Spanish America where printing was at its most vigorous, the percentage of religious titles, in 1804–7, still varied between 75 and 84 percent;[222] even after 1808, when patriotic and popular publications were flourishing, the percentage never fell below 28 (in 1814).

The gap is so obvious that no commentary is necessary. It becomes even more obvious if instead of percentages we examine the absolute figures of books and pamphlets or handbills printed in Spanish America: a little over a hundred during the best years, before 1808 in Mexico,[223] about twenty in Bogotá during the same period, and none in Chile. The vast majority of books read at the time in America came from abroad, mostly from the Peninsula: this was not only where most works originally in Spanish were printed, but also where foreign works were translated and the translations printed. Whether due to the authorities' reluctance or more probably to a lack of internal demand, printing in Spanish America, except for the old viceroyalties, was still scarce on the eve of the revolution. But a kind of effervescence could be felt, no doubt as a result of the rise in school attendance, which heralded its growth in a near future.

A study of newspapers and periodicals may supplement and clarify these observations in an area even more significant when it comes to the progress and dissemination of modernity. We cannot provide here an exact count of the periodical publications of the entire Hispanic world; we can only point out some trends and make some comparisons. The most important city in terms of the precociousness, number, and quality of its newspapers was undoubtedly Madrid. At the height of the Enlightenment, in the decade of 1780, this city's periodicals included, among others, the official newspapers the *Gazeta de Madrid* (founded in 1701), the *Mercurio de España* (1784–1830), and the *Diario de Madrid*

220 Dupront and Furet 1965–70.

221 See López 1976.

222 See chapter VIII.

223 A more exhaustive count would most likely give a slightly higher figure.

(1758–1918), the first newspaper on the continent; the *Semanario erudito* (1781–91), *El gabinete de la lectura española* (1787–93), the *Correo literario de Europa* (1781–87), the *Memorial literario* (1787–91), the *Espíritu de los mejores diarios* (1787–91), which was extremely influential in Spanish America; two more ideologically progressive newspapers, the *Correo de Madrid* (1786–91) and the *Diario de las musas* (1790–91), as well as the radical publications *El Censor* (1781–87) and Marchena's *El Observador* (1787), besides a few other more short-lived publications.[224]

In the face of this abundance of publications, the importance of the other regions of the Hispanic world was very minor. In peninsular Spain, there were few important newspapers in the provinces, except for a handful of rather ephemeral ones in Seville, Cartagena, Cádiz, Valladolid, and Barcelona, with its *Diario de Barcelona*, founded in 1791. In Spanish America, the geography of the press was fairly similar to that of the peninsular provinces: there were no newspapers before 1808, whether in Caracas or in Santiago de Chile, and only a few isolated and somewhat ephemeral titles in some other capitals. Among these, the most important were the ones published over a certain period by the patriotic societies—official or unofficial—of which we have already spoken: the *Mercurio peruano*, *La Gazeta de Guatemala*, *Las Primicias de la Cultura de Quito*, *El Papel periódico de Santa Fé de Bogotá*, *El Correo curioso, erudito, económico y mercantil de la ciudad de Santa Fé de Bogotá*, *El Telégrafo mercantil, rural, político-económico e historiográfico del Río de la Plata*, or *El Semanario de agricultura, industria y comercio*, in Buenos Aires.

From this point of view, the Spanish American capitals were quite similar to the peninsular provinces, though this does not diminish the importance of these few publications. On the contrary, their very scarcity certainly gave them greater weight in the formation of public opinion in their regions. The *Mercurio peruano*, for example, was read by half the white population of Lima.[225] The fact that most of these

---

224 On these newspapers and their editors, see Barrio, in Enciso 1991; Dérozier, in Tuñón de Lara 1980; Elorza 1970, Herr 1973; and Fuentes 1989.

225 See Clément 1983.

publications should have been the organ and extension of some patriotic society shows both the narrowness of the enlightened elite and the strong consciousness they had of their mission as leaders and teachers of society, as the independence period would show very clearly.

In this overview we have deliberately left out New Spain and more especially Mexico City, which reproduced on a smaller scale the role of Madrid by virtue of the precocity, diversity, and quantity of newspapers published. Besides other scientific and scholarly publications which began to appear in the second half of the eighteenth century,[226] in the same style as those of Madrid, and the various *Gazetas* that had begun to appear periodically since 1722, we find appearing in Mexico City on the eve of 1808 the following newspapers: the *Gazeta de México*, published twice a week; Mexico's first newspaper, founded in 1805, the *Diario de México*; and a weekly paper, *El Noticioso General*, devoted to advertisements and short pieces of news. As for Veracruz, it had one weekly paper, founded in 1806, *El Jornal económico de Veracruz*, which became a daily in 1807.[227] This shows the peculiarity of New Spain clearly; and after Madrid the cultural importance of Mexico City had no equal in the entire Hispanic world.

But curiously, though New Spain can be seen as the region with the highest levels of literacy and schooling in Spanish America, its political culture was not the most advanced, as would become clear during the crisis of the monarchy, when it displayed a very traditional ideological frame of reference.[228] The most advanced regions would be other areas, which until then had not come anywhere close to possessing as broad a cultural base; some of them, like Caracas, had not even a single newspaper. This paradoxical phenomenon makes it clear that there was no simple correlation between cultural institutions, the abundance of printed material available, and the press, on the one hand, and ideological modernity on the other. It would seem, on the contrary, that

226 Their main editors were José Antonio de Alzate and José Ignacio Bartolache.

227 Medina 1911; Miquel y Vergés 1941; and Bravo Ugarte 1966.

228 See chapter VIII.

in America there was a reverse correlation: the regions with the fewest modern elites turned out to be the most advanced.

One explanation might be that the reduced number of these elites, precisely, made their ideological evolution more coherent, something less likely to happen in a society with elites that were more numerous and more fragmented. An additional explanation might be that ideological radicalism can be expressed more easily in less literate societies, where there is less connection between elite and popular culture. In Mexico, on the contrary, the high levels of literacy and the widespread circulation of written materials meant that the elites' advanced ideas could more easily reach the masses and trigger strong negative reactions. We see this happening during the independence period, when both Hidalgo and his adversaries mobilized Indian populations by talking about the danger for traditional customs and religion implicit in the collusion with the French Revolution that Napoleon embodied.

The formation of the "republic of letters" certainly needed the self-affirmation and growth of newspapers and printing in order to create a "public space"; but this condition was not necessary everywhere and at all moments, as we can see from the Spanish American example and that of a great many peninsular cities. The fact is, as we have mentioned, in many of these regions the press was scarce or entirely absent, and the modern forms of sociability few and far between. Nonetheless, the revolutionary period would show that they did possess zealous modern elites and a seed of "public space" awaiting the right moment to come to light. In the meantime, this "public space" was organized by cultural practices more than by the press or an abundance of books. The networks of letter writers allowed many manuscripts and the little printed material available to circulate; and borrowing and shared reading increased the dissemination of documents coming from various places, mostly those where freedom of assembly and publication made possible the "progress of the Enlightenment." These places, which were often remote, made up for the structural deficiencies of the peripheral zones, or for the temporary obstacles imposed on other areas by restrictive political measures.

That is why we need to construct a historical geography of modernity that takes into account the type, density, and establishment of the modern groups; the number and print runs of enlightened newspapers;

the periods of greater or lesser freedom of assembly and the press. Then we will be able grasp precisely where the driving centers of cultural transformation were located and when.

There remains a great deal to do before we can achieve this result, but we can already attempt to construct a global model whose broad lines present a high degree of probability. France undoubtedly takes first place in the Latin world, whatever the criteria that we adopt. Richard Herr, assessing the size of the enlightened elite in peninsular Spain around 1788, estimated subscribers to newspapers at several thousands of people and institutions, something which meant several tens of thousands of readers; in France, these figures were in the tens and hundreds of thousands, which, considering the two countries' respective populations, meant four times fewer readers in Spain.[229] The Spanish American figures were even lower, though with regional variations: Mexico certainly came closest to the peninsular figures than to those of other regions in America. If we quantified all the forms of modern sociability, we would find an even greater discrepancy, if only because of the considerable number of Masonic lodges existing in eighteenth-century France.[230] These factors show the Latin world, by the late eighteenth century, organized in three concentric circles: the central one was France, the second was formed by the adjacent countries—Italy, Spain, Portugal—and the third was made up, with regional variations, of Hispanic America and Brazil.

Finally, only a few words need to be said—the subject having been already very widely studied—about the ideological evolution of the modern elites and their relations to the state. Modernity, whether in its absolutist or its new version, progressed continuously throughout the eighteenth century, though the circumstances of this progress varied. In peninsular Spain, the height of the Enlightenment was undoubtedly the period of Charles III, and more especially the decade of the 1780s. This was a golden age during which educational institutions would be founded or reformed, modern forms of sociability would multiply, the

229 Herr 1973, 162–65.

230 On this topic, see Halévy 1980.

publication of books and the founding of newspapers would increase. It was also a golden age because of the fairly easy circulation of books arriving from the European centers of the Enlightenment, the great delays in censorship on new books, and the reduced watchfulness of the Inquisition with respect to printed material so long as it did not attack absolutism directly. And also because the governing class, the servants of this absolutist monarchy, belonged for the most part to the modern elites, in some cases to their highest intellectual reaches.

Circumstances would change profoundly with the French Revolution, especially after 1791, not because the governments of Charles III's period were rejecting the legacy of the Enlightenment—in this area even the hated Godoy implemented enlightened cultural policies—but for political reasons.[231] The desire to prevent revolutionary contagion from the neighboring country while not complicating delicate diplomatic relations with powerful revolutionary France made the government distrust the nascent yet flourishing public opinion, expressed in the many publications founded during the reign of Charles III. The drastic suppression, in February 1791, of all the existing newspapers except the three official ones represented a decisive turn: though the different prime ministers who succeeded each other in office practiced varying degrees of severity in their "cordon sanitaire" policies, the press never recovered its earlier strength until the crisis of 1808.

This does not mean that the modern elite disappeared or that its numbers diminished; but for almost seventeen years it would lack these extremely important means to forge a "public opinion" in the full sense of the term. Of course, a social milieu continued to exist in which travel, letters, and the exchange of written material—manuscripts impossible to publish, forbidden books, foreign newspapers—fueled discussions among the modern groups and thus formed an "opinion" which, though it was not "public," was that of the "public" in the modern sense of the word.[232] A "public" that was obliged to remain, if not in the shadows—

---

231 On these topics, see Seco Serrano 1978; Dérozier in Tuñón de Lara 1980; and Elorza 1970.

232 For example, on the role played at the time in Madrid by bookstores in the clandestine dissemination of written material and as a place for political

since everyone knew quite well who its members were—at least in the half-light of the private sphere.

In this half-light, the great transformations caused by the French Revolution would take place. Not all these transformations would favor the progress of modernity: many enlightened thinkers, even radicals such as Olavide, would recoil in horror from the turn taken by the French revolutionary process. But clearly a crisis was beginning in the support that the modern elites had given to the absolutist government up until then. True, the doubts had begun before 1789; but that date is when the criticism of absolutism began to intensify, and solutions began to be sought for the regeneration or replacement of a regime that no longer seemed to represent the "spirit of the age." This change had an impact on all the enlightened intellectuals, but especially on the young people, more and more of whom had never known anything but a discredited regime, the criticism uttered against it by its predecessors and the more modern writings—including the revolutionary ones—being read in the various tertulias and societies where they met.[233]

When the crisis of 1808 broke out, they would be the most active agents of the revolutionary process. As if they were concluding a long interlude, the modern men and groups that had remained for so many years in the half-light would come out into the open, bringing with them ideas and imaginaries that seemed all the more modern because they had been taking shape in the private sphere. The interlude also came to an end for the press: the need to mobilize the people and promote patriotism made newspapers proliferate to an extent never seen before. Almost every capital or important city had its own newspaper. Not all these publications, by any means, propagated the ideas and imaginaries

---

conversations, see Elorza, "El temido árbol de la libertad," in Aymes 1989, 74.

233 The correlation between youth and cultural modernity is confirmed in every country. In prerevolutionary Spain, the most advanced tertulias and literary societies could be found mainly in the academic world, in Salamanca, Seville, Zaragoza, Murcia, Madrid, the Basque Country. A first count of these groups can be made thanks to Martínez Quintero 1977, Domergue 1984, and Pons 1990, vol. I.

of modernity,[234] but their number and diversity would enable the formation of a genuine public opinion, a public opinion in which the most advanced modern elites would soon play a dominant role, insofar as they themselves, by virtue of their social practices and ideas, had previously been the seeds of "public opinion" and the new society.[235]

In Spanish America, which was farther removed from the French revolutionary focal point, the crown's restrictive policy existed, but was not applied with the same rigor as in the Peninsula. The modern American elites thus encountered fewer obstacles to their development, though they suffered indirectly from the paler glow of the peninsular Enlightenment. Here the crisis of 1808 also caused a proliferation of published material, but unlike the situation in the Peninsula, there was no immediate surge in the number of available newspapers, since most of the royal authorities continued to govern and enforce the restrictions inherited from the previous period.

True, the *Gazeta de Caracas* was founded at the end of 1808; but we must wait for the first autonomous juntas to be formed in 1810 before we see newspapers multiply and, with them, the gradual birth of modern public opinion. This is when every important city in Spanish America would follow the road taken by the Peninsula in 1808. In Bogotá, for example, we see the founding of the *Diario político de Santa Fé* (1810–11), the *Aviso al Público* (1810–11), the *Gazeta ministerial* (1811), Nariño's *La Bagatela* (1811–12), and others. In Caracas, besides the *Gazeta de Caracas*, founded in 1808, we see appear successively *El Semanario de Caracas* (1810–11), *El patriota de Venezuela* (1811)—the organ of the recently founded patriotic society—*El Mercurio venezolano* (1811) and *El Publicista de Venezuela* (1811). In Río de la Plata, the *Gazeta de Buenos Aires* was created in 1810, followed a few months later by the *Gazeta de Montevideo*, and later, again in Buenos Aires, by *El Censor* (1812) and the *Grito del Sud*. In Chile, we must wait until 1812 to see the foundation of the *Aurora de Chile*.

234 See chapter V.

235 See chapter VII.

Spanish America would follow the evolution of the Peninsula with a time lag of almost two years; this makes it even more essential to understand how, during these two crucial years, the great ideological transformation then taking place in the Peninsula was propagated.[236]

236 See chapter VIII.

# IV

# Two Crucial Years (1808–1809)

The interval between the peninsular uprisings in the spring of 1808 and the dissolving of the Junta Central in January 1810 was undoubtedly the key phase of the Hispanic revolutions, both in the transit to modernity and in the shaping of independence. True, from a commemorative standpoint, 1810 is much richer in symbolic dates: the creation of the autonomous juntas in South America in the spring of that year; Hidalgo's insurrection in Mexico in September; the assembling of the Cortes in Cádiz a few days later, and their proclamation of national sovereignty. Yet we should mention, in defense of this less celebrated period, that the time lag in the transmission of news meant that the spring of 1810 in Spanish America was the equivalent of the peninsular January. The creation of the American juntas is contemporary, in political terms—and that is what counts—with the disappearance of the Junta Central.

The events and the change in mentalities that led to this first upheaval would take place during this short period between 1808 and 1809. Peninsular Spain would cover most of the distance still separating it from the victory of political modernity. The traditionalism still in force during the period of the uprisings would give way to a very modern kind of political debate. Later, military and political circumstances would interrupt the consolidation of the victory for a few months; but ideologically, the most modern elites had already carried the day by the end of 1809.

America would emulate the ideological evolution of the Peninsula, evolving at the same time, in less than two years, from unanimous and fervent pro-Hispanic patriotism to an explosion of grievances against the peninsulars which would cause a break that by then was almost irreversible.

To understand these crucial years, it is essential not to lose sight of the global perspective: that is, to see the monarchy for what it still was—a single whole—and analyze the consequences that events in one of its parts had for all the others. From this global perspective, it is normal that events in peninsular Spain should take on primary importance, since that is where we find the political center of the monarchy, where its fate would be decided in military terms, and where the general decisions were taken to which Spanish America would react. Thus, political circumstances in the Peninsula would define the timing of American changes.

In other words, the global perspective on the political circumstances of the time is indispensable for several reasons. First, because a study of local causes cannot explain the most spectacular feature of the period: the simultaneous character and the similarity of the processes leading to independence in the various countries. Internal causes, whatever they were, can only lead us to recognize diversity: diversity in social and economic structures, cultural levels, and the spread of awareness about those feelings of singularity that would later be called *national.* But diversity cannot explain either simultaneity or similarity: why, at the same moments, and following very similar processes, did the various regions of Spanish America react in similar ways? That is why we must give priority to the whole over its parts.

Second, all the sources of the period point in this direction. Even a superficial reading of these sources shows the central position occupied at the time by general problems and especially by issues related to the provisional governments established in the Peninsula for the whole of the monarchy. Gazettes, proclamations, the proceedings of the cabildos, private correspondence, all show, without a shadow of doubt, that the most urgent concerns for the Spanish Americans of the period were, for example, the struggle against Napoleon, the formation of the Junta Central in Spain, the election of American deputies to represent them in this junta, the convening of the future Cortes, the reform of the political system, and so forth. The realms and provinces of Spanish America—to use the names by which they referred to themselves at the time—participated, from afar, it is true, but just as passionately as the peninsulars, in the same political debate, and thus in the same revolutionary process.

This does not mean that local affairs did not count, but that they were seen and defined in relation to the monarchy as a whole. If we ignore this global perspective, then we must discard most of the sources as irrelevant, and limit ourselves to selecting, out of the enormous mass of available documents, every slightest expression of American particularism as a harbinger of the independence to come. It is often forgotten that even though particularism did exist, it was because of the existence of a broader political whole, and that the fundamental issue of the period was precisely how to combine the particular and the general. To ignore the whole would be like trying to study federalism in the nineteenth century by writing merely the local history of one of the states, without examining either the federal state and its constitution or its relation to the other states.

Such an approach can be justified for the period after 1810, though only very partially;[237] it is entirely inappropriate for the years between 1808 and 1810 and amounts to consigning these two crucial years to oblivion.[238] This perspective can undoubtedly be explained by the very "national" character taken on by historical studies. Every country born out of the former Hispanic monarchy—including peninsular Spain itself—has devoted itself first and foremost to its own "national" history. In Spain, Spanish America was quickly consigned to oblivion, and when discussing this period historians focused primarily on the liberal revolution. In America, the need to create a national imaginary for the new independent countries led historians to frame a vision in which internal causes took center stage; the rest of Spanish America, and most of all the Peninsula, became a mere backdrop in the historical narration, to which no clear causal function was assigned.

---

237 Even after 1810, when the creation of juntas in South America and Hidalgo's uprising seemed to give center stage to local events, the political debate continued to be global, as we may see in the Spanish American press. For example, in *El Despertador Americano*, published by the Mexican insurgents in Guadalajara in December 1810, we find many of the articles still debating the legitimacy of the governments formed in the Peninsula.

238 Curiously, the great disintegration of the monarchy, which culminated in the 1820s, did not cause in Spain a great moral crisis like the one triggered by the loss of Cuba in 1898.

And yet, the unity of the Hispanic world during this period was so strong that a systematic use of the Spanish American sources[239]—especially the press—and more particularly the Mexican ones, which were the richest, can be highly useful even for the history of Spain itself. Indeed, all the significant Spanish official documents, those of the Junta Central or the Regency Council, and most of the important political writings were reproduced and reedited at the time in New Spain. These highly coherent and continuous collections contrast with the fragmentation and discontinuity caused by the war in the Spanish sources. That is why our quotations from Spanish documents give precedence to American sources: not only as a matter of convenience, but also because they tell us about the knowledge that the Spanish Americans had of peninsular events. And these events—victories and defeats, political decisions, ideological transformations—as well as the Americans' knowledge of them were precisely what caused their actions and reactions.

## The Clash of 1808

The first among these events, which would leave a decisive mark on the entire Hispanic world, were the Bayonne abdications[240] of late May 1808, whereby the crown of Spain passed from the Spanish Bourbons to Joseph Bonaparte. Subsequent events are well known: as the May 25 *Gazeta de Madrid* announcing the abdications reached the Spanish provinces, uprisings against the French began, along with the creation of insurrectional juntas in the name of loyalty to Ferdinand VII. This very same reaction of loyalty to the captive king would occur everywhere in Spanish America. In Mexico, the news of the peninsular uprisings triggered popular demonstrations of a magnitude never seen before in the city.

239 This consideration holds until 1810: that is, until the formation of the first juntas in South America and Hidalgo's uprising in Mexico.

240 Abdications, in the plural: as a result of Napoleon's coercion, first Ferdinand VII abdicated in favor of his father Charles IV, then the latter did so in favor of Napoleon, who in his turn passed the crown on to his brother Joseph.

That these facts should be well known does not make them less surprising. There are various reasons for this. For one thing, there was no precedent for such a reaction. This was not the first time an ancien régime monarchy had changed dynasties, and never before had it caused such a commotion. Napoleon himself, who had previous experience with this type of operation, had foreseen merely minor disturbances in the case of the Spanish monarchy.[241] For another thing, the popular nature of the uprising was noteworthy: a considerable part of the Spanish governing elites, out of resignation or opportunism, had already accepted the new monarch. And finally, the identical nature of reactions in Spain and Spanish America was startling. The proclamations and manifestos being published at the time on both sides of the Atlantic were completely alike in their language, their topics, and the frame of reference used. Despite the tensions of all kinds that existed within the monarchy, it reacted to the external enemy as an extraordinarily homogeneous community.[242]

These surprising facts allow us to grasp a series of traits that were characteristic of the Hispanic world at the time. The first of these is that society, despite its highly traditional nature, was sufficiently acquainted with political events. It is difficult to speak yet, outside of the elites, of a public opinion in the modern sense of the word. But certainly, and especially in the cities, we find quite a broad dissemination of news as well as other forms of public opinion that would need studying. In these forms, transmission to the people of the seeds of public opinion existing among the elites played a crucial role. Even in the rural areas, among indigenous communities seemingly isolated from everything, there were always people who knew how to read, were able to receive written news, and had some knowledge, however distorted, of personages and events of a general order. For example, in a letter from the Mexican

---

241 All the reports Napoleon had received, except for one—Tournon's—came to the same conclusion: that there would be no reaction. See Lovett 1975, vol. I, 92.

242 The texts of these proclamations, which were coming from all the corporate bodies and authorities, filled the pages of the Spanish and Spanish American gazettes throughout the summer of 1808. For a more detailed study, see chapter V.

insurgents in 1810 addressed to the "Honorable Governors, Republics and Principals of the town of Ixmiquilpan," we can read: "let them get their whole pack of Indians together [...] it being understood that the *Gachupines* have sent a courier to the Frenchman Buena Parte [Bonaparte] so that he may come and finish off the Creoles, and this courier was captured in the Port of Tampico."[243]

All of this is closely related with the wave of school foundations during the late eighteenth century, and with the progress of literacy and the press. The Hispanic societies that were about to engage in the revolutionary process were ancien régime societies, no doubt; but they were also cultivated societies, equipped with education systems on the old model which were growing and flourishing.[244]

The second characteristic trait has to do with the values of the monarchy as a whole. The patriotic enthusiasm exuded by all the peninsular and Spanish American publications and by the civic ceremonies[245] was founded primarily on old-fashioned values: fidelity to the king and defense of religion, custom, and homeland.[246] True, there did exist at the time, and this would soon become clear in the press, men who took their inspiration from the French Revolution, just as there did exist in America some who aspired to independence; but during this initial period, society remained so strongly traditional that none of these groups could express their aspirations openly. Hostility to the French Revolution, seen as regicide, impious, and a persecutor of religion, had not been merely a topic for official propaganda: it was deeply rooted

---

243 In Alamán 1972, vol. I, appendixes, document no. 20.

244 See "Geography and Circumstances of a Cultural Area" in chapter III, and chapter VIII.

245 There are hundreds of pages in the gazettes and archives that narrate these ceremonies: *Te Deums* for victories, oaths of fidelity to Ferdinand VII or to the Junta Central, and so forth. For more details, see chapter V.

246 Jovellanos made this very clear to the French general Sebastiani: "Spain is fighting for its religion, its constitution, its laws, its customs, its uses: in a word, for its freedom." Reply of Jovellanos, in the *Gazeta de México*, July 8, 1809, 608.

in public opinion.[247] Personal bonds of vassalage to the king and the identification of Catholicism with everything Spanish, which for centuries had been elements essential to the unity of the monarchy, remained fully active.

And yet, this distinctly traditional system of values coexisted with elements that announced future changes. The unanimity and intensity of the patriotic reaction, the population's rejection of abdications to which it had not consented, pointed to something much more modern: the nation, and national feeling. The word "nation" appears in a great number of writings, sometimes in the modern sense, referring to the entire community of Spaniards; mostly, it appears with the definite connotation of the crown or the realm, as a political community in the old sense. Even though the ones who were acting and expressing themselves were the kingdoms, provinces, towns and other bodies of an ancien régime society, their very unanimity made them aware, sometimes with astonishment, of their extraordinary unity. In peninsular Spain, by this time, the word "nation" was never used to describe the particular communities within the monarchy; it only meant the "Spanish nation." The same thing was happening in Spanish America, where the entire frame of reference referred to a single nation—the Spanish nation—even when it was seen as made up of Europeans and Americans, spread over the two hemispheres, and even consisting of two peoples. The *nation*, a key word in the modern political vocabulary, which would later appear as equivalent to the old kingdoms or provinces, to whose independence it would provide a foundation, now made its first solemn appearance to describe the monarchy as a whole.[248]

Nor was traditionalism incompatible with a deep and universal desire for change. The clamor for Ferdinand VII, "the Desired One," possessed a messianic character, which in fact preceded his captivity. After the mutiny of Aranjuez in March 1808 had deposed the favorite Godoy and forced Charles IV to abdicate in favor of the prince of Asturias, an immense hope had sprung up in the entire Hispanic

---

247 See chapter I.

248 See chapter IX.

monarchy.[249] This is when the topic of "regeneration," widespread in all countries during the revolutionary period, made its appearance. The potency of this topic was proportional to the depth of the crisis and the diffuseness of the idea of "regeneration." This idea embraced concrete measures, such as cashiering the men connected to the favorite, restoring public finances, and ceasing to amortize the royal debt (the *vales reales*).[250] But it also included a broader aspiration: justice, prosperity, the battle against ignorance. And above all, the end of despotism: this meant not just suppressing the arbitrary power of an omnipotent minister, but also reestablishing direct bonds of trust between vassals and sovereign. The desire for social and political reform, in fact, was universal in 1808. Ferdinand VII was more than a concrete person: he was a symbol of regeneration, the promise of a new society where justice would reign, and which later would be embodied in the constitutions.

## Constituting a Legitimate Government

Rejection of the invader and fidelity to Ferdinand VII were very spontaneous manifestations,[251] as was, in many cases, the creation of the various Spanish provincial juntas. But from the very outset the problem arose which would dominate the entire political scene, both Spanish

249 We find the same reactions in Spain and in Spanish America. All the American gazettes of the period express their hostility to Godoy.

250 The suspension of this measure, which had played such a key role in the discontent in Mexico, was immediate and general, both in Spain and in Spanish America, from the very first moments of the crisis. See the order to this effect emitted by the Junta Central on November 18, 1808, published in the *Gazeta de México* XVI, no. 18, February 8, 1809, 120.

251 This spontaneity is not incompatible with a possible conspiracy on the part of Ferdinand's supporters, a theory which some historians defend, not unconvincingly. But if there was a conspiracy, it was merely the spark that ignited flammable material.

and Spanish American, over the following years: Who governs, and in whose name?

Using a diversity of terms, which shows the terminological instability of a watershed period, all the peninsular juntas resorted to arguments on pactist lines. In Asturias: "The general junta of this principality, having reassumed sovereignty on finding itself without a legitimate government…"; in Valencia: "The Supreme Junta of this realm which holds sovereignty by the decision of the people"; in Catalonia: "The Supreme Junta of government of the principality of Catalonia reassumes all the sovereign's authority and that wielded by all the councils and Supreme Juntas of His Majesty"; in Murcia: "the kingdom has been left an orphan and as a result sovereignty has fallen to the people, represented by the municipal bodies."[252]

The mutual bonds existing between king and kingdom—or nation—cannot be broken by only one of the parties. If the king disappears, power returns to its primary source: the people. These arguments sometimes used the vocabulary of Spanish Neo-Scholasticism or that of the modern sovereignty of the people; in other versions, we find judicial references to old medieval laws. Many other versions were a mixture of all these elements. But in every case we find a manifest and fundamental fact: the break with absolutist theory. The absolutist doctrine of the direct divine origin of royal power collapsed like a house of cards insofar as it offered no theoretical basis for resistance. The very fact of the uprising imposed pactist theories. By the force of circumstances, and without anyone having intended it, sovereignty suddenly reverted to society. What the French Revolution had wrested violently from the king was obtained in his name and without a fight in the Hispanic monarchy. True, for the vast majority at the time, this was merely something temporary, while they waited for the sovereign to return; but the fact is, from then onward, politics became accessible for all the social actors.

In fact, basing the legitimacy of provisional governments on the reversion of sovereignty to the realm or the nation immediately raised the issue of political representation. The formation of the first juntas in Spain took place in the heat of the uprising. The procedures for

---

252 Quoted by Artola 1968, 68.

appointing their members were improvised and diverse and were justified de facto by popular assent.[253] But this improvised representation could not be sufficient, and very soon means were sought to give the new authorities an indisputable legitimacy.[254] Hence, from the very first weeks of the uprising, the universal call for Juntas Generales, Congresses, or Cortes. Some provinces even convened old representative institutions that had died out or had never existed in isolation.[255]

In order to create a single government that would be capable of managing the war it was also necessary to overcome the fragmented nature of government. Indeed, the "people" which reassumed sovereignty was in practice the "peoples." The cabildo of Mexico City, for example, when rejecting the abdications, spoke of the need for the "universal consent of the Peoples."[256] In other words, these were political communities formed on the old model—kingdoms, principalities, provinces—represented by the capital cities, which considered themselves as their "heads."[257]

---

253 Sometimes the small group of conspirators who had launched the uprising occupied the main offices; in other cases, the most prominent authorities of the province were invited to do so, and in still other cases, the group in charge even included representatives of the popular mutiny. For these topics, see Artola 1968 and Martínez de Velasco 1972.

254 In Spanish America, this process gave rise to the convening of a Junta General of New Spain and to projects in Caracas and Buenos Aires that were temporarily suspended.

255 The kingdom of Aragon convened its Cortes, which had been suppressed by the Bourbons. Galicia, which had never had Cortes in its own right, but only a participation in the Cortes of Castile, now convened its own. New Spain, which had the right to participate in the Castilian Cortes, though it had never done so, assembled a Junta General of the kingdom. For this period, see Artola 1968 and Martínez de Velasco 1972.

256 Proceedings of the cabildo of Mexico City of July 19, 1808, in Hernández y Dávalos 1877, 477.

257 The uprising would normally begin in the capital of the kingdom or province, and once a junta had been formed there, its emissaries would promote the creation of others in the provinces or their dependent localities. The same thing would occur later with the creation of juntas in Quito, Upper Peru, Venezuela, Río de la Plata, Santiago de Chile, and New Granada.

The same thing was happening in Spanish America, where the cabildo of Mexico City, when calling in 1808 for the convening of juntas, described its action as "the will and decision of the realm, explained by means of the metropolis." The same justification would be given in South America for creating juntas in 1810.[258] In the imaginary that prevailed in the entire Hispanic world at the time, the "people" from which sovereignty derived was conceived primarily as a group of "peoples," that is, particular political communities with their capital cities.[259] The old medieval imaginary, still intact at the time of the Habsburgs, remained very much alive.[260]

The debate on how to constitute this single and indisputable government would dominate the Peninsula during the summer of 1808. It was a theoretical debate, which already involved examining the nature of the nation and therefore of representation; it was also a very concrete discussion concerning the exercise of power, between the various juntas and between the juntas and those royal authorities that had more or less collaborated with the usurper: basically the councils, especially the highest of them all, the Council of Castile. The juntas and their new legitimacy prevailed. As the Junta of Catalonia, quoted above, stated very clearly, no authority delegated by the monarchy, not even the highest of them all—that is, the Council of Castile—could rival the authority originating in the people.[261]

As we know, the solution that was found for these problems was the creation in Aranjuez, on September 25, 1808, of the Suprema Junta

---

258 Proceedings of July 19, 1808, in Hernández y Dávalos 1877, 477.

259 For the many meanings of the word "people," which was crucial throughout the nineteenth century, see chapter X.

260 Both in the Peninsula and in Spanish America, early in the eighteenth century, the basic political structure of society was still made up of a network of municipalities, in their turn hierarchically organized in main cities and the smaller cities and towns that depended on them. See "The American City as the Basic Political Unit" in chapter II.

261 For this topic, see for example the exchange of documents between the Junta Central and the Council of Castile, in the *Gazeta de México*, no. 145, December 24, 1808, 977 and the following pages; and no. 146, December 28, 1808, 1008.

Central Gobernativa del Reino, which would rule in the place and name of the king as the "custodian of sovereign authority."[262] The makeup of this Junta Central—two delegates for each junta created in the capitals of the old peninsular realms—showed that the nation was still conceived, implicitly, as a group of kingdoms, of old political communities, each of which carried the same weight even though the number of their inhabitants differed.[263]

## American Reactions

As we have already mentioned, all the Spanish American sources display the same enthusiastic patriotism, the same fidelity to Ferdinand VII, the same determination to resist the invader as in the Peninsula. The fears of some peninsulars that America might recognize the usurper would immediately be proved mistaken. The Spanish Americans rejected the abdications and proclaimed themselves Spaniards and patriots in every way they could think of. The cabildo of Chile, for example, made a very forceful pronouncement: "The loyalty of the inhabitants of Chile has not in any way degenerated from that of their fathers, who shed their heroic blood to save this country from the barbaric state in which it lay, and who, by uniting it to the Spanish Empire, made it civilized, populous, and religious. [We only] want to be Spaniards, and to live under the rule of our matchless king."[264]

The sense of identity is undeniable; precisely for this reason, the Spanish Americans would react to the crisis in the same way as the

---

262 See the installation of the Junta Central in the *Gazeta de Madrid*'s extraordinary issue no. 129, September 29, 1808, and in *Gazeta de México*, no. 133. "Orden de la Junta Central del 3 octubre de 1808," in Proclamation of Pedro Garibay, viceroy of Mexico, November 30, 1808, AGN, Historia, vol. 416, file I.

263 To this distribution of delegates, we must add two representatives of Madrid, as the capital.

264 Proceedings of the cabildo of Santiago, September 19, 1808, quoted by Collier 1977, 52.

peninsulars. Like the latter, they needed to have authorities who would be at the same time reliable—not suspected of collaborating with the invader—and indisputably legitimate. For this reason, just as in the Peninsula, patriotic enthusiasm went hand in hand with the questioning of the authorities, attempts to establish juntas, and even plans for independence. These various phenomena are not mutually contradictory, as was often believed later, on the basis of a teleological view of independence.

As in the Peninsula, the first reflex in the face of the abdications was to form juntas that would reassume the sovereign power left vacant by the king. The cabildo of Caracas prepared "a state junta to represent the sovereign authority";[265] only the persuasion of emissaries from the Junta of Seville made it desist from its plan while "reserving the city council's rights, for any event in which the state of things should depend on the hazard of the conflict."[266] The same thing occurred in Buenos Aires. The process went further in New Spain. The cabildo of Mexico City, based on arguments taken from the Partidas of Alfonso X the Wise,[267] declared the abdications null and void because they had been carried out without the consent of the nation, and called for the representation of the kingdom—that is, the Cortes or Congress of New Spain—to be convened. We know that this attempt, which had the support of Viceroy Iturrigaray, went as far as the convening of preparatory juntas and was only cut short by Yermo's coup d'état and its European equivalents in September of 1808.[268] The Spanish American problem was exactly the same as the Peninsula's: in the absence of the king, all delegated

---

265 Report from the captain-general of Venezuela of August 28, 1808, AHN, Secretaría de Estado records, vol. 60, file 66.

266 Letter from the town council of Caracas, August 29, 1808, AHN, Secretaría de Estado records, vol. 60, file 64.

267 We find the same kind of arguments, with quotes taken from the same laws, thousands of miles away in the manifesto of the Junta of Murcia. For a detailed statement of the arguments used by Mexico, see "Rival Conceptions of the Nation" in chapter IX.

268 Most of the relevant documents have been published in Hernández y Dávalos 1877.

authorities ceased to exercise their functions, and it became necessary to create juntas to embody the sovereignty reassumed by the people.

This quest for governments endowed with indisputable legitimacy provides the context for the independence that was often spoken of at the time, and which should not be confused with the one achieved some years later. The independence we find discussed in the documents of this first period was not an attempt to secede from the entire monarchy; on the contrary, it was a display of Hispanic patriotism, a means to remain free from French dominance, under which it was believed that the Peninsula was about to fall. This fear was not a pretext, as it has sometimes been argued, as if contemporaries could know that Napoleon would fall at the end of 1814. In 1808, Napoleon was at the height of his power, and was the master of Europe as few have ever been before or since. As we mentioned earlier, hardly anyone believed at the time that Spain could oppose his plans.

Thus, it was in no way unreasonable for the Spanish Americans, who found out about the abdications before hearing about the uprisings, to believe that peninsular Spain was lost and that the peninsular authorities were collaborating with the invader. For several weeks, the fluctuating state of communications created such confusion about the situation in the Peninsula that the Spanish American gazettes would be simultaneously printing dispatches from the usurping authorities[269] and news of the peninsular uprisings. A logical reaction, then, was to feel that the only way to save part of the monarchy was by proclaiming the independence of American Spain. Independence was conceived in relation to France and to those in Spain who were collaborating with the French. As Buenos Aires declared very bluntly to the junta in Seville: "in that province [Buenos Aires] enthusiasm for the freedom of Spain was general, it being the verdict of its natives and inhabitants to obey

---

269 Thus, in New Spain we find reprintings of the *Gazeta de Madrid* with Murat's proclamations after the May 2 repression, the official documents with the news of the Bayonne abdications, and even the call to convene the collaborationist Cortes of Bayonne. See *Gazeta de México*, no. 59, July 16, 1808, and no. 76, July 10, 1808. The same thing happened in the Andes, see Demélas 1990, vol. I, 33n2.

no authority but the legitimate one, and should this one be lacking, to declare their independence."[270]

In Mexico as well, Fray Melchor de Talamantes invoked identical arguments in documents addressed to the members of the cabildo of Mexico City in which he clearly mentioned independence. He expressed the conviction that the Cortes to be assembled in New Spain would represent the whole of the Spanish nation, and thus also the metropolis: "It will be declared as well that Spain, represented in its national congress [that is, the Congress of New Spain]…"[271] Independence was conceived as Spanish patriotism, intended to give Spanish America interim or residual representation for the whole monarchy.

However, though Spanish American reactions were the same as the peninsular ones, since the two political imaginaries were identical, the American attempts to form juntas like the Spanish ones were not successful in 1808. Though the issue of the legitimacy of government was the same on both sides of the Atlantic, circumstances were not. In Spanish America, there were no foreign troops, no popular uprising, no imminent war: that is, none of the circumstances which had given rise in the Peninsula to the insurrectionary governments and subsequently to the creation of the Junta Central. Nor do we find, despite the suspicions raised as to some people's loyalty, any collaborationist authorities like the ones existing in the Peninsula. This explains why it was difficult to overturn all at once the opposition of the royal authorities, who continued to rely on an absolutist tradition which had already collapsed in Spain. Moreover, as soon as it became known that the metropolis was resisting the invader, the Americans gave priority to the assistance that they could lend in the war. Thus, in South America, despite their doubts, the Americans ended up recognizing the Seville Junta, which

---

270 "Mensaje del cuerpo superior y autoridades de Buenos Aires" to the Junta of Seville, November 9, 1808, *Gazeta Ministerial de Sevilla*, no. 60, December 23, 1808. This was of course the insurrectional Junta of Seville and not the Junta Central, which had not yet been created.

271 Fray Melchor de Talamantes, "Idea del congreso nacional de Nueva España, individuos que deben componerlo y asunto de sus sesiones," undated [July 1808] in De la Torre Villar 1964, 121 and the following pages.

was pretending to be the legitimate government of the entire monarchy precisely in order to prevent the creation of juntas in Spanish America. Only in Mexico, for reasons we will explain below, did events take a different turn. This subterfuge would leave a deep legacy of distrust for the future whose effects would be felt in 1810 and would facilitate the creation of juntas in America.

## Uncertainties and Conjunctures

The confusion reigning in Spanish America during the summer of 1808 as to the real military and political situation in the Peninsula leads us to make some observations concerning a physical factor—distance—which would play an important role in how relations between Spain and America would evolve. The first consequence of this factor was the peculiar mode in which information circulated between the two shores of the Atlantic. Accustomed as we are nowadays to receiving information swiftly, regularly, and continuously, it is hard for us to imagine the effects of information, which, in contrast, arrived in ways that were slow, random, discontinuous, and unreliable. Not only must the transmission times always be counted in months[272]—from two months for Mexico to five for Peru—but these time lags also varied, as well as the places that the ships and news started out from. Moreover, when the news did arrive, it would all arrive in an undifferentiated bunch—packets of letters, dispatches, and gazettes—and the press would then disseminate it gradually, while they waited for the next installment. Depending on how this confused and disjointed information was put back together, very different versions of the most crucial events could be reconstructed. And of course, we also have the fake news, which always

272 Though the situation had improved since the sixteenth century, the space–time maps worked out by Pierre Chaunau in *Séville et l'Atlantique* had not substantially changed.

existed and for long periods of time was impossible to verify.[273] And the same was true in the Peninsula with the news coming from America.

Spanish American reactions to the events we have been describing and to those that would come later[274] were largely subordinate to the contingencies of information. The Mexican attitude, so different from that of South America during the summer of 1808, resulted largely from the fact that New Spain received the news of the abdications two weeks before anything had been heard about the uprisings. The ship *Ventura*, which brought news of the first on July 16, had sailed from Cádiz on May 26, before the city had heard about the insurrections.[275] For two weeks, in the midst of the most complete anguish and uncertainty, Mexico attempted to figure out what was happening in Spain and what decisions to make. When at last the news of the uprising arrived on July 29, it was brought by the schooner *Esperanza*, which had sailed on June 7 from Tarragona,[276] where no one had yet heard of any Spanish junta claiming to govern in the name of the entire monarchy.

From the beginning, New Spain had no doubts as to the headless state of the central government, and this may help to explain the convening of juntas aimed at preparing a Congress of New Spain. In South America, on the other hand, news of the abdications, the uprisings, and the creation of the Seville Junta, which called itself Junta Suprema de España y de Indias, all arrived almost at once, thus preventing the creation of

273 The topic of rumors and fake news—whether deliberate or not—and their consequences remains to be studied. Special attention should be paid to apocryphal documents attributed to Ferdinand VII.

274 At the beginning of 1810, when the Regency Council was being formed in Cádiz, orders were given to prevent ships from sailing for America until a manifesto had been written up informing the Spanish Americans of the latest political upheavals. This measure did not prevent the news from arriving by other channels and causing the creation of the Buenos Aires and Caracas juntas.

275 See *Gazeta de México*, 1808, no. 76, 551 and the following pages.

276 Among other documents, the ship carried manifestos from the Valencia and Murcia juntas, but not from that of Seville. See *Gazeta extraordinaria de México del viernes 29 de julio de 1808*.

local juntas. When Mexico finally learned, on August 29, of the arrival of emissaries from the Junta of Seville, messages from the Junta of Asturias had already arrived. Thus, New Spain would act autonomously, well aware of the plurality of governing bodies in the Peninsula.

All these communication problems, which were more or less tolerable in times of peace, became very serious factors in times of war and political crisis. On both sides of the ocean, decisions were being made based on very incomplete information. Speculation, imagination, and rumors played just as great a role as the reality of facts about which only doubtful knowledge was available.[277] This uncertainty, a key factor for understanding the Spanish governments' significant errors of judgment, was even more serious for the Spanish Americans. The course of the war, the formation of a new government, the new political or administrative measures were peninsular events on which their fate depended. For a complete picture of these variables, we would need to include along with these peninsular dates those of the alliances and battles taking place in the rest of Europe, which were very important for future predictions and were also being published in due time in the Spanish American gazettes.[278]

Among these events the military situation in the Peninsula played a crucial role. The military conjuncture largely determined the political one: after all, the prestige and the very existence of the peninsular governments depended on it. That is why the watershed dates of our period coincide with the main stages of the Spanish War of Independence. The summer and early autumn of 1808 were a time of optimism. The uprisings, the victory of Bailén on July 21, the evacuation of Madrid by the French troops and their retreat beyond the Ebro, the entrance of Castaños's troops into Madrid: all these events aroused enthusiasm.

---

277 The uncertain conditions in which the Spanish governments were making their decisions have been well analyzed by Anna 1986.

278 Demetrio Ramos made a groundbreaking analysis of this topic, in "Wagram y sus consecuencias, como determinantes del clima público de la Revolución de 19 de abril de 1810, en Caracas," *Estudios sobre la Emancipación de Hispanoamérica: Contribución al Sesquicentenario de la Emancipación* (Madrid: CSIC, 1963), 34–85.

They uplifted national pride throughout the monarchy, strengthened the English alliance, and furthered general recognition of the Junta Central. This stage would end with the counteroffensive undertaken by Napoleon himself in November of the same year, and the retaking of Madrid by the French on December 2. The Junta Central, which until then had convened in Aranjuez, would have to withdraw and establish itself in Seville on December 17.[279]

For nearly all of 1809 only Andalucía was continuously free from French occupation. The rest of the Peninsula witnessed a succession of victories and defeats, the timing of which precisely determined the evolution of the Junta Central and its main decisions, like the convening of the Cortes. The final military stage of our period, which was crucial for Spanish American events, began on November 19, 1809, with the great Spanish defeat of Ocaña, which forced Wellington to withdraw toward Portugal and left Andalucía wide open to the French troops.[280] The Junta Central fled Seville in the midst of a popular revolt that was accusing it of treason. A new provincial Junta of Seville reassumed sovereignty. The members of the Junta Central, now discredited and hunted refugees in Cádiz, would end up transferring their powers to a Regency Council on January 29, 1810. On February 1, Seville was occupied by the French, who shortly afterward set siege to Cádiz, where the Regency Council was established under the strict control of the city junta; in this Council, whose legitimacy was weak, resided theoretically the sovereignty of the monarchy.[281] We already know the consequences of this situation for the creation of the Spanish American juntas in 1810.

---

279 From this residence of the Junta Central in Seville from November 1808 until the end of 1809 derives the confusion, still very widespread among today's historians, between the Suprema Junta of Seville, which was a provincial junta, and the Junta Central, which was the central government of the monarchy established at the time in Seville.

280 In the Spanish historiography written immediately after independence culminated—regardless of political affinities—the French invasion of Andalucía always appears as the key landmark in this process.

281 For these events, see among others Lovett 1975.

We have discussed these events at some length, not only to establish the chronological framework of the political issues, but also to show to what an extent—and we have considerably simplified here the ups and downs of the war—the Americans were subjected throughout all these years to an avalanche of news which caused constant swings between hope and disappointment, optimism and gloom.[282] These feelings were all the more extreme in that the news of the period was distorted by war propaganda, always excessive and unreliable, given to inflating the smallest victory and downplaying the greatest defeats. The Spanish Americans' distrust of the news from the Peninsula would be the main unfortunate effect of distance and propaganda.

## Representing the Nation: The American Problem

The Junta Central provided a practical solution to the problem of the unity of government, which is why it was recognized both in the Peninsula and in Spanish America; but in the final analysis its legitimacy was precarious because it derived solely from the delegation of the peninsular insurrectional juntas. That is why, only a few days after its creation, it was already debating the convening of the Cortes and the election of Spanish American deputies to represent America in the Junta Central. Though for the time being, both the Cortes and the American representation before the Junta Central were still conceived in terms of traditional representation—that of the "peoples" expressing themselves through their municipal corporate bodies—the issues that would be discussed from then on were the key issues that would pave the way to political revolution and Spanish American independence. While the practical modes of representation were being discussed, the

282 A very significant illustration of these successive stages can be seen in the reactions of the remote city of Chihuahua in 1808, recorded in the *Gazeta de México* of November 23, 1808, 908–9, under headlines like "Surprise and dismay in Chihuahua," "Chihuahua gives itself up to prayer," "Chihuahua comforted."

real questions being raised over the following years were: What was the nation? And within it, what was the relationship between peninsular Spain and Spanish America?

The first question held center stage in the modern political imaginary and had been the main issue during the French Revolution. Was the nation made up of old political communities, with their estates and privileged corporate bodies, or of equal individuals? Was it the product of history or the result of voluntary association? Was it already there, or did it still have to be created? Did sovereignty reside in it? And if so, what sort of sovereignty[283]?

The second question—that of the respective positions corresponding to peninsular Spain and Spanish America in the national representation—publicly and forcefully raised the dangerous issue of equality between Spaniards and Americans which dated back to the period of the Conquest, had frequently come to the fore in quarrels about public offices, and was now acquiring crucial importance. The issue had to do with the very identity of the Indies. What were they? Kingdoms in their own right, subordinate realms, or colonies? It was, moreover, a very practical and very urgent problem since it would determine both the existence in America of juntas like those of the Peninsula and the possibility of a representation proportional to the region's population in the new representative institutions: first the Junta Central and later the Cortes.

Though the idea was constantly in everyone's thoughts, convening the Cortes would become a secondary concern until the spring of 1809, because of the pressures of the war and because there already existed in the Peninsula representative bodies of the realm—however imperfect—in the form of the insurrectional juntas and the Junta Central.[284] The issue of Spanish American representation was much more urgent, for a reason which the closest observers were well-acquainted with, and which was confirmed by the news from America: The Spanish Americans wanted to exercise the same rights as the other Spaniards. It was an

283 On this topic, see chapter IX.

284 The nature of this junta was ambiguous: though it governed in the name of the king, its composition—it was made up of a group of deputies from the provinces—made people tend to see it as a representative organ of the realm.

urgent problem, because even though their patriotism led the Americans to accept the Spanish provisional governments, the situation could not last for long without arousing serious tensions.

An urgent problem, then, but a tricky one to solve: in many peninsular circles, which were very ill-informed on American matters, there was a tendency to consider the Indies as colonies or at the very least as subordinate realms, which therefore had fewer rights than the peninsular kingdoms. The decree inviting the Americans to elect their spokespersons to the Junta Central was finally published on January 22, 1809, in Seville; this date constitutes undoubtedly one of the most important in the entire revolutionary period.[285]

The contents of the decree were a strange hodgepodge of good intentions and colossal blunders. It began with a preliminary declaration, which over the following years would be quoted again and again by the Spanish Americans:

> the Junta Suprema Central, organ of government of the kingdom, considering that the vast and beautiful dominions that Spain possesses in the Indies are not properly speaking colonies or factories like those of other nations, but rather an essential and integral part of the Spanish monarchy, and desiring to knit indissolubly the sacred ties uniting the two parts of these dominions, as moreover becomes the heroic loyalty and patriotism of which these realms have just given Spain such decisive proofs [...] H. M. has seen fit to declare [...] that the realms, provinces, and islands that make up the aforesaid dominions must have immediate representation before his royal Person through their corresponding deputies.[286]

---

285 Royal order, Seville, January 22, 1809 (AHN, Secretaría de Estado records, vol. 54, dossier 71). Like all government documents, this one was published in the various regions of Spanish America on various dates, according to the time lags in transmission. In Mexico, for example, it was transmitted by proclamation of Viceroy Garibay on April 14, 1809 (AGN, Historia, vol. 418, file V), and published in the *Gazeta de México* of April 15, 1809. For a more detailed analysis of this document, its consequences, and its implementation, see chapter VI.

286 Ibid.

Under a cloak of apparent generosity the text concealed profound ignorance as to what Spanish America was, as well as serious political mistakes. Though the royal order seemed to proclaim equality of rights between the two parts of the monarchy, the very fact that it thought in terms of "colonies," or even worse, "factories," went against everything that the Indies had always been in the laws and the imaginary of the Americans. A further insult was that participation in the national representation appeared, not as a right, but as a concession, a reward. Equality was denied in the very moment in which it was asserted. This inequality was also displayed in the number of deputies: nine for Spanish America and the Philippines, to thirty-six for the Peninsula, when both regions had more or less the same number of inhabitants.

The Americans' reactions were ambivalent. On the one hand, there was satisfaction at having a share, for the first time, in the sovereign power; on the other hand, there was deep frustration at the unequal treatment that they were receiving. The royal order catalyzed the silent discontent already existing in Spanish America since the creation of the Junta Central. Camilo Torres, one of the founding fathers of the independence of New Granada, expressed this feeling better than anyone, speaking in the name of the city of Bogotá. The cabildo of Santa Fe

> experienced a deep, heartfelt sadness to see that when the deputies of all the provinces of Spain were assembling in the national representation [the Junta Central], not a word was said of the vast dominions making up Ferdinand's empire in America, nor were they in the least taken into account [...].[287]

The entire document expressed the grievances of a wounded Spanish patriotism, precisely that patriotism which the uprisings had displayed with extraordinary force:

> We are the children, the descendants of those who spilled their blood to acquire these new dominions for the Spanish crown [...]. We are just as Spanish as the descendants of Don Pelayo, and

287 Torres (1809) 1960, 1.

> therefore have the same rights to the distinctions, privileges, and prerogatives pertaining to the rest of the nation [...] with this difference, if there is one, that our fathers, as has been said, with unspeakable trouble and toil discovered, conquered and peopled this New World for Spain.[288]

This was an open assertion of Spanish identity, then, but also an expression of the traditional imaginary, which saw the single Spanish nation as made up of realms with equal rights. Yet new elements were already surfacing, in the idea that this nation was also made up of two equal peoples, the Spanish and the American one. An equal status must be expressed in equality of rights: an equal right to form juntas like those of the Peninsula, and equality of representation, something which both political circumstances and the evolution of ideas made indispensable. The demand for equality and even for preference to be given to Spanish Americans in the assigning of "distinctions, privileges, and prerogatives" had existed since the days of the Conquest; now that the entire Hispanic world was entering the age of modern politics, this demand was becoming a cry for equality of representation. As Camilo Torres's words already portended when he invoked the independence of the United States, should this equality not be respected, now and later in the future Cortes, it would mean a violation of the pact binding the two peoples together:

> true union and fraternity between the European and American Spaniards [...] may never subsist but when founded on justice and equality. America and Spain are two integral and constituent parts of the Spanish monarchy [...] to exclude the Americas from this representation would be not only to commit the highest injustice against them, but to arouse their distrust and suspicion and forever to alienate their hearts from this union.
>
> [...] If the English government had taken this important step, perhaps it would not now be lamenting the separation of its colonies [...] those rich possessions could not understand why, when they were

288 Ibid., 9.

> vassals of the same sovereign, integral parts of the same monarchy, and when all the other provinces sent their representatives to the legislative body of the nation, this body should desire to dictate laws to them and impose taxes upon them which had not received their approval.[289]

For the time being, though the resentment continued to grow, all Spanish America threw itself passionately into the election of its deputies to the Junta Central. From the spring of 1809 to the winter of 1810, from north to south, from Sonora to Chile and the Río de la Plata, all America lived for the elections. For the first time, both in Spain and in America, a general vote was taking place which would pave the way for modern politics.

Studying these elections, and the instructions drawn up by the cabildos for their deputies, provides an extraordinary snapshot of the political and social imaginary and the aspirations of Spanish America in these years of transition from the ancien régime to modernity and from a shared Hispanic patriotism to independence. In these elections tradition still prevailed. The cities that did not have the franchise demanded it as a privilege. The nation was conceived as a whole made up of hierarchically organized bodies: realms, provinces, cities, and towns. The town councils almost always voted for the most prominent citizens, usually by order of precedence. The deputies' mandates were imperative and were written up as if they were proxies in private law. The instructions intermingled a desire for economic and administrative reforms very much along Enlightenment lines with demands for privileges of all kinds for the city or the region, and sometimes for a return to the state of things that had existed before the Bourbon reforms.[290]

In the political sphere, we find once again solemnly expressed the wartime patriotic aspirations: the monarch's freedom, military victory, and the prosperity of the nation. We also find in all these instructions a determination to protect the indissoluble union between the two parts

289 Ibid., 4–5.

290 For a more extensive study of these topics, see chapter VI.

of the monarchy, and in many cases, a call for equality of rights. The Spanish American cabildos were participating at a distance and with a certain time lag in the peninsular political debate: with rare exceptions, such as the cabildo of Zacatecas, they would turn out to be more traditional than the peninsular local governments, which at the time, as we shall see, were making the transition toward very modern positions.[291]

Thus, the American elections would reveal a very widespread traditionalism and a very deep-rooted Hispanic patriotism, but also fierce political struggles. They displayed external conflicts between the cabildos and the royal authorities—the viceroy, the audiencia, the *intendentes*, or the *tenientes letrados*—as well as internal conflicts between different parties, in the old sense of the word, consisting of oppositions between rival family clans, sometimes with ramifications in various peninsular regions, or of quarrels between merchants linked to Cádiz and other groups, or between Europeans and Creoles.[292] In other words, this was a public life along traditional lines, but charged with tensions that emerging modern politics would exacerbate.

## The Political Transformations of Peninsular Spain

This evolution was even more advanced in the Peninsula. Here all the conditions were fulfilled for an even more intense and freer debate. More intense, because during these years Spanish American political life still presented a provincial character, subordinate to the decisions being made at the heart of the monarchy. Freer, too, because in the Peninsula, with the collapse of the absolutist state, the existing limitations on freedom of the press in the political field had disappeared in practice, though not legally. A veritable avalanche of written material of all kinds, including a multitude of newspapers, was spreading throughout Spain.[293] They

291 See chapter VII.

292 For these conflicts, see "Parties in Conflict" in chapter VI.

293 See CDF.

were patriotic writings aimed at kindling people's spirits in the struggle against the invader, but also writings full of opinions of all sorts, from the most traditional to the most modern, concerning the political solutions to be applied in reforming the monarchy. This is when modern public opinion was being born in Spain, while in America, where these conditions did not yet prevail, censorship was still in force.

The political movements coming to light in the Hispanic world in 1808—they were not yet actual political parties, of course—may be divided into three general categories. The enlightened absolutists, represented by the elderly Floridablanca, the president of the Junta Central, were in favor of considering this body as a provisional government whose sole function was to stand in for the king and manage the war. The historical constitutionalists, whose central figure was Jovellanos, took their inspiration from the English model: they wanted to reform the monarchy and establish a constitutional system by restoring the old Cortes.[294] And finally, the most revolutionary group, whose éminence grise was the poet Manuel Quintana, would later be called liberals; they supported the sovereignty of the people and a constitution on the French model.

The same political movements existed in America, though not yet openly. The absolutists were represented by most of the metropolitan authorities, by the Europeans—though not all of them—and by a certain number of Creoles. The historical constitutionalists were undoubtedly the majority, as in the Peninsula: in Mexico, for example, we find men like Talamantes, Villaurrutia, and Verdad, or the aforementioned members of the cabildo of Zacatecas, or, later on, Father Mier. And finally, the revolutionaries, the future liberals who secretly supported the French Revolution, were, as in Spain, a small minority; they were young and generally belonged to the intellectual elites.[295] It goes without saying that the peninsular groups also included Americans, who would

---

294 See "The Political Frame of Reference: Pactism Reborn" in chapter V.

295 See, for example, for the Michoacán group, Carlos Herrejón Peredo, "México: Las Luces de Hidalgo y de Abad y Queipo," in Guerra 1989, vol. I, 107 and the following pages. In South America, Bolívar in Venezuela or Moreno and his friends in the Río de la Plata were representatives of this group.

reappear later in the Spanish American revolutions: men like Mexía Lequerica, from Quito, a future liberal leader in the Cortes of Cádiz, or Father Mier himself, who resided at the time in Spain.

The main debate among all these groups would gradually center—as had occurred before in revolutionary France—on the convening of the Cortes, their composition and powers, and how deliberations and voting should be handled. As we mentioned earlier, these were not only practical problems, but central political issues: for they pointed, via the question of national representation, to rival conceptions of the nation, sovereignty, and the institutions. The call to convene the Cortes made by Jovellanos early in October 1808 made no headway, probably because of the coalition formed by the absolutists and the revolutionaries within the Junta Central: the former were acting out of conviction, and the latter, most likely, for tactical reasons, since they still felt themselves to be too much in the minority in public opinion.[296] The time was not yet ripe.

Change would take place thanks to the growth of public opinion, especially with the flourishing of modern forms of sociability and the press. Quintana's role in these areas was undoubtedly crucial, thanks to his tertulia, his newspaper *El Semanario Patriótico*, and his position as first official in the secretariat of the Junta Central. In his tertulia, which accompanied the government's changes of location—first Madrid, then Seville, and finally Cádiz—the future leaders of the liberals met and trained themselves.[297] This was where the most advanced opinions were openly discussed, actions were coordinated, and the texts which the other two media would later propagate were written up. *El Semanario Patriótico* conducted the public opinion campaign efficiently and in a very free tone, and its influence in the entire Hispanic world needs to be studied from a global perspective. Shortly afterward, *El Espectador Sevillano*—published in the last three months of 1809 by Alberto Lista, another member of Quintana's group—took the public opinion campaign to a higher degree of radicalism; this in fact prefigured what the Cortes would later be and do. And finally, thanks to the position he

296 For all these topics, see Suárez's crucial study, 1982, 33 and the following pages.

297 On this group and their newspapers, see chapter VII.

occupied in the secretariat of the Junta Central, Quintana not only was able to place his friends in key positions, but he himself often wrote the documents produced by the junta. Though occasionally his inflammatory prose would be corrected by other members, on other occasions it managed to get past this filter, introducing into the most solemn documents of the supreme authority of the realm—later to be reprinted in Spain and in America by the authorities—ideas and expressions which would have gotten an American author into a good deal of trouble. This is why the very documents by means of which the supreme political authority of the monarchy expressed itself can also be counted among the most efficient vehicles of the most advanced ideas of the time.

In the manifesto of the Junta Central of October 26, 1808, written by Quintana, we already find the expression "Spanish revolution": "Yes, Spaniards, the great day will dawn when, in harmony with the desires of our beloved sovereign and his loyal people, the monarchy will be established upon solid and genuine foundations. Then you will have fundamental and beneficent laws, which will protect order and banish arbitrary power [...]. The Spanish revolution will thus present a completely different aspect from the French one."[298]

Using a language characteristic of historical constitutionalism—"fundamental laws" against "arbitrary power"—the author was already declaring that the ongoing events were in fact a revolution; and denying its similarity to the French Revolution only served to locate it within the same frame of reference.

A multitude of documents and articles of this sort would be produced throughout this period, preparing people's minds for the great changes of which we can only give a general idea here. The most important of these changes would occur in May 1809. Floridablanca's death at the end of 1808 left the supporters of the Cortes without their main opponent. The alliance between the historical constitutionalists and the revolutionaries in the Junta Central took advantage of the collapse in the junta's prestige resulting from several military failures to push through the fundamental decree of May 22, 1809. This decree gave official status

---

298 Manifesto of the Junta Central, October 26, 1808. Like all the other documents of this sort, this one was also reprinted and disseminated in Spanish America.

to a modern political explanation of the monarchy's ills. Everything was due to the loss of the old liberties: "the disasters that the Nation has been enduring have sprung entirely from the oblivion into which those wholesome institutions have fallen which in happier times made the prosperity and strength of the state."[299]

The perfect era was seen to be located in the past, in a Golden Age to which it was necessary to return in order for "the rights and prerogatives of Citizens to be delivered from fresh assaults, and [for] the springs of public happiness—once the obstacles have been removed that have obstructed them until now—to flow freely once more [...] and restore everything that inveterate arbitrary power has withered and present devastation has destroyed [...]."[300]

Hence the Junta Central's decision: "That the legal, well-known representation of the monarchy in its ancient Cortes should be reestablished."[301] This fundamental decree seemed to give the victory to the historical constitutionalists, whose explanation of the ills of the monarchy and the cures for them thus acquired official status. A few months later, another manifesto of the Junta Central already spoke of the reforms planned for restoring the Cortes in terms of revolution. The editor imagined himself addressing the deputies and declaring: "Here you are gathered together, oh founding fathers, with all your rights restored to you, three centuries after despotism and arbitrary power dissolved you and rained down upon this nation the full flood of misfortune and all the evils of bondage."[302]

This motif of the three centuries of despotism and bondage, which the American insurgents would later use freely to describe the colonial period, appeared in the official documents of the supreme government

---

299 Royal order of May 22, 1809, published in Mexico by proclamation of Viceroy Lizana, August 14, 1809 (*Historia*, vol. 455, file I). Concerning the origins of this decree, see Suárez 1982, chapter III.

300 Ibid.

301 Ibid.

302 Manifesto of the Junta Central, Seville, October 28, 1809, published in the *Gazeta del Gobierno de México*, January 12, 1810.

of the monarchy as a way of explicitly breaking with the laws and the political regime of the previous three centuries.

Other provisions of the decree of May 22, 1809, opened the way for the final victory of the revolutionaries. Simultaneously with the decision to convene the old Cortes according to the fundamental laws, a general consultation was also organized to allow all corporate bodies—Councils, provincial Juntas Superiores, courts of law, *ayuntamientos*, cabildos, bishoprics, and universities—as well as "wise and enlightened persons" to give their opinion as to the modus operandi and role of the future Cortes. As Tocqueville pointed out in relation to the exact same consultation carried out in France by Lomenie de Brienne in 1788, to make the constitution a topic of debate was already to move beyond the restoration of fundamental laws into modern politics, the realm of public opinion.[303]

Subsequent events would confirm this perception. The results of the consultation—quite widely publicized in Spain[304] and almost unknown in Spanish America[305]—show that while historical constitutionalism remained strong, the liberals were gaining ground. The cultivated elites were those who participated in the consultation, and they were evolving very swiftly toward a modern frame of reference very close to that of the French Revolution.

The debate that would take place in the following months, both in the preparatory commission for the Cortes and in the press, already confronted the historical constitutionalists and the future liberals. This was the same debate that had taken place in France in 1788 and

---

303 Suárez 1982, 507–8.

304 For this topic, see Artola (1959) 1968. Some of the results of the consultation have been published by Suárez 1967–68.

305 The Spanish American results have not been collected and are partly unknown. A series of various documents, such as the previously quoted one by Camilo Torres, certain representations like that of the cabildo of Guatemala (letter from the cabildo of Guatemala to the preparatory Commission of C, January 30, 1810, AHN, Secretaría de Estado records, file 20E) and some instructions to the Spanish American deputies to the Junta Central are in fact answers to the consultation.

during the first months of 1789. Rather than deciding who was to be represented in the Cortes—whether the estates or only the *communes*, or general population—and what modalities would regulate assembly and voting—whether by estate or not—the real topic of discussion was national sovereignty. Though Jovellanos would gain a temporary victory early in 1810, when he determined that the Cortes would be convened by estates, this victory never materialized. The Cortes that would meet in Cádiz in September 1810 would be composed entirely of members of the "common people." As in France, the victory of the revolutionaries stemmed from the impossibility of restoring the old Cortes unchanged. The fact that Jovellanos should propose to endow them with two houses, along the English model—something that had no precedent in the traditional Hispanic institutions[306]—clearly demonstrated the weakness of the argument for tradition, and the historical constitutionalists' limits. If circumstances were forcing a transformation of tradition, this meant that nothing stood in the way of the nation's providing itself with whatever institutions best suited its needs.[307]

The revolutionaries' political victory grew out of the ideological one, unequivocally and irrevocably signified by the transformation of language. Words were gradually acquiring a new meaning, and the new terms of the French revolutionary lexicon were beginning to prevail, with their dualistic oppositions: old and new, darkness and light, ignorance and enlightenment, despotism and freedom.[308]

306 More difficulties for this party lay in the question of which Cortes they should take as a model, whether the unitary Cortes of the eighteenth century or those of the old kingdoms, and in that case, which ones?

307 It is significant that no one should have considered restoring the eighteenth-century Cortes, which had convened for the last time in 1789.

308 For these changes, see "Victory of the Modern Nation" in chapter IX.

## American Disappointments

These years would see Spanish America out of step with the intensity of the peninsular debate and the depth of the Peninsula's ideological transformations. And yet, the peninsular debate crossed the Atlantic thanks to the handbills and gazettes arriving from the Peninsula, and against which the authorities, even those most hostile to the new opinions, were powerless. Indeed, how could they prevent the arrival and reprinting in America of these patriotic publications, which, moreover, were often produced by the Spanish authorities themselves?[309] Much of the Spanish American editorial activity consisted of the reprinting of these publications. Books, handbills, proclamations, and the main newspapers were reprinted as soon as they reached America or were published again in the press.[310] The new standards no longer needed to take such devious routes as smuggling and clandestinity: they arrived openly by way of peninsular publications. As a Mexican lampoon stated in 1809: "Let there be no further disputation about the peoples' rights: the veil that covered them has been torn aside. No one is unaware now that under present circumstances, sovereignty resides in the peoples. We learn this from the multitude of printed materials arriving from the Peninsula."[311]

For the Spanish Americans, ideological change went hand in hand with demands for equality in relation to the peninsulars. What before had been grounded in ancient laws and privileges would now gradually be supported by natural right and the peoples' sovereignty. But the basic issues had not changed. They had to do with ensuring equality of rights in practice, and not simply on paper. This would be achieved by forming juntas and obtaining fair representation in the new representative institutions being created in the Peninsula for the whole monarchy. The Americans' struggle for local power, unsuccessful in 1808, grew fiercer as time went on and more became known about the political

---

309 For a case study of these phenomena, see chapter VIII. The same situation existed in Buenos Aires up until 1810.

310 See chapter VIII.

311 Proclamation of the licenciado José Castillejos, in Miranda 1952, 256.

situation in Spain. When the equality of the two parts of the monarchy was being solemnly affirmed, on the basis of what principle could the Spanish Americans be prevented from having the same institutions as Spain? What kind of legitimacy other than that of the "peoples" could the peninsular governments invoke to prevent the Americans, too, from resorting to this principle in constituting their own governments? Why the tolerant attitude toward the Europeans who violated the legal order in America, like Yermo in Mexico? Why the unequal treatment—prison or exile—for the supporters of the American juntas when the peninsular juntas could quarrel among themselves, even refusing to obey the Junta Central and reclaiming their sovereignty?[312] Why such unequal treatment of Spanish America when it came to electoral arrangements?

Discontent and distrust toward the peninsular governments grew continuously throughout 1809 and led to attempts at forming Spanish American juntas. Some of these were merely that—attempts—as in Caracas and Buenos Aires; others, as in Quito and Upper Peru, succeeded at first, before being repressed by the royal authorities as if they had been vassals rebelling against the king.

The quarrels among the various Spanish authorities—the Junta Central, the provincial juntas, and the Councils—weakened in America, as they did in Spain, the prestige of a government that claimed to hold sovereign authority. By the end of 1809, the situation in Spain was critical. The French offensive led to accusations of treason against the members of the Junta Central, the creation of an independent junta in Seville, and the flight to Cádiz of part of the Junta Central. On January 27, 1810, the Cádiz Consulado took power in the city thanks to a conspiracy and imposed its tutelage on the remains of the Junta Central. English pressure would be needed for these remains to take the form, on the twenty-ninth, of a Regency Council that proclaimed itself to be assuming sovereign authority, while French troops marched on Cádiz.

On the very day on which it dissolved itself, the Junta Central established the rules for convening the Cortes. While a manifesto addressed

312 This occurred in the Peninsula in 1808 when the juntas of Seville and Granada found themselves almost openly at war, or in the fall of 1809 when the provincial juntas united in refusing to obey the Junta Central.

to the Americans was being drawn up to explain the latest events, the port was closed to prevent unmonitored news from reaching America. As we know, this precaution turned out to be useless. The recognition that Spanish America—whether out of patriotism or surprise—had granted to the new peninsular government in 1808 would now be refused by almost all of South America. For many Americans, the Peninsula was now irrecoverably lost, and the Regency Council was a mere phantom that would not last, or that would govern under the tutelage of the Cádiz Junta, the Consulado, and their correspondents in America.

The Regency Council in its manifesto, drawn up by Quintana, attempted to forestall a probable break by using the language of the most radical liberalism: "From this time forth, American Spaniards, you are elevated to the dignity of free men: you are not what you once were, when you bowed under a yoke that was all the heavier for your distance from the center of power; when you were viewed with indifference, vexed by greed, and destroyed by ignorance. Keep in mind that when you utter or write the name of he who will come to represent you in the national Congress, your destinies no longer depend on Ministers or Viceroys or governors: they are in your own hands."[313]

For the writers of the manifesto, it was an absolute indictment of ancien régime despotism, and a declaration of the freedom that the new regime was to establish. But it also amounted to telling the Spanish Americans that for the past three centuries they had been living in bondage. As a result, many Americans interpreted it not as a call to support the new political regime, but as an incentive to form their own governments; and this is precisely what the elites proceeded to do by creating their own juntas. In other cases, it even provided grounds for social uprisings. In the Andes, for example, shortly before the revolt of the Huamalies in 1812, a translation of parts of the document into Quechua was a powerful stimulus for the rebellion.[314]

---

313 Decree of the Regency Council, February 14, 1810, published in Mexico by proclamation of the governing audiencia on May 16, 1810 (AGN, Proclamations, vol. 25, file 80).

314 See Demélas 1990, vol. I, 443.

In any case, very probably the manifesto came too late. No one could know when the promised Cortes would convene, and the electoral provisions made at the time—twenty-eight deputies for Spanish America against more than two hundred for the Peninsula—once again enshrined, and deepened, the inequality between Spain and America.

Some American regions would accept once more, as in 1808, the new peninsular government and would continue to fight for their rights within the monarchy, without breaking with the Peninsula. The elections to the Cortes would take place in Mexico, Central America, and Peru; many American deputies would participate in the Cortes, where they would fight for complete equality between the two continents. The constitution which they would vote through in Cádiz with their peninsular colleagues would also be applied in these regions of Spanish America.

However, by now the moral unity of the Hispanic world was shattered, and modern politics was underway. The Americans were, in effect, beginning to take their own fate in hand, though many years would still pass before the complete establishment of modern politics in Spanish America, and a definitive and general separation from peninsular Spain. By then, these "two crucial years" would have been forgotten: the years during which the political grievances that led to independence would be born, arising from the end of absolutism and the sudden intrusion of the need for political representation of the various "peoples" of the monarchy. And they had to be forgotten: in order to construct a historical explanation of the break, it was necessary to invoke preexisting "nations," since from the standpoint of the modern frame of reference, only the nation could justify independence.

# V

# 1808: Imaginaries and Values

In every age of political upheaval, social actors tend to take the floor to justify their actions, but the period beginning in 1808 was, in this regard, exceptional. The progress of literacy and printing triggered a proliferation of all kinds of writing: proclamations issued by a variety of juntas and authorities, corporations of all sorts, as well as individuals; bishops' pastorals, sermons, public prayers, novenas; official reports, letters, and records... The greatest novelty, however, was the proliferation of newspapers across the Peninsula and, to a lesser extent, in Spanish America. These newspapers gave a wide circulation to all these documents while adding their own in-depth articles, very detailed accounts of popular reactions, and descriptions of the many ceremonies that marked the period: the oaths made to the king, the *Te Deums*, the various religious ceremonies, allegorical processions, parades, and a great variety of patriotic festivals also constituted, with their symbolic language, another form of expression.[315]

It seemed as if the whole of society, with all its many heterogeneous actors, was taking the floor to express its anguish and fears, its hopes and aspirations. These expressions show us how this society conceived itself, and how it conceived the legitimacy of its authorities, the values

---

315 There is a great abundance of available material, and although some works on the subject have already been published, we are still missing a systematic study. See, for example, the following master's theses from the Université de Paris I: Richard Hocquellet, "Le complexe de l'orphelin: Étude du discours patriotique espagnol au début du soulèvement: mai 1808–septembre 1808," 1990, 131; Béatrice Arabucki, "Les réactions mexicaines face à la crise monarchique, 1808–1809: L'imaginaire de l'union," 1990, 110; Isabelle Arasa, "L'imaginaire politique et l'opinion publique à Valence du 7 juin 1808 au 26 juin 1810 à travers la Gazette de Valence," 1991, 170 and appendixes.

it held, and the behaviors that can be deduced from these values. Obviously, we cannot expect this avalanche of discourses and images to work as a systematic philosophical or political doctrine. The characteristics of the materials varied according to their aims: some were essentially exhortations, primarily intended to inflame spirits and exalt patriotism; others, more historical in nature, sought to explain the causes of events, while a third type, of a more political character, sought remedies with which to achieve the reformation of the monarchy. Yet their overall coherence was considerable, as was the unexpected unity of feeling that erased the distinctions between the different peninsular kingdoms, and between them and the Spanish Americans. The Spanish monarchy appears as a human community of extraordinary cultural and political homogeneity.

## Images of the King and Duties of the Vassals

The most remarkable aspect of all these reactions is the central place the king occupied in this imaginary. The monarch appeared as the keystone of the monarchy, yet indissolubly bound to the nation: an offense to the king was an offense to the nation. As in all metaphorical discourse, the images used did not make up a coherent whole, though their meaning was coherent. The monarchy was conceived as a family comprised of several children (the peoples or individuals), of which the king was the head and father: "the King is a Father before he is a judge," he is "the universal father of our nation."[316] His disappearance left the nation orphaned and exposed to all the dangers this implied: possible discord among the children and the scattering of the family. Hence the constant calls for unity: the children must stand united and fight side by side to

316 "A los muy ilustres y nobles caballeros de Ciudad Real," in *Diario de México*, no. 1.141, November 14,1808, 567–68. In 1811 we can still read, in a speech presenting the project for the future constitution: "The Cortes, seeing the Nation's desire that the King should be the Father of its peoples," in *Discurso preliminar*..., 1811, 1989, 92.

defend their father. Differences disappeared in the face of this common duty: everyone must defend the monarch equally.

Another frequently used image was that of society, or the kingdom, conceived as a body whose head was the king. His disappearance was the supreme evil, for acephaly—headlessness—condemns the whole body to corruption, that is, to political dissolution: "Lacking a head, the limbs fail [...]. A vassal lays before you the horrid totality caused by disunity and the lack of a superior head: without it, there are neither limbs nor bodies; if they exist at all, they are stiff and as good as dead."[317]

This was a multiform dissolution, beginning at the territorial level, since it was feared (and with good reason) that the disappearance of the head would cause the monarchy to disintegrate into kingdoms, provinces, cities, and towns. It was also a social dissolution, affecting the heterogeneous social groups that hitherto had worked together, in their diversity, for the benefit of the whole body. Spanish texts often insisted on the need for order and the obedience due to provisional authorities in order to forestall or put an end to anarchy, not only political (as in the rivalry between the juntas) but also social. In America, more emphasis was placed on what appeared to be the most likely source of discord: the necessary union between Europeans and Americans. Hence, it was everyone's urgent priority to establish a provisional central power that could put an end to acephaly. Hence also the rejection of Bonaparte's usurpation of the crown, which amounted to the grafting of a foreign head onto the extant body—a monstrosity: "The monarchy is acephalous: a strange head has been placed upon its body, turning it into a monster, as if the human body were fitted with the head of an ass."[318]

In more political terms, the relationship between the king and his kingdoms was seen as reciprocal: that of vassals with their lord. The words *lord*, *vassal*, *vassalage*, *fidelity*, *loyalty* are omnipresent in almost all the documents of the period, starting with the call made on May 2 in

317 "A los muy ilustres y nobles caballeros de Ciudad Real," in *Diario de México*, no. 1.141, November 14, 1808, 567–68.

318 Proclamation inserted in the *Diario de Valencia*, June 6, 1808, in *Gazeta de México* XV, no. 90, November 7, 1808, 639.

Madrid: "Vassals, to arms!"[319] The king's bond with his kingdoms was one of vassalage and always referred to "sworn faith": sometimes this meant the oath sworn to the Prince of Asturias by the Cortes in 1789; more often, it meant the oaths sworn to Ferdinand VII after he rose to the throne: "King Ferdinand VII, to whom they have been sworn."[320] Resistance to Napoleon was simultaneously a defense of the homeland and a manifestation of the vassals' duties toward their lord, duties that applied to all without distinction.

On August 28, 1808, for example, the clergy of Guanajuato organized a patriotic event that "was attended by all the secular and regular ecclesiastics with sword in hand, bands and feathers, and the honorable badge of our vassalage."[321] To those who expressed surprise at this attire, the editor explained that "before consecration, ecclesiastics were vassals; and their duties as such, of which the most essential is the defense of the Church, their King, and their Country, far from being extinguished by the Priesthood, are further reinforced by it."[322]

Women participated in the same duties, and there was no lack of references to the "Spartan women of old."[323] When, on September 18, also in Guanajuato, the workers of the Valenciana mine paraded in an extraordinary procession, the different battalions included "one hundred and fifty women who worked in the mine lined up as a squadron, with naked swords in their hands, representing the Amazons, and marching to the sound of the drum, carrying a banner with the image of Our Lady of the Immaculate Conception."[324]

---

319 Quoted by Lovet 1975, 134.

320 "Manifiesto del superior gobierno y autoridades de Buenos Aires," November 9, 1808, in *Gazeta ministerial de Sevilla*, no. 60, December 23, 1808, 482.

321 "Relación de las demostraciones de lealtad y júbilo que dio la ciudad de Guanaxuato desde el 31 de julio [...] hasta el 18 de septiembre," in *Suplemento de la Gazeta de México*, XV, no. 147, December 28, 1808, 1013–25. See also Arabucki, op. cit.

322 *Suplemento de la Gazeta de México*, XV, no. 147, December 28, 1808, 1018.

323 Ibid., 1015.

324 Ibid., 1024–25.

All the estates and social or age groups were equal in their duty as loyal subjects. The indigenous peoples, like the other vassals, took part as a corporate body in the Spanish American ceremonies and proffered their help to the captive king. The governors of the native republic of Querétaro, after recalling the oath made to the sovereign, told the viceroy that

> all the Caziques of this same said City are ready to plant ten thousand men with slingshots and stones, and other weapons that can be acquired throughout the jurisdiction of this city [...] and we are resolved to shed the last drop of blood we have to forsake [*sic*] the defense of the law of God and of our Catholic Monarch.[325]

Likewise, in Mexico City,

> The Indian Districts of this jurisdiction, its towns and contiguous neighborhoods [...] believe it would be injurious to the laws to which they have sworn obedience, to the love they have professed for their Kings [...] that they should prove insensitive to the public calamities and not partake in them. [...]. The Indians will be the first to sacrifice their scanty possessions, both personal and common, their rest and their tranquility, their children and families, and unto the very last drop of their blood, rather than render vassalage to one who deserves naught but the righteous anger of our nation.[326]

The duty of vassals to defend their lord was expressed in a vocabulary that harked back to a very old frame of reference:

> [I proffer] to Your Excellency the most righteous and due tendering of my person, of my goods, and of all that I possess, in order to

---

325 "Representación de la República de Naturales, Querétaro," July 27, 1808, in *Suplemento de la Gazeta de México*, XV, no. 87, August 31, 1808, 624.

326 "Ofertas hechas al propio Exmo. Sr. Virrey por las Parcialidades de Indios de esta Capital," *Suplemento de la Gazeta de México*, XV, no. 87, September 10, 1808, 665–66.

> fulfill the duties appertaining to a vassal, the obligations of a true Spaniard [...] not I alone, [...] for I do it in the name of all the Parish Priests [...], of all the Ecclesiastics [...], of all the principal householders and commoners and, last, in the name of the Indians, for they are all determined, as am I, to sacrifice their lives and interests in so righteous a cause.[327]

Good vassals had to fulfill their duty of assistance to their lord and take up arms in his defense; battalions of "Ferdinand VII's Volunteers" were formed in both Spain and America.[328] Participants included, among many others, the merchants of San Luis Potosí, who created a cavalry battalion; the Mining Corps of the Valenciana in Guanajuato; the city council of Guadalajara, which announced on September 6 that 2,560 volunteers were already registered in its lists.[329] They also fulfilled another of the vassal's duties and contributed financially to the war with their donations, thus upholding the tradition of "service" due to the king. Donation funds opened up everywhere and immediately, and the newspapers of both continents were filled with donors from all ranks of society.[330]

A normal consequence of the bond of vassalage was that the relationship between the king and his vassals was necessarily reciprocal and, therefore, could not be broken by only one of the parties. Hence, the Bayonne abdications were illegitimate, even if the king had voluntarily consented. For this reason, among others, the illegitimate character of the Napoleonic regime was indisputable to all. And being illegitimate, it was necessarily tyrannical, not only in its exercise but, above all, in its origin. The word *tyranny*, echoed a thousand times, harks back

---

327 Letter to the viceroy of Mexico from the subdelegate of Malinalco, August 14, 1808.

328 Andalusia seems to have set the tone in this regard.

329 Arabucki, op. cit., 25–26.

330 For Buenos Aires, see "Manifiesto del superior gobierno y autoridades de Buenos Aires," September 9, 1808, in *Gazeta ministerial de Sevilla*, no. 60, December 23, 1808, 487.

primarily to this ancient meaning: the illegitimate government of one who is not the natural lord of the kingdom.

The linguistic spectrum of vassalage in itself explains why, among the virtues that were then exalted, loyalty, fidelity, and honor were paramount. The central idea was keeping the sworn faith. Honor was the vassals' vindication of their own being, of personal consistency and dignity. The adjectives used to qualify Napoleon created an inverted picture of these values. His actions were obsessively perceived, everywhere and by everyone, as felony, treason, and perfidy. Napoleon had betrayed the alliance, his sworn word, the friendship that the kings and the nation had extended to him.

As a result, as soon as news of the abdications and the aggression became known, one of the vassals' first reactions was to pledge their allegiance as soon as possible to the captive king. The ceremony in Madrid, held in the capital after the Battle of Bailén, was particularly solemn and was reported by a great many newspapers.[331] Then every city and every town on both continents proceeded in turn to solemnly proclaim the sovereign and take the oath of loyalty.

In Spanish America, physically removed as it was from the war, the public demonstrations were particularly solemn and lavish. In wealthy New Spain, for which we have plentiful sources, the festivities were innumerable: there were spontaneous demonstrations by the entire people upon hearing news of the Spanish uprisings, a variety of prayers and religious acts, allegorical processions and, at the end, the official proclamation of the king and the oath of allegiance, with all the ritual this entailed. The oath ceremony in Mexico City was particularly spectacular, but so were those in Puebla, Guadalajara, and Guanajuato. The latter, a very wealthy mining city, spent the exorbitant sum of 100,000 pesos on these formal events.[332]

It was through these manifestations, both spontaneous and ritualistic, that society expressed its patriotism, reaffirmed its identity, and

---

331 For this ceremony held on August 24, see *Gazeta de Madrid*, no. 120, September 6, 1808.

332 *Suplemento de la Gazeta de México*, XV, no. 147, December 28, 1808, 1013–25.

sought strength in unanimity in order to face the difficult circumstances of the times. The proclamation of the king and the oath of allegiance, which had always been central to civic ceremonies, now took on even greater importance. They reaffirmed, in a solemn manner sanctioned by the sacredness of the oath, the rejection of arbitrary power, the legitimacy of the monarch, and the commitment to defend him. They were also a way of reformulating the pact that indissolubly bound not only the nation to the sovereign, but each vassal to all the others.

The role played by the king's portrait, which was central to the entire ceremonial tradition of the oaths,[333] took on a new, more spontaneous and emotional tone: the royal portrait left its usual ceremonial position when it was reproduced in thousands of copies as a sign of personal adherence to the monarch, as if attempting to compensate for his physical absence by the multiplication of his image. In Mexico City, for example, on July 30, 1808, when the news of the peninsular uprising was received,

> rejoicing spread across the capital and throngs gathered in front of the royal palace, cheering and praising the cherished Ferdinand VII. A remarkably disorderly commingling of Europeans and Americans clamored for the repetition of the artillery salute and the ringing of the bells [...] an immense people, breathing nothing but patriotism, fidelity and deep love for their Sovereign [...]. In the ardor and enthusiasm of the salute, a group of the people brought with them the portrait of the beloved Ferdinand, and carried it to the royal palace while the troops found themselves unable to bring the multitude to order.[334]

After the viceroy had the portrait placed on the central balcony of the palace, held up to the veneration of the crowd, "the people asked him for it, to parade it in triumph through the streets of the city," which they proceeded to do amid overflowing enthusiasm. The city was adorned

333 See for these ceremonies in Caracas at the end of the eighteenth century, Leal 1990.

334 *Diario de México* IX, no. 1035, July 30, 1808, 115 and the following pages.

with tapestries, and "almost everywhere the portrait of the acclaimed Sovereign" was displayed. Later, "The entire people [...] gathered at 4 o'clock in the afternoon, some eighteen to twenty thousand persons of all classes, bearing the portrait of the Sovereign on a banner under a canopy. Many wore the same portrait on paper, tucked in their hats."[335]

The personal nature of each vassal's bond to the king and the oath each had taken thus help to explain the considerable difficulties that the partisans of independence later faced in America when seeking to achieve total autonomy—that is, open rejection of the king. These factors provide one of the main explanations for the mandatory reference to the sovereign that we find even among the most determined supporters of independence—a phenomenon some have described as "the mask of Ferdinand VII."

## The Monarchy and the Nation

In all these sources we find the king and the nation indissolubly joined. But what nation is it? In peninsular Spain, curiously, although the designation "Spaniards" was not absent, most of the proclamations and manifestos issued during the early days of the resistance were addressed to the inhabitants of the different kingdoms or cities: "Brave Cantabrians and Comrades,"[336] "Loyal Asturians and beloved compatriots,"[337] "Aragonese,"[338] "Alicanteans,"[339] etc. The words were immediate references to the political communities that had played the main roles in the uprising: the cities and the kingdoms. What is made fully manifest here

335 Ibid., 117.

336 "Proclama de la Junta de Santander," May 27, 1808, in *Gazeta de México* XV, September 10, 1808, 658.

337 "Proclama de la Junta General del Principado de Asturias," in ibid., 657.

338 "Manifiesto del Reyno de Aragón," in ibid., XV, no. 90, May 31, 1808, 641.

339 "Proclama de Alicante," in ibid., XV, no. 88, September 3, 1808, 631.

is the deep structure of the monarchy: unitary in the absolutist imaginary, plural in social reality.

In 1808, the identity of the inhabitants of the monarchy was defined by a pyramid of allegiances: at the base, the sense of belonging was to the towns and cities, then to the ancient kingdoms and, through them, to the monarchy. The ritual acclamations used in the oath-taking ceremonies were much more than mere relics of the past deprived of any current content. When, for example, people swore loyalty to Ferdinand VII in Guanajuato with the words "Castile, New Spain, Guanaxuato for Lord Don Fernando VII, [...] flying the Royal Banner,"[340] the hierarchy of belonging was quite clear: the crown (Castile), the kingdom (New Spain), the city (Guanajuato).

The same acclamations were heard across the cities of the Peninsula and Spanish America, even in indigenous villages, which resembled the other communities in this regard. When, in January 1809, the Indian republics of the region gathered in the city of Huexocingo,[341] in New Spain, to swear loyalty to the king, the archaic ceremonial refers us to the same imaginary:

> the following words were said by the Kings of Arms in loud voices (silence, silence, silence, hear, hear, hear, attend, attend, attend) [...] and the subdelegate received the Standard from the hands of the Royal Ensign, and holding it in his hands at the edge of the stage said in a loud voice: For the Spains, for Mexico and for Huexocingo, The Lord Don Ferdinand the Seventh Our Catholic Monarch—hail-hail-hail—and immediately, as a sign of rejoicing, many voices were raised among the populace repeating the same.[342]

---

340 "Relación de las demostraciones de lealtad y júbilo que dio la ciudad de Guanaxuato desde el 31 de julio [...] hasta el día 18 de septiembre," in *Gazeta de México, Suplemento* XV, no. 147, December 28, 1808, 1019.

341 Today the city is called Huejotzingo.—Trans.

342 "Representación del ayuntamiento de Huexocingo con el relato de la jura del rey y después de la Junta Central," May 4, 1809, in AGN México, Historia, vol. 417, file I.

The Crown of Castile has been replaced here by "the Spains," but the meaning is the same: the monarchy as a group of kingdoms, followed by their own kingdom and then the city.

This extraordinary strength retained by the identities of the ancient political communities was also displayed when the *fueros* (or territorial statutes)[343] and privileges of the kingdoms were invoked, or when old representative institutions were convened. It was also manifest in the invocation of local heroes: in Asturias, Pelayo, in La Mancha, Don Quixote and, above all, the different regional Virgins. Our Lady of Covadonga in Asturias, Our Lady of the Fuencisla in Segovia, Our Lady of the Pillar in Zaragoza and, in America, the many titles of the Virgin, especially that of Guadalupe.

This dispersion of the monarchy into diverse communities, however, does not mean that, in 1808, there was no sense of belonging to a single nation. Quite the opposite: paradoxically enough, fragmentation itself led to the emergence of a very strong idea of nationhood. After the initial period of isolation, during which each city and region had to decide, almost alone, what stance to take following the disappearance of the king, it would seem that each of these communities was astonished to discover, as they received news and correspondence from the others, the extraordinary unity of feeling and cultural and political references existing throughout the monarchy.[344] As an unexpected consequence of the invasion, the inhabitants of the monarchy discovered themselves a nation unanimously joined against the common enemy. The unity that had manifested itself in dispersion and isolation was the best proof that a single entity—the nation—did indeed exist. From then on, emphasis would constantly be placed on the idea that, in the name of this nation's higher interests, differences and partial interests should disappear or be postponed: there were no longer any Castilians, Galicians, Asturians, or Catalans, only Spaniards.

---

343 For example, the lordship of Biscay proclaims, "to our beloved Ferdinand VII, for our king and lord, in accordance with the charters and customs of this province." "Manifiesto del Señorío de Vizcaya" (Bilbao), August 6, 1808, in *Gazeta de México* XV, November 26, 1808, 911.

344 See Hocquellet, op. cit., chapters II and III.

This does not mean that the old vision of the monarchy—or the nation—as a group of kingdoms had disappeared but that, in fact, two levels of belonging were coexisting more or less coherently: one was political and remained plural while the other was emotional and patriotic, as well as profoundly unitary.

These two levels of belonging were also present in Spanish America, but they were understood in a slightly different way from what we see in the Peninsula. The nation was equally one for Americans and encompassed both hemispheres: none of the writings of this period mention a Spanish American nation. When the topic of the nation was addressed, it always referred to the monarchy as a whole. In America, as we have seen, the political structure was conceived as a gradation of kingdoms and city-provinces, but there was another level of belonging: Spanish America itself, which was identified with all the kingdoms of the Indies as a group, and whose makeup was a shifting combination of the political and the cultural. For this reason, American proclamations were frequently addressed to European Spaniards and to American Spaniards, or even to both peoples, thus marking the dual composition of the monarchy.

An allegorical engraving printed in Mexico in 1808 gives a good idea of this dual conception of a single nation comprised of two parts, Spain and the Indies:

> A *Lion* holding on its head the Portrait of the Young sovereign, and firmly grasping the two worlds in his claws [...].
> *Underneath, the following placard:*
> This *Lion* (which is the *Spanish Nation*) will never let the two worlds of Ferdinand VII fall from its claws.
> *Around the Portrait is written:*
> Beloved Ferdinand: Spain and the Indies will secure this Crown on your head [...].[345]

---

345 Advertisement in *Gazeta de México* XV, no. 73, August 5, 1808, 542. We have respected the graphic characteristics of the text. It was a very successful advertisement, for the *Gazeta* added: "So far, there are not many of these prints; but in order to satisfy as quickly as possible the desire of all those who have manifested their interest in acquiring one, they will be sold, starting

José Simón Larrea, engraver. Ferdinand VII, August 1808. Copper plate engraving. Half title of Juan López Cancelada, *Ruina de la Nueva España si se declara el comercio libre con los extrangeros*, Mexico: Imprenta de D. Manuel Santiago de Quintana, 1811. Biblioteca Nacional de España, 1/35515.

Yet this nation, which was already potentially modern insofar as it was founded on a uniformity of feelings and duties, was still conceived in both worlds as an ancien régime society with its estates and corporations. In all the ceremonies of this period, the ceremonial order expressed a very traditional view of a society still comprised of hierarchically organized groups. Each corporate body took its place by order of precedence: civil and ecclesiastical authorities, then privileged corporations, then age or gender groups (i.e., young people and women), indigenous people, etc.

The equality of all vassals in the defense of king and country, so often proclaimed and symbolically represented, nevertheless took the form of specific roles distributed according to the traditional view of society: the nobles fought and led the struggle of the people, the clergy prayed, the rich contributed their donations, the learned turned their pens into swords. Women encouraged their husbands and sons to fight

---

today, in the Office of the Gazeta and in our stalls for the cost of two pesos on vat paper."

and cared for the wounded,[346] but only took up arms when the men could not. However, there was an important development that heralded future changes: the people occupied a more central place in many of the writings of the time. This was due to their importance during the uprisings, in which they were the main (but not the only) actor. Some writings, such as the *Elogio de la plebe española*,[347] adopted a radical tone to vindicate the people's rights, exalting their patriotism vis-à-vis the passivity or complicity of the established authorities.

This same estate-based image of society can be found in the composition of the Spanish juntas or in those which the Spanish Americans were trying to create at the same time. Although the mechanisms for appointing members were not very clear, the results were, and they show that, despite these groups' revolutionary or at least extralegal origin, society was still conceived in accordance with an ancien régime imaginary. This might involve reviving old representative institutions based on the estates, or creating unprecedented compositions that tried to represent what were perceived as the most important authorities, estates, or corporations.

Asturias renovated an old representative institution that was still in existence, the Junta General of the Principality, with the participation of members of the Audiencia and also several nobles. Galicia had recourse to the Provincial Council (or *Diputación*) of the Kingdom of Galicia: seven councillors elected by the seven cities that took turns being represented in the Cortes. This council, in order to give it greater authority, was described as the Cortes de Galicia. In Aragon, Palafox convened the Cortes of the kingdom with its four traditional arms: the clergy, the nobility, the lower nobility or *hidalgos*, and the cities.[348]

In other places, where it was not possible to resort to old representative institutions, attempts were made to include in the juntas a fully

346 See, for example, "Proclama de Alicante," in *Gazeta de México* XV, no. 88, September 3, 1808, 631.

347 Quoted by Hocquellet, op. cit., 98, BN Madrid, R. 60.553.

348 See Antonio Peiró Arroyo, *Las Cortes aragonesas de 1808: Pervivencias forales y revolución popular*, Cortes de Aragón, 1985.

diversified sample of the most prestigious people and corporate bodies. In the Junta Suprema of Seville, for example, members were classified by estate: secular clergy, Audiencia, city council, nobility, regular clergy, members of the military, commerce. In still other places we find a varied combination of authorities—civil (intendants, *corregidores*), military (captains-general, military governors), and ecclesiastical (bishops)—as well as representatives of the main courts and bodies: the Audiencia, the city council of the regional capital and sometimes of the less important cities (Badajoz), the ecclesiastical chapter, the regular clergy, the bar association, the university (Granada), the military, commerce and even artisans (Valencia).[349]

The same concern can be observed in Spanish America. In Mexico, the junta convened by Viceroy Iturrigaray on August 9, 1809, to decide what stance to take in the face of events, brought together eighty-one individuals representing the most important people and corporations. They included the viceroy, the Audiencia and the archbishop, canons and inquisitors, religious prelates, the City Council of Mexico, delegates of the City Council of Jalapa, governors of the indigenous districts of San Juan and Santiago, the heads of offices of the viceregal administration and several employees, some titled nobility, and prominent householders.[350] The junta that convened for the same reason on September 5 in Santa Fe de Bogotá had a very similar makeup: the viceroy, the Audiencia, a judge from the Quito Audiencia and another honorary one from that of Charcas, various high officials, the city council, canons, soldiers, "illustrious vecinos," parish priests, lawyers, the head of the university, professors, provincials of the regular clergy.[351] The nation, seen as plural in its political structure, was also estate-based and corporate in its social constitution.

---

349 See Martínez de Velasco 1972, 81–90 and Artola 1968, chapter IV.

350 See *Junta General celebrada en México, El nueve de Agosto de mil ochocientos ocho presidida por Exmo. Señor Virrey D. Josef de Yturrigaray*, in AGN, Virreinato, Bandos, vol. 22 and for this episode, Alamán 1972, vol. I, 127 and the following pages.

351 AHN, Secretaría de Estado records, vol. 60, 1, 3.

## History and Religion

However, as we mentioned earlier, the community of feelings and values was so great and the rejection of the enemy so general, that this unity would serve as the basis for the construction of a modern national identity. Many of the elements of this construction have deep historical roots: Spanish virtues (a sense of honor, heroism, an aspiration to glory, perseverance), and the special protection Providence has always bestowed on the Spanish people. These elements, however, were now integrated into a totalizing, historically based discourse that can be traced to the first days of the uprising and that aimed both to exalt the past and lay the groundwork for a new future. History became the privileged instrument for creating a sense of belonging within this collective being—the nation.

The historical discourse was primarily intended to inflame patriotism by exalting past glories and exhorting the Spaniards to prove themselves worthy of their ancestry. The glories praised, however, were those of a single Spain, supposed to have existed from the dawn of time. In an 1808 text, Martínez Marina traces this nation's history and repeatedly contrasts the periods of unity, portrayed as periods of glory, with those of political division, seen as times of weakness and decadence.[352] He celebrates national heroism in the face of the Roman conquest: "The Spaniards waged the war for almost two hundred years: a resistance all the more prodigious because it did not include the whole assembled nation for, had that been the case, it would have been impossible for the enemies to proceed with their attempts."[353] The same rationale is used to explain the Reconquista era, which took so long because disunity "hindered military operations and sterilized the heroic but poorly joined efforts of the nation. Needless to say, the fundamental law of the Spanish monarchy—that the kingdom must be one and indivisible—was

352 Martínez Marina 1988. This text, published for the first time in 1813, was written, in fact, in two stages: the first, dating from the summer of 1808, was published in *El Español*, no. 1, 1810; the second dates from after the promulgation of the Constitution of 1812.

353 Ibid., 120.

forgotten."[354] For this reason, the Catholic monarchs are exalted as those whose "glory it was to elevate the Spanish monarchy to the point of its greatest splendor and grandeur."

In addition to this union-disunion opposition, Martínez Marina's historical scheme identifies another explanatory element behind the nation's moments of splendor or decadence: the periods of freedom or oppression (an issue we will not address for now, given its more specifically political character). In any case, in this, as in most documents of the period, the omnipresence of history responded, above all, to a need for intelligibility: to explain the catastrophe of 1808. The topic of Spain's backwardness vis-à-vis the rest of Europe and the examination of the causes for this lag harked back to the seventeenth century and took on renewed importance during the Enlightenment. What had hitherto been the subject of literary disputes became a vital experience shared by all—a scandal, in the strict sense of the word, produced by the clash between the celebrated and supposedly eternal glories of the past and the terrible humiliations of the present.

The historical discourse was intended, above all, to dispel scandal and prepare the ground for the restoration of former greatness. The abyss into which the monarchy had fallen was often perceived in a positive way: as an eye-opening confrontation with reality, an awakening that would enable the correction of those defects considered to be the cause of contemporary evils. This theme was most present in the more overtly political articles, especially those written by the future liberals. In this view, a new time, a new era, a new golden age awaited the nation: "everything is new."

A new era was beginning—that of regeneration—and some 1808 publications even identified this date as "the first year of the regeneration of Spain."[355] This is why we see such a strong historical consciousness

---

354 Ibid., 126.

355 *Proclama a los españoles del africano numido Abenumeya Rasis (6 de agosto primer año de la regeneración de España)*, in CDF, vol. 871, quoted by Hocquellet, op. cit., 98, 118.

from the very beginning of the uprising and why writings claiming to have been written for posterity were so numerous.[356]

Narrating the exploits of the War of Independence was not only a way of showing that the present generation was a worthy heir to its ancestors, but that it even amply surpassed them: in this version, the current age was superior to all others, and ages to come would see it as one of the most brilliant in history.[357] There was a clear intent to build a symbolic narrative of the homeland, with a pantheon of national heroes and great achievements, even to the extent of foreseeing the paintings that would one day depict the heroic scenes of the period. The *Semanario Patriótico*, for example, when reviewing the poems of Juan Nicasio Gallego that were read at the Royal Academy of San Fernando in August 1808, stated that "the paintings that will provide the Museum of Spanish Arts with the heroic and admirable deeds of today's warriors are announced in a prophetic tone."[358] The desire to create the historical imaginary of the new nation was explicit, and future commemoration was already clearly expressed in the present.

Curiously, however, despite the mood born out of the fierce struggle against a foreign enemy, which necessarily led to discourses whose patriotism adopted a very particularistic and even xenophobic tone, we find many others of a distinctly universalist character. Spain appeared as a beacon for all nations, setting the example by the resistance of an entire people who refused to be dominated by their oppressors. Spain, many writers said, was fighting for the freedom of Europe: it was the first free nation to raise the torch of independence, an example for all of Europe, and its struggle was a battle for the entire continent.[359] Spain could even help France free itself from serfdom:

> If, as is to be expected, she takes off her blindfold, she will see him in the same light as does all Europe, and perhaps she will join us

---

356 See the case of the *Gazeta de Valencia*, in Arasa, op. cit., 27.

357 *Gazeta de Valencia*, quoted by Arasa, op. cit., 85–87.

358 *Semanario Patriótico*, Madrid, no. VI, October 6, 1808.

359 *Gazeta de Valencia*, quoted by Arasa, op. cit., 85–87.

> [...] and she will be worthy of renown as both great and enlightened when she reflects on the principles of her revolution, meant to restore men to their just and estimable rights.[360]

The sympathy of many enlightened intellectuals, not only for French enlightened thought, the "*lumières*," but also for the early stages of the revolution understood as a vindication of the nation's rights against absolutism, can still be seen in many discourses. As a defender of the people's freedom and independence, Spain combined the purest love of country with that of reason in its fight against those who had declared war on the "light."[361]

It is clear, however, that these issues, so dear to the enlightened and the partisans of political reform, were secondary in relation to other topics, which were much more popular and thus attracted much more support. We have already mentioned the importance that defending the king and the nation's rights assumed in the hostility toward the invader. Now we can add to the discussion other, more emotional topics. The combatants were struggling for their homeland, in the most visceral sense of the word: they were fighting for their land—or for their small plot of land; for their wives and children; for their ancestral customs and their religion.[362]

Religion, side by side with king and country, occupies a central place in all the documents of the first period—central, but with different meanings and functions. First, religion was an essential part of the national identity—one of the elements that, alongside loyalty to the king, was shared by all members of the monarchy. It was a very traditional component when it came to defining the personality of the

---

360 "Manifiesto del superior gobierno y autoridades de Buenos Aires," September 9, 1808, in *Gazeta ministerial de Sevilla*, no. 60, December 23, 1808, 484.

361 *Gazeta de Valencia*, quoted by Arasa, op. cit., 29.

362 See, for example, the "Proclama de la Junta General del Principado de Asturias": "defending our unhappy Monarch, our homes, our children and wives [...] they have profaned our temples, assaulted our religion," in *Gazeta de México* XV, September 10, 1808, 657.

Hispanic monarchy.[363] The American insurgents would inherit it later on, along with the complication of declaring themselves at the same time Catholics, partisans of independence, and republicans.

Contrary to the version circulated by French military reports that portrayed the Spanish uprising as a revolt by "fanatical clergy" who aroused the masses in the name of essentially religious values, the defense of religion appears to have been inseparable from the defense of the homeland and the other elements that constituted it. In fact, the clergy were not usually a driving force behind the uprisings or the popular mobilizations during this early period.[364] Clerics intervened as just one more (albeit important) element of traditional social authorities and religion—they represented one of the values that was being defended.

That said, and although religion was inseparable from the other elements, it is clear that religious arguments considerably strengthened resistance to the invader and were therefore employed by both clerics and laity, though of course the former had a leading role to play in this struggle. Hence the multiplication of pastoral letters, sermons, supplications, funerals for fallen patriots, *novenas* carried out in great numbers by all the bodies and regions of the monarchy. America stands out in this regard.

In a different register from that of the struggle for independence and freedom, the defense of religion took on a universalist character too. The struggle against Napoleon also appeared as that of Christendom against the heir of the French Revolution insofar as the latter was perceived by contemporaries as impious and antireligious. This is why emphasis was placed, not only on the sacrilegious behavior of the French troops—who looted churches, destroyed images, and raped sacred representatives—but on the regicide committed against the sacred person of the king of France, Napoleon's persecution of the pope, etc.

Religion, even more than profane history (which was mainly accessible to the elites), also provided a historical explanation of the ongoing disaster. This disaster was given a religious reading: it was a consequence of men's sins, a punishment sent by God to his people so they would

---

363 David Brading has highlighted this peculiarity in several of his works.

364 Except, perhaps, in Valencia.

convert and do penance. Providence, then, had allowed these difficult times to happen so as to effect the people's conversion. This, in turn, would ensure the divine help and favor to the combatants. Hence all the analogies drawn from both the Old and New Testaments. The nation was presented as a new Israel, an implicit reference to Sacred History. While the chosen people's unfaithfulness was punished at first by the defeat of their armies, their return to Yahweh was rewarded with protection by the "Lord of Hosts." For example, the editor of the *Diario de México* (no doubt Carlos María de Bustamante) ended his description of the city's festivities after the news of the Spanish insurrection with an exhortation that was simultaneously a patriotic speech and a prayer filled with biblical reminiscences:

> Great God! Sovereign Father of the peoples, in whose hand resides the fate of Kings. Lord of Hosts, whose omnipotent arm has been, is, and will be the support and strength of Christianity, never forsake a nation that humbly professes your holy name, that upholds the rights of Religion as an infinite treasure that you yourself have entrusted it with to ensure its happiness, that calls for a Sovereign, that you, Righteous God, doth protect as the work of your hands, and save the fatherland, which knows how to immortalize your name even amid desolation. Mighty God, immortal God, in you alone do the two Spains put their trust, like another Israel: make our arms propitious, and we shall fear nothing, not even the abyss that conspires against us![365]

References to the Book of Revelation play a similar role: they also explain history in slightly different but complementary terms, by describing it as a struggle full of vicissitudes between the servants of evil and the hosts of good, which will end with the final victory of the latter. Revelation also had the advantage of providing a multitude of images, well known in religious iconography, that were suitable for stage representation and could

365 *Diario de México* IX, no. 1035, July 30, 1808, 118.

be immediately understood by all.[366] Alicante called Napoleon the "Antichrist of the Human Race."[367] The city of Ourense referred to the palaces of Paris and Versailles with the terms used in Revelation to describe Babylon,[368] the great whore, and proclaimed that her ruin was near.[369] In the *Gazeta de Valencia*,[370] the Lord was described advancing at the head of his troops, with a flaming sword ready for vengeance.[371] The allegorical procession with which Valladolid de Michoacán celebrated its loyalty to the king included a parade of the different bodies of society, the allegorical figures of four characters from antiquity—Ulysses, Hector, Cato, and Brutus—and an "angel of victory on a white horse [...] with a sword in his hand and [...] the motto: this is the prize."[372]

In this struggle against evil, the combatants sought the protection not only of the Lord of Hosts but also of their patron saints and, above all, that of the Virgin—in Mexico, the Virgin of Guadalupe:

> Mexicans, you are happily blessed with an august intercessor whose protection is infallible. To this precious image of the Most Holy Mary of Guadalupe your fate is tied [...] She has promised that she will listen to you constantly [...] you may count, of course, on an illustrious victory.[373]

---

366 Themes from Revelation had recently been exploited in the Peninsula by a popular preacher against the French Revolution, the Capuchin Diego José de Cádiz.

367 "Proclama de Alicante," in *Gazeta de México* XV, no. 88, September 3, 1808, 631.

368 Revelation, 17–18.

369 In *Colección de papeles interesantes sobre las circunstancias presentes*, Madrid, 1808, I, 8, in Hocquellet, op. cit., 22.

370 Arasa, op. cit., 88.

371 Revelation, 19, 11.

372 "La lealtad valisoletana celebra la heroicidad de la España," in *Diario de México* IX, no. 1064, August 29, 1808, 243–45.

373 *Diario de México* IX, no. 1035, July 30, 1808, 118.

In Asturias, the protector was the Virgin of Covadonga, Lady of Battles: "Let us invoke the God of Hosts; let us choose for an intercessor our Lady of Battles, whose image is venerated in the ancient temple of Covadonga, with the assurance that she will not abandon us [...]."[374]

At other times, the choice of words (the frequent invocation of the martyrs in the strict sense of the word, the portrayal of the king as "innocent," and the description of his sufferings) also refer us to the religious universe and the idea of restorative pain.

## The Political Frame of Reference: Pactism Reborn

If the social imaginary that suddenly came to the surface at the time was, as we have seen, extraordinarily traditional, both in Spain and in Spanish America, the same thing was true of the explicit political frame of reference that justified the peninsular uprising and American loyalty. Pactism, whether as the persistence of classical political doctrines or as the result of modern reworkings, was predominant throughout. The images took a great many forms, but what they expressed in a variety of ways was a corporate and estate-based image of society as well as a pactist conception of the political regime that was very much in contradiction with the imaginary transmitted by absolutism and the modern elites. What, then, explains the presence of pactism in 1808?

First, it was certainly due to the gap existing between the goals of absolutist modernity (as expressed in so many royal documents) and its achievements. The theoretical declarations of struggle against the particular privileges and statutes that hindered the power of the modern state were clear and conclusive, but their results were much more modest.[375] Despite its claims to absolute power, the state was, in fact, obliged to engage in dialogue with the social actors: to negotiate, make

374 "Proclama de la Junta General del Principado de Asturias," in *Gazeta de México* XV, September 10, 1808, 657.

375 For these plans and their limited results, see Domínguez Ortiz 1976, chapter 18.

concessions, compromise when these actors resisted measures that threatened interests or rights they considered fundamental. This is how we can interpret the well-known Spanish American phrase "*se acata, pero no se cumple*" (respect, not compliance): as an avowal both of the deference due to royal authority and of the rights that this authority could not disregard. More generally, it can be said that pactism, even when the term itself is not used, is the mode of relationship necessarily established between real actors of a collective type. The treaties or pacts between states in international life are an extreme example of this.

Toward the end of the eighteenth century, we can also observe the persistence or revival of pactism in the field of ideas. In some circles, this was owing to the endurance of classical Spanish thought (Vitoria, Las Casas, Mariana, Suárez, etc.) and its theories regarding the indirect divine origin of monarchical power—*a Deo per populum*—and the reciprocal duties and rights that pertained between king and kingdom, or between the king and his vassals, where noncompliance by the monarch could justify disobedience or even revolt.[376] Although these authors were not always known about firsthand but, rather, through systematic works of theology or canon law,[377] they were important enough that, during the last third of the eighteenth century, the crown repeatedly forbade the teaching of traditional doctrines of political power in universities or seminaries.[378]

The rebirth of pactism sometimes stemmed from the dissemination of modern jusnaturalist authors and books (Grotius, Puffendorf, and their disciples), which was favored by the creation of chairs of natural law in the universities during the last third of the eighteenth century.[379] Other influences were the social contract theories of Locke or Rousseau

---

376 For the persistence of these classical ideas in pro-independence America, see Stoetzer 1982.

377 This is how Hidalgo became acquainted with them. See Carlos Herrejón Peredo, "Hidalgo: La justificación de la insurgencia," *Cuadernos Americanos*, CCXLVI, no. 1, January–February 1983.

378 See Sánchez Agesta 1953, 109–113.

379 Ibid., appendixes.

and, after 1789, those derived from the French Revolution. Obviously, many of these social contract doctrines did not necessarily imply a traditional notion of society or political power, but many people before the great crisis of 1808 interpreted them traditionally so as to provide new foundations for the old pactist imaginary based on the reciprocal bond between king and kingdom.

Many of the controversies around the modernity or traditionalism of the ideas behind the Spanish uprising of 1808 and the subsequent movements for American independence stem from this kind of interbreeding of ideas and imaginaries. Most people during any given period, and even more so during a revolutionary one, are not specialists in the history of ideas or political science, with the ability to learn and adopt in all its completeness and coherence (supposing it to be coherent) a given form of political thought.

That is why, rather than attempt an impossible assessment of the theoretical influences of one school or another on a given statement of principles, we must try to apprehend the "spirit of an age"—*l'air du temps*. And this spirit, on the eve of the Hispanic Revolution, was clearly pactist in nature, implying a vision of society that was still largely traditional even if the concerns and ideas of many elites were already starting to address modern problems.

This is the context in which we must locate historical constitutionalism, which was so important in the Hispanic context at the end of the century. Its origin in Spain certainly predates the French Revolution and has to do with causes common to both countries. These causes undoubtedly included, first of all, the cost the modern elites had to pay, in terms of freedom, for the modernizing enterprise they embraced; and, second, a growing distrust in the ability of "enlightened despotism" to bring reforms to completion. As early as 1780, Jovellanos's admission speech before the Royal Academy of History defended the old representative institutions.[380]

380 This is the best-known speech, but there were others, such as those that Ibáñez de Rentería delivered at the Royal Basque Society of Friends of the Country (Real Sociedad Vascongada de Amigos del País) between 1780 and 1793, some of which were published in 1790.

However, it was not until after 1789 that reflections on "free government" and the barriers that had to be raised against "despotism" and "arbitrary power" came to the fore. The physical and cultural proximity to revolutionary France would of course prompt these discussions, irrespective of whether France was seen (depending on the different stages of the Revolution) as the country of freedom, of "anarchy" and terror, or of Napoleonic "despotism." To all these factors we must add the internal circumstances of the monarchy. The accession to the throne of the colorless Charles IV in 1789 and the murky origins that public opinion—both the general populace and the enlightened intellectuals—attributed to his favorite Godoy's hold on power, took some of the shine off "enlightened despotism." Although the frequent ministerial changes and the corresponding domino effect of misfortunes befalling the different political factions and clienteles (i.e., loss of office and sometimes even imprisonment or exile) largely responded to shifts in the challenging foreign policy of a revolutionary time, they were very often interpreted as a consequence of arbitrary power and signs of growing despotism.

Although Spanish reflections on the historical constitution of the monarchy have their origins in a time before the French Revolution, in the late eighteenth century they must be located within the framework of the great debate that this historical event triggered in Europe—more particularly, the controversy between Edmund Burke and the supporters of the Revolution. In his *Reflections on the Revolution in France*, which was immensely popular at the time,[381] Burke defends the concrete and historical character of English liberties against the abstract universalism of the Rights of Man and the French revolutionaries' aspirations to build an entirely new society by making a tabula rasa of the past. For Burke, the constitution of England was not a rational construction made by a single generation, but a set of fundamental laws condensing centuries of experience. The pact binding the king to the kingdom was, in England, mutual, and could not be broken by one of the parties

---

381 Published in 1790, Burke's book went through 11 editions during its first year, with more than 30,000 copies in print. The first French translation appeared in 1791. A clandestine translation, printed in 1790 in Tarragona, circulated in Spain. See Herr 1973, 245.

alone, as the supporters of the nation's radical sovereignty believed. The controversy provoked by Burke's book spread very quickly and Paine and Condorcet[382] responded to it, explicitly or implicitly, defending the idea of the nation's exclusive sovereignty.

Much like their Spanish adversaries, who supported the radical and exclusive sovereignty of the nation, the Spanish historical constitutionalists (including the greatest of them, Jovellanos) defended the future reform of the monarchy as men of their time, who were well informed about the disputes taking place in the enlightened Europe to which they belonged.[383] For this reason, Spanish historical constitutionalism was not fundamentally based on the revival of classical political thought proper, but on a conceptualization of what the monarchy should be; that is, on a "scholarly" investigation of the liberties contained in the ancient medieval laws of the various Hispanic kingdoms.[384] These laws were interpreted, along the lines of Burke's argument, as an implicit constitution of the monarchy based on custom and intended to regulate the relations between the monarch and his kingdom, with the latter represented in the Cortes. This historical constitution, embodied in the "fundamental laws of the kingdom," was primarily intended to guarantee the freedom of the subjects, prevent arbitrariness, and give voice to the kingdom in a new dialogue with the king. Although there was talk of restoring the old liberties, these

---

382 Thomas Paine replied a year later with *The Rights of Man*, which was also immensely popular; a French translation followed in 1792. Condorcet wrote his *Réflexions sur la Révolution de 1688, et sur celle du 10 août 1792*. For this topic, see Eduardo Muñoz, "Deux thèmes de l'Indépendance: Pacte social et constitution historique au Chili," in Guerra 1989, vol. II.

383 During the tertulias that took place at Jovellanos's home in Asturias, some of the books that were read and discussed included those of Burke, Barruel, and Bossuet on the one hand, and Paine and Condorcet on the other. See Herr 1973, 312.

384 Among these laws, those of the kingdoms of the Crown of Aragon or Navarre were frequently invoked, including some very ancient charters, such as the Fueros de Sobrarbve, which was published by *El Semanario Patriótico*, Madrid, no. X, November 3, 1808.

were interpreted from a modern individual viewpoint rather than in terms of the freedom of the kingdoms. These archaizing arguments should not, therefore, be taken at face value, since many of those who employed them were taking refuge behind old terms to express new ideas that were difficult to state plainly before 1808, first because of censorship, and later because of the spectacular rise of popular traditionalism. The same words referred to concepts that were actually very different. When speaking of the kingdom before 1808 (and, more frequently, of the nation after this date) some meant the traditional political communities structured as a body, whose arms convened in the Cortes, while others meant a nation formed, as in the French Revolution, by an association of citizens represented in Cortes that were not divided by estates—in other words, a national assembly. There were also differences when it came to assessing what remained of the ancient constitution of the kingdom. For some, the fact that many of its elements had been forgotten did not result in any profound alteration; for others, who would become more and more numerous, the old constitution had been radically altered, and the date of its death could even be given specifically: 1521, the battle of Villalar, in which the defeat of the Comuneros put an end to Castilian liberties.[385] The theme of the "three centuries of despotism," which would later enjoy great popularity in Spanish America, although with reference to the colonial period, was conceived at this time in the Peninsula.

In any case, by 1808, all these currents (which until then had been limited to the private sphere as topics of conversation in the tertulias or unpublished manuscripts circulating in these circles)[386] had made their mark on the opinion of the elites, to such an extent that the Secretary of Justice chose to surreptitiously suppress several medieval laws during the updating of the great Spanish legislative compendium *Novísima Recopilación de Leyes de España*, published in 1804. The suppressed

385 This is the subject of Quintana's ode to Padilla, written in 1797 and unpublished until the crisis of 1808.

386 On this period and this literature, see, besides Elorza 1970, by the same author, "El temido árbol de la libertad," in Aymes 1989, 69 and the following pages, and also Dérozier, in Tuñón de Lara 1980, vol. VII, chapter IV.

laws, which had appeared in the previous compendium, included, for example: "no new tributes or taxes shall be distributed in these Kingdoms without summoning the Procurators of the towns to the Cortes, where they will proceed to allow them."[387]

However, despite such vigilance, it was difficult to prevent the republication of the old legislative compilations, such as the *Partidas de Alfonso X*, reedited in 1807.[388] In 1808, Francisco Martínez Marina's *Ensayo histórico y crítico sobre la antigua legislación y principales cuerpos de los reinos de León y Castilla* was also published in Madrid. In this text, the author prudently addressed the essential aspects of the book he would publish in 1813, which would become the bible of historical constitutionalism: *Teoría de las Cortes*.[389]

Whatever the real intentions of those who appealed to the old liberties of the kingdom, the French Revolution inexorably led to more radical approaches. The institutional, social, and cultural similarities between Spain and France would very soon displace the problem of restoring the rights of the kingdom to that of the sovereignty of the nation. From 1789 onward, the Parisian press reported on the Spanish Cortes of that year as if they were a reenactment of the Estates General, also presenting Campomanes (much to his displeasure) as a champion of the rights of the people: "This intrepid protector of the Third Estate has earned the hatred of the Spanish aristocrats by his zeal in defending the cause of the people before the Assembly of the Cortes."[390]

Three years later, the Spanish authorities confiscated a pamphlet written by José Marchena in which he incited the Spanish people to revolution. The argument was based, precisely, on the need to convene the Cortes to reconquer the rights of the nation: "There is one means left to you, Spaniards, to destroy religious despotism: this is to convene

---

387 Note by the Marquis of Caballero, Minister of Justice, dated June 2, 1805, in Fernández Martín 1885, vol. I, 351.

388 Alfonso X, *Las Siete Partidas nuevamente glosadas*, Madrid, 1807, 3 vols.

389 Martínez Marina 1813.

390 Article from the *Courrier de Paris*, December 6, 1789, quoted in Domergue 1984, 20.

your Cortes. Waste not a moment: let 'Cortes, Cortes' be the universal clamor."[391]

For the most determined of the pre-liberals, the convening of the Cortes went far beyond reforming corrupt practices, satisfying specific grievances or recovering the old liberties. It was about establishing a nation and proclaiming its sovereignty, in order to build on this foundation a free government via the promulgation of a constitution. However, the strength of historical constitutionalism was so great that even the most radical would have to employ many of the traditional political terms, even when their true opinions were revealed in private documents. Thus, in 1809, when defending the convening of a representative body (which was in fact, a genuine national assembly) Blanco White confessed: "The national body that Spain now needs (a body that must retain the name of Cortes, not because that is what they were, but because this designation is sacred to the Spanish) [...]."[392]

In any case, and whatever frame of reference the words belonged to, on the eve of the 1808 crisis the all-encompassing power of the monarch had already been called into question in the minds of most of the elites, whether radical or moderate.

---

391 Reproduced in the appendix in ibid., 247–50. For this proclamation, see Fuentes 1989, 93 and the following pages.

392 José María Blanco White, "Respuesta de la Universidad de Sevilla a la Consulta sobre las Cortes," December 7, 1809, in Suárez 1967–68, vol. I, 269.

# VI

# Spanish America's First General Elections (1809)

In the complex and shifting relations between the Peninsula and Spanish America during the revolutionary era, the American elections organized to send deputies to the Junta Central in Spain represent an original, fundamental, and largely bypassed milestone. Original, because, for the first time in the Hispanic world—even before this happened in peninsular Spain—the whole of America was called to the polls for an electoral process that, taking place as it did over a whole continent, was unprecedented in world history. Fundamental, because, for the first time during the Hispanic Revolution, the representative principle around which the entire revolutionary process revolved was put into practice. And also because it posed, openly and irrevocably, the central political problem of the monarchy: that of political equality between the two continents.

Curiously, this pivotal milestone continues to be largely ignored.[393] First, because it takes place between two important moments in the American history of the time: 1808 (the Napoleonic invasion and the royal abdications, which gave rise to the first attempts to create juntas) and 1810 (the invasion of Andalusia by the French, the consequent dissolution of the Junta Central, and the establishment of the Regency Council, which in turn would lead to the great wave of autonomous American juntas). Second, because the deputies elected in America did

393 The only significant exceptions to this general silence among historians are González 1937, an old and very well-documented study that addresses these elections in Río de la Plata, and Pérez Gilhou 1981, which is more recent but limited to the relationship between electoral dispositions and Spanish and American public opinions, and Demélas 1990, for Peru (vol. I, chapter III, A, 2, 320 and the following pages).

not reach Spain in time to participate in the Junta Central, and this has diminished their importance in hagiographic terms. Third, because electoral studies had fallen into oblivion until recently. Finally, and perhaps most importantly, because what these elections reveal about the real state and aspirations of Spanish America at the time does not fit comfortably with the canonical vision of independence, a vision obsessed with America's modernity and with the teleology of a precocious search for independence.

And yet the importance of this historical moment appears quite clearly, not only in the archives but also in later pro-independence writings. Bolívar himself, when in 1815 he wrote a historical account of the independence process, spoke of this intermediate period in veiled terms that were nevertheless perfectly intelligible to his contemporaries when he affirmed that, at the time, they were "beguiled with the justice due to us and with flattering but continuously derided hopes."[394]

The elections are important for an understanding of the increasing process of moral estrangement between the two pillars of the monarchy, and also for what they tell us about the real actors in American political life, about their imaginaries and about certain political practices and behaviors that promised to be long-lived.

## The Necessary American Representation

As we have already mentioned, the problem of representation was, from the first peninsular uprisings, the central problem of the Hispanic Revolution.[395] In the absence of the king, the resistance to Napoleon and the existence of authorities in charge of leading this resistance could only be founded on the nation, however this word might have been understood at the time. In peninsular Spain, it was to this explicit founding concept that the different insurrectionary juntas resorted to justify their existence

394 "Cartas de Jamaica," Kingston, September 6, 1815, in Bolívar 1971, 75.

395 See "Constituting a Legitimate Government" in chapter IV.

and their exercise of power. However, it was also clear to everyone that this solution, a consequence of events, could only be temporary. And not only because the conducting of the war and the diplomatic negotiations required a unified command, but also because this nation, which had unanimously expressed itself in its rejection of the usurper, had to be endowed with a single authority that would symbolically assume both the sovereignty of the captive king and the unity of the monarchy.

The forming of the Suprema Junta Central of the Kingdom in Aranjuez on September 25, 1808, by the delegates of the peninsular provincial juntas provided a short-term solution to the problem. Its creation responded to the urgency of the situation, and that is why it was recognized as the supreme authority of the monarchy, first in the Peninsula and later in Spanish America; its nature, however, was profoundly ambiguous. On the one hand, the Junta Central governed in the name and place of the king and was the "depositary of sovereign authority" until his return. It represented the king in the literal sense of the word: that is, it made him present. Hence the importance of the royal attributes during its installation and in its ceremonial: it was addressed as "Majesty," was escorted by the king's guards, royal ceremonies accompanied its enthronement, etc.: "the Junta will receive the title and honors of His Majesty, in whose name it governs."[396] No wonder that after its installation the Junta Central should have demanded that the limited powers given by some juntas to their members be transformed into the most wide-ranging and unlimited powers, since they were supposed to be participating in the sovereignty of the monarch, which at the time, by definition, was unlimited.[397]

However, on the other hand and since there had been no explicit act of delegation on the part of the monarch himself, the Junta Central was

---

396 The installation of the Junta Central is described, for example, in *Gazeta de Madrid*, no. 129 special number, September 29, 1808, and *Gazeta de México*, no. 133 special number, November 29, 1808. On this topic, see Richard Hocquellet, "Le complexe de l'orphelin: Étude du discours patriotique espagnol au début du soulèvement: mai 1808–septembre 1808," I (master's thesis, Université de Paris, 1990), 131.

397 On this topic, see Martínez de Velasco 1972, 178 and following pages.

a body comprised of deputies from the insurrectionary juntas, who considered themselves de facto representatives of society. For this reason, it would soon come to be seen as an early form of national representation: "The members who make up the Supreme Junta of the Kingdom, united in body, represent the entire nation, and not the province of which they are deputies."[398]

Although this sentence in the regulations of the Junta Central was meant to counter the strongly autonomist leanings of the provincial juntas, the definition already points to a national representation, whose members were, so to speak, rough drafts of the modern deputy, endowed with unlimited powers and personal immunity. However, this representation of the nation, though made urgent and inevitable by events, was clearly imperfect and thus open to criticism. Imperfect from a legal point of view, insofar as neither the Junta Central itself nor the juntas from which its power arose had any historical precedent—a very serious flaw in a society where legality still rested on the stipulations of ancestral laws and customs. It was likewise imperfect in terms of representation itself, whether traditional or modern, insofar as the formation of the insurrectionary juntas which were its immediate origin had not conformed to regular and rigorous representative mechanisms either. That is why, even before the creation of the Junta Central, there was no lack of writings in peninsular Spain (some of them coming from the highest governing bodies of the monarchy, such as the Council of Castile) that pointed out all these failings.

Although no one actually or immediately rejected its authority, it was inevitable that, as soon as a more perfect form of representation was sought, the question of convening the Cortes as the acknowledged and legal representation of the monarchy would arise. Even though the project for convening the Cortes presented by Jovellanos on October 7, 1808, was not even examined by the Junta Central because of the opposition of Floridablanca and the supporters of absolutism,[399] the problem of the Cortes remained dormant and would finally come to the fore in May 1809.

---

398 Regulations of the Junta Central, cited by Artola 1968, 397.

399 See Jovellanos 1811 and Suárez 1982.

The imperfect representativity of the Junta Central, however, was also due to the absence of deputies from Spanish America. Although this second flaw was not very visible at the time for the nascent public opinion of the Peninsula,[400] the problem was evident to those in better-informed circles. For them, indeed, gaining and preserving American loyalty answered both to a vital need—that of securing American financial aid, which was crucial for the war—and to an obsessive fear regarding the possible birth of an independence movement.

Both these motives can be clearly seen in the behavior of the insurrectionary Junta of Seville, which, immediately after its constitution, not only sent emissaries to Spanish America to ask for help, but, in order to maintain the bond with the continent, went so far as to adopt the title of "Supreme [Junta] of Spain and the Indies." As the junta itself explained a few weeks later to justify its usurpation of this title:

> certain people, whether ignorant or malevolent, have tried to make the public believe that we were affecting superiority over the other provinces. We never entertained such a thought [...]. The Americas certainly drew all our attention as we sought to preserve that most important part of the Spanish Monarchy. We have sent notices and commissioners to it and to Asia asking them to join us, something that could not be achieved if we did not call ourselves the Supreme Government Junta of Spain and the Indies [...].[401]

This hoax made it clear that the Americans were not trusted, but were such misgivings justified? The answer must take into account both American realities and peninsular perceptions of them. The demographic and economic weight of Spanish America within the monarchy had certainly increased considerably. By the early nineteenth century, the population of the Indies exceeded that of the Peninsula, and a substantial part of the peninsular economy and the finances of the

---

400 The issue is not addressed in the many political plans published in the Peninsula in 1808.

401 "Manifiesto de la Junta de Sevilla," August 3, 1808, quoted by Martínez de Velasco 1972, 120.

monarchy depended on the Indies. The construction of an American identity was also well underway, both in its global "American" dimension and in the formation of those identities specific to each community which we have called "proto-national."[402]

The change in the way peninsular Spain perceived America was clear as well in the eighteenth century: as we mentioned before,[403] there was a growing tendency to view America as a group of "colonies"—that is, economic and political dependencies of peninsular Spain. It is true that this conception had not yet taken on legal form, and that the government of America had not changed substantially. Yet it is equally true that to this transformation in the peninsular vocabulary and imaginary (which explains many of the misunderstandings of the revolutionary era), would be added, in the early 1780s, the peninsulars' fear of a possible independence movement in America.

The "Great Rebellion" of Túpac Amaru in Peru in 1780 and that of the Comuneros of El Socorro in New Granada the following year, which took place, moreover, in the context of the emancipation of the United States, made many among the peninsular elite believe that the independence of the Indies was possible, perhaps even inevitable. In this context we find plans for an independence controlled by the crown, such as the one conceived by the intendant of Venezuela, Abalos, or the Count of Aranda's various schemes. American discontent with the reforms, as well as the social uprisings, were interpreted as preludes to independence movements.

In the light of current scholarship, which insists that these uprisings were of the old-fashioned kind—"Long live the king, death to bad government!"[404]—these fears now seem rather unfounded, as the extraordinary explosion of Hispanic patriotism in America as well as American loyalty to peninsular resistance also proved in 1808. There were certainly Spanish Americans who favored independence by the

402 See chapter II.

403 See "American Grievances" in chapter II.

404 See, for example, for New Granada, Phelan 1978, and for Peru, O'Phelan Godoy 1988, and Demélas 1990, vol I.

end of the eighteenth century, but they still represented a very limited minority, as Bolívar himself acknowledged in 1815:

> From all that I have said it will be easy to infer that America was not prepared to break away from the mother country, as suddenly happened, as a consequence of the illegitimate cessions of Bayonne and the iniquitous war that the Regency declared against us, without any right to do so, not only because of the lack of justice, but also of legitimacy.[405]

What would be true in 1810, during the Regency period, was not true in 1808, still less so at the end of the eighteenth century. However, the peninsulars' fear of independence, as foreshadowed by the example of the United States and by the Abbot of Pradt's analyses,[406] is a fact that needs to be kept in mind if we are to understand the attitudes of the peninsular governments.

Curiously enough, however, one response to the discontent aroused in Spanish America by the expulsion of the Jesuits—the first traumatic intervention of enlightened despotism on the continent—was a proposal by some ministers as early as 1768 that, among other measures designed to appease Creole resentment and "strengthen friendship and union, and [form] a single body of a Nation,"[407] deputies should be sent to the Cortes of Spain.[408] The proposal was not accepted at the time, but it is very similar to the one which the Junta Central would later adopt, and for which, in fact, it served as a precedent:

---

405 Bolívar, loc. cit., 72.

406 The Abbot of Pradt's book, *Les trois âges des colonies ou de leur état passé, présent et à venir* (Paris: Giguet and Co., 1801–2), 285 and 536, was well known at the time and announced that the destiny of colonies was to gain independence from their metropolises.

407 Dictamen al Consejo Extraordinario, March 5, 1768, in Richard Konetzke, "La condición legal de los criollos y las causas de la Independencia," *Estudios Americanos*, Seville, II, no. 5 (January 1950): 45.

408 This does not refer to the Cortes proper, but to the Diputación de Millones, an emanation of the Cortes, which administered the tax of the same name.

> The ninth means would be to establish a deputy for the district of each of the three Viceroyalties, and a fourth one from the Philippine Islands, with the principal cities taking turns in his election, and he would attend the Court during a six-year term in the manner of the Deputies of the Kingdom, and His Majesty would thus bestow on the Indies a grace equal to that which he has just bestowed on Catalonia and Majorca, incorporating these four deputies from the Kingdoms of the Indies with those of Castile, Aragon, and Catalonia [...].[409]

What some ministers had proposed during the absolutist era had become a necessity by 1808, as the desire for representation was impetuously reviving.

It was reviving all the more imperiously because Napoleon himself, desirous of winning America to his cause, had already set a precedent by having six Americans appointed to represent the continent in that "general deputation" of 150 people, later called Cortes, that met at Bayonne in July, 1808: one for each of the four viceroyalties—New Spain, Peru, Santa Fe and Buenos Aires—and two more for Guatemala and Havana.[410] Such a convocation was almost unprecedented, as was the Spanish Americans' active participation in the assembly, where they presented traditional grievances—especially the neglect in which they were held regarding the assignment of public positions—as well as proposals for reform that were of a modern nature: freedom of trade and industry, abolition of Indian tribute and of castes.[411]

The constitution promulgated at the time by the assembly of Bayonne devoted an entire title—"On the Spanish Kingdoms and provinces of America and Asia"—to the rights of Spanish America, with special emphasis on political rights. It declared that these kingdoms and

409 Ibid., 46.

410 Those who actually went to Bayonne came from the four viceroyalties and from Guatemala and Caracas.

411 See Pérez Gilhou 1981, 33–36; for the entirety of these Cortes, Sanz Cid 1922.

provinces would enjoy the "same rights as the Metropolis"[412] and would be represented by twenty-two deputies[413] in the future Cortes and also in the Council of State.[414]

In this regard, as in others, the real influence of this first modern constitution, which was never implemented, continues to be a matter of debate: it could hardly serve as a public model if we consider the climate of fevered patriotism prevailing at the time. It is clear, however, that American participation in the assembly of Bayonne and the clauses on the Indies contained in said constitution were a precedent with which the better-informed peninsulars were well-acquainted. The same can be said of many Spanish Americans, for even Murat's call, with its paragraph on American representation, was, in the confusion of the early days, published in its entirety by the *Gazeta de México*.[415]

Seen in this context, the summons for Americans to elect and send deputies to the Junta Central was not some startling invention coming out of nowhere. Rather, it was the first and most urgent manifestation of the need to perfect national representation and respond to Spanish American aspirations.

## "An Essential and Integral Part of the Spanish Monarchy"

Thus, it is no surprise that the Junta Central, deferring the problem of convening the Cortes, should have asked the Council of the Indies, as early as the end of October 1808, to study the modalities of American representation:

412 Constitución de Bayona, article 87.

413 Ibid., article 92.

414 Ibid., article 95.

415 "Disposiciones del duque de Berg, para que varios individuos de España pasasen a formar una Diputación general en Bayona de Francia," *Gazeta de México* XV, no. 76, August 10, 1808, 551–54.

> The Supreme Governing Junta of the Kingdom, desiring to acknowledge the sentiments of justice that inspire it and to further strengthen the bonds of love and fraternity that unite the Americas with our peninsula by admitting them, in a fitting manner, to national representation, decrees that each of the viceroyalties shall send a Deputy to the Junta Central.[416]

The language is clear and the tone is fitting: the monarchy is comprised of the Americas and the Peninsula, and a suitable way must be found "for the election to be held in the most appropriate terms so that it will constitute a true representation of those Dominions [...]."[417]

Even though the Junta Central appeared eager to make rapid progress in the matter,[418] its resolution was delayed by the French offensive that took place at the end of the year, forcing the Junta to take refuge in Seville. The royal order summoning the Americans to elect deputies to the Junta Central was finally proclaimed on January 22, 1809.

Its multiple implications make this undoubtedly one of the key events of the entire revolutionary process: for the first time, the debate concerning political equality between peninsular Spaniards and Spanish Americans was being publicly launched; with it began a fundamental controversy regarding the status of America within the monarchy, which would grow ever more acrimonious until it led to independence.

The impact of the royal order in America was extraordinary. Published as edicts by the viceroys and governors[419] and printed by different newspapers, the document was seen not only as a call to elections but as

---

416 De la Junta Central al gobernador del Consejo de Indias, October 27, 1808, AHN, Secretaría de Estado records, vol. 54, dossier 67.

417 Ibid.

418 The Council of the Indies was urged several times to speed up the process. The delay was also due to divergences among its members. See AHN, Secretaría de Estado records, vol. 54, dossiers 68 and 69.

419 In Mexico, for example, in a proclamation of Viceroy Garibay on April 14, 1809, AGN, Historia, vol. 418, file V, published in the *Gazeta de México* April 15, 1809, and in the *Diario de México* on the same date.

a declaration on the status and rights of America within the monarchy. For this reason, it has since been cited, explicitly or implicitly, in countless documents of all kinds. For all its contemporaries, ranging from the peninsulars José María Blanco White and Alvaro Flores Estrada,[420] to Camilo Torres in New Granada,[421] Gregorio Funes in Río de la Plata,[422] and Servando de Mier in Mexico, it represented a fundamental milestone in the history of the relations between the two pillars of the monarchy.

It was a crucial event, as much for what it granted to Spanish America as for what it withheld. What it granted was both ambiguous and fundamental: "the vast and beautiful dominions that Spain possesses in the Indies are not properly colonies or factories like those of other nations, but rather an essential and integral part of the Spanish monarchy [...]."[423]

The statement is ambiguous because declaring the Indies to be an essential and integral part of the monarchy was nothing new if viewed from a traditional perspective. It was new in relation to the new imaginary regarding Spanish America that, as we have mentioned, was becoming widespread in the Peninsula by the end of the eighteenth century. In this regard, the declaration was appropriate, and it affirmed, with the full weight of the monarchy's supreme authority, what all Americans so tenaciously defended.

Yet the very terms in which the declaration was formulated were deeply offensive and tacitly denoted the opposite of what was stated. To speak of Spain's "possessions" went against the Americans' almost unanimous feeling, as expressed in proclamations of the time, in which the Spanish nation was conceived as single and extending across the two hemispheres. Moreover, it also made the kingdoms of the Indies dependent not on the king, as had always been the case in the pactist

---

420 Flores Estrada 1812, 13.

421 Torres 1809, 1960.

422 Gregorio Funes, *Ensayo de la Historia Ovil del Paraguay*, Buenos Aires and Tucumán, 1817 ed., vol. III, 482.

423 Real orden, Seville, January 22, 1809, AHN, Secretaría de Estado records, vol. 54, dossier 71.

conception of the monarchy, but on a territory: peninsular Spain, that is, the peninsular kingdoms. This meant, at the very least, that the Indies were conceived as a group of subordinate kingdoms. As Camilo Torres, future hero of independence and the declaration's most exacting critic, put it at the time:

> What empire does industrious Catalonia hold over Galicia; or, what can this and other populous provinces boast over Navarre? Or be it the very center of the Monarchy and the residence of its highest authorities, what right does it have, for this reason alone, to dictate laws that exclude the others?[424]

A few months later, *El catecismo político cristiano* that circulated in Chile in 1810 expressed, even more radically, the Americans' plural conception of the monarchy with its pactist foundations:

> The inhabitants and provinces of America have only sworn allegiance to the kings of Spain [...] they have not sworn allegiance to, nor are they vassals of, the inhabitants and provinces of Spain: the inhabitants and provinces of Spain have therefore no authority, jurisdiction, or command over the inhabitants and provinces of America.[425]

It was even worse to say, even if only to deny this condition, that the Indies were not "properly colonies or factories[426] like those of other nations." Implicitly, this meant comparing the kingdoms of the Indies to the European colonies in the Caribbean. Three years later, the Mexican Mier, expressing the grievances of the Americans, still felt wounded by these words: "I cannot but be stung, whenever I hear, based on this

---

424 Torres 1809, 1960, 7.

425 *El catecismo político cristiano por Don José Amor de la Patria* (1810; Santiago de Chile: Ed. del Pacífico, Instituto de Estudios Políticos, 1975), 28.

426 In the medieval and early modern eras, a "factory" was an entrepôt, that is, a free-trading zone, trading post, or intermediary transshipment point.—Trans.

decree, not only in England but in Spain and in the Americas themselves, that we should remember that the Americas are no longer colonies. It was an insult to tell us that this is what they used to be [...]."[427] After quoting the royal order at length, Mier appeals to Humboldt's testimony:

> The learned Baron von Humboldt [...] wrote [...]: "The kings of Spain, taking the title of Kings of the Indies, have rather considered these possessions to be integral parts of their monarchy than as colonies in the sense ascribed to this word by the merchant peoples of Europe [...] These vast regions cannot be governed like islets scattered over the West Indies."[428]

There was an aggravating circumstance: the representation to which Spanish America was being called also appeared, in the very same document, not as the recognition of a right but as a concession, granted "to reciprocate the heroic loyalty and patriotism of which they have just given Spain such decisive proof."[429]

The inferior status attributed to America, which was hidden behind the egalitarian language of the royal order, also appeared clearly in the number of deputies assigned to the region: nine, plus one for the Philippines. Each of the four viceroyalties (New Spain, Peru, New Granada and Buenos Aires) was asked to send one, as well as the five independent captaincies general (Cuba, Puerto Rico, Guatemala, Chile, and Venezuela). The inequality vis-à-vis peninsular Spain was patent and pointed out at the time—and later—by the Spanish Americans: Why only one deputy for each kingdom or province, instead of the two sent by the peninsular juntas? Why have deputies for the aforementioned territories and not for others that were just as important?

---

427 Mier 1813, 1990, book XIV, 525.

428 Ibid., 526. The Humboldt quote is from *Ensayo político...*, book V, chapter XII, 450.

429 Real orden, Seville, January 22, 1809.

> So the provincial juntas of Spain do not agree on the formation of a Junta Central except on the express condition of an equal number of deputies; and when it comes to the Americas, shall we find this odious restriction? Thirty-six or more members are needed for Spain, and for the vast provinces of America, a mere nine are deemed sufficient—and this with the risk that should their representatives die, fall ill, or be absent, their representation will be null and void.[430]

True, it could be argued that what was represented in the Junta Central were the kingdoms and provinces, without regard to population, but the argument was unconvincing in the light of such a disparity in representation. This was especially true if we consider that, even taking into account only the representation of kingdoms and provinces, some of those whose existence was undeniable—such as Upper Peru or Quito—were missing. (This certainly had an impact on the creation of the latter's precocious junta in the summer of 1809.)[431] Another aggravating circumstance was that Americans tended to reason in terms of global equality between peninsular Spain and Spanish America, seen as two parts of the monarchy that were equal in both population and rights: "The Junta Central has promised that everything will be established on the basis of justice, and equality [...]. America and Spain are the two bowls of a weighing scale: the more load the one takes, the more the other's balance will be disturbed or impaired."[432]

The electoral provisions and the proclamation of equality in the royal order were, to the Americans, "a play on words, a false proclamation of justice at the same time that its principles are abjured, and its practice is violated."[433]

The demand for equality between peninsular Spain and American Spain, which harked back to the time of the Conquest itself and until then had focused on access to public office and the demand for equal

430 Torres 1809, 1960, 20.

431 This explanation is already given in ibid., 27.

432 Ibid., 21.

433 Funes, op. cit., 482.

economic rights, now burst into the political field and became, for the Spanish Americans, their fundamental demand and main grievance: "just and competent representation of their peoples, without any distinction between subjects where no law, custom, origin or right decrees it [...]. Equality! The sacred right of equality, for justice lies in this, and in giving to each what is his own."[434]

It was a fundamental grievance, that came to affect the very legitimacy of the Junta Central even if, for the time being, the Americans continued to obey the provisional government of the monarchy:

> The Supreme Junta has only been able to rule in America on the one condition that its kingdoms and provinces should agree to appoint deputies to represent them in the selfsame Junta, and that the head of the government should be located in the other world; but the number of deputies should then have been determined with precise consideration to the size of the population, and since that of America is greater than that of Spain, the number of American deputies should have been greater, or if not, equal, to the number of Spanish deputies.[435]

## Imaginaries, Actors, and Behaviors

Despite the disillusionment and resentment caused by the royal order among a large part of the American elites, the call to elections was still an extraordinary novelty for America, which was being summoned for the first time in its history to send its deputies to the center of the monarchy not only to be represented, but to participate in the sovereign power itself. For this reason, and even while they protested and tried to obtain better representation, an electoral process was also being launched, which would mobilize all the regions and political actors in Spanish America, from northern Mexico to Chile and the Río de la

434 Torres 1809, 1960, 35.

435 *Catecismo político cristiano...*, 28–29.

Plata. From the spring of 1809 to the winter of 1810, the whole of America lived in the fever of this first experience of general elections. This was, in fact, something unprecedented in the entire Hispanic world: hence, it provides valuable lessons regarding the real actors of social life, their aspirations and frames of reference.

The electoral system established by the Junta Central was of a traditional type, since the election of deputies was entrusted to the *ayuntamientos* of the "capitales cabezas de partido" (capitals of administrative and judicial districts) and largely reproduced the method used in the Peninsula for the election, by the cities, of the *procuradores* to the Cortes. The novelty of the phenomenon, however, lay in the number of cities called to participate in the electoral process: more than one hundred in America, at a time when elections had not yet taken place in the Peninsula and when the number of cities that had a vote in the Cortes was limited to thirty-seven.

The electoral procedure comprised two stages. First, the *ayuntamientos* of the main cities voted to elect three individuals, from among whom one was then drawn by lot. When all these elections had taken place, the viceroy or the governor, in consultation with the Real Acuerdo, repeated the process with the names selected: a shortlist of three candidates was chosen from among whom one name was drawn once again, and this person thus became the kingdom or province's deputy to the Junta Central. The deputy would then receive his proxy and instructions from the different municipalities.[436]

The whole system was pervaded by a traditional, corporate conception of representation. The representation of the kingdom was identified with that of the principal cities, since each of these cities, as the capitals of their respective territories, was considered responsible for representing them; the cities, in turn, were represented by their *ayuntamientos*. Since the idea was to select *procuradores* from a series of bodies (cities, provinces, and kingdoms) by which they were to be charged with specific instructions, candidacies and electoral campaigns were banned. The theoretical ideal was unanimity, since the goal was to choose "individuals of widely acknowledged probity, talent, and education, exempt

---

436 Real orden, Seville, January 22, 1809.

from any fault that might discredit them in the eyes of public opinion."[437] That is, the choice was to be made on the basis of a dignity and a series of intellectual and moral qualities which it was assumed must be recognized by all. However, this ideal was tempered by the experience of the many conflicts previously sparked by elections in the various bodies of the ancien régime (civil and ecclesiastical cabildos, chapters of religious orders, confraternities, guilds, etc.), and by a vision of man in which "passions" occupied a very important place.

Hence the drawing of lots, intended to avoid "the partisan spirit that usually prevails in such cases";[438] it was also a way of involving Providence—the ultimate guarantee of the social order—in the human choice.[439]

The traditionalism of the proposed system was evident and, later on, there would be no lack of more modern spirits, like that of Camilo Torres, who would criticize the oligarchic nature of the cabildos. However, and despite these criticisms (we do not know how widespread they were), the elections took place according to the rules that had been established. The only significant changes in electoral procedure were belated effects of the experience of elections that had already been held, as well as the result of a series of consultations addressed to the Junta

---

437 Ibid.

438 Ibid.

439 The city council of Mexico, for example, after their elected candidate was designated deputy for New Spain in the drawing of lots in the viceroyalty, declared its satisfaction "on seeing their election approved anyway, and preferred by the powerful hand of the Highest, who was pleased to grant them this grace; and that there should be given so indubitable a sign of the correctness with which the election was conducted and the high dignity that, as Capital and Head of these Kingdoms, belongs to it, even as fortune has decided," "Poder e instrucciones de la Ciudad de México," AGN, Historia, 417, vol. 417, file II, folio 270. The same reaction can be found in the Andes, where the cabildo of La Plata, now Sucre, claimed that "the election [of its deputy] had been confirmed by the fate of providence" (ACE, actas, dossier 3, file 11).

Central. The new regulations were only applied in regions that had yet to vote, basically Río de la Plata.[440]

Let us add, to qualify the oligarchic character of the cabildos, that many of them in New Spain included *diputados* and *síndicos* representing the commons: these positions had been established by Charles III's municipal reforms, and they were elected by all householders (*vecinos*).[441] And a municipality like Zacatecas enlarged the electoral body on its own initiative, adding a series of supplementary electors to the members of the cabildo.[442]

However, in most cases, the imaginary revealed by the sources is quite traditional. Representation, for example, was seen as a privilege, granted on the basis of merit and pre-eminence. In New Spain,[443] the call to elections immediately sparked a wave of protests on the part of the excluded cities. Villahermosa (Tabasco), Campeche, Chihuahua, Monclova (Coahuila), Monterrey (Nuevo León), Santa Fe (New Mexico), Bejar (Texas), Arizpe (Sonora), Querétaro, and Tlaxcala submitted multiple documents to substantiate their right to vote. Only the last three succeeded: Arizpe, because it was the capital of the vast province of Sonora-Sinaloa and already had an intendant,[444] and the other two on the strength of their merits and dignities, which they presented with all the pride of their old titles.[445]

---

440 The publication of the new regulations seems to have been very closely related to the lawsuits brought by Buenos Aires.

441 There were *síndicos personeros del común* in Querétaro, Puebla, Zacatecas, Guanajuato, San Luis, Veracruz, and four *diputados del común* in Zacatecas, Guanajuato, Veracruz, and also Mexico City.

442 See AGN, Historia, vol. 418, file V, folio 64 and the following folios.

443 Most of the concrete examples are taken from Mexico, for Mexico has preserved almost intact all the records of these elections.

444 The right to vote was not so much requested by the city as it was granted by the Real Acuerdo so that Arizpe might represent the whole of northwestern Mexico.

445 The final decisions were made by the viceroy on September 11, 1809, after lengthy procedures and serious differences between the members

Thus, Tlaxcala expounded its rights in a long document signed by the members of its cabildo, many of whom belonged to the indigenous nobility:

> The Most Noble, Illustrious, and Ever Loyal City of Tlaxcala [...] declares: That among the various graces, honors, and favors with which the Royal Mercy of our Monarchs has wished to distinguish it at all times, is that of having declared it to be the first and principal of this America, as stated in one of the Laws of the Kingdom [...].
> Tlaxcala, from the happy moment of the glorious conquest of this vast Empire [...] has been able to preserve its loyalty and obedience [...] which has inclined the merciful spirit of our sovereigns to enrich it with the exquisite graces and privileges that no other City enjoys [...].
> They may be blessed with greater riches and opulence, but Tlaxcala, despite the poverty to which the vicissitudes of time have reduced her, will always be famous among the splendors of America: she will retain the renown of Auxiliary and protector of the conquest of these Kingdoms [...].[446]

These arguments were completely relevant in the legal and mental register of the ancien régime. Despite its slight contemporary importance, the city obtained the right to vote.

Querétaro adduced very similar reasons for participating "in this election, the most interesting offered in the almost three centuries that have elapsed since the conquest of this Kingdom" and gave an account of the popular reaction to its exclusion from the vote: "It is to be wished that the Superiority of Your Excellency had witnessed the huddles and gatherings that formed immediately in the shops and in private abodes, everywhere lamenting the exclusion of this City." This was followed by a list of its privileges and the argument, also convincing for the traditional

---

of the Real Acuerdo. The determination was taken mainly for reasons of urgency, because of the remoteness of the cities in question.

446 Representación de la Ciudad de Tlaxcala, May 30, 1809, AGN, Historia, vol. 418, file XIII.

mindset, of the difference between a city's dignity and its administrative status, since

> it is well known that, when designating these [the capitals of Intendancies], no attention was paid to the intrinsic merit that makes a city higher or lower, more or less worthy of consideration; only its local position was taken into account, so that each one should attend to the territory assigned to it; but if this was a good reason for dividing the Intendencias, it cannot be one for depriving the Cities of the privileges and rights corresponding to them, whose location did not allow them to become Capitals of an Intendancy.[447]

The "statutes and rights" of the city as an acknowledged social actor did indeed prevail over administrative rank, and Querétaro was admitted to the vote.

Analyzing who the councils voted for across the different regions provides us with other information regarding both the political life and the American imaginary of the time.[448] If we consider, first of all, the number of different people who were voted for, we can see a very clear difference between the four regions for which we have complete data (see Table I).

---

447 Representación de la Ciudad de Querétaro, April 22, 1809, AGN, Historia, vol. 418, file XII.

448 It is better to consider the shortlist chosen by the cabildo—and the order in which it was determined—than the individual that each cabildo elected, since the drawing of lots introduced an element of uncertainty and did not necessarily reflect the preferences of the voters.

**Table I.** The Elected: Dispersion of the Vote[449]

| Elected | Possible Candidates | Different Names | % Dispersion |
|---|---|---|---|
| Venezuela | 18 | 16 | 88 |
| New Spain | 42 | 38 | 79 |
| Peru | 51 | 28 | 56 |
| Chile | 45 | 17 | 37 |

Venezuela's vote was extremely dispersed, indicating a high degree of localism. Only the governor and intendant of Maracaibo, Brigadier Fernando Mijares, and the canon of Mérida, Luis Ignacio Hurtado de Mendoza, were voted for twice. This localism undoubtedly favored the maneuvers of the *visitador regente* of the Audiencia of Caracas, the powerful and quarrelsome Joaquín de Mosquera y Figueroa; he was elected once in second place on the Barinas shortlist, and then "chance" selected him twice: the first time in Barinas and the second time in the final election for the whole of Venezuela. The fact that the candidate chosen by the cabildo of Caracas was not selected for this last shortlist by the Real Acuerdo was seen as an affront by the Caracas elite. This further embittered the already tense relations between the city and the authorities.[450]

In the Mexican cities the vote was also highly dispersed. Only Manuel de Lardizábal, a member of the Council of Castile, his brother Miguel, of the Council of the Indies, and Manuel Abad y Queipo, capitular vicar of Valladolid de Michoacán, were voted for in two different cities.

449 Table based on the total votes of the cabildos: for Venezuela, ACE, General, file. 7, no. 99 and *Diario de México* XI, no. 1451, September 21, 1809, 340–41; for Mexico, AGN, vol. 418, files V, VII, VIII, X, XII and XIII; for Peru, AHN, Secretaría de Estado records, vol. 58, file 156; for Chile, Amunategui 1911, vol. I, 346–61.

450 See also Parra Pérez 1959, 365 and the following pages.

Mexico's strong localism is evident, as well as the existence of very heated quarrels between factions—the "European" against the "Creole" party—that reached all the way into the highest levels of the viceroyal administration, something that undoubtedly prevented a concerted vote.

In Peru, the votes appear more grouped, as if the cabildos had received instructions to vote for a series of names in a certain order.[451] The judge of the Audiencia of Lima, José Baquijano, Count of Vista Florida, was selected ten times; Brigadier José Manuel Goyeneche, interim president of the Audiencia of Cuzco, and Lieutenant Colonel Simón Díaz Rábago, secretary of the viceroyalty, five times; the Marquis of Casa Calderón, *alcalde ordinario* of Lima, four times; and Colonel Marquis de Feria y Valdelirios, three. The power and influence of the Lima elite over the whole of Peru thus appears clearly,[452] and even more so when we see that, during the last phase of the vote, the Real Acuerdo did not appoint any provincial on its shortlist. However, as an unforeseen consequence of the draw, the elected candidate was not Baquijano but the candidate who had obtained the fewest votes, cantor José Silva y Olave.[453] The phenomenon was even more marked in Chile, a kingdom with a small and homogeneous population that was well under the control of the Santiago elites.[454]

---

451 The fact that cities so far removed from each other should have voted, in the absence of any electoral campaign, for the same people, can only be explained either by the existence of networks based on connections or the influence of the political elites, or by the concerted action of the authorities, or the widespread prestige of these men. The three explanations are probably valid, and especially the first two.

452 The exception was Goyeneche, a native of Arequipa, but trained in the Peninsula, whose presence was owing to his capacity as an emissary of the Junta Central.

453 See Demélas 1990, vol. I, 323.

454 Manuel Manso y Rodríguez, General Customs superintendent, and canon Santiago Rodríguez were selected six times; Nicolás de Cruz, five times; Manuel de Salas, José Santiago Concha Lobatón, a senior judge of the Audiencia of Santiago, Miguel Eizaguirre, of the Audiencia of Lima, and Juan Martínez de Rozas, colonel of the cavalry militia regiment of Concepción, three times; three others were selected twice each.

We know that in New Granada, of the twenty cities that voted, four appointed lawyer Camilo Torres to their shortlist, which indicates that he was quite well known. However, during the final phase, the Real Acuerdo designated a shortlist in which he did not appear at all; this evidently contributed, later, to his reflection on the electoral system as it appears in his *Memorial de agravios*. The final shortlist was made up of Count Puñoenrostro, a native of Quito, field marshal Antonio de Narváez, of Cartagena, and lawyer Luis Eduardo Azuola, a native and elected candidate from Santa Fe. The final draw appointed the second candidate as deputy.[455]

If we examine the social status of the elected candidates, we can see what sort of men the urban patricians considered worthy to represent society. In all three kingdoms, the elected were among the most prominent personages, by virtue of their rank and the offices they held (civil, military, or ecclesiastical) in ancien régime society; the order of the votes even followed the scale of dignities. Thus, in New Spain, the first place was occupied by two members of the central councils of the monarchy (the two Lardizábals); three bishops (the bishops of Guadalajara and Tlaxcala, and the auxiliary bishop of Oaxaca); one judge, Aguirre; five governors and titular or interim intendants; a brigade commander, Calleja; only one prebendary of the Puebla cathedral and the royal ensign of Veracruz. In the second place, besides Miguel Lardizábal, another judge, Foncerrada, and an interim intendant, we find the secretary of the chamber of the viceroyalty, the advisor to the city of Puebla, the *corregidor* of Querétaro, Domínguez, a vicar general, two canons, a parish priest, and two *regidores*. Third, and still descending in the scale of dignities, besides two interim intendants we find four canons, three cabildo members, four employees of the finance administration and two members of the military.[456]

---

455 Antioquia, Popayán, Pamplona, and Santa Fe voted for Torres as the third name on the shortlist. See Abelardo Forero Benavides, *El 20 de julio tiene 300 días* (Bogotá: Ed. de la Universidad de los Andes, 1967), 57 and the following pages, and Restrepo 1827, 1969, 104–5.

456 Ibid., Table I.

Mexico presented a peculiar situation: since the royal order had not stipulated conditions of geographical origin, the "European party," which had dominated New Spain since the Yermo coup d'état of September 1808, managed to elect a majority of peninsulars—eight to six Americans—a fact that also eloquently demonstrates the weight of the Europeans in the Mexican cabildos and the rancor that this predominance could not but arouse. This does not mean that most of the population already favored independence, as we shall soon see when we analyze the instructions of the cabildos. The resentment had to do with the Americans' expectation that they should be preeminent in public office and elections, given that they were natives of the Kingdom and descendants of the conquistadores. This condition continued to be one of the most highly valued qualities, as the cabildo of Mexico manifests when describing the lineage of one of its elected candidates:

> Lieutenant Colonel Don Ignacio José de la Pesa [...] perpetual *regidor* of this Most Noble City [...] of widely known ancestry and nobility, is a descendant of Conquerors of these Kingdoms, counting among his forebears the distinguished hero Hernán Cortés [...] and Captains Francisco de las Casas, first *alcalde ordinario* of this City, Andrés de Tapia and others of equal merit, and is connected with very illustrious families of this Kingdom and of ancient Spain.[457]

In Peru and Chile the predominance of Spanish Americans was almost complete, although, in terms of the quality of those elected, the two kingdoms followed the same pattern as New Spain: they also chose the highest-ranking personages by order of dignity.[458] In Peru, the abundance of noble titles says a great deal about the lineage of the local elites.

American society chose candidates based on what it was and how it saw itself: as an ancien régime society in which the highest ranks of society were regarded as its natural representatives.

---

457 AGN, Historia, vol. 418, file V, folio 119.

458 Naturally, in the smaller and more distant Chile, these dignities were less numerous and, as a result, the rank of those elected was also proportionately lower.

## Parties in Conflict

The aspiration to unanimity did not mean that this was a unanimous society devoid of conflicts. Quite the opposite. In this regard, an examination of the vote itself, of possible fraud and electoral complaints sheds a very vivid light on the actors who participated in political life and on their confrontations. In the three regions studied, complaints were generally few—perhaps because most of the cabildos were well under the control of a powerful clan and its allies—but elections were rarely unanimous. In New Spain, only Tlaxcala and Oaxaca voted unanimously and in a single session. In all the other the cities, elections were held on the basis of a "plurality of votes"; that is, by relative majority, which shows that in most of the cabildos there were at least two opposing groups. In most cases, the impression given by the electoral records is that of a very intense local political life that, however, was of a very different kind from that which would characterize modern politics shortly afterward. It was an ancien régime political life, in which very coherent and diverse actors confronted each other: public authorities, great family clans, various clientelist networks, Creoles and Europeans, etc.

Complaints, when they existed, reflected various types of conflicts. In Tlaxcala, for example, the governor opposed a unanimous cabildo with which he had undoubtedly been in conflict for some time and which he had managed to exclude from the vote, despite the latter's protests.[459] We find a similar conflict in Peru during the Ica elections, in which the subdelegate asked that the vote of the cabildo—controlled by a family-based clan, which met with its friends and relatives in a tertulia led by a lady of good family—be annulled.[460] Elsewhere, the large number of sessions required for the election—three in Puebla, four in Mexico, five in Valladolid (Michoacán)—shows that there were clear divergences within the cabildo and that long negotiations were undoubtedly required in order to reach an agreement.

---

459 See AGN, Historia, vol. 418, file XIII, folios 20–43.

460 See AHN, Secretaría de Estado records, vol. 58, file 151 and Demélas 1990, vol. I, 326 and the following pages.

In Valladolid (now Morelia) no compromise was ever reached; on the contrary, a very bitter conflict took place, in which the whole city participated, with pamphlets and anonymous leaflets, and, in the end, a petition to the Real Acuerdo for the annulment of the elections on grounds of fraud. This episode deserves a more detailed analysis, not only because Valladolid would be the city where, in December of this same year, the first plot to form a government of its own for New Spain would be discovered, but also because of everything it tells us about the workings of local political life, divided here between two "parties" which, at first glance, would seem to pit Creoles against Spaniards.

First, we see the importance of procedural issues in the conflict. The cabildo met five times between April 18 and May 20, 1809, and the two sides clashed over every possible and conceivable point of electoral procedure. It was initially decided to set up a preliminary list with the names of those who deserved to be voted for, and this led to a violent argument regarding European eligibility. The "Creole party" asserted that the "zealous patrician" of the royal order could only be an American, for an American "would promote better and with greater zeal the branches and objects of national interest than a European, especially with respect to matters of commerce."[461]

To which the other party retorted that Europeans who had been settled in America for a long time were as "patrician" as the Americans, since America was the homeland (*patria*) of their children. The president, José Alonso de Terán, a deputy jurist and *asesor ordinario*, interim intendant and the uncontested head of the "European party," tried to put an end to the debate on the matter in order "to avoid feelings," but the argument about the meaning of "Americans" persisted: Should the term only cover the children of the province or also those of the kingdom—perhaps those of any other kingdom in America? Each of the sides, "lacking any party spirit," kept up the debate around the definition of "patrician" adducing arguments taken from the dictionary of the Spanish language.[462] The next point of contention was whether the

461 AGN, Historia, vol. 418, file V, folios 124–98.

462 The idea was to include Judge Manuel de la Bodega, a native of Peru, in the list.

vote should be public or secret—in the end, they decided on the latter. A preliminary list of eligible candidates was drawn up,[463] and four sets of ballots, marked with all these names, were prepared.

The names on the list clearly show the selection criteria applied by the members of the cabildos. In the first place, we have a compendium of the local elites: a bishop, canons, different officials, soldiers, lawyers, and various notables such as José Joaquín Iturbide, but also other distinguished figures from the rest of New Spain, such as Manuel de Lardizábal, Judge Foncerreda, the *corregidor* of Querétaro, Miguel Domínguez, or the intendant of Guanajuato, Juan Antonio de Riaño. Significantly, the list already included the names of future supporters of independence, such as the Michelenas and the *corregidor* Domínguez, which points to the formation (though still under the guise of a network of relationships) of the future pro-independence party.

The vote finally took place during the May 17 session. After a mass invoking the Holy Spirit, the ballots were distributed and a vote was also taken to find out if there would be three different votes, one for each name on the shortlist, or a single vote with three ballots. The latter method was adopted, and Manuel de Lardizábal obtained six votes out of seven, Judge Foncerrada five, and in third place, tied with four votes, the Peruvian Judge Bodega and the canon penitentiary Manuel Abad y Queipo, the learned prelate so admired by Alexander von Humboldt. The president broke the tie in favor of the latter, and it was then discussed whether the final draw would be made by a child or by the notary. In the end, the choice fell on the notary, and Abad y Queipo's name was drawn.

When the process appeared to be over, the conflict was embittered by accusations from the "Creole" side that someone had voted twice for Abad y Queipo. The quarrel became so violent that on May 20 the decision was made to appeal to Mexico, to the Real Acuerdo, which received, in addition to the official documents, a series of anonymous handwritten texts, some of which were signed "The Public." The disagreements between the

463 The process of drawing up a previous list that was used in other places, such as Querétaro, seems to have been intended to measure the influence of the different parties before the vote itself.

two parties then moved on to Mexico, giving rise to a clear division within the Real Acuerdo, which eventually validated Abad y Queipo's election[464] so as not to delay the entire electoral process in the viceroyalty.

The arguments adduced by the judges of the Real Acuerdo demonstrate a profound knowledge of the mechanisms of voting and of fraud. It is a timely reminder that the ancien régime societies constantly practiced voting within the various bodies, both civil and ecclesiastical, of which they were composed; as a result, there was a whole jurisprudence on these subjects.[465] This knowledge about voting and fraud, and the accompanying jurisprudence, should not be forgotten when analyzing the "modern" voting of the nineteenth century.

What we have, then, is a traditional way of doing politics, but a very rowdy one, as evinced by its description. Chile, too, sought to guard again this problem:

> The squalls and partisan quarrels experienced every year in the elections for *alcalde* are the almost necessary forerunners of the greater discord we may suspect will take place during the present election, in which strong influences will operate, even in this capital, and perhaps in other governorates [...]. It is very difficult to keep [the cabildo members] away from particular arrangements and

---

464 Decision of August 23, 1809. An analysis of the arguments seems to indicate that there was indeed premeditated fraud in the election of Abad y Queipo. That is why the single-vote, secret ballot was used: it was enough that one of the voters should cast two identical votes for the third name, and only one for the first two, to obtain the desired result. This hypothesis is confirmed by the existence of four sets of ballots when only three names were to be voted for. These arguments were presented by two judges in Mexico. Archbishop-Viceroy Lizana adopted the opinion of the majority (regent Catani and judges Aguirre, Calderón, Mejía, Bataller, and Villafane); the minority was undoubtedly made up of Judges Bodega and Foncerrada. AGN, Historia, vol. 418, file V, folio 188 and the following folios.

465 For voting in the Peruvian cabildos of the ancien régime (whether indigenous or Spanish), see for example Demélas 1990, vol. I, 308 and the following pages, and for the Indian cabildos of New Spain, Carmagnani 1988, IV.

> the lure of private gratuities, and for this reason we may presume voting fraud and maneuvers [...].[466]

As we have just seen, "squalls and partisan quarrels" did indeed manifest themselves in quite a few places. The Valladolid case allows us to grasp what these "partisan quarrels" were about. The first surprise is that the appellations "European" and "Creole" do not refer to the real origin of the *regidores* since, as a matter of fact, they were all European except for one, the royal ensign, Huarte. What we have are two groups based on geographical origin and common business interests. The dominant one was comprised of "highlanders" (Asturians and Santanderinos), while the other was not really made up of Creoles; rather, it was a coalition of all the others, united by a network of correspondence and commercial relations with all the malcontents of New Spain. The head of the first party in Valladolid, advisor José Alonso de Terán, was a relative of the prior to the powerful Consulate of Mexico and a highlander like Abad y Queipo. As his adversaries put it: "they have connections with Señor Abad and with the Advisor, because they are *compadres* and dependents, and most of them are highlanders, the party that the Advisor protects, looking upon everyone else as enemies."[467]

This kind of local division became more complicated when it mixed with other, broader party divisions, such as the one that, after the Yermo coup d'état, pitted two sides against each other within the Mexico Audiencia. The Valladolid opponents, precisely, voted for Judge Bodega, who at the time, was seen in Mexico as the head of the "American party."[468]

---

466 Statement sent to the Captain General of Chile by José Teodoro Sánchez, a tax agent in civil matters concerning the Royal Treasury, proposing a series of measures to prevent fraud—measures that were clearly insufficient since the elections in Chillán had to be annulled. See Amunategui 1911, 341–44.

467 Anonymous text signed "The Public," Valladolid, May 19, 1809, AGN, Historia, vol. 418, file V, folio 194 and the following folios. This rivalry is reminiscent of the one between the highlanders and the Biscayans in the Mexican Consulate, a rivalry so intense that the regulations of the Consulate required that its leadership alternate between the two parties. See Hamnet 1978, 28.

468 See Alamán 1972, I, 195.

The parties were, therefore, networks of men joined by very diverse ties (kinship, *compadrazgo*,[469] patronage, interest, common geographical origin) and defined, above all, by their opposition to a rival network.

Another magnificent example of the struggle between parties, and of the nature of these parties, is the one presented by the elections in Córdoba, in Río de la Plata, which were even more conflictive than those in Michoacán, with the quarrel lasting from June 2, 1809, to January 17, 1810. This was a tenacious struggle between two rival "parties," one led by the *gobernador intendente*, the brigadier of the Royal Navy Juan Gutiérrez de la Concha, and the other headed by future independence leader Dean Gregorio Funes. The struggle, which had begun in 1805, had so far centered on the bishopric of the city, to which Funes aspired. His party was supported by the wealthy merchant Letamendi and had ramifications as far away as Buenos Aires, where it was supported by Álzaga. His opponents, who were in the majority in the cabildo at the time, were trying to obtain the transfer of the bishop of Paraguay to the bishopric of the city and had a number of ties to the Buenos Aires Audiencia and the former viceroy Sobremonte. The struggle between the factions mobilized all the means usually employed in these circumstances: pamphlets and anonymous leaflets, official accusations and petitions, etc.[470]

The election of a deputy to the Junta Central was just another episode, though perhaps the most bitter, in the rivalry between the two parties. As in Michoacán, the conflict crystallized in a long quarrel over procedure, with constant comings and goings to Buenos Aires to ask for

---

469 The practice of *compadrazgo* ("co-godparenthood") was a "form of ritual kinship" imported from Andalusia that functioned as an important instrument of social cohesion in Spanish American society (see J. H. Elliott, *Empires of the Atlantic World: Britain and Spain in America, 1492–1830* [Yale University Press, 2006], 157–58).—Trans.

470 Funes prevented his opponent (the bishop of Paraguay) from taking office once he had been appointed, and Letamendi is said to have offered him money if he would resign from the bishopric. On these topics, see Enrique de Gandía, "Primeras ideas políticas del deán Gregorio Funes," in *Revista de Historia de América: Instituto panamericano de Geografía e Historia*, Mexico, no. 49 (June 1960): 173 and the following pages, and especially González 1937, vol. I, 143–82, whose very detailed analysis I summarize here.

a resolution of the disputed issues. It began on June 17 with an appeal to the viceroy to prevent the governor from attending, alleging a Royal Order of 1783 regarding the annual elections of the cabildos; the appeal was granted to Funes's party. While this consultation was being carried out, the cabildo unanimously appointed Funes as the first name on the shortlist, followed by the judge of the Audiencia of Chile, Manuel de Irigoyen, with six votes, and the honorary judge of the Audiencia of Buenos Aires, Miguel Gregorio de Zamalloa, with five. Of the three, only Funes was a resident of the governorate, and for this reason, the draw was suspended in order to consult on the matter. When the reply was finally received, the presence of the governor and the election of non-residents were both declared invalid. On July 15, during another impassioned meeting, the sides were already much better defined. As the first voter cast his vote, an objection was raised, this time against one of the candidates, Zamalloa, on the grounds that he was not a native of the province—even though the previous consultation had been about residence. Two cabildo members voted for this to nullify the candidacy, three voted against, and two asked that a local jurist be consulted; shortly afterward, said jurist ruled in favor of eligibility. Both sides continued to allege all kinds of grounds of nullity in each of the subsequent votes. In the end, the same three names chosen a month earlier were selected again; but this time there was a tie for the third name on the shortlist, and the viceroy had to be consulted once again.

Three months went by without a reply for, in the meantime, Cisneros had replaced Liniers as viceroy. The new meeting of October 10, which was to break the tie on the third name by one vote, was attended by members who had been absent until then, and who therefore proceeded to request the nullification of the previous acts, alleging moreover that there were ties of kinship between the voters and the elected candidates.[471] The argument grew more and more acrimonious; as one of the few neutral parties commented, "since everyone was voting for their

471 This allegation appealed to the provisions on the ineligibility of relatives contained in the electoral provisions of Charles III's municipal reforms.

relatives, he took the opportunity to do so for his brother." Indeed, the parties were made up of brothers, first cousins, and brothers-in-law.[472]

After two hours of wrangling, they ended up voting for the third name—not one of the two previously elected, but Funes's brother, Ambrosio, who lived in Buenos Aires—while at the same time asking for legal arbitration from several jurisconsults. This did not satisfy them either, and they ended up rejecting the jurisconsults' opinion, which in turn led to a new appeal to Viceroy Cisneros, who had already taken sides with Funes's party. The viceroy's ruling arrived two months later, ordering that Ambrosio Funes be third on the shortlist. The new meeting of the cabildo again led to endless disputes and legal maneuvering and concluded without any decision having been taken. In the meantime, on January 1, the cabildo was renewed, and it was finally a fresh order from the viceroy, during January 1810, that commanded the election to proceed. The draw took place on January 17, 1810, and Dean Funes was elected, putting a temporary end to the struggle between the two parties. A few months later, after the formation of the Junta of Buenos Aires, its troops were sent against Córdoba and would bring the matter to a conclusion at the battle of Cabeza del Tigre, with the execution of Funes's adversaries. Thus ended a quarrel that was, in fact, typical of colonial society long before all the sectarian divisions of independence arose.

The structure and strength of these parties or factions were manifest on the eve of independence: they were vast coalitions that brought together great family clans and were organized by traditional ties. Certainly, the ideas of many of their members were already changing fast, and their discourse would very soon begin to show their adherence to modernity. The question arises, however, as to whether the structure of these parties, the ties that constituted them and their behaviors, were undergoing the same transformation. There is no reason to think so, and this is undoubtedly one of the keys to explaining the particularities of modern political life in all the new countries: the existence of traditional actors, imaginaries, and behaviors in contradiction with the new principles that appeared in the texts.

472 González 1937, vol. I, 169.

## Instructions to the Deputies: The Political Demands

This picture that the Spanish American elections provides us—of a society still mostly traditional in its conception of representation, its actors and behaviors—needs to be supplemented and nuanced with an examination of the proxies and instructions that the cities prepared for their deputies. Exceptionally, we have almost complete records of those for New Spain; our analysis here will center on this material.

We must first consider the fact that the deputy, though elected to represent the whole kingdom, had to receive powers and instructions from all the cities that had participated in his election. It was an ambivalent role: on the one hand, he was a member of the Junta Central and therefore had a share in the sovereign power; but on the other, he continued to represent each of the cities that had elected him—that is, he was a *procurador* of the old type. As the cities' *procurador*, the deputy had to receive from them the powers and instructions that he needed to carry out his mission. He represented a pyramid of territorial communities: the kingdom, the city-provinces and, through them, the secondary cities, as well as the towns of lesser importance. As Guanajuato forcefully stated, "this Most Noble Capital City of its Province, on behalf of the other subordinate Cabildos of the Cities, Towns and places included in its demarcation [...]."[473]

The identity of these key political entities of the ancien régime was so strong that, in the case of New Spain, cities that had been excluded from voting, such as Campeche, nevertheless obtained the privilege of sending their own instructions to the deputy.[474] In other cases, such as San Luis Potosí, the main city even consulted the most notable civil or ecclesiastical personalities in its territory when drawing up its instructions.[475]

---

473 Poder de Guanajuato, October 12, 1809, AGN, Historia, vol. 417, file II, folio 295 (122).

474 See AGN México, Historia, vol. 416, file, folio 41 and the following folios, and vol. 418, file VIII.

475 AGN Mexico, Historia, vol. 417, file II, folio 318 and the following folios.

The powers confirm this ancient conception of representation. Although most of them contain clauses such as that of Mexico City, which conferred on the deputy "faculties and full powers insofar as possible and lawfully necessary,"[476] other formulas employed make it clear that these are private powers in which, for example: "said capitular lords or each one of himself *in solidum*[477] waiving the Laws of community [...] bestow, give, and confer all their power, ample, complete [...]."[478]

Many of these powers also included clauses on the correspondence that the deputy was to maintain with the city[479] in order to receive more instructions, transmit official information and relevant documents,[480] submit petitions (*memoriales*) to the central government with their respective supporting arguments ("*relaciones de méritos*"),[481] and receive the money necessary for all these dispatches.[482]

The deputy remained, in practice, an old-fashioned type of *procurador*, bound to his principals by an imperative mandate, stated in both his powers and his instructions. Hence the importance of the latter and the considerable amounts of time spent drawing them up—a time that greatly exceeded that devoted to the elections themselves.

Although the practice of sending *procuradores* to court to defend the interests of the city was commonplace, the circumstances of the time, when the reform of the monarchy was already being discussed,

---

476 Poder e instrucciones de la ciudad de México, January 15, 1810, in ibid., folio 275 (104).

477 This refers to a legal figure under which a faculty or obligation held in common by two or more people must be fully exercised or honored by each of the individuals involved.—Trans.

478 Poder de San Luis Potosí, October 12, 1809, in ibid., folio 321 (149).

479 See, for example, Poder e Instrucciones de la ciudad de México, November 15, 1810, in ibid., folio 275 (104).

480 Instrucciones de Guanajuato, December 6, 1809, ibid., folio 300 (128).

481 Ibid.

482 Poder e instrucciones de Guanajuato, October 19, 1809, ibid., folios 289–300. Poder e instrucciones de Valladolid (Michoacán), February 1, 1810, ibid., folios 283–88.

meant that these writings took on particular importance.[483] In some cases, such as San Luis Potosí or Arizpe in Sonora, the cities produced veritable synthetic treaties on the region's condition and needs.[484]

An examination of the instructions thus provides us with a very concrete picture of the political, social and economic demands of New Spain at the time.[485] Politically, the first declarations, and those with the broadest scope—so broad that noncompliance rendered the powers null and void—[486] were the affirmation of unfailing loyalty to King Ferdinand VII, the defense of the Catholic religion, and the preservation of an indissoluble bond between the Old and New Spains. All the elements of the patriotic explosion of 1808 were still in force.

The deputy's chief goal must be the following:

---

483 While the election of the deputy for New Spain, Miguel de Lardizábal, took place on October 4, 1809 (AGN, Historia, vol. 418, file V, folio 1 and the following folios), by February 1810, Puebla, Veracruz, and Tlaxcala had yet to send their instructions, which arrived on March 3; Mérida and Arizpe signed theirs on March 12. See AGN, Historia, vol. 417, file II, folios 175–77. Some cities did not manage to draw up their instructions; this was the case of Valladolid, which adopted, in summarized form, those of Guanajuato. Poder [January 22, 1810] e instrucciones [February 1, 1810] de Valladolid de Michoacán, AGN, Historia, vol. 417, file II, folios 285–88 (114–17).

484 For these instructions, see AGN México, Historia, vol. 417, file II, folios 187–224 and 145–72.

485 We still do not know whether, politically speaking, there was complete freedom in the writing of these documents, since the instructions were submitted to revision by the audiencia and the viceroy. In some cases, there are traces of their fear regarding what these documents might express; thus, in a note addressed to the viceroy in response to a request from him concerning the examination of Mexico City's instructions, "with regard to the aspirations of this same City [of Mexico]", the officials considered that there were indeed some expressions of this kind but "we do not think it necessary or useful to raise such issues." Confidential report to Viceroy Lizana, February 9, 1810, in Poder e Instrucciones de la ciudad de México, in ibid., folio 263 (90).

486 See Instrucciones de Zacatecas, November 13, 1810, in ibid., folio 354 (181).

> [to devote] before all things his attentions and labors to promoting, by all possible means and with the greatest effort, the increase and defense of Religion, the liberty of our beloved Monarch Lord Don Ferdinand the Seventh, that he may be restored to his throne, and to the bosom of his faithful vassals, the defense and preservation of the Crown, the honor of its Arms and of the Nation that [...] sacrifices itself, after the example of its elders, to the sustaining of its liberties, charters and privileges.[487]

The causes of the king, religion and the nation, along with their rights, were seen as one cause. Expressions of loyalty to the monarch belong to the same register as the oath and the duties of vassals: "the loyalty, love and obedience that this most noble city of Mexico has sworn to the King Our Lord and to the Supreme Junta Central that happily governs us in his Royal name."[488]

Guanajuato says the same thing in different terms, reaffirming

> the solemn oath that with the most plausible demonstrations of joy it has sworn [...] to its King and natural Lord, the much beloved and desired Lord Don Ferdinand of Bourbon, Seventh of that name in the Kingdoms of Castile [...] and the perpetual recognition of the Sovereignty of the Dominions of Spain and the Indies by this same Lord Don Ferdinand the Seventh and his august and legitimate successors descended from the house of Bourbon, may neither the vicissitude of the times nor the contingencies of war [...] lead him to change his dynasty nor force him to render vassalage to any other sovereign.[489]

---

487 Poder e Instrucciones de la ciudad de México, November 15, 1810, in ibid., folio 272 (101).

488 México, ibid., folio 272 (101).

489 Instrucciones de Guanajuato, July 6, 1809, in ibid., folio 299 (127). Puebla expresses the same feeling, referring to the "solemn oath of fidelity and obedience that this Most Noble city has publicly sworn to him in accordance with the fundamental Laws," Poder de Puebla, February 15, 1810, in ibid., folio 180 (6).

Many of these statements expressed a certain fear and disappointment. Fear that the American kingdoms might be used as trump cards in the diplomatic game or handed over to the usurper should ancient Spain be defeated: "whatever may be the final fate of the Peninsula, or of any other portion of the Spanish Empire, Valladolid de Michoacán must always be the patrimony of Lord Don Ferdinand the Seventh, and his legitimate successors to the Crown."[490]

The disappointment, which was more or less openly displayed, was a reaction to the royal order's declaration of Spanish America's non-colonial status. All of the terminology employed—"kingdoms of Castile," "natural lord," "vassalage"—refers to a traditional conception of America as a group of kingdoms belonging to the Crown of Castile and united with the king by an indissoluble bond that must be defended "by preserving these kingdoms inseparable from the Crown of Castile."[491] For this reason, almost all of these documents emphasized the indissoluble ties that united "one and the other Spain," which together formed a single nation; when this term appeared, it always referred to the whole of the monarchy. Hence the total equality of rights that must obtain among its inhabitants. The deputy of New Spain would have to defend

> that this America should be considered not as a Colony, but as a very essential part of the Monarchy of Spain, [that] New Spain should be considered exactly like the old without any distinction, since for both there is one Legislation, one honor, one esteem, and all without any difference, exactly on the same terms as all the natives of the Provinces of Spain.[492]

490 Poder [January 22, 1810] e instrucciones [February 1, 1810] de Valladolid de Michoacán, in ibid., folio 285 (114).

491 Poder e Instrucciones de la ciudad de México, February 15, 1810, in ibid., folio 268 (97).

492 Instrucciones de Guanajuato, July 6, 1809, in ibid., folio 300 (128) and Poder [January 22, 1810] e instrucciones [February 1, 1810] de Valladolid de Michoacán, in ibid., folio 285 (114).

This equality must be manifested not only by the equality of the laws governing both parts of the monarchy, but also, very practically, by equal access for Americans—or rather, due preference in their access—to public office. This long-standing demand was expressed with varying degrees of clarity. Mexico City did it diplomatically:

> Given that the Royal Clemency has always dispensed its mercies, graces and protection to the natives of these Kingdoms and all their inhabitants, [...] may the Deputy make such reverent petitions as he deems appropriate, so that they may be attended and clerics as well as political and military figures be chosen to occupy the employments [...].[493]

In its long instructions, San Luis Potosí devoted an entire chapter to the "Merits and Services of Employees in America," asking that there should be no "odious distinction between the Gachupines or Europeans and Creoles"; the document complained about the obstacles many civil and ecclesiastical employees encountered when it came to promotions and asked that these be given according to the merits of each person. This would enable Americans to occupy some of the highest positions in the monarchy, while peninsulars would occupy medium-level positions in America. For the highest positions in the latter, the most suitable candidates would evidently be those who knew these provinces best, that is, primarily the Americans.[494]

However, once these fundamental principles had been proclaimed, the strictly political part of all these documents appears to have been relatively limited, at least in comparison with the intensity of the political debate in the Peninsula. This makes it difficult to grasp America's attitude to the political reform of the monarchy and the great ideological transformation then taking place, both of which were at the center of the peninsular political debate at the time. Only the cabildo of Zacatecas, as we will see shortly, expressed itself clearly and in detail

493 Poder de Guanajuato, October 12, 1809, AGN, in ibid., folio 296 (124).

494 Instrucciones de San Luis Potosí, October 24, 1809, in ibid., folio 324 (152).

on these issues. The other cities limited themselves to a few general considerations without going any further in their reflections. How are we to explain these mysterious silences? They may have been owing to the political situation in New Spain, then dominated by the "European party." This imposed an implicit censorship on the editors, something that did not affect the cabildo of Zacatecas, given its composition and power: it was made up largely of the great mining nobility, often of peninsular origin. In fact, these silences undoubtedly had more to do with the scant development of public opinion, in the absence of such a complete freedom of the press as the Peninsula enjoyed. This entailed an obvious disparity between the two continents in their evolution toward political modernity. By the end of 1809, New Spain was still reasoning in terms of traditional pactism or, for the more enlightened, in terms of historical constitutionalism.

Mexico City, for example, showed itself politically prudent, speaking first of the "wise and holy Laws that govern us," and then of "the observance of the Laws, the reform of some, and the addition of others that may prove more useful than the old ones."[495]

Puebla spoke in passing of "fundamental laws" and of "the indemnity of our laws, customs, and traditions."[496] San Luis Potosí alluded to the "reforms required by the present constitution of this America," but then went on to ask for concrete reforms for its region and concluded with the statement "that our wise Government and Your Excellency know the need for further establishments and reforms, which will dispel in the political sphere the deathly disease that afflicts the Vassals of both Worlds."[497]

Only Zacatecas, as we mentioned, spoke clearly and proposed precise political reforms for "good government in the Monarchy [...] its universal interests and particularly those of the country it represents."[498] It

495 Mexico, ibid., folio 273 (102).

496 Poder de Puebla, November 15, 1810, in ibid., folio 180 (6).

497 Instrucciones de San Luis Potosí, October 24, 1809, in ibid., folio 341 (169) and folio 343 (171).

498 Poder de Zacatecas, December 29, 1809, in ibid., folio 345 (173).

spoke clearly in that it began by expressing "its inestimable satisfaction at being able to freely express the sum of its ideas without having to come up against the obstacles that three centuries of erroneous policy have little by little raised up between the nation and the sovereign."[499]

The "three centuries of erroneous policy" that would so often be evoked during the independence era to designate colonial times, were here (as in peninsular Spain) still those that, according to historical constitutionalism, had elapsed since the loss of Castilian liberties in Villalar. Hence the constant reference to the "fundamental laws of the Kingdom," "whose abandonment in the past [...] is the most certain source of the evils and calamities that now afflict the Nation."[500] Hence, also, logically enough, the demand that "the legislative power be restored to the Nation assembled in Cortes, that the abuses introduced by the executive be reformed, and that the King's Ministers be responsible for those that may be introduced."[501]

Although expressed in the language of the recovery of ancient rights, these were demands for constitutionalism, for a division and balance between the powers of the king and those of national representation, and also, perhaps most importantly, a request for equality in this representation between the two parts of the monarchy:

> May the most perfect, just, and inviolable balance be established, not only between the two powers, but also in the national representation in other Cortes, by the increase that should be the consequence of the above-mentioned Sovereign declaration that the Americas are an essential integral part of the Monarchy, accommodating, with the prudence and sound judgment that the importance of this matter demands, the spirit of the Ancient Laws to the present circumstances.[502]

---

499 Ibid.

500 Instrucciones de Zacatecas, November 13,1810, in ibid., folio 353 (180).

501 Ibid., folio 355 (182).

502 Ibid.

Zacatecas's reformist aspirations did not stop there; they also extended to religion and morals, and to the reestablishment of ecclesiastical discipline, with a request for the convocation of "Provincial and National Councils with the frequency prescribed by the Sacred Canons," a request that was also typical of the so-called Spanish Jansenists.[503]

Even though Zacatecas mentioned the "supreme being," this does not mean that there was the slightest tolerance for new ideas in this field. The city asked that, when peace with France should be concluded by the restoration of the king, "political relations with her be restricted as much as possible." They also made a demand that the peninsular liberals never would have made: "that the Holy Tribunal of the Faith and the civil magistrates keep a scrupulous watch over the introduction and propagation of anti-political and irreligious Books and Doctrines, foreign uses and customs, and that their introducers and followers be punished with the utmost rigor."[504]

Zacatecas thus confirms, despite the ways in which it was ahead of the other cities, the political time lag between Old and New Spain. Modernity was still incipient.

## Local Interests

Finally, we must examine the precise demands that the different cities charged their deputies with presenting and defending before the supreme power of the monarchy. Naturally, the diversity in this regard was great; the length of the instructions also varied considerably. Some, after addressing the matters of principle already discussed above, limited themselves to general statements asking for measures beneficial to their inhabitants.

At most, some additional clarifications brought the specific interests of each region to the fore. In this vein, Guanajuato expected measures

503 Instrucciones de Zacatecas, November 13, 1810, in ibid., folio 354 (181).

504 Ibid.

aimed at promoting the mining industry.[505] Mexico City, in keeping with an enlightened perspective, asked that "the Arts and industries and all useful establishments be protected,"[506] but also, in much more traditional language, called for the preservation and increase of its "graces, honors and privileges."[507] Puebla spoke of the "encouragement of such factories as there may be, and the establishment of new ones" and, more generally, of measures in favor of "Agriculture, Commerce, Mining, Arts, and Industry."[508]

Three cities, Oaxaca, Arizpe, and San Luis, sent very detailed reports concerning the situation in their provinces, along with precise instructions regarding what they wished to obtain. These were three cities in very remote areas, which present a kind of sampler of the concrete concerns of Mexicans on the eve of the independence movement.

Oaxaca, in the distant indigenous south, painted a rather gloomy picture of its situation, which it blamed on the reforms carried out under Charles III; it proposed to abolish most of them. They claimed that the production of cochineal, a fundamental element of their economy, was in decline because of the disappearance of the *alcaldías mayores*. Ever since, "the Indians do not work as they used to" and this has affected the collection of the *alcabalas*[509], the tribute and the parochial obventions. To improve this situation, they called for a reestablishment of the *repartimientos*[510] in order to remedy the scarcity of labor. They

505 Instrucciones de Guanajuato, July 6, 1809, in ibid., folio 300 (128).

506 Poder e Instrucciones de la ciudad de México, November 15, 1810, in ibid., folio 273 (102).

507 Poder e Instrucciones de la ciudad de México, November 15, 1810, in ibid., folio 272 (101).

508 Poder de Puebla, November 15, 1810, in ibid., folio 180 (6).

509 A sales tax.—Trans.

510 This was the practice of distributing the indigenous population as a workforce among the colonists, especially on the haciendas or in the mines.—Trans.

also asked for the suppression of a series of taxes[511] or the granting, to the city, of others[512] that could be destined to public works, since the city had very few taxes of its own. This would enable them to build a bridge and water piping for their growing population. They also asked that the *ejidos* (common lands) that they had previously lost should be restored for pasturing the city's cattle, taking these lands from the domains of the Marquis del Valle in exchange for state lands given as compensation. They demanded the establishment of a university for the progress of the sciences, given their remoteness from Mexico City; the creation of a Consulate of Commerce; free trade with the ports of Peru and Guatemala, and, on the pretext of simplifying the Royal Treasury, the abolition of the intendencias.[513] The "modernity" of this demand for free trade goes hand in hand here with the desire to return to the administrative and social situation prior to the reforms.

The situation of San Luis Potosí was markedly different. Their instructions, which make up a veritable treaty, give us the picture of a region seemingly in full expansion, with elites full of dynamism and initiative. They began by calling for a series of measures in the ecclesiastical field, starting with the establishment of a bishopric in the city with jurisdiction over the entire intendencia—Nuevo León, Santander, Coahuila, and Texas. This was justified by their distance from the bishopric of Valladolid, on which the city depended: they had only seen their bishop once in 58 years. They also called for the creation of new curacies to remedy the neglect and ignorance of the faithful; a seminary college for the training of the clergy and a hospital, each time providing the appropriate statistical data and a study of available fiscal resources.[514]

---

511 The tax financing the military picket stationed in the town and the one on grocery stores.

512 The *medio real de Hospital*, paid by the indigenous population for the maintenance of indigenous hospitals, or the *sisa*, a tax on goods.

513 Poder e Instrucciones de Antequera de Oaxaca, October 18, 1809, in ibid., folios 302–16 (130–44).

514 Instrucciones de San Luis Potosí, October 24, 1809, in ibid., folio 325 (152) and following folios.

They then requested the establishment of a cigar and cigarette factory in the city to alleviate the idleness of many of its 25,000 inhabitants, taking advantage of the house of "*mujeres recogidas*"[515] and their labor.[516]

They went on to request the construction of a port in Sotolamarina[517], on the grounds that "it is the reciprocal communication between Ports by means of navigation that gives vigor to and sets in motion Agriculture and commerce, comprising the main portion of the springs of wealth."[518] Follows a description of all the types of production in the region that would benefit from this venture, all thanks to the thriving breeding of mules in the province. This request was supported by very precise, city-by-city calculations of profit margins. The greater ease of communication would have a positive impact on the sparsely populated interior and exterior provinces, that lived in fear of the "barbaric Indians" and in need of more inhabitants to maintain the borders with the United States. To make their arguments still more convincing, the instructions cite the evils caused by the monopoly of Veracruz, presented as analogous to those caused by the monopoly of Cádiz.[519]

We then find some extremely modern propositions on agrarian questions in which the influence of Jovellanos's report on agrarian law and the Spanish experience of colonization in the Sierra Morena were noticeable. There is a proposal to make over ownership of state lands to members of the indigenous population who were landless. The situation of "poor Spaniards, free mulattoes, and other castes" who live on the haciendas as laborers, tenant farmers, or squatters arouses some harsh criticism concerning the evils caused by large property and a proposal that land should be sold to them in emphyteusis. There is even a request

---

515 The "*casas de recogidas*" were shelters for women considered to be in need of social or religious redemption. Whether corrective or penitentiary in nature, these homes covered the women's basic needs and sought to keep them from engaging in prostitution.—Trans.

516 Ibid., folio 329 (157) and the following folios.

517 Now Soto la Marina.—Trans.

518 Ibid., folio 331 (159) and the following folios.

519 Ibid., folio 331 (159) and the following folios.

that, in sparsely populated areas, the land of unoccupied haciendas be given for nothing to new settlers. Alongside these very new measures, there is also a request for the reestablishment of the *repartimientos* of "*mulada y reales*,"[520] the abolition of which had led to the decline of trade; it was expected that, by means of the debts incurred, the indigenous population would be stimulated to work.[521]

The instructions then move on to the "Factories of Goods made with materials from the Earth," defending, in a very modern tone, the freedom of manufacture for cotton, wool and linen textiles, many of which were not produced in Spain or were produced in insufficient quantity. Thus, "industry, without which work makes little progress for want of consumers," would be encouraged.[522] This is followed by requests for a reduction in taxes on grocery shops, and, above all, the abolition of the tribute paid by "Indians, mulattoes and castes," not only because of its fiscal weight, but also

> because of the stigma implied in the name of tribute-payer, and because of the many humiliations they suffer in the manner of its collection, for in this regard, everyone wants to be free and held to be Spaniards, as they truly are, and faithful Vassals of the King, as all the rest of us are.[523]

The very foundations of the estate-based society were beginning to be called into question. The equality of vassals could only be conceived with equality of statutes; the old principles regarding the rights and duties proper to each estate—in this case, to the two "republics"—had become incomprehensible.

The elevation of the neglected condition of the indigenous inhabitants and the various castes now required the suppression of their

520 The compulsory provision of mules by indigenous communities ("*mulada*"), and the payment of tribute in silver coinage ("*reales*").—Trans.

521 Ibid., folio 335 (163) and the following folios.

522 Ibid., folio 337 (166) and the following folios.

523 Ibid., folio 339 (167) and the following folios.

difference from the "Spaniards." To compensate for the fiscal deficit, it was proposed that the *alcabala* be increased and the indigenous population be required to pay it; a supplementary tax on tobacco was also proposed. Curiously, this modernity goes hand in hand with the above-mentioned demand that the *repartimientos* be reestablished in order to force the indigenous population to work: these blatant contradictions among the enlightened elite would persist well into the nineteenth century.

Following other demands, including the control and payment of certain public employees and the appointment of the intendant, the instructions end as they began, on another topic concerning religion: the convocation of a national council to reform customs, return "the ancient cult to its primitive rigor" and increase the zeal among the ministers of the altar.[524]

And finally, in faraway Sonora, Arizpe appears as the capital of a pioneering area in need of resources for its future expansion. It was, in fact, a capital, though it was no more than a village and had no *ayuntamiento*. As a result, and by order of the higher authorities, the election and the instructions were prepared by a junta that included the main authorities and by some of "the most distinguished individuals of this capital."[525] Their instructions are presented as a book divided into chapters in which the different issues of interest to the provinces of Sonora and Sinaloa are dealt with topic by topic.

The document begins with an idyllic geographical description of the provinces and their potential production while at the same time stating "the most deplorable misery" of their inhabitants (chapter 1). To remedy this situation, they first ask for a free port to encourage trade, concluding that Guaymas would be the most suitable place for it; then they request that, in order to promote the future port, it be exempted from duties on goods for 10 to 12 years (chapter 2). To endow Sonora with a bishopric, it is requested that one be created in Culiacán (Sinaloa)

---

524 Ibid., folio 343 (171) and the following folios.

525 Poder e Instrucciones de Arizpe, November 12, 1810, in ibid., folios 197–24 (23–50).

so the region can have two bishops, one in each province, and so that the bishop of Sonora may take up residence in Arizpe, in order to be closer to California as well. The instructions also request that a cathedral be built, an ecclesiastical chapter be established, and a seminary college be created, both for the good education of the clergy and for that of the young men in general, who have hitherto been forced to travel very far to get an education, with all the dangers this entails (chapter 3). Still on the topic of the promotion of religion, it is requested that the parish priests, a key element in the relations with the indigenous population (so much so that the instructions propose uniting the spiritual and temporal jurisdictions in the mission towns), be endowed with proper salaries: their poverty has been forcing them to exact high emoluments from the indigenous peoples, which has caused these populations to flee and has proved detrimental to evangelization. In fact, they advocate for the restoration of the old system of missions, citing the prosperity of the California missions as a model (chapter 4).

The cultivation of cotton is then praised and its promotion requested,[526] as well as that of looms with which to weave it (chapter 5). The instructions also ask that an audiencia be established, since the one in Guadalajara is 500 leagues away, making the administration of justice very difficult (chapter 6). Also, that the intendants may not have judicial powers: Arizpe complains of the favoritism prevailing in the appointment of subdelegates and proposes that judges be elected annually (chapter 7). They advocate for the creation of two additional military companies to fight the nomadic indigenous groups and for these companies to be made up of men from the Opata tribe "because they are the most faithful, the bravest and the most practiced in the wiles of the barbarians" (chapter 8). Regarding the mines, the great wealth of the region, complaints are made about the non-observance of the ordinances on stowage and drainage, the cause of many accidents and ruined mines (chapter 9). They also propose the establishment of a

526 By temporary exemptions from "*pechos y gavelas*" (direct and indirect tax) and a ban on imports of cotton produced in other places.

"*quinta y ensaye*"[527] for precious metals given that the creation of a Mint was impossible for the time being (chapter 10).

Here, then, was a whole series of very diverse requests that sometimes seemed to be in line with progress as conceived by the Enlightenment while others revealed a desire to return to the era that had preceded the reforms.

## A Mixed Balance

The Spanish American deputies never became part of the Junta Central. The fact is, the latter was dissolved in the midst of the French invasion of Andalusia at the end of January 1810, when the American electoral process was not yet everywhere complete. By then, the following kingdoms and provinces had elected deputies: Venezuela had elected Joaquín de Mosquera y Figueroa, regent of the Audiencia of Caracas, on June 20, 1809;[528] Puerto Rico had elected Ramón Power, the commander of the naval division blockading Santo Domingo, on July 17;[529] New Granada, Field Marshal Antonio de Narváez, on September 16;[530] Peru, José Silva y Olave, cantor of the cathedral of Lima, on September 19;[531] New Spain,

527 The collection of the 20 percent royal tax on precious metals ("*quinta*") and the official assaying process that determined the value of the metals for said taxation ("*ensaye*").—Trans.

528 See ACE, General, file 7, no. 99. The news was published in the *Gazeta de Caracas* on June 30, 1809, and by the *Diario de México* XI, no. 1451, September 21, 1809, 340–41.

529 The election took place on July 17, 1809. See letter from Ramón Power, in AHN, Secretaría de Estado records, vol. 60, box 50.

530 See Abelardo Forero Benavides, op. cit., 57 and the following pages, and Restrepo 1827, 1969, 104–5.

531 AHN, Secretaría de Estado records, 58, folio 157.

Miguel de Lardizábal y Uribe on October 4, 1809, and Guatemala, the merchant José Pavón in March 1810.[532]

In Chile, the elections in most of the cabildos had taken place between November 1809 and February 1810, but Santiago was still missing. No doubt it was keeping itself for the end of the process and the kingdom's final vote, which never took place. The same thing happened in Río de la Plata, where the electoral process was enormously delayed by the internal quarrels of Buenos Aires and the consultations sent to the Junta Central; when the electoral process was interrupted, the vote of some cabildos was still missing—among them the most important of all, Buenos Aires.

None of the elected deputies made it to Spain before the fall of the Junta Central except for the one from New Spain, who was already residing there. The fact that he had been elected by Mexico was undoubtedly one of the most important factors behind his appointment, on February 4, 1810, as one of the five members of the new Regency Council that replaced the Junta Central.

Beyond this aspect, however, these elections represented, on the one hand, an extraordinary novelty that excited and mobilized all of Hispanic America for months, and on the other, a profound trauma that would constitute a crucial milestone in the estrangement between peninsular Spain and Spanish America.

This first statement is hardly an exaggeration: we have already seen the extent to which the elections rallied the elites of the most important cities. But not only the elites: through them, entire cities—and this was a common feature of ancien régime politics—took part in what was happening. Though the members of the councils might be very few, they polarized the rivalries among the other actors, among whom the main role fell to the family clans, with their extended networks of clients and relatives.

The people itself also participated as a spectator: a necessary spectator of this theater of power, manifesting with its presence and acclamations its approval—and, at times, its disapproval—of the elites' actions. On October 4, 1809, when the Real Acuerdo in Mexico held the final

---

532 See Rodríguez 1984, 65–66.

election that designated Miguel de Lardizábal y Uribe as New Spain's deputy to the Junta Central, the notary left the room

> to publish [the news] to the great multitude that was outside the hall [...] it was resolved that a halberdier of the guard should be sent to notify the Dean of this Holy Cathedral Church so that at once a solemn, general ringing of the bells should be carried out in celebration, to which all the other churches of this Court responded.[533]

The cabildo, for its part, "in order to further express its joy, and that all the *vecinos* of the city might join in the celebration, requested and obtained permission from the Most Excellent and Illustrious Lord Viceroy for the streets to be embellished with hangings and general illumination, as was indeed done."[534]

We should mention a further aspect of the importance that these elections took on: not only was this the first time that Spanish America was sending representatives to an assembly that represented the entire monarchy, but moreover, the elected deputy was to form part of the supreme sovereign power. In December 1809, when Mexico heard of the arrival in Acapulco of the deputy for Peru, José de Silva, who was on his way to Spain, the authorities' reaction illustrates the enormous importance given to this unprecedented event—the presence of a depositary of the sovereignty. The governor of Acapulco made it known that

> on his entry and exit, he was given the honors of an active Captain General, having brought to this effect an order from the Commander of the Navy in Cayao in Lima, the captain of the ship, and

533 Acta de la elección del diputado de la Nueva España a la Junta Central, AGN, Historia, vol. 418, file V, folio 2.

534 Poder e Instrucciones de la ciudad de México, November 15, 1810, in AGN, Historia, vol. 417, file II, folio 270 (99).

> announcing his arrival with a square flag hoisted on the top of the mast as soon as she entered the Bay.[535]

The deputy was lodged in the governor's palace, and instructions were given to the subdelegates for his reception on his way to Mexico, where the viceroy himself prepared to entertain him in his palace.[536]

When we consider these elections as the first step in the direction of modern politics and representative regimes, we can see how the electoral process itself gradually brought on the evolution of mentalities toward a progressive improvement of representation and its evolution toward modern forms.

These phenomena can already be seen in the shift that took place regarding which cities had the right to vote. In the first regions that voted immediately after receiving the royal order of January 22, 1809, we find that the number of cities granted the right to vote was very small: 14 in Mexico, which housed almost half the population of Hispanic America,[537] 17 in Peru,[538] 20 in New Granada,[539] six in Venezuela.[540] So the document, in this early period, was being interpreted in a very restrictive sense.

---

535 Acapulco, January 16, 1810, AGN, Historia, vol. 416, file III, folios 173–83 (126–36).

536 In the end, he lodged him in a private house, that of the "Icaza knights [...] because of my family relations, which are not easy for me to forgo," in ibid., 182.

537 The elections took place between April and October 1809. The cities that voted were Arizpe, Durango, Guadalajara, Guanajuato, Mérida, Mexico City, Oaxaca, Puebla, Querétaro, San Luis Potosí, Tlaxcala, Valladolid de Michoacán, Veracruz and Zacatecas.

538 The last election was held in September 1809. The cities that voted were Arequipa, Carmona, Cajamarca, Chachapoyas, Cuzco, Guayaquil, Huamanga, Huancavélica, Huánuco, Ica, Lambayeque, Lima, Moquegua, Piura, Puno, Tarma and Trujillo.

539 The last election took place in September 1809.

540 The last election took place in June 1809. The cities that voted were Asunción de la Margarita, Barina, Caracas, Cumana, Guyana, Maracaibo.

We have a very different situation with those provinces that, for one reason or another (probably because they appealed against their scanty number of voters) waited several months before proceeding to elections. Thus, in Guatemala 14 cities participated—more than in New Spain, despite the enormous difference in population between the two.[541] In little Chile, sixteen cities and small towns voted, and many of them had very small populations.[542] This was even more marked in Río de la Plata: when the electoral process was interrupted, 12 cities had already voted and as many more remained pending,[543] because Río de la Plata had obtained a new royal order, dated October 6, 1809, which gave all localities that had an *ayuntamiento* the right to vote.

This last royal order is informed by the experience of the electoral process in those kingdoms and provinces that had voted first, as well as by the consultations submitted to the Junta Central.[544] The new regulations included some novelties that implied expanding the number of cities with the right to vote as well as increasing the autonomy of the vote.

To begin with, it extended the franchise to a greater number of cities because of the uncertainty prevailing in Spanish America concerning

---

541 The last elections took place in March 1810. See Rodríguez 1984, 65–66.

542 The elections took place from November 1809 to February 1810. The Chilean towns that voted were Concepción, Mercedes (Cauquenes district), San Agustín (Talco district), San Bartolomé (Chillán district), San Felipe el Real (Aconcagua district), San Fernando (Colchagua district), San Francisco de la Selva (Copiapo district), San Martín de la Concha (Quillota district), San Rafael de Rozas (Illapel district), Santa Ana de Briviesca (Petorca district), Santa Cruz de Triana (Rancagua District), Santa Rosa (Andes district), Serena, Valdivia, Valparaíso. Santiago did not get to vote.

543 According to the calculations of González 1937, vol. I, 215 and the following pages, the following cities had voted in what was then the territory of the viceroyalty: Asunción, Córdoba, Corrientes, La Plata, La Rioja, Mendoza, Montevideo, Mizque, Potosí, San Luis, Santa Cruz de la Sierra, Santa Fe. We are missing data for Catamarca, Cochabamba, Jujuy, La Paz, Oruro, Santiago del Estero, Tanja, etc.

544 The royal order of October 6, 1809, is reproduced in González 1937, 269–70.

what qualified as a "*cabeza de partido*" ("district capital"). This expression, which in the Peninsula designated a subdivision of the province, was misleading in America, and it was not clear to what circumscription it corresponded.[545] In New Spain the phrase had been applied to the intendancy capitals, but there was so much doubt in other places that in the end the new provisions granted the right to vote, as we have said, to all cities in possession of an *ayuntamiento*.[546]

Another modification responded to American protests regarding conditions for eligibility. The first regulations only contemplated the "good citizen and zealous patrician" as a candidate, which meant, as we have already seen, that in New Spain, where the peninsulars controlled quite a number of cabildos, many of those elected by the *ayuntamientos* were not natives of America. The new provisions required the deputy to be "American by birth." They also forbade—again, on the basis of the experience gleaned from the initial elections—that the elected candidates should occupy some of the so-called first offices: governor, intendant, judge, *asesor*, royal official, administrator.

Finally, also as a result of several conflicts with the higher authorities, the final electoral board had less of an administrative nature because it excluded the viceroy, while including representatives of the ecclesiastical and civil cabildos.[547]

By the end of the electoral process, once the problems deriving from its defects had been experienced in practice, there was already talk of the future elections to the Cortes, which had been announced by the Junta Central on May 22, 1809. This is also why the political debate was progressing, and harsh criticism was beginning to attack the restricted

545 The same problem would arise during the elections to the Cortes in 1810. For the latter case, see the report of the Consejo pleno, Cádiz, November 27, 1810, AHN, Consejos, 17795.

546 In Chile, voting was carried out in accordance with the royal order of January 1809, but now district capitals were understood to be cities and towns that had an *ayuntamiento*.

547 It was made up of two ministers appointed by royal agreement, two canons appointed by the ecclesiastical chapter, and two *regidores* appointed by the *ayuntamiento*.

nature of an electoral body limited to cabildo members appointed for life. It was in this context that Camilo Torres drafted his aforementioned statement, which protested less against the fact of representing the cities than against the limited number of cities that had the vote, as well as the small number of deputies. As he saw it, every provincial capital and every episcopal seat should elect one. He also objected to the oligarchic nature of the *ayuntamientos*:

> These deputies must be appointed by the towns themselves so as to deserve their confidence and so that they may have true representation, of which the cabildos are only a very disfigured image, because they have not been created by the public vote but by inheritance, renunciation, or purchase of degraded and venal offices.[548]

When the first autonomist juntas were formed a few months later, this last demand would be adopted in most cases for the election of juntas and congresses. And yet, curiously, along with this "democratization," the cities, now called "*pueblos*" or towns, would persist as the basic electoral unit, something which continues to refer us to a traditional social imaginary. This was the case of Río de la Plata, where only the cities would be allowed to vote in the election of the Buenos Aires Junta, to the exclusion of small towns that were not "district capitals." At the same time, the vote now extended to all *vecinos* assembled in open cabildo.[549]

However, the shift in mentalities toward ever broader representation was irreversible. The disappointment was therefore all the greater when, in January 1810, the Junta Central, before it was dissolved, published its regulations for the election of deputies to the Cortes. Not only would Spanish America and the Philippines elect a mere 30 deputies compared to more than 250 in peninsular Spain, but these deputies would be elected in America following the same regulations that had been used for the election to the Junta Central. Meanwhile, in the Peninsula,

548 Torres 1809, 1960, 28.

549 González 1937, vol. II, 57 and the following pages.

most of the deputies were already to be elected by a very broad suffrage of all householders and in a number proportional to the population: one for every 50,000 inhabitants.

The unequal political treatment given by the central government to an America whose political equality it had proclaimed—and continued to proclaim—further fueled American grievances and turned the demand for equal representation into one of the main causes behind the incipient independence movements.

# VII

# The Political Pedagogy of the Spanish Revolutionary Press

Over two years (from 1808 to 1810), the transformation that took place in the ideas and imaginaries of the Hispanic elites was considerable. The traditionalism of the mental universe belonging to the vast majority of the monarchy's inhabitants was evident in the months following the insurrection.[550] Yet two years later, when the General and Extraordinary Cortes met in Cádiz, the revolutionary group that was to play the driving role in the Cortes—soon to be termed "liberals"—would impose itself; its mental references were, by then, totally modern. This victory can be partially explained by the peculiar character of the city of Cádiz, which at the time served as a refuge for the cream of the Spanish intellectual elites, but it was also the consequence of a more global evolution in mentalities over the previous two years.

Two simultaneous phenomena played an essential role in this extremely rapid transformation: the proliferation of printed matter—especially the press—and the expansion of new forms of sociability.

With them, modern "public opinion" truly comes into being, as well as what we can describe, in Habermas's terms, as "the public political space." It is true that what he calls a "literary public space," or what Cochin terms "the republic of letters," already existed: a social milieu, a network of men gathered in societies and tertulias of a literary, economic, and scientific character, where free debate on all kinds of topics, including political ones, began to emerge as a moral agency independent of the state—one that judged, in the name of "reason," not only the

550 See chapter V.

validity of the government's measures, but that of the general principles that should regulate society.[551]

Although the "republic of letters" was relatively widespread by the end of the eighteenth century and had produced a great many publications in the 1780s, the measures taken by the state against the influence of the French Revolution confined it to its private spaces of sociability and to a network of private connections and correspondence that lacked public expression. The events of 1808 provided these circles with an unexpected opportunity to burst into the open:

> If anyone had said, at the beginning of last October, that before a year had elapsed we would be free to write about government reforms, plans for a constitution, scrutinizing and limiting power, and that hardly any writings would be published in Spain that did not address these important matters, he would have been taken for a fool.[552]

The "divine surprise"—the sudden collapse of absolutism—would allow the "republic of letters" to constitute a "political public space" via two different but parallel paths, the study of which is still largely pending.[553] On the one hand, through the multiplication of modern forms of sociability and a much greater freedom of speech in these spaces; on the other, through the proliferation of printed matter and newspapers with patriotic aims that sprung from the de facto disappearance of censorship.

Indeed, the new press gave many of its members the opportunity to express their ideas publicly, albeit very cautiously at first, so as not to

---

551 For these topics, see chapter III.

552 "Reflexiones acerca de la *Carta sobre el modo de establecer un Consejo de Regencia con arreglo a nuestra constitución*," *Semanario Patriótico*, Madrid, no. IV, September 22, 1808, 62.

553 The first—that of the forms of sociability—undoubtedly presents greater difficulties given the more scattered sources. The work of Martínez Quinteiro 1977 constitutes a first and indispensable approach to the best known of these groups. The second—print—is more readily available given that most of the newspapers and a multitude of miscellaneous printed publications have been preserved. This second aspect is the one we will address here.

offend the sensibilities of readers who still adhered to traditional imaginaries and values. However, this diffuse influence in a press whose primary goal was to mobilize the population in the fight against the invader was insufficient.[554] The modern groups, obsessed both with the urgency and immensity of the work of regeneration that needed to be carried out and by people's real state of mind, which was still far removed from modern principles, soon provided themselves with media through which to express their ideas.

Certainly, to find an already constituted modern public opinion with a plurality of newspapers of different tendencies, we must wait at least until the summer of 1810 and, above all, until after the convening of the Cortes in Cádiz during the autumn of that same year. However, even before this period of maturity, three newspapers played a significant role in the evolution of mindsets by virtue of their precocity, the quality of their editors, and their broad circulation: the *Semanario Patriótico*,[555] *El Espectador Sevillano*,[556] and *El Voto de la Nación española*. It was these publications, during the period of the Junta Central—the key period of the Hispanic Revolution—that drove the ideological transformation of the elites. They not only bear witness to the chronology of this transformation, but they also show us the strategy used to promote it, as well as a very complete exposition of the project of the Hispanic Revolution.

---

554 For the newspapers of the period, see Gómez Imaz 1910. Although in need of an update, this work is still indispensable.

555 The *Semanario Patriótico* of these years, whose chief editor was Quintana himself, was a weekly consisting of two series. The first was published in Madrid, from no. I, dated September 1, 1808, to no. XIV, dated December 1, 1808, when the members of the group fled to Seville as French troops advanced on Madrid. The second series, published in Seville, ran from no. XV, dated May 4, 1809, to no. XXXII, dated August 30, 1809, when the newspaper chose to suspend publication rather than give in to pressure from certain members of the Junta Central. Its main editors were José María Blanco White for political topics, and Isidoro Antillón for military ones.

556 *El Espectador Sevillano* was a newspaper that ran from no. 1, dated October 2, 1809, to no. 114, dated January 23, 1810, when publication ceased due to the advance of the French troops on Seville. Its main editor was Alberto Lista.

The study of these newspapers helps clarify two phenomena that are still partly unexplained. The first is the extraordinary speed and coherence with which the Cortes of Cádiz carried out its destruction of the ancien régime: to a great extent, the main ideas of the constitution and the reforms had already been publicly set forth in these papers. The second is the transformation, over this same period, of the American elites: in 1808, these elites had seemed even more traditional than those of the Peninsula, whereas by 1810 they were as modern as the latter and were handling the same ideas with the same ease. The circulation of these newspapers in Spanish America and reprints that were made of them help to explain this phenomenon, which cannot be simply attributed to direct foreign influence.[557]

## Strategy and Tactics

On September 1, 1808, the first issue of the *Semanario Patriótico* was published in Madrid, which had been liberated a few weeks earlier by Bailén's victorious troops. Although its main editor was the poet Manuel José Quintana,[558] the newspaper can be seen as the organ of a group: Quintana's tertulia, the most famous among those existing in Spain at the time. Established at the end of the eighteenth century, this tertulia had since then become the main meeting place for the most radical intellectuals of the day, where they discussed all kinds of literary, philosophical, and political questions. In 1808, many of those who would later become key figures in the Hispanic Revolution were part of this

557 The *Semanario Patriótico*, for example, was reprinted in Mexico as soon as several issues were available: "No. 3 of the *Semanario Patriótico de España* is being bound this morning. Several issues have been compiled," *Gazeta de México* XVI, no. 111, November 9, 1809, 836. See also ibid., February 6, 1810, which inserts an article from the November 7, 1808, issue of the weekly. As for *El Espectador Sevillano*, the main political articles received up to September 7, 1810, were printed together in a volume of 147 pages.

558 For Quintana, see Dérozier 1968.

group; they were known as "Jacobins" because of their radical ideas.[559] Its members came from different milieus and would follow diverging paths: some would become "Frenchified" and collaborate with the government of Joseph Bonaparte;[560] the patriotic majority would follow the provisional governments as they moved, first from Madrid to Seville, and later to Cádiz, where they would be among the best-known deputies and publicists.[561] Another member, Blanco White, would settle in London where, from April 1810 onward, he would publish the newspaper *El Español*, which would serve as the most important link between the Hispanic revolutionaries, both peninsular and American.[562]

The motley origins of its members made this group the center of a network of societies and tertulias extending throughout the peninsular geography. If a seed of the "liberal party" existed at the time, it was really this network of modern forms of sociability: a group of societies (generally tertulias) linked by personal acquaintance between members as well as by frequent exchanges of correspondence, which contributed to the circulation of the press and to the exchange of writings and reflections. As the *Semanario Patriótico* stated clearly upon receiving an article from Zaragoza: "I am not surprised, sir, that, you tell me, your *tertulia* [italics are the author's] only speaks of plans for reform and constitutions."[563]

Ideological modernity is inextricably linked to modern forms of sociability. And in this milieu, and up until early 1810 and the Junta

---

559 See Pons 1990, 63, quoting one of the participants, Blanco White.

560 The case of Alberto Lista, the main editor of *El Espectador Sevillano*, is perhaps one of the most striking.

561 We are not writing a history of this group here, merely analyzing the content of their newspapers. For the makeup and political sensitivities of the group, see Martínez Quinteiro 1977, 41 and the following pages, and Pons 1990, 63 and the following pages.

562 On Blanco White and his importance, see the fundamental work of Pons 1990.

563 Introduction to "Carta sobre la antigua Constitución del Reyno de Aragón," *Semanario Patriótico*, no. X, November 3, 1808, 163 and the following pages.

Central's flight to Cádiz, Quintana's tertulia played the main role in the Hispanic Revolution due to the personality of its leader and its main members, its duration, its publications, and its wide-ranging connections. As Blanco White stated shortly afterward, they formed "a sort of Club without formalities that was known as the Little Junta, a reference to the influence in matters of opinion that it hoped to have on the Big One [the Junta Central] in favor of right-minded ideas."[564]

The press was but one of the means employed by this group in its many-sided action. There were other means that were just as important: for one thing, they functioned as a pressure group on the Junta Central via some of its members, such as Calvo de Rozas, who belonged to Quintana's group. They also influenced the language of the official documents of the Junta Central since Quintana was the main author of these documents. And finally, there was the increasing presence of the group's members in the government's auxiliary organizations: the secretariat of the Junta Central, the Constitutional Commission in charge of preparing the convocation of the Cortes, the official gazette, etc.

Among these varied modes of action, the primary purpose of the press was political pedagogy. Indeed, an analysis of the content of these newspapers reveals, beneath the apparent jumble of articles—since information also occupied an important place—a plan, clear and tenaciously pursued, to transform the mindsets of its readership. Such an analysis reveals not only a gradual radicalization of the language and ideological frames of reference used, but also the increasing multiplication of explicitly political articles. We might think that this merely reflects the general evolution of mindsets, but this hypothesis does not stand up to careful scrutiny: from the very beginning of their publication, these newspapers clearly stated the principles that would be discussed in detail a year later.

Thus, starting with the first issue of the *Semanario Patriótico*, we find clearly formulated, as if they were obvious propositions, the basic principles of modern politics that would only prevail with the convening of the Cortes. Speaking of the provisional power which ought to govern the monarchy, we already find it stated: "Are they unaware that

564 *El Español*, London, II, no. 10, January 1811, 288, quoted by Pons 1990, vol. I, 132.

the supreme power, the true sovereignty, resides in the Nation assembled by means of its representatives?"[565] And, shortly afterward, criticizing the project for a Regency Council:

> every constituent power emanates from the people and can have no other origin [...]. But who should form and constitute this Regency, properly speaking? To the Nation alone, through its Representatives, falls the task of reconstructing the executive Power, now disrupted by the King's absence. Hence the need to instantly convene a national Representation, call it Cortes or what you will.[566]

The foundations of the revolution are already clearly expounded here: sovereignty resides in the nation and is exercised through its representatives; there must be a division of powers,[567] the future Cortes must not part "until it has secured the ship of the State with the anchor of a good constitution."[568] The forceful sentences that conclude the article are like a blueprint for what would be accomplished during the following years:

> The supreme Junta that is to be formed [...] must at once call the Nation to convene in Cortes [...] to determine not only the formation and establishment of the Regency Council [...] but the reforms that are absolutely necessary to our political, civil, and economic Laws. In a word, this representation must give us a constitution at once [...], which will make of all the provinces composing this vast Monarchy a Nation, truly one where all shall be equal in rights,

565 *Semanario Patriótico*, Madrid, no. 1, September 1, 1808, 15.

566 "Reflexiones acerca de la *Carta sobre el modo de establecer un Consejo de Regencia con arreglo a nuestra constitución*," *Semanario Patriótico*, Madrid, no. IV, September 22, 1808, 63 and 65.

567 Ibid. The king appears as the "Executive" and in footnote 1, the text speaks of the "legislative power" of the Cortes and the "balance between the powers." The whole article is an implicit critique of the historical constitutionalists. For example, it quotes Martínez Marina with esteem, but confines him to the role of a respectable, erudite scholar.

568 Ibid., 67.

> equal in obligations, equal in burdens. With it, in the eyes of the law, the distinctions between Valencians, Aragonese, Castilians, Biscayans must cease: all must be Spaniards.[569]

The contrast between this and the ideas that were predominant among the elites—let alone those prevailing among the general population—is obvious. This contrast explains the pedagogical priority of these newspapers: to transmit the new ideas and foster an ideological mutation into modernity.

The existence of this pedagogical project from the very beginning is not a delusion fabricated by today's reader. The "Prospectus" of the *Semanario Patriótico* frankly expressed this, explaining that its political segment would consist of two sections, "one historical and the other didactic": "The didactic section will be sometimes deduced from the news, sometimes it will address general issues to establish principles, dispel errors, destroy concerns. In this subdivision we will speak of any reforms to be attempted in our internal government."[570]

The editors modestly introduced themselves as "some studious Spaniards" who "have decided to create a newspaper meant to foster public spirit."[571] In fact, their ambition was much greater: "to establish principles, dispel errors, destroy concerns." Although they praised public opinion as "stronger than unpopular authority and fortified armies," this public opinion did not reflect the feelings of society; it was a preexisting moral entity to which the press gave expression: "there are no better means than those provided by the printing of newspapers, destined by nature to excite, sustain, and guide public opinion."[572]

The editors saw themselves as the "guides" of public opinion, or rather, as the demiurges who would create it out of the mass of common

569 Ibid., 69–79.

570 "Prospecto," *Semanario Patriótico*, Madrid, late August 1808, 5.

571 Ibid., 4.

572 Ibid., 1.

concerns.[573] Because they were aware of the distance that separated their own ideas from those of most of the population, they would employ a gradual strategy, a "didactics" by means of which they could gradually impose their ideas. An examination of the type and order of published articles shows how they did so.

During the first period of the *Semanario Patriótico*, that of the autumn of 1809 in Madrid, the articles in the "Politics" section were mostly[574] chronicles, narrations, reflections, and comments on events and publications related to the immediate, ongoing situation. As the "Prospectus" announced, "didactics" did not mean defending essential principles directly, but, instead, making them appear self-evident through articles connected to the circumstances.

The means employed were diverse. One of the most widely used was to transform the usual meaning of words, carrying them through successive semantic shifts into a modern sense. The word "homeland," for example, shifts from its most common meaning as a place of birth to signify a human community that governs itself with the laws it has given itself. The struggle for freedom and independence, which in the proclamations of the time referred to a defense against the foreign invader, moves into the vocabulary of domestic politics to demand the freedom of the nation or of the citizens in relation to the government.

The words "people" and "nation," in particular—the terms par excellence of the new legitimacy—were subjected to a special effort that used their multiple connotations as a means to shift them to the modern register without making these different meanings in any way visible. By a slippage in the meaning of words, "the people," as a population in all its heterogeneity but unanimous in its rejection of the invader, becomes a people somewhere between the abstract and the homogeneous; from there, it shifts to meaning a unitary nation, freely constituted by a new

573 This awareness is not exclusive to Spain. Habermas 1961, 1978, also points to it as one of the common features in his studies of other European countries.

574 There is a very important exception: the article entitled "Reflexiones sobre el patriotismo," *Semanario Patriótico*, Madrid, no. III, September 15, 1808, 47, which we will analyze later.

pact and with no room any longer for distinctions of class or estate, nor for the differences that stemmed from belonging to the various kingdoms and provinces: henceforth, there were only Spaniards.[575]

Another frequently employed procedure was the surreptitious introduction of terms hitherto considered taboo because of their revolutionary connotations. These words suddenly appear as the evocation of something obvious that needs no explanation. This is the case with the word "revolution," used to describe the events in progress: "the first scene of our revolution,"[576] "the March revolution,"[577] "the historical recapitulation [...] of this political revolution,"[578] etc.

Another example: the appearance of "the rights of man and of the citizen," which emerge as if by surprise in a sentence about the courage of the Spaniards in their struggle against the invader—these "armies of free men [who] had committed the crime of raising the banner of independence, of resisting heroically [...] of upholding, in short, with magnanimity, the imprescriptible rights of man and of the citizen [...]."[579]

Essentially, as we shall see in more detail shortly, the newspaper, having announced its intent in the "Prospectus," was using history as a pedagogical instrument and striving to construct a new vision of the past that foregrounded the new actors it had gradually defined: the people, the nation. This new version of history served, at the same time, to legitimate the new principles, conceived as the recovery of those that existed before the establishment of despotism, as an explanation of present circumstances and as a project for the future.

During the newspaper's second period, that of Seville, from May to August 1809, it would seem that the editors of the *Semanario Patriótico* felt that circumstances allowed them to expound their ideas much more

---

575 For a detailed analysis of this slippage of meaning, see the case of the oath of allegiance to Ferdinand VII in Madrid, "Victory of the Modern Nation" in chapter IX.

576 *Semanario Patriótico*, Madrid, September 8, 1808, 26.

577 Ibid.

578 "Prospecto," *Semanario Patriótico*, Madrid, late August 1808, 4.

579 *Semanario Patriótico*, Seville, no. XV, May 4, 1809, 2.

clearly.[580] The time was indeed ripe for it. On April 15, Calvo Rozas, inspired by Quintana, had presented a motion to the Junta Central in favor of convening the Cortes and, since then, this key issue had been under discussion inside the government. The death, a few months earlier, of Floridablanca, the most determined supporter of absolutism, and the pressure from the provincial juntas on the Junta Central, which was accused of perpetuating itself in power, helped the campaign of those who supported convening the Cortes, whether they were Jovellanos's historical constitutionalists, or the "Jacobins" of Quintana's group. Undoubtedly, it was the alliance of these two groups that made possible the decree, published on May 22, 1809, announcing that the Cortes would be convened and the nation consulted as to how they would be held. It is quite possible that the reappearance of the *Semanario Patriótico* served as an additional means of action for the radical group at this important juncture.

In any case, the political project became more and more explicit and, as if following a plan sketched out in advance, readers were gradually led to make the newspaper's solutions their own. This began with the article "Del egoísmo político" ("On Political Selfishness"), which lashed out at those who argued for focusing on the war and leaving reform for later:

> They shudder at the name of reforms of the kingdom, because they live off the evils hitherto suffered [...]. Let's throw out the French, they say; as if our only affliction were the French; as if closing the doors on the bad government that brought them to Spain would distract us from pursuing them [...] as if, after throwing them out, we could be sure our rights would be established amid the intoxication of triumph.[581]

In "De los nombres de libertad e igualdad" ("On the Names of Liberty and Equality"), the paper went on to openly defend the great principles of the French Revolution, while explaining that these principles

---

580 For this period of the newspaper and the role of Blanco White, its main editor and the author of these articles, see Pons 1990, vol. I, chapter II.

581 *Semanario Patriótico*, Seville, no. XVI, May 11, 1809, 1.

had been distorted by this same revolution and that these were "terms unjustly called revolutionary."[582]

The titles and content of the articles in the successive issues are like an inexorable chain of reasoning in which each conclusion serves as a starting point for new progress. "Sobre la oportunidad de mejorar nuestra suerte" ("On the Opportunity to Improve Our Lot") asserts the need for present union in the fight against tyranny.[583] "La España necesita un remedio general y poderoso" ("Spain Needs a General and Powerful Remedy") is a direct attack on the ancient fundamental laws so revered by historical constitutionalists. The article titled "¿Cuál puede ser el remedio más general de nuestros males?" ("What can be the most general remedy for our ills?") comes to the logical conclusion that this remedy is the convening of a "legitimate representation" of the nation, so that "the foundations of a liberal constitution may be laid."[584] "Problema político" ("Political Problem") already addresses the issue of the balance of powers in the future constitution.[585] "Continúa el problema político. De la elección de los cuerpos nacionales" ("Political Problem Continued: On the Election of National Bodies") reflects on the rationale of representation and on electoral systems.[586] "Continúa el problema político. De la organización de los cuerpos nacionales" ("The Political Problem Continued: On the Organization of National Bodies") examines their periodicity and combats the imperative mandate."[587]

The *Semanario Patriótico* then ceased publication, a victim of the hostility of some members of the Junta Central who were offended by its attacks against "despotic governments." When *El Espectador Sevillano*, an organ of the same group and written mainly by Alberto Lista,

---

582 Ibid., Seville, no. XVIII, May 11, 1809; XIX, June 1, 1809; and XXII, June 22, 1809.

583 Ibid., Seville, no. XXIII, June 29, 1809.

584 Ibid., Seville, no. XXV, July 13, 1809, and XXVI, July 20, 1809.

585 Ibid., Seville, no. XXVIII, August 3, 1809.

586 Ibid., Seville, no. XXX, August 17. 1809.

587 Ibid., Seville, no. XXXI, August 24, 1809.

began publication two months later, the pedagogical project became increasingly overt. After three weeks of issues dealing with various topics related to the ongoing circumstances, the doctrinal articles took over the newspaper to such a degree that it seemed a mere medium for the publication of a book in installments.[588] This last feature was so clear that all the longer, reflective articles would be reprinted in Mexico a few months later as a book with continuous page numbers.[589] Only the difficulties of communication with the Peninsula prevented publication of the last chapters.

A series of very long articles presented reflections on the solutions to the political problems of the moment in a less combative style than had characterized the authors' predecessors, adopting an academic, analytical tone to address the comparative advantages of the different political systems, public opinion, the demands of modern representation and, increasingly, as time went by, the Cortes, with a very well-documented and sometimes very technical analysis of all the problems to be solved in order to convene them: the type of suffrage, the elections, the character and modalities of their meeting, their powers, etc.

So, the revolutionary group's political project unfolds with great coherence. It begins with a "Discurso sobre el espíritu público de las naciones" ("Discourse on the Public Spirit of Nations")[590]; then, in succession, "Discurso sobre la reforma de las costumbres" ("Discourse on the

---

588 Thus, incidentally, completely contradicting the prospectus that launched the new paper: "The best plan there can be for a newspaper of this kind is to observe none with regard to the matters that are to compose it." *Prospecto al periódico intitulado El Espectador Sevillano*, Seville, 1809.

589 *El Espectador Sevillano*, reprinted in Mexico by Casa de Arizpe, 1810. This volume collects only the political speeches from the Seville publication, which are given numbers (I to IV), while the book has continuous page numbers, from 1 to 144. It concludes the publication of the first three "Qüestiones sobre las Cortes" with an optimistic "To be continued." *Diario de México*, September 7, 1810, explains that "The reprint of *El Espectador Sevillano* with its questions on the Cortes, which has been received so appreciatively by the public, has been suspended for lack of the December 24, 1809, issue." A week later, the Hidalgo uprising broke out.

590 *El Espectador Sevillano*, Seville, nos. 20–22, October 21–23, 1809.

Reformation of Customs"),[591] "Discurso. El poder arbitrario es funesto al mismo que lo ejerce" ("Discourse: Arbitrary Power Is Fatal to the Very One Who Exercises It"),[592] "Discurso sobre el modo de formarse la opinión pública" ("Discourse on How Public Opinion Is Formed"),[593] and "Discurso sobre los gobiernos representativos" ("Discourse on Representative Governments").[594] And finally, over a month and a half, interrupted only by a series of articles on freedom of the press,[595] we find the long series of "Qüestiones sobre las Cortes" ("Questions regarding the Cortes"),[596] in which the problems posed by the convocation of the latter are addressed with great technicality and solutions are proposed. In most cases, these would be the ones adopted in the Cortes of Cádiz.

## New Times, a New History, New Virtues

In this civic pedagogy, however, the institutional issues that gradually occupied the central place in these newspapers were not the most important. The constitutional issue was, so to speak, the last stage of a much larger undertaking: the construction of a new society. These men held the very distinct conviction that humanity had entered a new era. As heirs of the Enlightenment, they certainly thought of this new era as one of reason, but a reason that did not confine itself, as it had for their predecessors, to working slowly and silently to change society little by little: this reason has burst right into history to liberate the peoples: "Reason, dreadful against wickedness and misgivings, will dispel

591 Ibid., Seville, nos. 23–28 and 30–31, October 24–November 1, 1809.

592 Ibid., Seville, nos. 35–36, November 5 and 6, 1809.

593 Ibid., Seville, no. 3847, November 8–17, 1809.

594 Ibid., Seville, nos. 48–53, 55 and 56, November 8–26, 1809.

595 Ibid., Seville, nos. 98–102, January 7–13, 1810.

596 Ibid., Seville, nos. 60–76, 82–97 and 108–14, November 30, 1809–January 23, 1810.

the darkness of ignorance, break the chains of despotism, and erect the monument of good legislation to the glory of the Spanish nation."[597]

"Reason" has become politics and, since the French Revolution, revolutionary politics. Against the Enlightened view of history, conceived primordially as evolution, the revolutionary generation foregrounded rupture. Whether we call this "revolution" or, more prudently, "regeneration," the insistence on the novelty of the times is one of the leitmotifs in all of these writings. From the beginning, one of the main goals of these publications would be to construct a new history, both in terms of its "periodization" and of its actors: "one of the topics we will explore most carefully will be the historical recapitulation of everything that has happened in Spain since the memorable day of October 31, when our foolish oppressors signaled the start of this political revolution, until we pick up the thread of present events."[598]

Revolution, before being a program, was a rupture that launched a new historical moment. Hence the immediate publication of articles narrating the "present revolution." True, the chronicle of these events was recorded in traditional language: as the narration of heroic deeds so that posterity would remember the exploits of the present generation. However, it was also much more than that: it was an explanation *per causa* of the extraordinary events of the age, destined, by the continual repetition of the explanatory model, to become a canonical version of the nation's history. The same phenomenon would be repeated in America from 1810 onward to legitimize the ongoing revolutionary process.[599] What all these publications said, above all, was that the history of the revolution was understood as rupture, even though the content of the new times varied as the revolutionary process progressed.

---

597 "Discurso sobre el modo de formarse la opinión pública," *El Espectador Sevillano*, Mexico, 110.

598 "Prospecto," *Semanario Patriótico*, Madrid, late August 1808, 4.

599 For example, the *Diario Político de Santa Fe de Bogotá*, which appeared from October 1810 to February 1811, devoted several issues to recording the history of the revolution in Bogotá in each of its episodes.

In the model adopted by Quintana's group, the symbolic date of this rupture varied. We have seen references to the date of October 31, 1807, which corresponds to the publication of Charles IV's decree announcing the arrest of the Prince of Asturias, accused before the nation of conspiring to dethrone him. The "Relación de los principales sucesos ocurridos en Madrid y en las provincias de España desde el 31 de octubre de 1807 hasta el 1 de septiembre de 1808" ("Narrative of the Principal Events Occurring in Madrid and the Provinces of Spain from October 31, 1807 to September 1, 1808")—which the article calls the "first period of the Spanish revolution,"[600]—repeats the same date, now clearly explaining what it symbolized: the first appearance on the stage of public opinion battling against arbitrary power. "The struggle was between public opinion, which held the accused to be innocent, and the absolute power of the Queen and her favorite, which sought to incriminate them."[601]

Public opinion triumphed and the Council of Castile acquitted the accused of conspiracy. In other places, the revolution's foundational moment was established as March 1808—that is, the mutiny of Aranjuez, which overthrew the favorite and forced the king to cede the crown to the Prince of Asturias. Here, the people was manifesting itself directly in action and imposing its will by placing the idolized prince on the throne.

The people thus began to emerge as an actor in the history of the nation, eventually becoming its protagonist during the uprising against the invader, thanks to which it regained its sovereignty. This was a role of which it was still largely unaware, but of which its pedagogues constantly sought to remind it: "Great and generous people! Admire the unexpected and rapid series of events that have brought you to the happy moment of regaining your sovereignty: enjoy it with temperance; but do not allow yourself to be deprived of it again."[602]

---

600 *Semanario Patriótico*, Madrid, no. XII, November 17, 1808, 201 and the following pages.

601 Ibid., no. XIII, November 24, 1808, 227.

602 "Los tres días de Madrid: Conclusión," *Semanario Patriótico*, Madrid, no. 5, September 29, 1808, 81.

The perception of time changed radically with the nation's awakening from the slumber in which it had been plunged.[603] The present, like a watershed, reorganized history entirely: it looked to the past to explain the lethargy and evils of despotic times (thus, the "ancien régime" of later writings made its appearance) and to the future to paint the coming era in idyllic, utopian colors.

Both reconstructions, of the past and of the future, were based on a redefinition of the notion of "*patria*" (homeland):

> The word *Patria* had a narrower meaning among the ancients than the one commonly given to it by the moderns. By it we designate the birthplace of one or many individuals: they called *Patria* the state or society to which they belonged, and whose laws ensured to them liberty and well-being.[604]

Appealing to the authority of classical antiquity, the homeland was presented as a free community living under laws that ensured freedom, to the extent that

> where there were no laws aimed at the general interest [...] where all wills, all intentions, and all efforts, instead of moving toward a center, were enslaved to the will of one [...] there was certainly a country, a people, a gathering of men; but there was no *Patria*.[605]

The true homeland, then, stemmed from a union of wills, not from a mere geographical or historical inheritance. The role of the will, so important to the nation according to the French Revolution, now appears in the foreground, with its egalitarian corollaries. The true homeland is "a tender mother who loves all her children equally"; that is why she sees to it that they are "equal before the law," have access to the same positions,

603 See ibid.

604 *Semanario Patriótico*, Madrid, no. III, September 15, 1808, 47.

605 Ibid.

and enjoy "well-being."[606] The new homeland implies a radical sovereignty to which all authorities are subordinated:

> The *Patria*, in short, they said, is a superior power, as old as societies, founded on nature and order; she subjects to her laws those who command just as much as to those who obey: a power superior to all those that she herself establishes in her bosom, be they Archons, Ephors, consuls, or kings.[607]

Classical antiquity was more than a rhetorical device with which to better defend these new principles: it was also a return to a notion of politics conceived as active and voluntary participation in the life of the *polis*.

A new homeland came with new virtues. The sublime passion of patriotism was defined as the source from which sprung all civic virtues: that is, favoring "the public interest over the individual," "terrible hatred of all tyranny," "courage and daring" to defend independence. Many of these virtues were compatible with common values, but it is clear that the new notion of homeland was very different from that conceived as a compendium of traditional values, as expressed, for example, by a Yucatecan woman addressing her children:

> Yes, my children, the homeland, the amiable homeland, is no other than the sweet union that binds one citizen to another through the indissoluble ties of a common soil, a common language, laws peculiar to them, an immaculate religion, one government, one king, one body, one spirit, one faith, one hope, one charity, one baptism and one God, the universal father of all."[608]

---

606 Ibid.

607 Ibid., 48.

608 "Copia de una carta que la viuda del Sr. Coronel Don Ignacio Peón, Doña María Josefa Maldonado, escribió a sus hijos Don Alonso y Don Felipe, que sirven en el regimiento de Vitoria, desde la ciudad de Mérida, capital de Yucatán," *Diario de México* XI, no. 1450, September 10, 1809, 298.

Logically enough, the new notion of homeland implied that it did not yet exist, although the patriotism that would serve to build it was already being reborn. Hence, the goal that the authorities of this heroic age had set themselves was "the founding of a *Homeland*,"[609] for its absence had brought about the ruin of the monarchy.

All these definitions provided a logical explanation of the crisis and the military disaster, but since it was somewhat difficult to get the readers, full as they were of the patriotic enthusiasm of those days and the pride of being Spanish, to accept that Spain had never been a homeland, it was necessary to corroborate this explanation with a new vision of the past.

The periodization used for this was, at first, not very different from that of the historical constitutionalists, perhaps so as not to frighten readers with excessive novelty. The revolutionary writers agreed with their predecessors in locating the beginning of Spanish misfortunes in the disappearance of the different kingdoms' liberties: "That flame was extinguished when Villalar saw Padilla expire in unworthy torture: in Aragon when Lanuza was beheaded in Zaragoza: in Catalonia when Pablo Claris died."[610]

The men and symbolic images employed by Quintana in his patriotic poems were, as might be expected, the same ones used by the newspapers.[611]

From this disastrous time onward, the history of Spain had been nothing but suffering and injustice: "our fathers succumbed in the glorious struggle to defend their privileges and liberties and bequeathed

---

609 Ibid., 51.

610 Ibid., 49. In other articles, the end of Aragon's freedom is even located in its union with Castile under the Catholic monarchs. See "Carta sobre la antigua Constitución del Reyno de Aragón," an article published by "an Aragonese patriot" in *Semanario Patriótico*, Madrid, no. X, November 3, 1808, 166 and the following pages.

611 Moreover, the *Semanario Patriótico* (Madrid, no. X, November 3, 1808, 184) announced the publication of these poems: odes to the vaccine, to Juan Padilla, "the defender and martyr of Castilian freedom," to the "Pantheon of the Escorial."

us monstrous arbitrariness [...] three centuries of suffering on the one hand, and of usurpations and injustices on the other."[612]

These "three centuries of despotism," so important to the legitimization of American independence, came into being at this time to designate the era of despotism. Since then, "arbitrary power" had reigned—the origin of all evils both in France and in Spain. That there might be no doubt as to the different names this omnipresent enemy might assume, the writer added: "absolute power, arbitrary power, tyranny, despotism, are all one and the same thing."[613]

The rejection of absolutism was total and, in order to strip it of the legitimacy it had enjoyed among a considerable segment of the enlightened elites, it was identified with arbitrary power (the opposite of justice, the supreme attribute of traditional power), with tyranny (that is, a power illegitimate in its origin), and with despotism (a power illegitimate in its exercise). Absolutism usurped the rights of society and could not be justified by anything, whether conquest, an ancient concession on the part of society, or centuries of peaceful possession.[614]

However, alongside this explanation, which could be called institutional, there was another one, of a cultural and moral nature, which was intimately connected to the first; by virtue of its suggestive power, it was undoubtedly just as important. This explanation painted a dualistic picture of the opposition between the evils and vices of the ancien régime and the happy state to which society would gain access once the homeland was built. The starting point of this analysis, which was strongly inspired by Montesquieu,[615] was the connection existing between the type of government and the public spirit of nations: "Each kind of government produces in the general mass of citizens certain habits, certain

---

612 *Semanario Patriótico*, Madrid, no. IX, October 27, 1808, 149–58.

613 *Semanario Patriótico*, Madrid, no. IX, October 27, 1808, 149–50.

614 See ibid.

615 His theory of climates was rejected, however. See "Sobre el espíritu público de las naciones," *El Espectador Sevillano*, Mexico, 33. For the correspondence between the Mexican and Spanish editions, see supra, note 589.

modes of thought, certain needs and affections, which compose the public spirit of the nation."[616]

The corruption of the Spanish public spirit was due not only to the "establishment of arbitrary power," but also to "the immense accumulation of wealth, caused by the discovery and conquest of America."[617] This reflection was premised on the corrupting effects of the Conquest and the riches so abruptly gained. To support it, both ancient and modern references were employed. This condemnation of the Conquest of America did not choose the terrain of indigenous rights—that of the just titles of the Conquest, as they were discussed in Castile in the sixteenth century—but focused on the modalities of the undertaking and its effects on Spain:

> The discovery of America, which in a century of Enlightenment and under a liberal administration would have furnished us with commercial colonies to enliven and enrich the manufactures and agriculture of the nation, served us for nothing but to acquire heaps of gold that we scarcely knew what to do with.[618]

The possession of colonies was not only legitimate but beneficial, provided that their fruits were well employed. True, there is a paragraph that presented these evils as a punishment for the "nation that enriches itself through the ruin of other states," but the central argument is still the nefarious effect of ill-gotten wealth. Wealth in itself is not corrupting, provided it comes from commerce and industry, as demonstrated by the example of the United States, "an opulent and virtuous people," and that of England "as famous for its riches as for the decency of its customs." This was not what happened in Spain: rather, the sudden wealth perverted customs.

---

616 Ibid.

617 "Sobre la reforma de las costumbres," *El Espectador Sevillano*, Mexico, 45.

618 Ibid., 49.

> The government and those who participated in its favors enriched themselves in an enormously unequal manner over the mass of the nation; the only ones who achieved opulence were those whose thirst for gold tore them from their homeland to go in search of it amid the devastation of Mexico and Peru.[619]

If the customs of Rome and Greece, which were free states with a great patriotic spirit, were corrupted by the riches obtained in conquests and lost their liberty to them, what would not happen to Spain which, at the same time, was seeing the establishment of a despotic government? Hence, too, the censure of Habsburg foreign policy and the subjugation of Italy and the Netherlands as futile undertakings "in which we uselessly shed the most precious portion of our blood."[620]

Subjected to such powerful causes, it was no surprise that the public spirit of the Spaniards should have declined over three centuries. The most curious thing for the writers was that, despite all this, they should have retained, "in the midst of corruption, their ancient love of virtues and the primitive honesty of their character." A case of *Captatio benevolentiae*,[621] given the impossibility of fitting the reality to the explanation, this strange phenomenon was explained, without much conviction, by the limited intermixing of Spaniards with foreign nations.[622]

Whatever the reason for the preservation of certain virtues, the general explanation continued to be the correlation between public and private virtues, on the one hand, and the type of political regime, on the other. The reflection on the virtues proper to each regime was, to a certain extent, classic and followed Montesquieu very closely. Democracy produces in every citizen a fervent love of country and leads him

---

619 Ibid.

620 Ibid., 53. See also, "La España necesita de un remedio general y poderoso," *Semanario Patriótico*, Seville, no. XXIV, July 6, 1809, 153–54.

621 *Captatio benevolentiae* ("winning of goodwill") is a rhetorical strategy aimed at gaining the sympathy of the audience or readership.—Trans.

622 "Sobre la reforma de las costumbres," *El Espectador Sevillano*, Mexico, 49–50.

to sacrifice himself for the glory of his city. Belonging to the nobility gives lords "an appearance of reserve and dignity" that earns them the respect of the people. "Temperate monarchy" shows the latter's most brilliant aspect and is based on "the great principle of honor, which is nothing else but the awareness of one's own merit."[623] This homage, however, was quite formal, and the preference that the author claimed to express for the monarchy was, in fact, an apology for its constitutional variety, and even more than that, for representative regimes, whatever form they might take. The virtues and advantages attributed to the latter appeared as a summary of those belonging to all the others and made it an ideal form of government:

> Honor, public virtues, the respectful audacity with which representatives oppose the unjust desires of the sovereign [...], the general love of useful talents, of true patriots, of domestic virtues, without which there are no civil virtues. The citizen who participates in legislation by means of elections and by public opinion, while paying his magistrates the deference due them, also knows how to show them that he is a part of the greater whole, and that his opinion has a right to be heeded.[624]

In contrast to this paragon of good qualities, despotism annihilated all the moral powers of man, and domestic virtues, too, decayed as a consequence of the disappearance of public ones.[625] If despotism was odious, this was not only because it deprived society of its rights, but also because it debased men. Servility figures prominently in the extremely sinister description that is given of its corrupting effects:

623 Ibid., 35.

624 Ibid., 35.

625 "El espíritu público, padre de las virtudes políticas, es también el origen de las virtudes domésticas," "Sobre la reforma de las costumbres," *El Espectador Sevillano*, Mexico, 55.

> Arbitrary power, erected on the ruins of our Cortes, by destroying in Spain all the intermediate powers between the king and the people and annihilating any kind of representation, reduced the Spaniards to the necessity of seeking fortune solely in the favor of the prince or his ministers.[626]

The indignation at "the baseness of soul and the complete denial of the manly character" is strenuous and certainly reflects memories of Godoy's favoritism: servility, the "spineless ambition of slaves," flattery, bribery, avoidance of public burdens.[627] Curiously, clientelism, which would later become one of the most marked features of politics in Hispanic countries, and, in general, all the phenomena linked to a kind of politics based on personal ties, appear as a consequence of despotism and destined to disappear with it: "How long will Spain see perpetuated this yearning for protection, this urge to deliver itself up to chains, this love of vain distinctions, this desire to be freed from laws and public burdens by the influence and power of a patron?"[628]

The description of the private vices caused by the degeneration of public virtues seems more artificial, as does the proposed remedy. By a kind of mathematical deduction, since these vices were a consequence of despotism, abolishing it would restore domestic virtues. Liberty and love of country would purge men of whims and vanity, would make them less susceptible to amorous dalliances, incite them to become fathers and encourage marriage, "the safeguard of morals." Respect for other people's property would prevent adultery, "a crime that is the most general source of corruption." Children would then obey their fathers and respect their mothers. Civil liberty would discourage the corruption of public employees, private thefts, slander, the influence of fashion, and extravagant customs.[629]

---

626 Ibid., 45.

627 See, for example, *Semanario Patriótico*, Seville, no. XVIII, May 25, 1809, 62–63.

628 "Sobre la reforma de las costumbres," *El Espectador Sevillano*, Mexico, 55.

629 Ibid., 55–59.

Since these equations were, however, visibly too simple, other variables were added. First and foremost, there was public education, because "it is impossible for a nation ignorant of its duties and rights to be virtuous;" but material factors—"subsistence"—were also considered, since poverty is a cause of vice. Yet even in this case, moral arguments predominated. The excessive inequality between rich and poor led to the conscience of the latter "[being bought] with the money of the former."[630] The idea was not to eliminate inequality, for "inequality of property [arises] from inequality of character and talent," and "to attempt to abolish it would be the same as annihilating property rights."[631] It was necessary, however, to fight the poverty that led parents "to incite their sons to steal and give their daughters up to prostitution." A fair distribution of taxes and economic reforms was required: the net product of the land and luxury goods should be taxed; customhouses should be banished to the borders of the monarchy; "proletarians" should be exempted from taxation. This last measure would allow day laborers to support their families with their work, and—in an unacknowledged quote of the *poule-au-pot* formula attributed to Henry IV of France—would enable "the most unhappy laborer to cook a hen in his pot every Sunday."[632]

Curiously, none of these articles, full as they were of references to the virtues and to public or private morality, made the slightest reference to religion, and it is not clear what its future place could be in a society designed according to the principles of a natural right valid for all peoples, regardless of faith: a natural right constructed *etsi Deus non daretur*,[633] as if God did not exist. Religion was a topic conspicuously absent from all these issues, with one isolated but significant exception: when Madrid, in November 1808, was about to succumb to Napoleon's

630 Ibid., 63.

631 Ibid., 64.

632 Ibid., 67.

633 According to Grotius's classical expression in *De jure belli ac pacis*.

troops, the people were called "to defend Religion and the Homeland," a clear sign of this invocation's function as a rallying cry.[634]

This silence on religion is thunderous if we consider its universal presence, not only in society but even in the traditional definition of Hispanic identity. Compared to the centrality of religious themes and language in the vast majority of the period's writings,[635] this feature alone shows how particular these men were, and what a minority they represented. Their personal beliefs were far removed from those of the larger mass of the population. Quintana was undoubtedly an agnostic; Blanco White, at the time, was not only anticlerical but deeply hostile to Catholicism;[636] and almost all of them certainly considered religion to be one of the main obstacles to the building of the new society. Their silence regarding this topic was part of their civic pedagogy: they considered, as they later would in the Cortes, that people were not yet prepared to address this subject. We find the same situation at this time on the other side of the Atlantic. When Mariano Moreno, one of the most radical among the Buenos Aires revolutionaries, published his translation of Rousseau's *Social Contract* in 1810, he suppressed all the passages on Christianity and civil religion.[637] The virtues, so constantly invoked, had been secularized; now they are correlated, not with religion but with the law: "there are no good laws without virtues; but there can be no virtues where there are no good laws."[638] Since the law had to emerge from society, the focus of these groups' action, for the time being, was politics.

---

634 *Semanario Patriótico*, Madrid, no. XIV, December 1, 1808, 3.

635 See "History and Religion" in chapter V.

636 See Pons 1990, vol. I.

637 Concerning this edition, see Furlong 1950, vol. III, 271–79.

638 "Sobre la reforma de las costumbres," *El Espectador Sevillano*, Mexico, 69.

## An Original Political Moment

For this reason, politics occupied the foreground in their reflections: this was the sphere that would eventually transform society and mindsets. Economic and social thought played a very limited, indeed a subordinate, role. The revolution was, first and foremost, political, in the strongest sense of the word: that which concerned the principles that should organize society, the authorities that should govern it, and the ends to be attained.

The Hispanic revolutionaries fully belong within the great revolutionary era, but their situation, compared to that of their French predecessors, was peculiar. What had to be destroyed was clear: the ancien régime, identified with despotism and ignorance. The ultimate goal was equally discernible: a society of free men, from which the evils currently afflicting it would have disappeared. However, the path ahead was less clear. There was no doubt about some of the steps involved: convening the national representation—Cortes that were, in fact, a national assembly—to restore the nation's prerogatives, drawing up a constitution that might include both the division of powers and the rights of man and of the citizen, destroying the ancien régime by means of adequate legislation, and so forth. At the same time, however, many of these steps, so clear in theory, were less so in practice: the shadow of the French Revolution, at once the central model for the revolutionary process and an example to be avoided because of its deviations, hung over them constantly and explicitly: "Let the French Revolution be to us as the wreckage of ships broken up in the shallows, which teaches the navigator to steer clear of dangerous reefs, but does not distract him from his journey."[639]

The Spanish revolutionaries had to carry out two different tasks at the same time: on the one hand, they had to achieve the revolution and, on the other, prevent it from following in the footsteps of the French one. We might say that their situation was similar, on the one hand, to that of the French revolutionaries in 1788–89 as they struggled to impose the

639 *Semanario Patriótico*, Madrid, no. X, November 3, 1808, 163 and the following pages.

sovereignty of the nation in both ideas and actual fact; and, on the other, to that of the generation of the Thermidorian Republic, pondering, like Benjamin Constant, on how to build a regime founded on the principles of the revolution, yet stable and respectful of law and liberty.[640]

This double goal gave rise to many of the revolutionary group's ambiguities and its double-faced, Janus-like nature. Given their radical principles, the group's members were revolutionaries ("Jacobins," as their adversaries called them). But their constant concern with building a representative regime certainly made them moderates, and in fact, the first modern constitutionalists to embody their aims in a constitution and, for a time, in actual reality. Hence their European importance and lasting influence in Portugal, Italy, France itself, and even faraway Russia.[641] Hence also the contradictions between their moderate intentions and their radical stance in the face of society's resistance to their enterprise. Their originality lay less in the sources and authors that inspired them[642] than in the peculiar way they combined these sources in the service of their double purpose: to impose the revolutionary imaginary and principles while, at the same time, conceiving and constructing a viable political system.[643]

---

640 On this French generation and its questions, see Furet 1988, 176–79. Although there is no absolute certainty as to their direct knowledge of Constant, it is very likely, given the topics they had in common, that the editors of these periodicals were familiar with Constant's writings of the period: *De la force du gouvernement actuel de la France et de la nécessité de s'y rallier*, 1796, *Des réactions politiques* and *Des effets de la Terreur*, 1797.

641 On the influence of the Cádiz Constitution in Europe, see "La Constitución de 1812," *Revista de Estudios Políticos*, Madrid, no. 126, commemorative issue, November–December 1962. In France, several translations of the constitution were made during the Restoration.

642 Essentially, the political writers of the eighteenth century—Locke, Montesquieu, Rousseau—and for economics, Adam Smith, with an added assortment of texts from and about the French Revolution. See, for example, for the sources of the *Semanario Patriótico* in Seville, Pons 1990, chapter II.

643 Although these two purposes are constantly interconnected, the *Semanario Patriótico* focused more on the first, and *El Espectador Sevillano* more on the second.

We have already explained how, to attain the first of these ends, it was necessary to make the public aware of the deplorable state in which the country found itself and to provide a convincing explanation of the source of its ills in order to convince readers of the need for radical reform.

The critical state in which the monarchy found itself did not, at first sight, require lengthy descriptions: the king was a prisoner; the country had been invaded and its existence threatened; war was everywhere; political power was uncertain and scattered. However, though the ills were visible to all the political groups of the time, differences arose in the analysis of the causes and, consequently, in the remedies proposed. Almost everyone agreed that bad government during the Godoy period was greatly to blame, but this explanation was not enough. Quite a few invoked moral causes pertaining to the traditional mental universe: the corruption of ancestral customs or the progress of impiety. Others—the historical constitutionalists—used a political terminology to attribute bad government to neglect of the old legislation. Our editors, as we have already seen, blamed despotism and the resulting corruption of the public mind.

The second goal—to build a political system combining freedom with a stable government—was much more difficult to achieve and occupied an increasingly important place in their reflections. In the search for this system, history did not provide solutions, only experience. Against those in favor of restoring the old Spanish legislation, they argued that, if it "has been violated for two consecutive centuries, it must have contained some principle of destruction."[644] It was necessary to start from other bases: "Following the general and primordial principles of natural law, let us establish society, if not on the bases that it has had in other ages, then on those that it should have had in all ages."[645]

Well supported by these universal principles, reflection must proceed in the manner of a "political arithmetic." Thus, many articles were entitled "Political Problem" in the mathematical sense of the word, and would address, for example,

---

644 "Sobre el Espíritu público de las naciones," *El Espectador Sevillano*, Mexico , 40.

645 Ibid., 41.

> the most important and most difficult problem of politics: one that, expressed in simple terms, may be posed in this manner: *How can the power of he who exercises sovereignty be balanced in such a way that taking away his power to injure a nation does not diminish his power to govern it?*[646] [emphasis in the original]

The construction of the political system was, therefore, a question of method, of reasoning based on indisputable premises. The general admiration for science meant that political problems were seen as belonging to a new category of the same, "the moral and political sciences," ignorance of which suited the despots and explained the apathy in which the population was plunged.[647] This political arithmetic, very much like that of Benjamin Constant, came from two sources: principles on the one hand,[648] and historical experience on the other. The importance of reasoning from history, so essential in both the Scottish Enlightenment and Constant, was also one of the fundamental pillars of the Spanish revolutionaries' argumentation.[649] This history was, of course, the history of Spain, but unlike the French Thermidorians, the Spanish revolutionaries, in their construction of the free government, could not yet refer to their own experience and could only be guided by the experiences of others; hence the sometimes very bookish nature of their reflections.

Among these experiences, two were key: that of classical antiquity, in keeping with these men's learned education and their favorite political authors; and, above all, that of revolutionary France. The presence of the latter was predominant and almost obsessive. In addition to the

646 *Semanario Patriótico*, Seville, no. XXVIII, July 3, 1809, 220.

647 See "Sobre la reforma de las costumbres," *El Espectador Sevillano*, Mexico, 60. Here, as in many other places, we find the implicit reference to France and its "Académie des Sciences morales et politiques."

648 In the latter period of their publications, they also distinguish, much as Constant did (*Des réactions politiques…*, chapter VIII), "the local and adventitious causes that modify the influence of the main ones" (ibid., 95).

649 On this subject, see Marcel Gauchet, "Constant," in Furet and Ozouf 1988, 952.

articles explicitly intended to analyze it,[650] we find countless references to it in many others. This is not to say that the editors had unbounded admiration for the French political regimes of the revolutionary era. On the contrary, their criticisms were constant, and they felt more sympathy for the English political system. However, this admiration had its limits. English civil liberties, balance of powers, and stability were admired, but not the principles on which they were founded. Above all, it would seem that the editors saw the English system as inaccessible. The duration and influence of absolutism were such that for them a break with the past was indispensable, and in this regard, the only existing experience was that of the French Revolution. Spain's cultural and political kinship with the neighboring country led the Spanish revolutionaries, willy-nilly, along the same paths: toward the invention of a new political system. France, even more than classical antiquity, played the role of a laboratory in which solutions to problems very similar to Spain's had been tried out, sometimes with success, and many other times, very mistakenly. In this sense, it was the only country that could provide them with real experience. Which is why their project was deeply dependent on the French one while being, at the same time, very original.

In the social imaginary as well as the basic principles that were to support the political system, identification with France was total: the nation is one and indivisible, and sovereignty resides in it; its elemental components are the individuals, united by voluntary association; the law is the expression of the general will; only individuals can be represented, not estates, bodies, or provinces; these individuals have equal rights and enjoy, alongside civil liberty and property, inalienable rights.

This list of principles, tirelessly repeated until they became self-evident truths, shows the distance separating the English model from these men's political projects. We are plainly in the universe of the French Revolution, and they were so well aware of this that part of their

---

650 See, for example, in the *Semanario Patriótico*: "De la ilustración francesa bajo el imperio de Bonaparte," no. VI, October 6, 1808; the review of *The Revolutionary Plutarch*, no. X, November 3, 1808; "De los nombres libertad e igualdad," nos. XVIII and XIX, May 25 and June 6, 1809.

pedagogy consisted of showing that liberty and equality, considered central principles of the new imaginary, did not necessarily lead to the French excesses:

> The French Revolution invoked them from its first beginnings and devoted them to establishing the primitive rights of man; but the frightful upheavals that accompanied this political explosion, the horrors that followed upon it, and the excesses carried out in the name of *liberty* and *equality* caused the discredit of the righteous principles they represented in their origin.[651]

Faced with the need to defend "these words unjustly termed revolutionary," they had to carefully explain that liberty did not mean disorder, nor did equality mean anarchy. Liberty was not debauchery: "*Political freedom* consists in a nation being subject only to the laws which it has willingly recognized. This *general freedom* lives only at the cost of the freedom of each individual."[652]

The first freedom, then, was that of the nation, of the collectivity constructed (the reference to Locke was explicit in other articles) by the ceding of a part of each citizen's freedom. To speak of this liberty was as much as to speak of free government, the opposite of absolutism, which had made "of the monarch an invisible divinity"; it was to speak[653] of the homeland as it was defined above, and of all the virtues it implied: "What zeal, what anxious care in a free government! Attention to the public interest occupies even the humblest individual."[654]

Rightly understood, equality was not the total equality of material conditions, as some people conceived it during the French Revolution: "The blood has yet to dry that we saw flow in the attempt to establish

---

651 "De los nombres libertad e igualdad," *Semanario Patriótico*, Seville, no. XVIII, May 25, 1809, 60.

652 Ibid., 62.

653 "La libertad política no se opone a la monarquía," ibid., no. XIX, June 1, 1809, 77.

654 Ibid., 63.

that absolute equality that flatters the unfortunate, makes the powerful tremble, and that philosophers regard as impossible"[655]

The memories of the Reign of Terror were still vivid and, while acknowledging that excessive inequality stirred up "the unquenched war between the class that has nothing and the one that enjoys everything,"[656] the Spanish revolutionaries used this argument to convince the privileged classes of the need to establish civil equality and the destitute of the need to "remain in the place that providence" had assigned them so that everyone might enjoy the same rights. Rights to the "preservation of acquired property, and the ability to increase it according to the natural dispositions, fortune, and industry of each individual";[657] to equality before the courts, to the same rewards and punishments,[658] to the same respect, and to the same opportunities in the career of honors.[659] General freedom was embodied in individual freedoms.

The moderate nature of these aims was clear, but less so were the reasons why these "primitive rights of man" should have led, in France, to those excesses that the paper had criticized so forcefully. The only explanation given for this slide was "the character of the two nations. The Frenchman is rash and prone to extremes [...] the Spaniard moderate and circumspect."

This explanation, though to be found in many other places, is conceptually very weak: in much the same way, the French would soon be attributing the political instability of nineteenth-century Spain to the "exalted and ardent" character of the Spaniards. The editors of the newspapers knew this, in fact, and to this character-based explanation they would add the need to set limits to those principles—limits that could only be those of "reason." It was necessary, however, to define where this reason was to be found and by what means it expressed itself. For

655 Ibid.,124.

656 Ibid.

657 Ibid., 127.

658 Ibid., 128.

659 Ibid., 129.

them the answer was clear: "The dictates of human reason expressed by the opinion of the peoples have an irresistible power."[660] The primacy of opinion, however, could not suffice either given that its nature, beyond the suggestiveness of the term, raised very diverse problems that could not be dissociated from the political regime adopted. For this reason, the Spanish revolutionaries' enterprise of political invention would be founded on two different but closely linked solutions: representative government and the reign of public opinion.

## The Defense of the Representative Regime

Representative government was, for our editors, the great discovery of modern times and corresponded to an advanced stage of human history, one in which it was necessary to "secure liberty and temper the power of kings [...] in monarchies extending over vast territories."[661] The debate about the political regime—whether monarchy or republic—was never explicitly addressed, no doubt because they adhered very firmly to the common feeling regarding the impossibility of a republican regime in a vast state.

The representative regime was a great discovery because it put an end to arbitrary power thanks to the manifestation of the national will, while at the same time making it possible to avoid democracy, understood as direct democracy: "The essence of representative government consists in the nation expressing its will only through the organ of its deputies: The essence of democratic government lies in the nation remaining assembled and making laws on its own."[662]

---

660 "La libertad política no se opone a la Monarquía," in ibid., no. XIX, June 1, 1809, 73.

661 "Discurso sobre los gobiernos representativos," *El Espectador Sevillano*, Mexico, 4.

662 *El Espectador Sevillano*, Seville, no. 84, December 24, 1809, 331.

The representative regime made it possible to reconcile the radical sovereignty of the people with the exercise of power by a few: "The name of representation makes it clear that not everyone can have a direct share in public affairs; in what way they can have it indirectly will be addressed in another discourse."[663]

The representative system had the enormous advantage of preventing any slide into democracy, which was seen as impossible in large states because of its dangers. Here, too, the example of revolutionary France was conclusive:

> The spirit of republicanism took possession of every mind, and in the century of greatest enlightenment, the greatest political absurdity in living memory was undertaken—namely, the establishment of democracy in a nation so vast, so populous, so corrupt.[664]

The terms *republic* and *democracy* are practically interchangeable here, and refer to something very dangerous for freedom, since democracy leads first to anarchy, then to a new despotism, as the case of France continues to show:

> all the evils of France arose from the fact that the constituent assembly, while feigning to organize a representative regime, actually formed a republican government [...]. Pure democracy took the place of the throne; the most terrible convulsions were followed by political chaos, and the French people, shortly tiring of the abuse of liberty, threw itself at the feet of the first tyrant who wished to oppress it without causing a stir, and purchased tranquility at the expense of its independence.[665]

The existence of a republic with a representative regime that respected freedom was never explicitly taken into account, and the positive experience of

---

663 *Semanario Patriótico,* Seville, no. XXV, July 13, 1809, 177.

664 "Qüestión III [sobre las Cortes]...," in *El Espectador Sevillano,* Mexico, 139–40.

665 *El Espectador Sevillano,* Seville, no. 84, December 24, 1809, 330.

the United States went unanalyzed, perhaps because of its remoteness and because it was a new country. Whatever the other reasons for not addressing the question of the republic, the most important was undoubtedly that merely to raise this possibility in the climate of monarchical exaltation prevailing at the time would have appeared sacrilegious.

However, given the type of arguments and language used, this reflection on representative government could lead with no great difficulty to substituting a republic for the monarchy and another type of executive power for the king. To attribute radical sovereignty to the nation as the only source of legitimacy explicitly made the king a magistrate; this led implicitly to the possibility of replacing him with another. "Sovereignty is one and indivisible in its essence; and yet, its different functions must be performed by different magistrates."[666]

Monarchy was accepted more through social inertia than the exigencies of theory. The rejection of any legitimacy of a historical kind enabled the transition to a republican regime. This is what the Spanish Americans would do a few years later when, based on the same principles, they would find the path of historical legitimacy closed to them by independence. The transition would be all the easier since the virtues that were being praised as proper to a liberal monarchy were rather of the republican kind.

Indeed, when reconciling demands that until then had seemed contradictory was also taken as a specific quality of the representative regime, the balance was unstable. The representative system, they said, made it possible to reconcile the liberty and civic virtues of the ancient republics—Greece and Rome—with the demands of governing the vast modern states. In the former, the citizens participated, physically and directly, in the making of laws and the government of the city. In the latter, the people's election of its representatives led to the same result: the citizens' participation in public life. The election of representatives enables the constitution of "a corporation which plays the role of a people" and performs the functions that fell to the people in the ancient republics: the making of laws by the collectivity—the first freedom of all—and the control of the government, always tempted to abuse its power.

666 "Sobre el espíritu público de las naciones," *El Espectador Sevillano*, Mexico, 9.

As far as virtues were concerned, and if we consider the comparison (still unpublished at the time) made by Constant between the freedom of the ancients and that of the moderns,[667] we could say that the Spanish revolutionaries, though coinciding with him as to this distinction, were inclined to see the representative regime as a synthesis of the virtues of both. So great, in fact, was the strength that they attributed to the construction of a symbolic people by means of representation that they tended to think that modern representative regimes would possess the virtues that classical political literature attributed to the ancient democratic ones: "the first effect of the spirit of liberty inspired by liberal governments is the union of all wills toward the objects of common usefulness and the good of the homeland."[668]

We see, as it were, a swing of the pendulum between, on the one hand, a tendency to extol the virtues and heroic examples of antiquity, which demanded active and continuous participation by all citizens in public affairs and seemed to tip the balance toward a republican regime and, on the other, the need, imposed by the dimensions of the state and the passions of men, to reserve active participation in politics to a few, a tendency that seemed to favor a monarchical regime. This unstable equilibrium explains why some regions of Spanish America—Caracas and Buenos Aires above all—oscillated between the republican enthusiasm of the early days of independence and the monarchical temptation of a second phase, when the goal was now to stabilize the political system.

In 1809, this problem had yet to arise. The representative regime that needed building was, therefore, that of a constitutional monarchy in which national representation might counterbalance the power of the king and his ministers. Of all the qualities attributed to the representative regime, this was undoubtedly the most important, since the first enemy to be fought was absolutism, despotic government, "arbitrary power." National representation was the most powerful check on the abuse of power, whether it arose from historical circumstances—the corruption of the public spirit brought about by the conquest of

667 See Constant 1980.

668 "Sobre el espíritu público de las naciones," *El Espectador Sevillano*, Mexico, 35.

America—or from permanent tendencies in human nature: those who wield power are prone to abuse it.

This goal determined how the Spanish revolutionaries analyzed the powers and composition of the national representation. Very much in the manner of Montesquieu, it was considered that "every authority must suffer the supervision of others and be modified by their action."[669] The division of powers in order to ensure liberty had already become a political cliché: "The division of these different powers constitutes liberty: their union tyranny."[670]

The scrutiny of the respective powers of the king and the national representation was extremely detailed and based as much on principles as on the functions that each was called upon to perform. Principles dictated that lawmaking should be the responsibility of national representatives, since, as we have already said, a politically free collectivity can be recognized precisely by the fact that it obeys only the laws that it has given itself. "The power to make laws is the sovereign faculty par excellence: because expressly or implicitly it contains in itself the general will of the whole republic."[671]

The king, or the executive, was in charge of governing: enforcing the laws, directing the administration of the state, managing public affairs. Functional logic reinforced this distribution of tasks. Using analogies drawn from physics, it was emphasized that the work of legislating and that of governing operate to different rhythms. "A law is an abstract maxim, and as such, it is subject to the examination and discussion required by general truths before they can be established."[672]

The drafting of a law requires reflection, discussion, deliberation by many so that the best solution may emerge from the diversity of perspectives. Governing, on the contrary, demands quick decisions, which can only be taken by a few or by a single person. "How different from

669 "Discurso sobre los gobiernos representativos," *El Espectador Sevillano*, Mexico, 10.

670 Ibid., 11.

671 Ibid., 10.

672 Ibid., 14.

the slow and distrustful pace of the legislators must be the swift and vehement movement of the government."[673]

However, this clear division of functions did not lead them to reject any intervention by the king in the work of legislation. The one who governed should also be able to suggest legislative projects to the national representation, since "no one can better know the nation's needs than the agents of the executive power." The reference to the French experience was explicit: "The fact that it deprived the monarch of this right was one of the greatest defects of the French Constitution of 1789."[674] To safeguard the representative regime, it was necessary for the king to have real powers. In the same line of thinking, it was also concluded that, for the same reasons, the king should have right of veto over laws he deemed harmful. This was not a mere technical provision, but a means to introduce public opinion into the representative system as a regulating force. The royal veto served to:

> inform the nation that there is discord between the opinion of the prince and that of the representation on a certain matter of public usefulness. This discord [...] will give rise to discussions in which, the press having its due freedom, the reasons for each opinion can be made known. The impartial public will judge, and universal opinion [...] will have occasion to form itself.[675]

This veto, however, must be temporary, to be maintained at most for two legislatures. If the national representation should persist for a third time in its purpose, the law would then be adopted, for the last word belonged to the will of the nation as manifested in the elections.[676]

We have here a whole complex system for distributing responsibilities and functions among different bodies, which the editors carefully

---

673 Ibid., 14.

674 Ibid., 22. However, if only the executive has this initiative, freedom will be lost, as in Bonaparte's France. See 23.

675 Ibid., 24.

676 Ibid., 25.

examined and for which they proposed a series of solutions that, in most cases, would be adopted item by item by the Cortes of Cádiz. But here, too, the editors wavered between two opposing attitudes: on the one hand, confidence in the rationality of men, who must surely appreciate the advantages of this wise constitution; and, on the other, their distrust of a human nature governed by passions and tempted by abuse of power. Hence their reflections on the possible excesses into which each of the actors in the political system might fall.

The excesses of the executive, which could trample on the rights of the national representation, led them to raise the issue of the responsibility of the king and his ministers. Being well-acquainted with Montesquieu and his description of the English constitution and, as always, with the French experience, they reached the very classical conclusion that every royal decree must be signed by the royal ministers, who must be responsible for their actions, not before the national representation, but before a special tribunal, "the supreme court of reversal," whose members would be appointed by the "nation itself."[677]

A more difficult question was the responsibility of the king himself, should he decide—a prophetic example—to use force against the national representation. The very fact that this possibility was raised shows clearly how little stock the Spanish revolutionaries put in their ability to convince the king that "arbitrary power is disastrous for the very one who wields it."[678] The solution they arrived at gives a clear idea of the discomfort aroused by a particular kind of legitimacy that did not fit well with the theoretical scheme that inspired them. The king was a sacred person and, therefore, in such a case, the only reaction possible would be to consider him insane and "entrust the reins of the monarchy to his heir if the latter is capable of governing, or to a regency council until he is able."[679]

Other abuses were also possible, this time by the national representation. In the case of individual abuses, the solution lay in elections: the freedom of the national representation demanded the immunity of the

---

677 Ibid., 27.

678 *El Espectador Sevillano*, Seville, nos. 35–36, November 5–6, 1809.

679 *El Espectador Sevillano*, Seville, no. 94, January 3, 1810.

representatives. Should the deputy prove himself unworthy, the voters would sanction him by failing to re-elect him. The possibility of a collective abuse by the national representation appeared less likely (while not impossible) because they believed that in a large body reason would predominate.

Constitutional mechanisms were not a sufficient barrier against the "arbitrariness" of one or many as the French Revolution had shown. The invariability of constitutional laws was also necessary: "The lesson that history gives us in this matter is thus very clear: [...] Let all the forms under which the national representation is to be organized be established by clear and strict laws; and let no leeway be allowed to the arbitrariness of the prince or of the nation."[680]

This invariability not only fulfilled a preventive purpose, but it was also pedagogical: it aimed to make the laws known to the citizens so that they could, through public opinion, set limits to the ever-possible abuses of power.

## The Makeup of the National Representation

If the division of powers was important to avoid "arbitrariness" and despotic government, the makeup of the national representation and the way its members were elected were no less vital to ensure the proper functioning of the political system.

The debate on the makeup of the national representation focused on several issues that shed a very bright light on the social imaginary and values of the revolutionary group.[681] The first question was, whom

---

680 "Discurso sobre los gobiernos representativos," *El Espectador Sevillano*, Mexico, 8.

681 The discussion of these issues takes up many pages in the long series of articles entitled "Qüestiones importantes sobre las Cortes," which were presented as a response to the publication of a pamphlet entitled *Observaciones sobre las Cortes*. The context of these articles, which appeared from the end of

the Cortes were to represent: whether the estates or individuals without distinction of class. The answer was obvious:

> our representatives cannot be the depositories of the public trust except insofar as they represent the general will of the nation. If there are privileged corporations among us, their privileges must be relative to the functions of their ministry: but the giving of laws to a nation cannot be the work of particular wills.[682]

The new conception of the nation was now so entrenched that the answer is almost a tautology. If the nation was the union of the wills of equal individuals, the will of any particular group could only be an obstacle, not only to representation but even to the very unity of the nation. Although the functional legitimacy of some privileges was recognized for the time being, their existence originated in a concession by the nation, and this prepared the ground for their future abolition. The modern nation inherited absolutism's hostility to the privileges of corporate bodies, conceived as obstacles to the very conception of absolute sovereignty. Privileges, the *fueros*, appeared as a "feudal and monstrous" legacy, which made them incapable of rising to the general interest and subjected their holders to "pride of *corps*." The distance between this view and Montesquieu's reflections on the function of privileges and honor in the moderate monarchy is evident, as well as its difference from the English system, seen as a mixed structure of government in which the powers of the king, the nobility, and the people contributed to the safeguarding of liberty. Our editors' view is that of the French Revolution, even in their vocabulary: "In a national assembly, no other voice should be heard but that of the nation."[683]

---

November 1809 onward, was the increasingly lively debate on the convening of the Cortes.

682 "Qüestion I: ¿Las cortes deben representar la nación dividida en clases, ó deben representarla entera e indivisible?," *El Espectador Sevillano*, Mexico, 122 and the following pages.

683 Ibid., 126.

There was radical homogeneity, then, in the elementary makeup of the nation, which admitted neither bodies nor estates: "Spain is an indivisible nation: thus, its representation must be indivisible."[684] This also entailed territorial homogeneity: the nation was one, hence there could be no representation of the provinces or kingdoms.

When considering the possibility that deputies might receive imperative instructions and mandates from their provinces, the conclusion was categorical. The provinces, however respectable their specific characters might be, were nothing more than particular bodies that must yield, like the others, to the general interest.[685] Nor could deputies be fettered in their freedom of deliberation by imperative instructions. The freedom of their decisions was a condition for the freedom of the national representation.

To these arguments of principle was added another, social, and more modern argument: the conciliation of interests and the importance of learning about the general one. "Nobles, plebeians, ecclesiastics, peasants, merchants, and artists, come together full of the sense of their own classes' needs: they will see how the good of each depends on that of the nation they represent: there they will recognize the advantages of mutual sacrifice."[686]

However, and in keeping with these men's continual oscillation between experience and the logic of principles, they concluded that if representation by estates were to be adopted in the future Cortes (something undesirable), it would be convenient that they meet in two separate chambers, with the representatives of the privileged classes in one and those of the commons in the other. In defense of this solution they adduced the English example, on the one hand : "England is the only nation that has been able to preserve her liberty when, in the other nations, the Estates General have either been abolished, or have only

684 Ibid., 130.

685 *El Espectador Sevillano*, Seville, no. 83, December 23, 1809, 325 and the following pages.

686 *Semanario Patriótico*, Seville, no. XXVI, July 20, 1809, 187–88.

retained a precarious authority."[687] They pointed, on the other hand, to the French experience, in which the victory of the Third Estate and the mixture of estates had brought about partisan struggle and the "republican convention": "this meant bringing together in a single body parties whose aspirations were different; it meant provoking struggle, stirring up hatreds and enmities through the debates; it meant corralling together in the circus the wild beasts who were ready to devour each other."[688]

This obsession with discord, the inevitable byproduct of the struggle between parties so typical of traditional societies, served as a background for their reflection. It is not clear, however, why the danger of division and discord should disappear in the single assembly that the editors had defended previously and which, in fact, would be the one that convened in Cádiz. The two explanations provided are either incidental or circumstantial. According to the first, the Spanish situation was different from that of France in 1789 because "feudal privileges were never so absurd and unjust among us as in France," which, though true, left out another cause of discord that was just as important or more so: that is, the opposition between two forms of legitimacy—the traditional one, that of the king, which was very powerful in a society that still thought in terms of personal ties, and the new legitimacy of the Cortes. The second explanation asserted that, in Spain, there was "a bond of union that was lacking in the early days of the French Revolution, this being the great enterprise of driving the enemy from our soil."[689] This explanation was valid, no doubt, during the war against the invader, and it partly explains why the clashes between parties in Cádiz were comparatively limited; but it would be much less so later on, when there was no longer any need to remain united against an external enemy.

---

687 "Qüestión II: En el caso de la representación por estamentos, ¿deberá reunirse en un solo cuerpo o dividirse en dos cámaras?," *El Espectador Sevillano*, Mexico, 131 and the following pages.

688 Ibid., 134.

689 Ibid.

Finally, there was one last point of discussion regarding the composition of the future Cortes: "What should the proportion of representatives be in regard to the general population?"[690] Here we see the political arithmetic displayed in all its glory. The Cortes must not have so few deputies that they can be easily bribed, nor so many that, as in France, "the excessive number of deputies" might lead to the "spirit of republicanism." The number of deputies must be fixed a priori (in this case, there were to be four hundred).[691] This number would then be distributed proportionally to the population of each province. Since the population of Spain was estimated at eleven million, this meant "one deputy for every 27,500 souls." The calculation is convincing and impeccable, but it includes a dreadful omission. These computations took into account neither the population of Spanish America nor its necessary representation. This omission is dramatic given that these newspapers are known to have been read and reprinted in America, and considering that by the hazards of communication, this very page of *El Espectador Sevillano* was the closing page of its reprint in Mexico.[692] Sophisticated political arithmetic, in this case, went hand in hand with a colossal political mistake.

When it comes to how distinctly the Spanish revolutionaries conceived the modern nation and its representation, the debate on elections sheds a much dimmer light on what actually constituted the real nation that was to participate in politics. Considering their rejection of democracy, the proposed electoral system should, logically enough, have been one of limited suffrage, as in the case of the French Revolution during its Thermidorian era. It was difficult, however, after the almost mystical exaltation of the people as the savior of the homeland and the central protagonist of the Spanish Revolution, to exclude its lowest and most numerous segments from this essential manifestation of citizenship.

---

690 "Qüestión III," ibid., 138 and the following pages.

691 This would be the approximate number estimated in the Cádiz Constitution, this time with the addition of the American representation: that is, one deputy per fifty thousand inhabitants.

692 *El Espectador Sevillano*, Mexico, 144 and the last page.

That is why, almost from the beginning, a very broad, almost universal form of suffrage was proposed: the vote of all men who were heads of families—that is, the *vecinos*, excluding only those individuals whose dependent condition prevented them from enjoying the autonomous will that was indispensable for the citizen to be able to construct the general will.[693]

This broad suffrage, however, had to be accompanied by mechanisms that might avert the danger of democracy or, at least, popular turmoil. Studying English direct suffrage, the editors acknowledged that this form was more respectful of "the equality of rights of all citizens in choosing the protectors of their interests," but this quality was nullified by the fact that it favored "tumultuary seditions." Indirect suffrage, therefore, seemed a more suitable means for preserving the order that should prevail during elections. And above all, it was fundamental for men who knew how much in the minority were the adherents to this new imaginary of the citizen: such a system enabled the formation of "a more select, more enlightened congress, of more liberal principles."[694] Here we see, quite undisguised, the cultural pride of this revolutionary group and its elitist nature.

Indirect suffrage, then, it must be. There had been previous experience of this system with Charles III's municipal reforms, which established the election by all householders, or *vecinos*, of *síndicos* and *procuradores del común* in the main cities.[695]

The final precaution against any possible slide into democracy was the immediate dissolution of the primary electoral assemblies: "for the primary assemblies do not represent the nation: they are the nation

693 *El Espectador Sevillano*, Seville, no. 71, December 11, 1809, 281. For an overall reflection on these topics, see chapter X.

694 *Semanario Patriótico*, Seville, no. XXX, August 17, 1809, 255.

695 Ibid., 253. This was the system adopted by the Cortes of Cádiz—and with the same terminology—in the Constitution of 1812.

itself."[696] To maintain them any longer would be a direct negation of the representative regime,[697] as had already happened in France:

> The deputies of the constituent assembly did not represent the nation, which constantly held together, but the electoral sections of Paris, whose furious cries almost always led to the decisions of that body. From this arose the confusion of powers, the part that the representative body suppressed of itself in the functions of government.[698]

## The Rule of Opinion

Finally, we must examine the other important element that, together with representative government, was one of the keys to the new political regime. As we have already stated several times in passing, all sophisticated constitutional mechanisms had to be supplemented by something much more impalpable and fundamental: public opinion, "this great agent of liberal governments, this gentle queen of the world, a thousand times more powerful than the weapons and the force of tyrants."

Certainly, freedom of the press was one of its indispensable foundations and had to be guaranteed by law under all circumstances for, without it, freedom could neither triumph nor even exist. The march of the revolutionary process since 1808 and the pedagogical work of our newspapers were based on a de facto freedom of the press. But it needed to be institutionalized, and that is why its official establishment was one of the first goals of the revolutionary group—one that would give rise to the first great political battle of the Cortes of Cádiz, when the two

---

696 *El Espectador Sevillano*, Seville, no. 70, December 10, 1809, 277.

697 *El Espectador Sevillano*, Seville, no. 72, December 12, 1809, 287.

698 Ibid., no. 75, December 15, 1809, 295.

groups of antagonists, the liberals and the *serviles*, would take shape for the first time.[699]

However, beyond this necessary medium, public opinion appeared as a concept presenting different facets and fulfilling multiple functions, to such an extent that our newspapers entrusted it with the ultimate role in resolving the essential problem of good administration:

> to combine [...] the greatest possible force in government and the greatest possible freedom among the citizens. [...] If we do not wish to be forever wavering between anarchy and despotism, a bond must be formed to unite these two extremes, whose opposition is only apparent, and this bond can be none other than public opinion.[700]

Being consecrated to so lofty a function, public opinion had to be defined and distinguished from other manifestations of the common feeling. It could not be identified with the mere "universal voice" of the people, for a corrupt and debased people was ignorant of its primary interests. The first feature that distinguished public opinion from the cry of "a degraded people" was its conformity to freedom—that is, to the new values[701] and, we might add, to the social practices of the modern forms of sociability: "public opinion [...] is the general voice of a whole people convinced of a truth, which it has examined through discussion."[702]

Discussion was the indispensable mechanism that enabled the alchemy that transformed "particular opinions [...] into a truth of which all are convinced." Through discussion, one arrived at the truth—a

---

699 For the makeup of these groups during the vote on freedom of the press, see DSCE, no. 25, October 19, 1810, 53–54.

700 "Discurso sobre el modo de formarse la opinión pública," *El Espectador Sevillano*, Mexico, 78.

701 The example used is that of the Roman people. When they retired to the sacred hill "to assert their liberty upon the ruins of aristocracy," they were expressing the public vote, but when they celebrated the death of the Gracchi, they were merely uttering degrading cries. Ibid., 79.

702 Ibid., 81.

social truth, as Cochin defined it, that is, a truth whose validity originated in the process of its own production: consensus arising from the confrontation of diverse opinions. If the common way of thinking or feeling did not obey this mechanism of production and, even more, if the values expressed were not in accordance with freedom as understood in modern terms, they could not be considered public opinion. Hence, in the clash between the traditional values of the social majority and the new ones, to which the modern elites adhered (something that happened very frequently during the nineteenth century), the latter opposed to the former the authority of opinion.

The discussion from which opinion emerged was not the "dangerous and tumultuary one [of] the ancient republics," but a complex process that began in private conversations and then flowed, thanks to the printing press, into the public sphere before returning to the private sphere, where it could then "speak in the silence of solitude with all our fellow citizens, listen to their answers and objections, quietly and, without the heat inspired by love of one's personal opinion, give air to the public interests."[703]

The old public sphere, or the one that still existed in traditional society—that of the town square, or the meeting of *vecinos*—was replaced by two different spheres: the private one, that of domestic intimacy, and a new public one, different from the old sphere and consisting mainly in the circulation of writings. These two new spheres interacted and complemented each other to produce an opinion that was elevated to a dignity equivalent to that of the general will: that is, the very principle of the new legitimacy.

According to this logic, against an opinion thus produced no appeal could be made to any other tribunal than the "supreme tribunal of reason and men's general common sense,"[704] that is, to itself. No one could judge opinion, for it was itself the supreme judge before which everything had to appear: values, ideas, behaviors. It was at once legislator and supreme judge.

---

703 Ibid., 83.

704 Ibid., 82.

We must not think, however, that these enormous powers were entrusted, in practice, to anyone and everyone. Just as the representative regime made it possible to reconcile the sovereignty of all with the exercise of power by a few, public opinion also demanded a distinction between its active agents and a passive and silent public, from which, nevertheless, the former derived their legitimacy:

> Most of the citizens, being absorbed in their domestic duties, though they are capable of knowing the truth when it is presented to them clearly and exactly, are not capable of proposing political ideas, because neither have they undertaken the necessary studies to acquire them, nor are they in the habit of putting them in order.[705]

The active role in shaping public opinion belonged to the "learned." The catalogue of sciences that a man needed to master in order to gain access to this driving role was impressive and disheartening for any ordinary citizen: "History, jurisprudence, political and moral studies have provided them with the means to acquire them [ideas]: logic and the art of writing have taught them how to express them. The learned, therefore, must be the first organ of public opinion."[706]

Thus, "in civilized countries" there existed a moral magistracy of opinion entrusted to a select few: "a body consecrated by the nature of its occupations to teaching and proposing the means to make the homeland happy." The elitist character of this leading group and its sense of superiority over the uneducated masses are evident.

To this body belonged the supreme regulatory function of the representative system, and its action unfolded in two directions: toward the government and toward the mass of the population. They provided the government with "new lights, new ideas, new combinations in the complicated science of administration." To the rest of the population they proffered their enlightenment by educating them: "they form public opinion, inspire in all minds the love of justice, promulgate the liberal

705 Ibid., 84.

706 Ibid.

principles dictated by the universal reason of the human race, and pave the way for the necessary reforms and the establishment of good laws."[707]

Their role was so lofty that they did not hesitate to affirm that they were the ones who "instruct[ed] the nation," its pedagogues. In an exalted eulogy, they are credited with civilizing the barbarian peoples, with being "those who taught the first arts, those who formed the embryo of the nascent society, those who dictated the first laws of the peoples." An imperceptible shift has occurred, from public opinion conceived as the result of the confrontation of opinions to the active group that must direct it and, from there, to the mythology of the legislating heroes, the founders of new societies. Models of this kind provide the construction of the modern nation's national pantheons with part of its inspiration.

Such lofty missions entailed, on the part of governments, a series of obligations toward the "learned." First of all, that of ensuring their freedom of expression, listening to them, and protecting them; then, that of making their own actions public so that the "learned" might examine these actions before the tribunal of reason. This demand for publicity was both a struggle against absolute power (to which secrecy was consubstantial) and a guarantee of the rationality of the decisions, since they could be examined by many.[708]

Curiously enough, this theory of public opinion, the modern character of which is in many respects self-evident, presents other aspects that are much less so. The most striking is the conception of opinion as necessarily unanimous.[709] True, we find much praise for the spirit of tolerance—"Woe to us if we despise he who tells us a useful truth merely because it does not agree with our way of thinking!"—but they immediately go on to criticize the partisan spirit: "Woe to us, if sects and parties form among the writers who are to enlighten the nation!"

707 Ibid., 85.

708 On the subject of publicity in modern politics, see Ronsanvallon 1990.

709 A conception exalted by the example of the United States, in which, as soon as the people became acquainted with its rights, there was but "one will [...] one will, one desire:" "Discurso sobre el modo de formarse la opinión pública," *El Espectador Sevillano*, Mexico, 96.

The criticism, once again, was based on an analysis of the French experience: on the struggle between "the philosophical party, very different from the philosophical spirit," formed in the eighteenth century, and the party of the Court. Except for the brief parenthesis of 1789, when a real public opinion existed, the confrontation between the two parties led opinion astray and as a result, "popular seditions [. . . were given] the name of the *voice of the nation.* [...] The laborers from the slums and the corps of Paris harlots became the organs of the popular voice."

To avert the risk that diversity of opinions might lead to party wars, a surprising solution was advocated: the creation of a national party. "Learn, you nations wishing to be free: form a national party, and let this party be made up of the total sum of the citizens: of this general mass of proprietors, of this people which is educated or capable of being so."[710]

Unanimity remained an ideal goal. Many of the ideological conflicts that would later tear the Hispanic countries apart are already implicit here. This includes the conflict between those who, by virtue of their values though not their numbers, constituted the national party—the true people—and those who, by virtue of their adherence to other values, were yet unable or unwilling to achieve this condition of "a learned people." Real political pluralism was not yet a part of the spirit of the age.

710 Ibid.

# VIII

# The Spread of Modernity: Literacy, the Printing Press, and Revolution in New Spain

Speaking of the revolution as a radical cultural mutation immediately brings up questions about where that transformation occurred, who experienced it first, and the means and pace with which it was transmitted to other places and social groups. In this regard, we must also inevitably consider the conditions that enabled or not the spread of said mutations. Literacy and the printing press predominate among these factors. These last two cannot be seen as issues related only to the history of culture, as they in fact affect political history.

Quite possibly, a modern revolutionary process—beyond popular revolts, no matter how large—requires a relatively high degree of literacy and a significant development of the printing press.[711] However, even though these variables were a necessary condition for the victory of modernity,[712] it is also very likely that, in and of themselves, they might not have been sufficient: both European and American political geography present multiple examples across the nineteenth and twentieth

711 Years ago, Lawrence Stone suggested a correlation between the European revolutions (English, French, and Russian) and a male literacy rate of around 50 percent. See "Literacy and education in England, 1640–1900," *Past and Present* (February 1969).

712 E. Todd, *L'Enfance du Monde: Structures familiaires et développement*, Paris, 1984, 170 and the following pages, relates literacy to a mutation in behaviors and values seen as a possible source of the democratic age.

centuries of regions that, from this point of view, were modern, while ideologically they remained quite traditional in their values.[713]

The era of the Hispanic revolutions is a privileged moment during which all these factors can be seen in action. And Mexico, given the complexity of its society and the wealth of historical sources, is an excellent field of observation. New Spain was then crossing the threshold that separates societies with a predominantly oral culture, in which writing is marginal, from societies in which writing is widespread, implying both extensive literacy and printing. It is precisely these developments at the end of the ancien régime that made the revolution of independence possible, as occurred in Mexico.

We must therefore analyze New Spain within the framework which was its own, that of a cultured society belonging to the European ancien régime, and then examine the reaction of this distant kingdom of the Hispanic monarchy to the revolutionary dynamics that began taking place in the Peninsula in 1808. For, beyond increased knowledge of the independence process, what is at stake here is the endogenous or exogenous, plural or singular character of the Hispanic revolutions.

---

713 In Mexico during the twentieth century, for example, the states that were the cradle of the Mexican Revolution were, indeed, among the most literate (the north, the Federal District and Morelos), as well as those that had the highest number of newspapers. However, a more precise examination of these variables shows a notable exception in the west of the country (Jalisco, Michoacán, Colima, Aguascalientes). This region resembles, in terms of literacy and press, the revolutionary areas but differs from them in its political behavior: it was passive during the time of the Revolution and would become a Cristero bastion during the religious conflict. Guerra 1985, vol. 1, 378–79, and vol. II, 196–98.

## A Cultured Society of the Ancien Régime

A very quick look at the schooling establishments of New Spain at the end of the eighteenth century shows the density and diversity of the educational network and its similarity to the contemporary European context.

At the summit is a set of higher education establishments, whether old or modern. Among the first, we can mention those in Mexico, Guadalajara and, in the most important cities, the seminaries, including the Tridentine Seminary of Mexico. Among the latter, the Royal School of Surgery, the Academy of San Carlos, the Botanical Garden, the School of Mines (the second to be founded in the world, after the one in Paris). It was this density that led Humboldt to write that "no city on the new continent, without excepting the United States, has scientific establishments as large and solid as those of the capital of Mexico."[714]

This observation is well known but also important since it places Mexican education within its own framework: that of Europe and that of the United States. But also, by drawing our attention to the top of the educational pyramid, this observation forces us to examine the foundations that made it possible.

The network of schools, including the former institutions of the Jesuits, who had been expelled in 1767, covered almost the entire center of the country. Practically all intendencia capitals had one. Here too Mexico held a privileged place with several great schools, including the famous one of San Ildefonso.[715] The basis of upper secondary education that would enable the scientific and literary institutes of the nineteenth century already existed at the end of the eighteenth. It would be no surprise if a quantitative study of the number of students were to show, in the period preceding independence, a figure of many thousands of pupils, comparable to that of Mexico at the beginning of the twentieth century but for a much smaller population (six million inhabitants in 1808, compared to fifteen million in 1910).

---

714 A. Humboldt, *Essai politique sur la Nouvelle-Espagne*, Paris, 1811, book II, chapter VII.

715 J. A. Manrique, "Del barroco a la ilustración," *Historia general de México*, vol. 2 (Mexico: El Colegio de México), 384 and the following pages.

Finally, at the base of this structure, many primary schools enabled the existence of the higher levels we have just briefly described. We are now getting to know this multiform education, which was analogous to that of Spain or France during the eighteenth century.[716] To the general pedagogical desire for literacy characteristic of the Enlightenment we should add, in the case of Mexico, the goal of Hispanicizing the indigenous population.[717] Although this purpose was rooted in a distant past, it gained force in the mid-eighteenth century, when the church launched the first great wave of primary schools. In 1756, the archbishopric of Mexico already had 262 schools in 61 of its 202 parishes.[718]

The reformist measures of the enlightened monarchs[719] reinforced, after 1760, the actions taken by the church and what we could term the natural evolution of traditional society. The essential characteristic of this education, which grew considerably during the last third of the eighteenth century, was the extreme diversity of its actors. Although the fundamental impulse came from above (that is, from the church and the state), education in fact depended on society: on its corporate bodies, those collective actors that formed its fabric. There were parish schools, schools belonging to the various ecclesiastical institutions, town schools, schools in indigenous communities financed with communal assets or through special contributions, schools in the haciendas and in the ranchos, as well as various education systems in crafts guilds, etc. The whole depended largely on mortmain assets, whether civil or ecclesiastical.[720]

---

716 For the evolution in France, see Furet and Ozouf 1977.

717 See on this topic Silvio Zavala, *¿El castellano, lengua obligatoria?* (Mexico: Centro de Estudios de Historia de México, Condumex), 1977; and Serge Gruzinski, "La segunda aculturación: El Estado ilustrado y la religiosidad indígena en Nueva España (1775–1800)," in *Estudios de Historia novohispana*, Mexico, VIII (1985): 175–201.

718 Gruzinski, loc. cit., 185.

719 The legal provisions are very numerous. See for example the references to the royal decrees of October 10, 1769, April 16, 1770, January 28, 1778, January 24 and November 5, 1782, etc., in AGN, Historia, vol. 493.

720 Guerra 1985, vol. I, 184, 230–31, 241–43, and Tanck de Estrada, "Las cortes de Cádiz y el desarrollo de la educación en México," *Historia Mexicana*, no. 113

By the end of the century, the number of schools undoubtedly exceeded one thousand, although it is difficult to arrive at a global sum.[721] In the Valley of Mexico, between 1784 and 1785, Xochimilco had 29 schools with 2,906 students, and Teotihuacán had 14 with 1,000 children, which totals some 4,000 students for a total population of approximately 25,000 inhabitants. And although there is data on less educated areas, even peripheral zones had numerous schools. Thus, in 1787 there were 11 schools with 742 students in the jurisdiction of Huatulco (on the Pacific coast); 44 schools and 2,370 children in Miahuatlán (Sierra Madre del Sur), and 21 schools and 2,950 children in Yahualica (Sierra Madre Oriental).[722] In Yucatán in 1791, 175 towns had schools, with a total of 35,906 students.[723]

Schools were everywhere, even in the smallest rural towns, and formed a natural part of the landscape: there were 94 inhabitants and a school teacher in 1799 in Anenecuilco (which, a century later, would become Zapata's hometown).[724] In the 1790s, they could be found in practically all the towns and distant mountain villages of what is currently the state of Guerrero.[725] In 1828 and despite crises, there were numerous schools in the district of Amatepec, in towns and ranchos

---

(July–September 1979): 3–35.

721 Aside from the global statistics on Yucatán, it is currently impossible to calculate global figures because our sources are fragmentary and essentially deal with towns that had difficulty maintaining their schools.

722 Gruzinski, loc. cit.

723 Statistics in AGN, Historia, vol. 498, file 7. For tables summarizing the information and a rectification of the figures, see Anne Gambino, *Les écoles primaires en Nouvelle-Espagne à la fin du XVIII et début du XIX siècle* (graduate thesis, Université de Paris I, 1991).

724 1799 register of Anenecuilco, reproduced in J. Sotelo Inclán, *Raíz y razón de Zapata,* 2nd ed. (Mexico: 1970), 151 and the following pages.

725 This information can found in D. Dehouve, *Production marchande et organization sociale dans une province indienne du Mexique (XVI–XXe. siècle),* vols. 1 and II (Paris: EHESS th. d'Etat, 1985), 158 (vol. I); 604 and the following pages (vol. 2).

that barely comprised 170 inhabitants. By then, however, this old education system was already in decline.[726]

This density of schools, so remarkable in the countryside, was even greater in the cities. In Mexico in 1820, between 48 and 62 percent of children were enrolled in schools, and two-thirds of these were free of charge.[727] In 1900, the era of great *porfirista* prosperity, instruction at the same educational level was below 50 percent.[728] As for the countryside, how many villages of the mid-twentieth century had yet to recover the schools they had at the end of the colonial era?

It is this vast educational edifice that allows us to understand the events of the independence era: not only the existence of new intellectual elites, both ecclesiastical and civil, that became the engine of American demands, but also that of a society that was literate enough for writing to become a weapon of civil war.

Is it legitimate to move from schooling to literacy? It is difficult to provide a quantitative answer, not only because of the lack of direct statistical data, but also because, in many of these schools, catechism may well have been been the main subject. Nevertheless, there is also an abundance of data showing that reading, writing, and basic arithmetic were taught in these schools. The measure of literacy might perhaps be indirect at first, as there are many indications that education did bear fruit both in the countryside and in the cities.

The propaganda wars waged from 1810 onward by insurgents and royalists further attest to the existence of a highly literate population. In 1811, for example, the dean of the chapter of Mexico was concerned about "the profusion of pamphlets, leaflets, letters, and other means to corrupt the loyalty and patriotism of Americans, especially of the *Indians and rancheros* [author's emphasis]."[729]

---

726 *Boletín del Archivo del Estado de México* (September–December 1981), 9 and the following pages.

727 Tanck de Estrada 1977, 242.

728 Estimates based on *Estadísticas sociales del Porfiriato: 1877–1910* (Mexico: 1956), 43 and the following pages.

729 "Informe sobre la libertad de prensa hecho por los Venerables Deán y Capítulo de la sede vacante de México al Virrey Don Francisco J. Venegas,

These same indigenous people were sometimes mobilized by writings in Spanish, but also by others in Nahuatl.[730] Viceroy Venegas took great care to make Nahuatl printed editions of his fiscal proclamations intended to contain Hidalgo's revolt.[731]

How many people in indigenous communities could read? At least some and, no doubt, many more. The report of a lawsuit between the parish priest and the inhabitants of the indigenous village of Xapaltlahuac, near Tapla in present-day Guerrero during the years 1803–6, offers some clues:

> the parish priest [...] asked the notary of the republic, [...] who read the paper in which he summoned them to come to Zacatipan? And being answered, it was the schoolmaster, he sent him the priest [...]. He then sent the previous notary.[732]

In addition to the parish priest, at least three other people in this village could read: the schoolmaster, the two notaries, and, no doubt, others. We can also see how, through public reading, the world of writing is articulated with the world of oral culture which, we may assume, would be that of a substantial part of the village.

Although the figures are unknown to us, there are indications pointing to a high degree of literacy in the cities and, above all, in Mexico City. For example, on November 4, 1811, the *Diario de México* published three editions with a total circulation of over 7,000 copies, an enormous figure for a city that, at the time, housed some 140,000 inhabitants: these figures give us one newspaper for every twenty inhabitants

---

el 14 de junio de 1811," in García 1910, 173.

730 A very eloquent example of this insurgent propaganda is the letter in approximate but effective Spanish that Alamán, 1972, publishes in vol. I, annex 20, 351–92.

731 See, for example, the proclamation "in Aztec and Spanish" in Medina, 1911, vol. VII, 554.

732 For the full text, see D. Dehouve, op. cit., vol. II, 561.

(children included).[733] In addition, the print runs during this period of works issued in Mexico and not intended for the general public ranged between 700 and 3,000 copies.[734] This is considerable and seems to be of the same magnitude as what would be observed a little later in Spain for texts of the same type.[735]

The December 1812 elections to select Mexico's new constitutional City Council provide other clues. These elections, which recognized a practically universal but indirect suffrage, were held by means of a vote on handwritten ballots. The strong electoral turnout meant the urban "plebs" participated, as the witnesses confirmed. None of the numerous inquiries into electoral irregularities carried out at the time alleged that voters were unable to write the candidate's name themselves on the ballot. This clue, which might seem weak at first sight, is much less so when one considers the thoroughness of the investigation and the wide range of irregularities registered.[736]

Although none of these clues can be taken as definitive proof, they nevertheless show the emergence of a society that, while still ancien régime, was undergoing a rapid process of schooling and literacy: a society that was following an evolution parallel to that of Spain and France, though with a clear time lag.[737]

---

733 Alamán 1972, vol. II, 282.

734 Seven hundred copies of *Las cuatro columnas del trono español*, an allegorical work, were printed in 1810; *Desengaños que a los insurgentes de Nueva España seducidos por los francmazones* [*sic*] by Agustín Pomposo Fernández de San Salvador was issued in 3,000 copies in 1812 (admittedly for free); *Los jesuitas quitados y restituidos...*, by the same author, was issued in 1,000 copies in 1816. Medina 1911, vol. VII, 512 and 614, and vol. VIII, 96.

735 *La muerte de los justos*, for example, which recounts the death of Louis XVI, was printed in Madrid in 1793 with 1,500 copies. See Domergue 1984, 84.

736 The official proceedings of these inquiries have been published in large part in *La Constitución de 1812 en la Nueva España...*, vol. I, 1912, 330 and the following pages.

737 See, for this difference, Furet and Ozouf 1977.

## The Development of Printing

The above statements are reinforced by the development of the printing press and the production of the books and periodicals it made possible. The origins of printing in New Spain date back to the sixteenth century, but its development was initially slow. It picked up in the second half of the eighteenth century, despite the obstacles presented by the official licensing regime.

In Mexico, only two major printers operated with a royal license between 1796 and 1806. Everything changed after this date: there were three in 1807, four in 1808, and five in 1809. From 1815 to 1819, during the period of the return to absolutism, there were only three, but they had increased to seven by 1820, after the reestablishment of the Constitution of 1812 across the monarchy.[738]

This applies to the large printing houses, which had several presses and extensive staff, as Fernández de Lizardi points out in his quarrel with the printer Mariano Zúñiga y Ontiveros: "As if in said printing house there were only one box of type, one typesetter, and one press [...]."[739] However, next to these we find other workshops (the *imprentillas* or *imprentitas*) that worked on a small scale with limited materials to produce administrative forms, lottery tickets, invoices, etc.,[740] and probably also *canciones de ciego* and other productions pertaining to

---

738 Calculations based on Medina 1958, vol. I. The main printers of the independence era are Mariano José de Zúñiga y Ontiveros, María Fernández Jáuregui, Alejandro Valdés Arizpe (from 1814 to 1817 his shop run by José María Benavente) and Manuel Antonio Valdés.

739 J. J. Fernández de Lizardi, *Aviso al público: Sobre el despotismo de imprentas*, September 7, 1820, reproduced by Medina 1911, vol. VIII, 204.

740 Like Gerardo Flores in Calle Escalerillas, or José Antonio Hogal in the years 1770–80. See Medina 1911, vol. I. In the previously cited notice, Fernández de Lizardi states that, to resolve the issue of printing his paper, "the newspaper will be suspended, printed in Puebla, or finished by a small printing press."

the *literatura de cordel*.[741] The market for printing presses went beyond "licensed" printers and incidentally enabled the existence of a literature that partly escaped official control—the literature that the viceroy tried to prohibit (in vain, no doubt) by banning the *imprentillas* in 1809: "In order to avert several inconveniences that might originate from the use of handheld or portable printing presses, I have resolved that all individuals who have them for use or sale should deliver them within the precise and peremptory term of three days [...]."[742]

The development of printing was not exclusive to Mexico City. At the turn of the century, it spread throughout the provinces. Puebla, which had housed a printer since the mid-seventeenth century, had three at the time of the crisis of independence. Guadalajara had had one since 1792; Veracruz, since 1794; Oaxaca, since 1810; Mérida, since 1813.[743]

The existence of abundant and widespread printing material would allow the insurgents and their supporters to publish those "pamphlets and leaflets" that worried the dean of the chapter of Mexico. The insurgents would thus set up their various war presses, which would issue the newspapers that we will discuss below.[744]

---

741 *Canciones de ciego* were popular lyrics sung by blind performers, usually as entertainment for the lower classes; *literatura de cordel* is popular printed, illustrated material sold by street vendors and mainly targeting the lower classes.—Trans.

742 "Bando del virrey Pedro Garibay," April 27, 1809, in *Diario de México*, vol. X, 508.

743 Medina 1911, vol. I, 91 and the following pages, 445 and the following pages, 453 and the following pages, and 597 and the following pages.

744 *El despertador americano* was printed in Guadalajara at the José Fructo Romero printing house; *El ilustrador americano* and the *Semanario Patriótico Americano* in Sultepec, at the Imprenta Nacional, which used types clandestinely bought in Mexico; *Sur* and *El Correo Americano del Sur*, in Oaxaca, in the printing house of Father Idiáquez. See Miquel y Vergés 1941, 17 and the following pages.

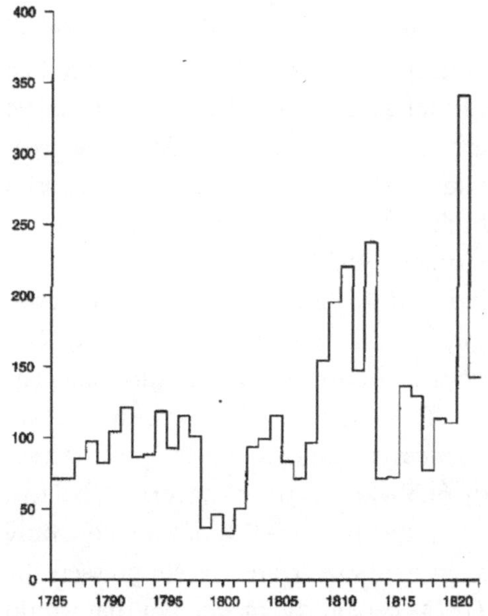


**Figure 1.** Books and pamphlets printed in Mexico: number of titles.Source: Data based on Medina 1911, and F. González de Cosío, *La imprenta en México (1553–1820)* (Mexico: 1952), 345.

An examination of the production of these printing houses allows us to complete our understanding of the cultural development of New Spain at the end of the ancien régime. Let us start with the books and pamphlets printed in Mexico City. Though these do not cover the entirety of Mexican editions (they leave out imported books, especially those from Spain), the titles printed in the capital still allow us to determine the essential trends. This is due both to the overwhelming percentage of the capital's production in relation to the provinces (Mexico City comprised close to 80 percent of total production) and to the fact that the most widely read Spanish works were quickly reprinted in the city.[745]

745 The data employed to create the following tables and graphs are based on an examination of the eight volumes of the classic work by Medina 1911, and completed with F. Fernández de Cosío, *La imprenta en México (1553–1820), 510 adiciones de la obra de José Toribio Medina en homenaje al primer centenario de su nacimiento*, Mexico, 1952, 345. We have not considered works of unknown date—465 titles from the eighteenth century—as they would not have substantially altered the trends, except to further increase the growth toward the end of the century.

At the end of the seventeenth century, specifically, during the period from 1685 to 1694, the number of titles printed in Mexico averaged 26 annually. A century later, the annual average for the period 1785–94 was 92 titles: it had tripled in one century (see Figure 1). After the great decline of 1798–1801, which was due to the limited paper supply caused by the war with England, the high figures of the end of the century returned at the beginning of the nineteenth.[746]

The great Hispanic crisis began in 1808, and with it, the number of publications multiplied. Following the example of the Peninsula, New Spain first entered a period of wounded patriotism and, subsequently, moved into that of modern politics. The existence of a new audience and the technical means with which to meet demand, alongside greater freedom of the press as far as patriotic publications were concerned, led to a very rapid growth in the number of published titles. From then on, only during the periods in which governments restricted or suppressed the publication of political writings (1813–19) did the movement that would accelerate with the Spanish Revolution of 1820 come to a halt. Thus, the birth of modern Mexico began in 1808.

However, the publication of books and pamphlets alone does not constitute the totality of the noble production of the printing press. We must add the newspapers: this is where the transformations were felt most strongly. Although several newspapers had been published sporadically during the eighteenth century (with the first *Gaceta de México* being, since 1722, the most important), these publications were subject to eclipses. There was no clear change until the early years of the nineteenth century. In 1805, the *Diario de México*, the first newspaper, made its appearance. Two years earlier, a weekly broadside, *El Noticioso General*, had already begun publication and was devoted to advertisements and brief notes.

Since 1806, Veracruz had also had a weekly newspaper, *El Jornal Económico de Veracruz*, already published daily by 1807. From 1809 onward, two new newspapers appeared in Mexico: the weekly *El Correo Semanario Político y Mercantil*, which became a daily

---

746 All these figures are far below actual numbers if we consider that the studies on which they are based are already quite old.

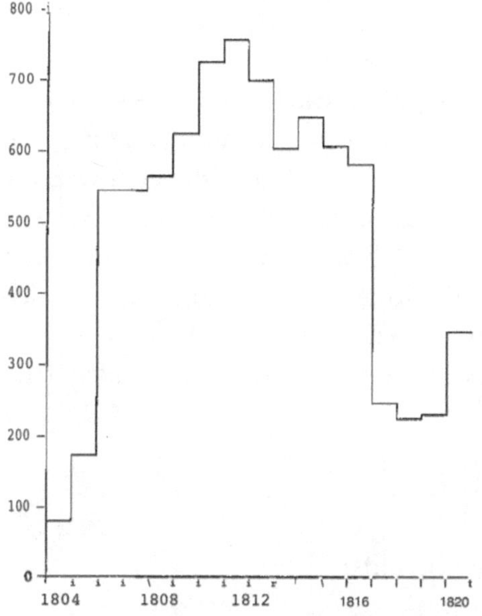


**Figure 2.** Newspapers in Mexico: total number of copies. Source: Data based on Medina 1911, and F. González de Cosío, *La imprenta en México (1553–1820)* (Mexico: 1952), 345.

newspaper at the end of 1811 under the title *El Telégrafo Mexicano*, and another, official publication issued three times a week, *La Gaceta del Gobierno de México*.[747]

This means that, by the time of the 1808–10 crisis, we have moved from almost a single newspaper, with 26 issues per year at the end of the century, to six titles in 1809, with an annual total of issues surpassing 600 (Figure 2). As in the case of books and pamphlets, the years 1810–11 saw the very rapid growth of titles and total issues printed: 10 different titles and 723 issues in 1810, 16 titles and 754 issues in 1811. These figures can be explained both by the reprinting of Spanish patriotic newspapers and by the wave of newspapers trying to fight insurgency with the pen. These same reasons explain the figures of 1812, but it is important to add the multiplicity of often ephemeral titles that arose as a result of a short period of freedom of the press, which was also enjoyed by certain

747 Medina 1911, Miquel y Vergés 1941, and Bravo Ugarte 1966.

supporters of independence. The abundance of titles paid for itself with smaller print runs.[748]

To this, let us add the insurgent press, which was of great political importance even though its publications were ephemeral and its print runs were very short.[749] Let us add, for the period of the civil war, the publication of two newspapers in Guadalajara and two more in Mérida. A phenomenon analogous to that which we have observed for books and pamphlets occurred with the restoration of absolutism, which led to a fall in the figures, lowering them to the level of the first years of the century. The freedom of the press, restored in 1820, immediately triggered a resurgence.

## Reading, Culture, and Sociability

Is it possible that this proliferation of printed matter concerned only a very restricted elite? An example taken from another region of Spanish America may provide some clues. In the Río de la Plata, a few years later, the young Sarmiento, who was then taking his first steps in journalism, estimated that 30,000 people could read in his province of San Juan and but 50 were able to take an interest in a newspaper.[750] Both figures seem exaggerated, but they draw our attention to the high degree of literacy arising from traditional education as well as to the minority

748 In the data in Figure 2, the total of issues mostly corresponds to a few newspapers. Thus, for 1810: 365 issues for the *Diario de México*; about 160 for the *Gazeta del Gobierno de México*; 52 for the *Correo Semanario político y mercantil*; 52 for the *Noticioso General*; the rest (13 percent of total) is distributed among six different titles. The phenomenon intensified in 1812, when the *Diario de México, El Telégrafo americano*, the *Gaceta del Gobierno de México* and the *Noticioso General* alone constituted 89 percent of the total issues; the remaining 11 percent was distributed among twelve other titles.

749 For this insurrectionary press, see the always useful work of Miquel y Vergés 1941.

750 See Verdevoye 1963, 37–38.

character of the elites. While it is not possible to posit an analogous gap for New Spain, the above-mentioned 7,000 copies of the *Diario de México* for November 7, 1811, or the 2,000 copies of the last issue of the insurgent newspaper *El Despertador Americano* of 1811 in Guadalajara can be illuminating.[751] These figures require a very large base of literate people and a fairly large group of elites capable of buying a newspaper. The gap presumed by Sarmiento is not applicable in this case; there was, undoubtedly, an extraordinary mobilization of "opinion" across New Spain during these years, and this went far beyond the elites.

The problem of cultural elites, of "opinion," and social mobilization naturally leads us to consider the different cultural levels of the Mexican population at the time. Let us try to approach this by looking at the topics addressed by the publications we have already considered from a quantitative viewpoint (Table 1).

The first observation is their traditional character, evidenced by the overwhelming presence of religious topics, which comprise between 75 and 84 percent of the titles published between 1804 and 1807. These percentages are, admittedly, excessive and largely due to crown policy. From 1789 onward, the crown imposed countless bans and controls on both sides of the Atlantic to prevent the spread of French revolutionary ideas.[752] Even after the relaxation of administrative controls following 1808, the proportion of religious subjects remained significant: an average of 31 percent of titles between 1808 and 1814. There is an evident gap when compared with eighteenth-century France, which had 40 percent of religious titles at the beginning of the eighteenth century, 30 percent by the middle of the period, and 15 percent between 1784 and 1788.[753] The traditionalism of New Spain is, then, very clear in relation to France, but certainly also with respect to the intermediate position occupied by peninsular Spain.

751 Miquel y Vergés 1941, 42.

752 See, for example, for Spain in the years 1792–95, Domergue 1984.

753 Dupront and Furet 1965–70.

**Table 2.** Titles Published in Mexico (Excluding Newspapers)

| | 1804 | 1805 | 1806 | 1807 | 1808 | 1809 | 1810 |
|---|---|---|---|---|---|---|---|
| 1. Total Number of Records | | | | | | | |
| Totals | 107 | 82 | 68 | 92 | 153 | 244 | 275 |
| Religion | 90 | 62 | 52 | 72 | 69 | 78 | 69 |
| Corporations and Individuals | 3 | 7 | 7 | 7 | 6 | 2 | 2 |
| Public Administration | 1 | 1 | 1 | 1 | 2 | 1 | 9 |
| Literature (Elegies) | 5 | 1 | 1 | 5 | 3 | 40 | 5 |
| Sciences, Technology, Law | 3 | 5 | 1 | 3 | 2 | 3 | 3 |
| Education | 1 | 1 | | | | 1 | |
| Catechisms | 1 | 1 | | | 1 | 2 | |
| Calendars, Almanacs | 3 | 3 | 2 | 3 | 3 | 3 | 3 |
| Political and Patriotic | | 1 | 4 | 1 | 67 | 114 | 184 |
| -Reprints | | | | | 23 | 54 | 29 |
| -Spain | | | | | 15 | 50 | 25 |
| -Hispanic America | | | | | 5 | 3 | 2 |
| -Other | | | | | 3 | 1 | 2 |
| 2. Total (in percentages) | | | | | | | |
| Totals | 100 | 100 | 100 | 100 | 100 | 100 | 100 |
| Religion | 84 | 76 | 76 | 78 | 45 | 32 | 25 |
| Corporations and Individuals | 3 | 9 | 10 | 8 | 4 | 1 | 1 |
| Public Administration | 1 | 1 | 1 | 1 | 1 | 0 | 3 |
| Literature (Elegies) | 5 | 1 | 1 | 5 | 2 | 16 | 2 |
| Science, Technology, Law | 3 | 6 | 1 | 3 | 1 | 1 | 1 |
| Education | 1 | 1 | 0 | 0 | 0 | 0 | 0 |
| Catechisms | 1 | 1 | 0 | 0 | 1 | 1 | 0 |
| Calendars, Almanacs | 3 | 4 | 3 | 3 | 2 | 1 | 1 |
| Political and Patriotic | 0 | 1 | 6 | 1 | 44 | 47 | 67 |
| -Reprints | 0 | 0 | / | 0 | 15 | 22 | 11 |
| -Spain | 0 | 0 | 0 | 0 | 10 | 20 | 9 |
| - Hispanic America | 0 | 0 | 0 | 0 | 3 | 1 | 1 |
| -Other | 0 | 0 | 0 | 0 | 2 | 0 | 1 |

(Roman characters = absolute figures; italics = percentages).

| 1811 | 1812 | 1813 | 1814 | 1815 | 1816 | 1817 | 1818 | 1819 | 1820 |
|---|---|---|---|---|---|---|---|---|---|
| | | | | | | | | | |
| 167 | 137 | 75 | 70 | 131 | 124 | 87 | 92 | 109 | 454 |
| 42 | 46 | 15 | 28 | 77 | 99 | 68 | 64 | 94 | 75 |
| 5 | 1 | 4 | 2 | 5 | 3 | 1 | 9 | 4 | 16 |
| | | | | | | | | | |
| 3 | 1 | 7 | 2 | 11 | 3 | 2 | | | 1 |
| 23 | 11 | 6 | 1 | 3 | 1 | 2 | 7 | 6 | 12 |
| | | | | | | | | | |
| 1 | 4 | 5 | 4 | | 4 | 2 | 4 | 1 | 6 |
| | | | 1 | | 1 | | 1 | 1 | |
| | | 1 | | | | 4 | 1 | 1 | 1 |
| 2 | 3 | 2 | 3 | 2 | 2 | 2 | 3 | 2 | 2 |
| 91 | 71 | 35 | 29 | 33 | 11 | 6 | 3 | | 341 |
| 12 | 10 | 13 | | 4 | 2 | 2 | 1 | | 91 |
| 11 | 9 | 11 | 0 | 4 | 2 | 2 | | 0 | 78 |
| 1 | | 2 | | | | | | | 10 |
| | 1 | | | | | | | | 3 |
| | | | | | | | | | |
| 100 | 100 | 100 | 100 | 100 | 100 | 100 | 100 | 100 | 100 |
| 25 | 34 | 20 | 40 | 59 | 80 | 78 | 70 | 86 | 17 |
| 3 | 1 | 5 | 3 | 4 | 2 | 1 | 10 | 4 | 4 |
| | | | | | | | | | |
| 2 | 1 | 9 | 3 | 8 | 2 | 2 | 0 | 0 | 0 |
| 14 | 8 | 8 | 1 | 2 | 1 | 2 | 8 | 6 | 3 |
| | | | | | | | | | |
| 1 | 3 | 7 | 6 | 0 | 3 | 2 | 4 | 1 | 1 |
| 0 | 0 | 0 | 1 | 0 | 1 | 0 | 1 | 1 | 0 |
| 0 | 0 | 1 | 0 | 0 | 0 | 5 | 1 | 1 | 0 |
| 1 | 2 | 3 | 4 | 2 | 2 | 2 | 3 | 2 | 0 |
| 54 | 52 | 47 | 41 | 25 | 9 | 7 | 3 | 0 | 75 |
| 7 | 7 | 17 | 0 | 3 | 2 | 2 | 1 | 0 | 20 |
| 7 | 7 | 15 | 0 | 3 | 2 | 2 | 1 | 0 | 17 |
| 1 | 0 | 3 | 0 | 0 | 0 | 0 | 0 | 0 | 2 |
| 0 | 1 | 0 | 0 | 0 | 0 | 0 | 0 | 0 | 1 |

Sources: Data based on Medina 1911, and F. González de Cosío, *La imprenta en México (1553–1820)* (Mexico: 1952), 345.

The lives of saints, lists of indulgences, sermons, doctrinal works and various devotional books, including novenas, speak of a society completely permeated by religion. The very diverse formal aspect of these publications, beyond their common topics, suggests a great homogeneity in the deep religious values. Within this common framework, the difference between the elites and the people lies in the forms of piety.[754] Even when, from 1808 onward, politics (in the broad sense of the term) began to pervade everything, many of the titles counted under this heading were sermons, rogations, novenas, pastoral letters, etc. In them, Providence was invoked for aid or forgiveness, and conflicts were placed in the religious register of heresy, irreligion, and defense of the faith.

The different bodies that most frequently gave rise to this literature or those that published its statutes, discourses, or composition[755] shared similar religious references in the same way that they met in the civic-religious festivals of the ancien régime and during the first years of the independent regimes.

Among this mass of titles, a large part of the literature addressed to the general public certainly escapes us. Our sources include calendars, catechisms, and alphabets, but we have less information about the *literatura de cordel* that peddlers, who were very abundant at the end of the eighteenth century, carried to rural areas. Happily, we have more information on satires and anonymous pamphlets, which were highly appreciated in cities and seem to be tied to the student environment.[756]

In addition to contents, we can try to locate the places where all these writings were disseminated, even though we know that every typology is somewhat arbitrary.

---

754 These impressions, gleaned from a quick reading of the titles, should be verified by a qualitative study.

755 We have counted this under the heading "bodies and individuals" in regard to the corporate part of its publications.

756 J. Miranda and P. González Casanova, *Sátira anónima del siglo XVIII* (Mexico: 1953), 20 and the following pages.

At the very top, the meeting places of the cultivated elite had long been the tertulias, increasingly organized in modern forms of sociability. As in Europe, there was a multiplication of enlightened associations, academies, and literary societies such as that of Querétaro, which served as a meeting point for the conspirators of the 1810 insurrection.[757]

This was also where the subscribers of the newspapers[758] gathered: those who frequented the fourteen bookstores of the kingdom (most of them in Mexico City), those who discussed the arrival of Spanish or foreign books. This world of "lights and enlightenment" would shortly become that of modern politics; as in the Peninsula, this was the world of cafés and tertulias, so much so that, in 1808, after Yermo's coup d'état, access to the cafés of those thought to support a General Junta of the kingdom was barred.[759]

Moving by degrees, as prompted by this last example, we can then shift to cultivated circles that were somewhat less restricted. The cafés served as a connecting point between the most distinguished milieus and more popular ones, both because they were open to a general public and because they were places for public reading of newspapers and printed material. In Spain, Alcalá Galiano explained how this articulation between the written and the oral worked in occupied 1808 Madrid:

> In the poor cafés of that time, where it was customary to read the *Gaceta* by the side of the brazier in winter and near the window in summer, people spoke with the same ease, so much so that there seemed to be no fear regarding the dangers posed by the oppressors; [...] This production [a proclamation] was read and admired in the Corredera Baja de San Pablo café in the middle of the day and, as often was the case, it was my role to read it aloud for all those present.[760]

757 See Alamán 1972, vol. I, 225.

758 A restricted but already broad milieu, as can be seen from the list of its subscribers that the *Diario de México* publishes at the end of each volume.

759 See Alamán 1972, vol. I, 163 and the following pages.

760 Alcalá Galiano (1878) 1955, 37.

The same phenomenon (printed propaganda, public reading in cafés) would be seen in Mexico City a few months later, in May 1809, when a series of anonymous printed cards appeared in the city with phrases such as "Freedom, you cowardly Creoles" or "Long live Religion and Independence." All these publications were discovered

> in the cathedral church, in its semetery [*sic*] and in those of other parishes, some leaflets and other seductive papers [...]. Don Nicolas Calero, a business agent, was accused of having taken an anonymous paper to the Café de Medina, where it was read aloud, and which was the same in substance as the cards and papers mentioned.[761]

There was, in short, a hierarchy of places and establishments that ranged from the most elegant cafés to inns and, even lower on the social scale, to the grocery shops that seem to have played an important and little studied role in forming the "opinion" of the lower classes.[762]

In this urban world, where there were multiple transitions from the highest to the lowest social groups, students (many of whom were clerics) or employees who had received a certain amount of education played an important role. It was partly these cultivated, intermediate groups that sometimes bought newspapers or pamphlets from the "*puestos*," "*caxones*" or "*estanquillos*" (stands and kiosks) of which the sources speak.

In the publication notices of the time, the "noble" sales points are well differentiated from other, more popular ones. For example: "this notebook will be found, from today, in the bookstore of D. Mariano Ontiveros [...] and at the stands of the *Gaceta*."[763] These were also the

---

761 File "Papeles aparecidos en las Iglesias y tarjetas satíricas a la Junta Central," 1809, AGN, Historia, vol. 415, file VIII, folio 218.

762 See for Mexico, *Reglamento para el gobierno y dirección de las tiendas de pulpería*, decree of February 20, 1810, Mexico, in the office of Don Mariano de Zúñiga y Ontiveros, 1810, and for Río de la Plata, the reflections of P. González Bernaldo, "Sociabilité démocratique et idéologie nationale. Le Río de la Plata de 1820 à 1853" (graduate thesis, Université de Paris, 1985), 26–30.

763 *Diario de México*, September 17, 1810, in Medina 1911, vol. VII, 544. Other notices of this type: "at the portal, at the stand of the Gazette is the tome";

same media and places where a portion of the anonymous or picaresque satirical literature circulated. These materials were politicized during the most turbulent times, such as 1820, which saw the proliferation of this type of printed materials.[764] It was also this medium that allowed, during major events, the spread of the widely circulated special editions we have mentioned. We also know that the sale of newspapers could take place in the streets and that the practice was banned in March 1821 to avoid the disorders it sometimes caused.[765]

Finally, there was the lowest level—that of the streets and squares. Those places of "tumults" in which text became speech through the public reading of lampoons, pamphlets, or newspapers. A few years later, in Veracruz, the authorities were concerned because "the most alarming and incendiary pamphlets, the most inflammatory libels, were carefully spread and read in public places to deceive the unwary."[766]

Let us add to these secular places the churches and their dependencies, the confraternities, the pious and charitable institutions, which by means of the pulpit or social conversations at the end of services became sounding boards for news and sentiments. This also explains the clergy's considerable capacity to mobilize.

---

*Diario de México*, February 14, 1812; "at the newspaper stand, Portal de Mercaderes"; "at the *caxón* of D. Domingo Llanes, Portal de Mercaderes and in the bookstore of Captain D. Manuel del Valle, Calle de Tacuba," *Diario de México*, XVI, 650; "It is on sale for half a real in the bookstore on the first street of Monterilla and in the stands where the newspaper is sold," *Diario de México*, October 28, 1808, in ibid., vol. VII, 604, vol. VIII, 10, vol. VII, 354 and 415.

764 Here are some titles selected at random: *La chanfaina se quita*, *El lechuzo descubierto en el pobrecito holgazán*, *Es Friegas y friegas y empacho pegado*, *La cola de las zorras de Sansón o defensa de su autor*, *La empanada y arroz*. For complete references, ibid., vol. VIII, 1820, 198–212.

765 Alamán 1972, vol. V, 115. The viceroy's edict of March 9, 1821, is found in *La Constitución de 1812…*, vol. I, 130–31.

766 *El Sol*, June 7, 1827, quoting *El Veracruzano Libre*, May 31, 1827, in Costeloe 1975, 122.

In all these cases except for the last one, which was common to the countryside, we are speaking of a highly socialized urban world in which "public opinion" was beginning to emerge, even before 1808. Is it not significant that the *Diario de México* had already contemplated the need for mailboxes in which to receive articles, information, and announcements sent by readers?[767] This was a very socialized world, with multiple channels for the dissemination of news across very diverse places of sociability, whose articulation is still mostly unknown to us. More research on this topic, however, would greatly contribute to the understanding of the great "popular" movements in the cities of the nineteenth century, whose origin does not appear to be as "popular" as one might think. Oftentimes, behind the anonymous "plebs," we can detect the urban clienteles of the powerful, the influence of certain priests or religious figures and, later, forms of mobilization directed by political elites grouped into modern forms of sociability.[768]

From a similar perspective, further study of the countryside is also pending. We cannot venture far on a topic that remains quite unexplored. This is, however, an essential issue when it comes to understanding social movements beyond the framework of elites and cities, given that it entails, more so than in the case of urban contexts, the connection between the worlds of written and oral culture.

We would simply like to point out the role played by the local elites and spaces of small-town sociability in the articulation of these two spheres. The elites, first and foremost, beginning with the clergy, whose role in the insurrection is well known, which is not surprising given they belonged to the cultural elite.[769] In this sense, the priests were the first to be affected by movements of opinion, but they also served as

---

767 Bravo Ugarte 1966, 30.

768 Some examples of this can be found in the 1812 Mexican elections; the influence of the powerful and the priests shows in the surveys of the time (see *La Constitución*..., vol. I, 230 and the following pages). The same thing happened in 1823 with the mobilization of the indigent population in favor of Iturbide (see Alamán 1972, vol. V, 455 and 463, for example).

769 We apply this term to people who stand out for their culture in the environment to which they belong. It is, therefore, a relative notion.

mediators for the opinion of the elites. This was even truer for the countryside than it was for the cities. In the villages, a substantial portion of the news passed through them.

The most important factor was that they legitimized (or not) movements and actions. In a deeply Christian society and at a time of crisis, the problem of the legitimacy of governments and its corollary, the right to revolt, occupied a central place in the conflicts. An example of this phenomenon is the battle of opinion that would be waged around the excommunication of insurgent leaders or the trial by civil tribunals of insurrectionary clerics, as seen both in newspapers[770] and in the many edicts and pastoral letters written and published by the bishops. These were meant to be read from the pulpit, and certainly played a crucial role both in the 1808-9 patriotic campaign and in the civil war.[771]

It was more difficult to assess the role of local personages, including indigenous caciques or municipal authorities—not in and of themselves (we have the correspondence they received) but in their relations with the urban elites and the clergy.

It was the clergy and local authorities who communicated official documents to the population of the villas and towns, almost always by organizing a public, and in some cases, solemn reading. We have spoken of pastoral letters, but we might add, given their importance in the transmission of modern ideas, the ceremonies that took place in 1812 to take the oath to the constitution:

> When the Constitution is received in the towns of the kingdom, the head or judge of each one, in agreement with the Town Council, shall appoint a day for the solemn publication of the Constitution in the more public and convenient place or places, [...] the

770 This is one of the most controversial topics in the newspaper *El Juguetillo,* published by Carlos María de Bustamante.

771 See, for example, those of Archbishop F. J. Linaza y Beaumont, in Medina 1911, vol. VII, 439, 440, 537 and 538; those of the bishop of Antequera de Oaxaca, Monsignor Antonio Bergosa y Jordán, ibid., vol. VII, 523 and 571, vol. VIII, 110, 11, 28–30, 53–57, and those of the bishop of Puebla, Manuel Ignacio González de Campillo, ibid., 616–17.

> whole Constitution shall be read aloud, followed by the writ of the Regency of the Kingdom, for its observance [...].
> A solemn mass of thanksgiving shall be celebrated, the Constitution shall be read before the offertory and the parish priest, or whomever he shall designate, shall make a brief exhortation corresponding to the object [...].[772]

This was done in all the localities controlled by the royalists.[773]

Finally, we must evaluate the spread of the insurgent leaflets that were circulated in the ranchos and among the indigenous populations. Their circulation likely followed the traditional routes of the *literatura de cordel*: the itineraries of the peddlers and those members of the general population who journeyed as part of their activities of exchange. These movements were so plentiful that, by the end of the eighteenth century, New Spain registered two hundred thousand donkeys, eighty thousand horses and one million mules.[774] Where did this printed material go? The answer will remain uncertain as long as we lack information, in this respect, about forms of village sociability as important as the confraternities.

At the end of the colonial period, New Spain thus appeared as a society that was both traditional and modern. It was traditional because of its corporate structure, the predominance of religious topics, and the homogeneity of the population's core values, despite cultural differences. It was modern given the intensity of its exchanges, the speed and extent of literacy, and the intense expansion of printing and printed matter. Let us now try to assess how these variables played out during the great revolutionary crisis that began in Spain in 1808.

---

772 "Decreto de la Regencia del Reino a los Intendentes," May 25, 1812, in *La Constitución de 1812…*, vol. I, 3.

773 See the proceedings of several of these ceremonies in ibid.

774 D. Dehouve, op. cit., vol. I, 333.

## From the "War of Words" to the Reign of Opinion

The Napoleonic invasion of Spain and the abdication of Ferdinand VII inaugurated the great crisis of the Hispanic world in May 1808. The consequences would be both the Spanish liberal revolution, leading to the Constitution of 1812 promulgated by the Cortes of Cádiz, and the Spanish American independences, which were largely its offspring.

This was a paradoxical crisis: in a relatively short time, we see a shift from loyalty to a Spanish nation comprising "the two hemispheres" and which, as Jovellanos clearly stated at the time, "is fighting for its religion, its constitution, its laws, its customs, its uses: in a word, for its freedom,"[775] to the sovereignty of the people and independence.

The issues we have discussed so far—i.e., the existence of highly developed modern means of communication—are one of the explanatory factors behind this paradox. The Spanish Revolution and the American Revolutions are but one and the same phenomenon.

During a first stage, which we could term that of wounded patriotism, as news arrived from the Peninsula, Spain and, later, America, reacted with equal indignation and identical fervor.

The power vacuum created in Spain by the loss of the king and the crisis of most of the traditional institutions resulted in the disappearance of the majority of legal barriers that had so far limited the printing press. Without official provisions, freedom of the press began its de facto existence from the moment the Spanish juntas were constituted. At the beginning of the uprising, the problem was not theoretical. It was, above all, a question of inflaming spirits in the fight against the invader, of proclaiming fidelity to the king, painting the perfidy and disloyalty of Napoleon and of the French in the darkest colors.

The manifestos, messages, proclamations, and patriotic sermons through which the various actors of the uprising expressed themselves multiplied and were printed as leaflets or broadsides, pasquinades, and newspapers, frequently published later in the form of booklets. The result was an extraordinary abundance of printed matter of all kinds.

775 Jovellanos to the French general Sebastiani, reproduced in the *Gazeta de México*, July 8, 1809, 608.

The proliferation of newspapers, above all, was extraordinary. As one of them states in September 1808 when speaking of the importance of public opinion to sustain the fight:

> There are no better means than those provided by the printing of newspapers; destined by their nature to excite, sustain, and guide public opinion [...]. This has been known to the Provinces of Spain, in whose capitals, after the generous resolution was formed to shake off the abominable yoke intended to subject us, *Gazetas* and *Diarios* immediately came out to exalt patriotism, and to communicate illumination and news.[776]

Sent everywhere immediately, all these printed materials were so many incitements to struggle assurances that people were not alone in their resistance, testimonies of the unanimous rejection of the invader by the nation. In the absence of institutions accepted by all, these texts expressed, in the unity of their themes, the unanimity of the nation and thus played, along with other means, a role in unifying the partial revolts.

Often, these texts were also reprinted as soon as they were received. Some examples show the trajectory of these texts and the very short time frames of their transmission. Thus, the issue of the *Correo de Gerona, del martes 28 de junio de 1808. En el que se da puntual noticia de la expedición del exército Francés contra dicha Ciudad y del resultado que tuvo*, was reprinted for the first time in Cádiz and then in Mexico, still during 1808. The issue of the *Correo Político y Literario de Salamanca* of Saturday, June 11, 1808, was also immediately reprinted in Cádiz and Mexico.[777]

Very soon, compilations of these printed materials would be published, giving patriotism new impetus. We have, for example, the *Colección de papeles interesantes sobre las circunstancias presentes*, published in three volumes in Madrid by Fuentenebro y Compañía during the

776 *Semanario Patriótico*, prospectus, Madrid, August 1808, 1.

777 Complete references in Medina 1911, vol. VII, 415 and 416.

summer of 1808.[778] This gathers manifestos of the juntas, speeches, messages, newspaper articles, reprinted pamphlets, etc. Another compilation, also from 1808, titled *Colección de bandos, proclamas y decretos de la Junta Suprema de Sevilla y otros papeles curiosos*, was reprinted in Cádiz by M. S. Quintana.[779]

All this was done spontaneously during the early days of the uprising, but awareness of the role played by the printing press in this revolutionary war was so clear that the Regency Council did not hesitate, a little later, to codify it as one of the duties of the intendentes, required to:

> report every month [...] what is the public spirit in them [the provinces], inflaming it and always working to electrify it to the greatest degree, scattering our public papers, which will be sent off by every post, reprinting what is in them most interesting relative to the resolute establishment of our Independence, hatred for the tyranny of the enemy and the abasement of his pride, issuing proclamations [...] that may help to convince young people that they must die alongside their brothers for their parents and families [...]; in short, the pen of the Intendentes must prepare the glories and laurels which the armies are to obtain once they defeat the enemy in campaign.[780]

Aware of the influence that writing, multiplied by the printing press, had on this literate society, the Regency Council did not hesitate to consider it indispensable in the preparation for military victories. The Mexican insurgents employed the same kind of language when they wrote, some time later: "the aid of the printing press [is] perhaps of greater need [to us] than cannons."[781]

---

778 Comprising 388, 438 and 176 pages, respectively.

779 See 64 where the same diversity of documents is found.

780 "El Consejo de Regencia del Reino a los Intendentes," May 25, 1810, in Gómez Imaz, *Guerra de la...*, pamphlet no. 63.

781 *Correo Americano del Sur*, February 25, 1813, quoted by Miquel y Vergés 1941, 17.

In this manner, a whole network of news circulation and a first outline of public opinion were constituted. Cádiz, as the above cited examples demonstrate, was an essential crossroads for the transmission of Spanish events and debates in the Americas. Its status as an important financial center, a great port for the Indies, and a cosmopolitan city with a strong foreign colony gave it, even before the meeting of the Cortes, a leading role in the shaping of American opinion.

The American reaction to the crisis of the monarchy was no different than the Spanish one. In New Spain, too, wounded patriotism lay at the very origin of a proliferation of publications that can be considered, in a broad sense, to be political. During the five months between July 1808 (when the king's abdication was made known) and the end of the year, so much patriotic material was published that it overturned the percentages of the titles printed. From 78 percent of religious titles and 1 percent of political titles in 1807, we see a shift to 45 percent of religious titles and 43 percent of patriotic and political ones in 1808. In absolute numbers, although the number of religious titles remained constant (72 in 1807, 69 in 1808), patriotic and political titles rose from 1 to 67. The following years only confirm this explosion: 114 patriotic titles accounted for 46 percent of total publications in 1809; 184 titles comprised 66 percent in 1810 (Table 1). Despite an inevitable lag and the coninued presence of the traditional institutions whose disappearance had enabled freedom of the press in the metropolis, New Spain followed in the footsteps of peninsular Spain.

We say that it followed in Spain's footsteps, because it is clear that the driving force was the Peninsula, not only chronologically, but also in terms of the origin of the published texts. Thirty-four percent of patriotic titles published in Mexico in 1808, and 48 percent in 1809,[782] were reprints of original Spanish publications. Cádiz above all, followed by Madrid and Seville, takes first place; there were also reprints of publications issued in other American cities, especially Havana, because of its role as a maritime stopover. The same thing happened, simultaneously,

782 The figures for 1810 are not significant, as Hidalgo's uprising gave precedence to the events taking place in New Spain, with 50 percent of the total number of titles.

in Buenos Aires. The reprints of the the papers (essentially political and patriotic) that arrived from the Peninsula represented about 50 percent of the total number of publications in 1808 and 1809.[783]

These proportions become even more impressive if we involve the newspapers. Not only did a substantial share of the articles and news published in Mexico come from Spain (usually reproducing newspaper articles, especially from Cádiz), but often complete issues of the Spanish newspapers would be republished in their totality as they arrived. Thus, in 1810, during the great period of the debate on the convocation of the Cortes, seven issues of *El Espectador Sevillano*, six of *El Voto de la Nación Española*, and twelve of *El Conciso* of Cádiz, were republished in Mexico.[784] The *Diario de México* clearly expressed the echo raised by the events in Spain and the dependence of Mexican opinion on that of Spain: "The reprint of *El Espectador Sevillano* with its questions on the Cortes, which has been received so appreciatively by the public, has been suspended for lack of the December 24, 1809 issue."[785]

The phenomenon is all the more relevant in New Spain because, after the coup d'état of September 1808 carried out by Yermo, which was supported by a portion of the peninsular colony, the times were not conducive to freedom of expression. And yet, how could the authorities oppose the patriotic expressions of the Creoles regarding the king and the occupied portion of the Spanish nation? How could they oppose these Spanish papers, aglow with patriotism, but also, as we shall soon see, filled with new ideas?

Wounded patriotism cried out loud and clear and was mutually inflamed by the unanimity of the protestations expressed in the texts that circulated from one Spanish city to another and, then, to America.

In terms of content, there is nothing very novel regarding old values and practices except for the breadth of the phenomenon. As in the France of the Fronde, the goal of this combat literature was to make

---

783 Calculations based on Romero 1959. Patriotic and political papers here accounted for 79 percent of the total in 1808 and 88 percent in 1809.

784 For bibliographical details, see Medina 1911, vol. VII, 510, 520, and 507.

785 *Diario de México*, September 7, 1810, ibid., vol. VII, 510.

people believe, to spur them to action.[786] It must therefore be analyzed in terms of its effectiveness: words were the weapons employed by the social actors in their struggle. It was through words that they strove to exalt their supporters, denigrate their enemies, mobilize the lukewarm.

However, this fight was not solely about battling the external enemy and vindicating wounded patriotism. There were also intense internal conflicts in which various actors confronted each other. At the center of the struggle was the creation of a legitimate interim power; the goal was to form, starting from the different insurrectionary authorities (i.e., the juntas), a unified governing body to lead the struggle against France and preserve the crown for Ferdinand VII.

During a first stage, in Spain and even though the new authorities had an insurrectionary origin, they all tried to appeal to traditional forms of legitimacy. In Aragon, the old Cortes had been summoned; in Galicia, the deputation of cities with a vote in the Cortes gathered; in Asturias, the former junta of the Principality had become a governing junta. Elsewhere, cabildos, sometimes enlarged or expanded, had formed other juntas.[787] Alongside these there still persisted key, though discredited, institutions of the ancien régime, such as the Council of Castile.

The "war of words," in the traditional sense, can also describe the rivalry between all these traditional and modern institutions during the period that preceded the meeting of the Cortes. The conflict was governed by very classical references: jurisprudence, ancient freedoms, traditional orders of precedence, immemorial procedures. Alongside this rivalry, however, there was already a modern conflict: that of opinion. And, beyond this seemingly innocent word, the key conflict of modern legitimacy: that of the sovereignty of the "nation."

The word, spoken and written, soon ceased to function as a mere weapon; it became the very essence of power: what the people or the nation said or wanted. The term "opinion," one of the key words of modern politics, quickly invaded patriotic discourse. The "unanimous voice of the nation" that rejected the usurper and proclaimed its allegiance

---

786 See C. Jouhaud, *Mazarinades: La Fronde des mots*, Paris, 1985.

787 Martínez de Velasco 1972, chapter III, and Artola 1959, vol. I.

to the captive king, its "unanimous action" to fight the invader, became the will of the people—the nation that acts.

The authors of this transformation were, precisely, the men of words and texts: the modern intellectual elites. An extreme minority at first, these men who had internalized modern politics and the ideas of the French Revolution regrouped in the modern forms of sociability. It was they who had mastered the language of the "citizen," of "despotism" and "liberty." In short, they were the ones who, as men of the spoken and written word, often occupied the most important positions in the progressive creation of patriotic propaganda. Quintana, a senior official of the Junta Central, is an example.[788]

Through them, the new language and the debates on opinion, which were revolutionary in their goal, came to the fore. As stated in the decree of the Cortes of November 15, 1810, which legally established freedom of the press:

> The general and extraordinary Cortes have considered that the individual faculty of citizens to publish their thoughts and political ideas is not only a check on the arbitrariness of those who govern but also a means of Enlightening the Nation in general, and the only way to gain knowledge of true public opinion.[789]

Here, public opinion plays the legitimizing role of the voice—the will, in fact—of the people. In this way, we cross the threshold into modern politics. And the Valencian patriots were quite right to see this step as irrevocable: "Only opinion, rooted in people's hearts and handed down from father to son, resists the woodworm of centuries and the insults of tyranny, and the devouring erosion of decay."[790]

In the face of this irruption of modern politics in the Peninsula, New Spain appeared, for a long time, as a very traditional region. This

---

788 See for this group, chapter VII.

789 "Decreto de las Cortes sobre la libertad de prensa," *Gaceta de la Regencia*, no. 95, November 15, 1810, in Gómez Imaz, *Guerra de la…*, pamphlet no. 77.

790 "Manifiesto de la Junta Suprema del Gobierno de Valencia," 1810, ibid., no. 79.

is not to say that the conflicts seeking to fill the power vacuum or the tensions between the different social actors should be dismissed. They existed to such a degree that they would lead to the great insurrection of 1810. For quite some time, however, the conflict took place within the old framework—that of the "war or words", of a world predating modern politics. The threshold would only be crossed progressively and thanks to the massive arrival of the publications that echoed the peninsular debate.

It was in this old-fashioned context that the debates of the summer of 1808 took place, with the presence of traditional corporate actors and constant references the traditional legitimizing theories. The confrontation pitted the cabildo of Mexico, supported by the viceroy, against the audiencia, which was controlled by the peninsular. The argument for the rights of the kingdom to convene a Junta General of New Spain responded to that of the inferior rights of a "colony" to passively maintain its constituted authorities. In short, the usual confrontation of Creoles and peninsulars. The conflict led, in September 1810, to the Hidalgo uprising, the great social revolt and the civil war.

This war mobilized, as in the Peninsula in the war against the invader, all the resources available to the contenders including, the press. It is because of the place words occupied in this struggle that the clash can be described as traditional. The issue is not the existence of modern technical means: we have already mentioned their abundance and the large number of readers. The issue is that of modern political culture and the number of new forms of sociability (the tertulias and the different societies) that were indispensable for the elaboration and transmission of new ideas.

The number of publications, as we have already shown, increased considerably after 1810, and even more so after 1812, the year in which freedom of the press would be briefly implemented. On both sides, writing was primarily a tool to mobilize supporters and condemn adversaries by referring to values that remained essentially traditional and still made religious orthodoxy the supreme argument. Accusations of treason against the king were answered by charges of wanting to hand the kingdom over to the French; those of disobedience to the legitimate authorities were countered by charges of complicity with that supreme evil, the ideas of the French Revolution. In 1812, the viceroy was still being called "Vizir, new Robespierre, atheist, materialist and Freemason" by the insurgent newspaper *Ilustrador Nacional*.[791]

The discourse of the insurgent publications was not that of a precocious Mexican liberalism, but that of the grievances, values, and utopias of a traditional society. The grievances: for the indigenous peoples, their communal lands usurped and their subjection to the tribute; for the mestizos, the tribute and racial discrimination; for the Creoles, their claim to preferential access to offices and employments. The values: loyalty to the imprisoned king, the defense of religion against the dangers of tolerance, the patronage of the Virgin of Guadalupe. The fears: the arrival of the French and their impiety, the treachery of the the peninsulars who wanted to hand the kingdom over to Bonaparte, enemies who poisoned springs. In short, the utopias of an egalitarian Christian millenarianism.

Are these messages taken from the insurgent literature a mere "mask" intended to mobilize a very traditional population, a tool employed by elites who had already crossed the threshold of modern politics? Except for the ritual reference to Ferdinand VII, considered very early on in the insurgents' private correspondence as "a pure entity of reason,"[792] there seems to be no voluntary concealment of values on other topics. Essentially, the elites and the general society shared the same mental universe during the early days of the revolt. Only later did modern elements progressively appear in the discourses of the insurgent elites. Was this then an internal evolution among the insurgents, which led led them to manufacture, according to the circumstances and needs of the moment, an early Mexican liberalism?

791 Facsimile page in Miquel y Vergés 1941, 65.

792 Letter from the Junta of Zitacuaro to Morelos, cited in ibid., 65.

## Center and Periphery

The answer, based on what has been said so far, is no. Not in terms of the origin of words, concepts, and institutions: this was a local version of the single great political debate taking place throughout the Spanish monarchy. It was also an outdated version: it took time for the ideas coming from the Peninsula, the center of the revolution, to arrive in America.

When one examines the more theoretical writings of the insurgents, one can see both the similarities and differences with the Peninsula. Thus, Ignacio Rayón speaks of the constitution and the sovereignty of the people, but he does so two years after the inaugural declaration of Cádiz stating that sovereignty corresponds essentially to the nation, two years after the beginning of the work of the Constitutional Commission in the Cortes, and in the very year of the promulgation of the Constitution of the Monarchy. Rayón speaks, indeed, of American citizens, but he clearly says that only "patricians" will occupy positions and that representatives to the Supreme Congress will be appointed by the municipal bodies. He speaks, indeed, of freedom of the press, but also of the restoration of the tribunal of the Inquisition.[793]

This delay is not surprising given that the insurgents were fighting in the countryside, and modern politics travelled by sea, and to the cities, thanks to the peninsular publications. We have stated before that, since 1808 and, above all, during 1809–10, patriotic publications multiplied in New Spain and that, for the most part, they were peninsular pamphlets and newspapers coming mainly from Cádiz. It was impossible for zealous authorities, even if they had wanted to prevent the entry of new ideas into Mexico, to make a distinction between patriotism and modern politics. The two were intimately intertwined in peninsular Spain as well as in Mexico. Since to effectively oppose the invader it was necessary to constitute an indisputable unified power, should this power not also transform the aging institutions that had enabled so many abuses, made all the more vividly present by the proximity of Godoy's tenure? The authors might differ on the extent of the reforms and the institutions

793 Ignacio Rayón, *Elementos constitucionales*, 1812, in De la Torre Villar 1982, vol. II, 423 and the following pages.

that should prevent arbitrariness (the majority wanted a restoration and reform of the old institutions, the liberal minority a constitution), but the debate was inevitable.

This debate crossed the Atlantic, how could it not? In 1808, a pamphlet entitled *Gobierno pronto y reformas* (Speedy Government and Reforms) was published in Cádiz and reprinted in Mexico.[794] Also reprinted, as we have said, were many manifestos of the Spanish juntas,[795] and, especially later, the manifestos and decrees of the Junta Central and the Regency Council of the Kingdom,[796] which were thoroughly pervaded by the radical language of the poet Quintana, whose *España libre. Odas* (Free Spain: Odes)[797] was also published in Mexico. The debate on the convocation of the Cortes, which was the central point of the peninsular political debate, was closely followed in Mexico and we have already quoted the observations of the *Diario de México* regarding how the reprint of the issues of *El Espectador Sevillano* on the Cortes had "been received so appreciatively by the public."

Under this avalanche of papers, the references of those Creoles who were in favor of independence or New Spain's autonomy evolved. The lampoon posted by the licenciado José Castillejos in 1809 clearly exposes the origin of the mutation: "Let there be no further disputation

---

794 Printed in Cádiz and reprinted in Mexico, "in the office on Santo Domingo Street," 10; in fact, the original had appeared first in Madrid.

795 The proclamations of the Junta of Cádiz in 1810 are of particular importance, both for the speed of their transmissions and for their liberalism, which was the most advanced in the whole Peninsula. They were published in Mexico as: *Colección de providencias dadas en la ciudad de Cádiz para el establecimiento de su Junta Superior de Gobierno para la defensa, provisión y conservación de la tranquilidad y buen orden en aquella plaza*, 24, and *La Junta Superior de Cádiz a la América española*, Isla de León, February 28, 1810, 8.

796 See, for example: *La Suprema Junta Gobernativa del Reino a la Nación Española*, October 26, 1808, reprinted "by order of the authority" in Mexico in January 1809; *La Junta Suprema del Reino a la Nación Española*, November 21, 1809, reprinted "by order of the authority" in Mexico in 1810.

797 Reprinted by the editor of the *Gaceta de Nueva España*, Mexico, 1809, 14.

about the peoples' rights: the veil that covered them has been torn aside. No one is unaware now that under present circumstances, sovereignty resides in the peoples. We learn this from the multitude of printed materials arriving from the Peninsula."[798]

To all these peninsular newspapers would be added, from 1810 onward, *El Español*, published monthly by José María Blanco White in London. The former editor of the Seville edition of the *Semanario Patriótico*, Blanco White would soon share the views of the American insurgents and meet their sympathizers in London. From that strategic place, his newspaper would henceforth prove an indispensable vehicle for news of both worlds and both sides, becoming a vital mediator and a sounding board for the spread of information and debates from all over the Hispanic world.[799]

The movement accelerated even more at the start of 1810, when the Junta Central, before dissolving, decided to convene the Cortes. From then on, the political debate in the Peninsula would revolve around the Cortes: first, around their meeting and powers and then, around their debates on the reform of the monarchy. The problem of American representation, which had already begun to poison the atmosphere between peninsular Spain and America since the elections of the American deputies to the Junta Central the previous year, now became vitally important: everyone understood the importance the future Cortes would have for the whole of the monarchy.[800]

The peninsular revolutionary language, which had always been ahead of American political discourse, once again opened the way for another step toward modern politics.

The creation of the Regency Council that succeeded the Junta Central even appeared officially as a demand made by public opinion: "the urgency of the evils that afflict us, and the public opinion that is

---

798 Quoted by Miranda 1952, 256.

799 Blanco White was able to build a whole network of correspondents, many of them secret and largely linked to the network of the Lautaro Lodge. For this key figure in the Hispanic revolutions, cf. Pons, 1990.

800 See chapter VII on these topics.

regulated by them, demand the establishment of a council of Regency and demand it now."[801]

In the manifesto appended, on February 14, 1810, to the decree of the Regency Council summoning America and the Philippines to send their deputies to the future Cortes,[802] a radical critique of the institutions that had governed the Indies was formulated to exalt the present, and this critique went much further than what had been said and published until then.[803]

The most extreme liberal language, the kind no one would have dared employ in America, was employed by the government of the monarchy itself:

> from this time forth, American Spaniards, you are elevated to the dignity of free men [...] your destinies no longer depend on Ministers, Viceroys, or Governors; they are in your own hands [...].
> It is necessary that in this act [the elections to the Cortes], the most solemn, the most important of your civil life, each elector should say to himself: [...] this man is the one who will expose and remedy all the abuses, all the extortions, all the evils that have been caused in these countries by the arbitrariness and nullity of the rulers of the old government: it is he who must contribute to the shaping, through just and wise Laws, of a well-ordered whole out of so many, so vast, and such separate domains.[804]

---

801 "Real decreto de la Junta central," January 29, 1810, published in Mexico by proclamation of the Archbishop-Viceroy Francisco Javier de Lizana, May 7, 1810, AGN, Historia, vol. 446, file 111.

802 Royal decree of February 14, 1810, Cádiz, 1810, 3, in Gómez Imaz, *Guerra de...*, no. 53. For the decree of convocation in Spain, see Fernández Martín 1885, vol. II, 571 and the following pages.

803 *El Consejo de regencia de España e Indias a los americanos españoles*, Real Isla de León, February 14, 1810, 8. The manifesto was drafted by Quintana and published in Mexico by proclamation of the Archbishop-Viceroy Francisco Javier de Lizana, on May 16, 1810, AGN, Bandos, vol. 25, file 80.

804 Ibid.

We have quoted this essential text at length, for it was issued, let us remember, ten months before the Hidalgo revolt. It was reprinted, of course, in New Spain[805] and widely disseminated; it would serve as the basis for the elections that would take place very soon afterward.

The impact of this type of text could not but be very great. Modern ideas came with all the authority of the central government. They were not seditious theories arriving clandestinely from France, but the very standard of the legitimate government of the monarchy. The discontented Creoles had only to refer to them, reproaching the authorities for mocking the principles to which they should be faithful.

Three years later, the Audiencia of Mexico, in a representation addressed to the Cortes to oppose freedom of the press in America, sums up this phenomenon:

> Eagerness for imitation provided an opportunity to gather this set of ineptitudes and delusions. Drawing on similar propositions printed elsewhere, with another motive, and by persons whom this court, giving them the benefit of the doubt, believes were spurred by the sincere desire that these countries should remain ever united with the Peninsula, have been transplanted here for a contrary purpose; thus, the vivid phrases of patriotism and eloquence Your Majesty heard regarding how tyranny had reigned in America, introducing slavery, oppression, vexations, bans on everything, humiliation, injustices as old as the establishment of the Spaniards, etc., etc., were copied here in isolation and twisted against the sound intention of their authors, propagating the evil they had sought to prevent.[806]

Very soon it was no longer the declarations of intent by the highest Spanish authorities that were disseminated in this way; the electoral process of the Cortes began. On different dates, but essentially through

805 Reprinted at the Arizpe press, "by order of the government," Mexico, 1810.

806 Representation of the Audiencia of Mexico to the Cortes, November 18, 1813, on the impossibility of enacting the constitution and the freedom of the press, in *La Constitución de 1812...*, vol. II, 226.

the spring–summer of 1810, election of deputies to the General and Extraordinary Cortes that would meet in Cádiz on September 24, 1810, took place in all the cabildos of the provincial capitals.[807]

Even though it was an old-fashioned electoral process, like the one employed for the elections to the Junta Central, the cabildos deliberated, voted, and prepared the mandates of their deputies. The principle of representation was again put into practice, and the deputies of New Spain arrived in Cádiz at the end of 1810 and the beginning of 1811. A new link was created, this time direct and institutional, which meant that New Spain would participate for over four years in the debates of the revolutionary Cortes of Cádiz.

This period, from 1810 to 1814, would be the privileged moment for the spread of new ideas and the mutation of the Mexican elites. Although Hidalgo's insurrection polarized the attention of the inhabitants of New Spain, the other inseparable center of their interest was, as for the entire Hispanic world, this great constituent assembly.

It was constituent and revolutionary, in the proper sense of the term, and would tear down, in the space of three years, the edifice of the Hispanic ancien régime. From the opening declaration of the first session, in which it was decreed that "sovereignty resides essentially in the Nation," a whole series of fundamental provisions followed: freedom of the press, suppression of the Inquisition, suppression of lordships, measures for the establishment of modern, individual, and full property, etc. These provisions would be duly published in Mexico and incipiently enacted in New Spain.[808]

Not only the dispositions of the Cortes, but the debates themselves were assiduously followed, as far as maritime communications permitted. It can be confirmed, for example in examining the 1811 *Correo Semanario Político y Mercantil de México*, that political articles on the debates in Cádiz were frequent. Sometimes these were extracts from the *Diario de las Sesiones de las Cortes*, but even more frequently, articles

807 ACE, Credenciales, file 3.

808 The main decrees for their application in New Spain can be seen in *La Constitución de 1812...*, vol. II, book VIII.

would be drawn from the Cádiz press or from other newspapers of the Hispanic world. There were articles from *El Conciso*, *Diario de Cádiz*, *El Observador*, *La Tertulia de Cádiz*, *El Patriota en Cortes*, *El Redactor General*, *El Hablador* and *El Diario de La Habana*.[809]

These texts dealt with the most explosive topics, sometimes cautiously (this took place, after all, in the middle of a civil war), and sometimes in extremely radical terms, as in this text taken from *El Redactor General* and entitled "Derechos del hombre". It is an article of extreme revolutionary inspiration that follows very closely, sometimes quite literally, the French Constitution of 1793. Not even the Constitution of 1812 dared formulate such ideas:

> I. The common good is the goal of society; and that of the government instituted therein is the preservation of the rights of its members. These rights are *equality*, *liberty*, *security*, and *property*.
> II. Since nature has endowed all men with the same organs, the same sensations, and the same needs, God, their eternal author, has thus declared [...] that all were equal in the order of nature.
> III. Being equal to one another, men are also independent in the order of nature: they are free [...]. Society, then, is the work of the will of men.
> IV. The law in society is the free and solemn expression of the general will. [...]
> VI. Security [...]. The law must protect public and individual liberty against any kind of aggression. [...]
> XI. The right to property is the right of every citizen to enjoy and dispose of his goods and income, the fruits of his labor and industry. [...]
> XIII. Every man may hire out his services, his time, but he can neither sell himself nor be sold; his person is not property.
> XIV. [...] The people has the right to concur in the appointment of contributions, to watch over its investments, and examine the corresponding accounts. [...]

809 List made from vol. III, January 2–October 30, 1811, of the *Correo Semanario político y mercantil de México*.

> XVII. Sovereignty resides essentially in the people; its exercise in those it elects.
> XVIII. No individual, nor any portion of the people, may exercise sovereignty without election by the entire people, in whom it essentially resides; [...] but every citizen has the right to freely express his will in the choice of those who are to exercise it.
> XIX. A people always has the right to revise, reform, and change its constitution; one generation cannot subject future generations to its institutions. [...]
> XXIV. [...] Public happiness is the composite and sum of individual happinesses.[810]

The interest with which the work of the Cortes was followed is also shown by the fact that the constitutional project, as prepared by the Constitutional Commission, was immediately printed.[811] The constitution itself was obviously published in New Spain immediately after its promulgation in 1812 "by order of His Excellency the Viceroy."[812]

This would be followed by the printing of the most important decrees and speeches of the Cortes. The suppression of the Inquisition and the ensuing controversy in both Spain and America occupied a very particular place.[813] New Spain participated, both because of the loyalty of one of its parties and the common shared culture, in the ideological debates of the Hispanic Revolution.

The promulgation of this constitution and the oath to uphold it, enacted in Mexico City on September 30, 1812, gave the movement new

---

810 Ibid., vol. III, no. 39, November 25, 1811, 307–9.

811 *Proyecto de Constitución política de la Monarquía española presentado a las Cortes generales y extraordinarias por su Comisión de Constitución*, Cádiz, royal press, 1811, and in Mexico, by Manuel A. Valdés, in the same year.

812 *Constitución política de la Monarquía española...*, reprinted in Mexico "by order of His Excellency the Viceroy," September 8, 1812.

813 The liberal *El Conciso: Sesiones de las Cortes sobre el tribunal de la Inquisición, desde el 8 de diciembre de 1812 hasta el 20 de febrero de 1813*, for example, was reprinted. Mexico, 1813, 38.

impetus. What until then had been an important but theoretical event that the cultivated elites had followed through the press and publications now became the new legal standard of the kingdom. The constitution was promulgated with all the solemnity we have described above across all the cities and towns controlled by the "royalists." Henceforth, there was no need to travel to the big cities in search of the modern ideas coming from Spain. The constitution was everywhere and accessible to any curious person. And very soon, not only as a doctrinal text of reference, but as the supreme law that would progressively be implemented–even those articles that were the most dangerous for the "royalists."

Freedom of the press, for example, which the Cortes had decreed on November 15, 1810, had yet to be applied in New Spain because of the viceroy and the audiencia's resistance, which was due to the civil war. When they could no longer oppose the orders of the Cortes, it was promulgated on October 5, 1812. With it began a new stage for the massive spread of liberal ideas.

The main impact of the freedom of the press was, above all, the use of this new weapon (the printing press) in the very heart of the "royalist" zones, by the hitherto hidden supporters of the insurgency. New newspapers, openly sympathetic to the insurgents, appeared in Mexico, and the authorities could do very little about it. This was how Carlos María de Bustamante's *El Juguetillo*, and José Joaquín Fernández de Lizardi's *El Pensador Mexicano,* appeared alongside numerous works that, in one way or another, defended the insurgents.

When we try to assess the nature of these publications and the real effects of freedom of the press in Mexico, we find ourselves torn with contradictory impressions that are also evident in the reports made by the royalist authorities. Viceroy Calleja, the following year, in his account of the months during which freedom of the press was in force, seems to believe, at first, in the considerable influence of Spanish liberal ideas:

> The very Diaries of the Cortes have supplied materials for the rebellious writers to wage an unstoppable war against us; and using the light of their reason in a malignant manner, for example presenting the liberal principles of the Congress in a dislocated way, distorting their foundation and sense and considering themselves as a

> separate nation in applying the consequences of these principles, this means has afforded them more proselytes than the advantages that their weapons have ever been able to obtain.[814]

Some articles from the insurgent newspapers the *Semanario Patriótico Americano*, *El Ilustrador Americano* and *Correo Americano del Sur* are cited,[815] as are some from newspapers published in Mexico City, such as *El Juguetillo* and *El Pensador Mexicano.*[816] But the main focus, even more than new arguments for independence, is the denunciation by these newspapers of the restrictions imposed on the freedoms recognized by the constitution. As Calleja himself states:

> complaints against a measured despotism were reproduced, restrictions that no longer existed were exposed, and necessary measures were distorted [...] all kinds of precautions were maligned, painted as the most extraordinary arbitrariness and as the distortion of the laws and the Constitution[...].[817]

However, regarding the actual content of these texts, a cursory examination shows, rather than a multiplication of modern references, the continuation of the old-style "war of words", now openly carried on by the formerly clandestine literature of the supporters of the insurgency. For example, the issue that led to the most bitter disputes was the order issued by the viceroy to treat insurgent clerics like the rest of the leaders of the uprising. This measure, which attacked the privileges of the

---

814 "Carta del Virrey Félix María Calleja al Ministro de Justicia," June 20, 1813, in De la Torre Villar 1982, vol. III, 491.

815 Ibid.

816 The Audiencia of Mexico also reproaches Bustamante for applying, in *El Juguetillo*, no. 5, the idea of the sovereignty of the nation to Mexico. Report of the Audiencia of Mexico to the Cortes of November 18, 1813, in *La Constitución de 1812...*, vol. II, 224.

817 "Carta del Virrey Félix María Calleja al ministro de Justicia," June 10, 1813, in De la Torre Villar 1982, vol. III, 491.

clergy, was opposed first by a group of clergymen in Mexico City; then several polemical pamphlets appeared, defending the immunity of the clergy and painting the measure as an attack on religion.[818] These were polemics and arguments of an old type, but their effects on the people were considerable. As Calleja's document states:

> the people [...] listened incessantly to the commentaries made in those writings [...] and absorbed the ideas intended to inspire them [...]. [They were led to believe] that some resolution was an attack on the purity of religion and the rights of the Church, as was argued in printed matter of those days, among which are those already mentioned, and especially a representation called Of the Mexican Clergy, which, multiplied and circulated in copies, was afterward printed at Tlalpujahua [...] these ideas having been disseminated among the multitude, canonized by the authority of an ecclesiastical author or apologist and by the validation of the printing press, caused an inexpressible increase in the indisposition of spirits [...].[819]

With this defense of ecclesiastical jurisdiction, we are far from a modern political register. Paradoxically, this freedom of the press that the liberals used in Spain to achieve the "kingdom of opinion," led at this time in New Spain to the mobilization of the people using traditional arguments. These were, however, no less effective:

---

818 See for this subject the above cited audiencia report. Among the incriminated pamphlets: José Julio García de Torres, *Vindicación del clero mexicano vulnerado en las anotaciones que publicó el M.R. P. Fr. José Joaquín Oyarzábal contra la representación que el mismo clero dirigió al Ilmo y Venerable Cabildo Sede-vacante, promoviendo la defensa de su inmunidad personal*, Mexico, published by M. A. Valdés 1812, 16. Fernández de Lizardi also intervenes in the controversy in *El Pensador mexicano*, no. 9, reproduced in *La Constitución de 1812...*, vol. II, 206–13.

819 "Carta del Virrey Félix María Calleja al ministro de Justicia", June 10, 1813, in De la Torre Villar 1982, vol. III, 494.

> all their papers [...] unfortunately circulate surreptitiously in this capital and other large towns, and continual vigilance and multiplied precautions are powerless to put a stop to it, and yet it is not possible that their venom should spread across the whole of the people, into whose hands they will find it difficult to arrive; however, the liberty of writing having been established, the wicked found the desired means with which to stir the ignorant multitude while combining the efforts of external enemies with the prevarication of the capital, now covertly pouring the spirit of those newspapers into the public writings of the capital, now inspiring hatred and abhorrence of the government by means of pictures of oppression and tyranny [...].[820]

The widespread literacy of New Spain favored this new weapon of the supporters of independence. The Audiencia of Mexico would say that "seditious and incendiary pamphlets were distributed even in the poorest and most humble homes."[821] The observation may appear exaggerated but, after the first elections for the new constitutional Ayuntamiento of Mexico that took place in the parishes on November 29 and 30, 1812, the disorders that broke out in the city provide a measure of the influence of these publications. A witness affirmed that: "among the various expressions heard among the rabble were those of long live the authors of *Juguetillos* and *Pensador Mexicano*, because they tell the plain truth."[822]

One of those elected was also heard saying, in order to justify the agitation, "that the people who were present 'were sovereign' and entitled to any demonstration, all the more so during the initial moments when they began to the exercise the rights of their sovereignty."[823]

---

820 Ibid., 492–93.

821 Report of the audiencia in *La Constitución de 1812*..., vol. II, 240.

822 Declaration of Don Manuel de Larragorta, ibid., vol. II, 216.

823 Declarations made to the mayor of district no. 9 on December 3, 1812, ibid., vol. II, 248.

In fact, we can see here the popularity of the journalists, which seems, however, to be of the old type, alongside the very modern justifications given by leaders who are essentially intellectuals. The viceroy pointed to this phenomenon in the report we have already quoted at length, in which he paints a portrait of those responsible for the pro-independence propaganda and the reasons for their superiority:

> almost all the Europeans in these countries are merchants, landowners, and clerks, and consequently very few of them have the ability or occasion to engage in political controversies for want of education or time; among the Americans, there abound literate blusterers, idle priests and corrupt schoolboys who, while they fail to produce anything original, know how to copy, truncate texts written by others, hallucinate, and pervert [...].[824]

The viceroy's judgment certainly reflects the passions of the time, but the identity of the group that supported the new ideas is perfectly defined: lawyers, priests, students—that is, the intellectual elites. As in Spain, they were the first to cross the threshold of modern politics, though they still used the ancient references to mobilize a society whose mental universe remained traditional.

For now, the downward spread of the new political culture was just beginning, especially since the restoration of absolutism in 1814, in Spain and in America, deprived the liberals of any means of public action. It was not until the Spanish liberal revolution of 1820 that the process would begin again and again, we will see the driving force of peninsular Spain, the multiplication of political publications on both sides of the Atlantic, the mobilization and acculturation of society by the intellectual elites. Public opinion, still in embryo in 1814, would then at last be truly born thanks to the growth of modern forms of sociability. It was then that society would truly enter political modernity, at least as far as the elites were concerned, with newspapers of opinion, journals of opinion, high-quality constitutional debates, incipient political parties. The 1820s would also see the progressive access of a significant part of

824 Report of Viceroy Félix María Calleja..., loc. cit., 494–95.

the urban lower classes to the new political universe, as shown by the popular language that the elites strove to employ in their pamphlets.[825]

We will pause here, having attempted to show that, if we are to understand it fully, the whole process of independence presupposes the prior existence of a cultural and technical modernity. While it is true that society still belonged to the ancien régime, rapid cultural modernization was enabling both the spread of an old-style type of revolt and the intellectual elites' access to modern political culture thanks to the influence exerted on them by the peninsular revolutionaries.

---

825 Alamán 1972, vol. V, 37, lucidly points out this phenomenon with the example of Azcárate, who was known for his culture and also authored pamphlets written in picaresque language such as *La chanfaina se quita*, *Las zorras de Sansón*, *Al que le venga el saco, que se lo ponga*, etc.

# IX

# Mutations and Victory of the Nation

Among the most important problems of the revolutionary era were, without a doubt, those pertaining to the nation. They were first and foremost political problems, given that many of the battles to be waged by the opponents of absolutism would concern the nation and its rights. As in the case of the French National Assembly of 1789, the proclamation of national sovereignty by the Cortes in Cádiz in 1810 would be the first and foundational act of the Hispanic Revolution. But what kind of nation are we talking about? The nation, as it was conceived in the late eighteenth century, was still a far cry from the modern nation as it would be envisioned after the revolution. One of the key points in the cultural and political mutation to modernity can be found precisely here: in the transition from the old conception of nation to the modern one.

The first conception, despite the changes it was already undergoing, referred to the diverse and heterogeneous political communities of the ancien régime, born of the long common existence of a group of people and the formulation by the elites and the state of a history and imaginary specific to this group. In the old sense, the nation referred to the past, to the history—real or mythical—of a human group that felt itself to be one and different from the *others*. The second conception—the modern nation—alludes to a new community, founded on the free association of the inhabitants of a country. In essence, this nation was already sovereign, and for its framers, it was, obviously, identified with freedom. While the first looked to the past, the second looked to the future: one was the recognition of a historical fact; the other, a project.

But in our case other problems appear that have to do with the emergence in America of new independent states that would justify their existence by their achieving the status of nations. The appearance of "nations" in Hispanic America is largely a historical enigma: America appears within the ensemble of the monarchy as a region of extraordinary cultural, political, and religious homogeneity. Everything that would serve as a basis for the affirmation of "nationality" in the contemporary world was common to the future Hispanic American countries. One might almost say that, if the great problem of nineteenth-century Europe was that of the diverse nationalities attempting to achieve an independent existence, that is to say, to become nation-states, the problem of Hispanic America was, first, how to build different states based on a single nationality, and then a single nation-state for each.

Moreover, most of the elements that normally constitute nationality were not only common to all of Hispanic America but also to much of peninsular Spain. The impassioned patriotism with which the Americans reacted in 1808 in the name of a single "Spanish nation" is a clear sign of this extraordinary cohesiveness of the Hispanic monarchy. And yet, a few years later, these same Americans would justify their struggle on the basis of a "national" demand. Analyzing the mutations in the concept of nation is also an attempt to understand Independence.

## Rival Conceptions of the Nation

By the late eighteenth century, one might have said, at first glance, that absolutism had managed to impose an image of society and political power that already was, in a way, modern. The realm—the word is more and more often used in the singular replacing the traditional "realms"—tends to be considered as a homogeneous group of individuals, the subjects, equal in rights and duties before the higher authority of the king, ever more often conceived as absolute.

True, this image was more of an objective to be achieved than an actually existing reality. For one thing, society was still structured in kingdoms and cities, estates and corporations, and the political and social imaginary of the majority of the population pertained more to this reality than to the homogenizing discourse of absolutism. For another, during the reign of Charles IV some of the enlightened elites had already begun to question the all-encompassing power of the king and to demand the rights of a nation.[826]

The first effect of the events of 1808 was to clearly reveal how fragile the absolutist conception of the monarch's power really was. Its fragility was due not only to opposing doctrines or political imaginaries but also to its inability to provide a conceptual basis for rejecting the usurper. Though we still do find proponents of absolutism, such as the Count of Floridablanca, what the innumerable writings of 1808 primarily show is a general rejection of the unilateral relationship between the king and the nation. In this sense, we can speak of a victory of pactism insofar as society was asserting its possession of such robust political rights that they were able to legitimize both the rejection of a new sovereign and the creation of provisional powers.

The terms used to describe this society, and therefore its nature, were very diverse and still largely traditional. Nonetheless, beyond the terminology, the reality they referred to was that of a political community tied to the monarchy by reciprocal bonds ruled by a multitude of ancient laws forming part of its very identity. When the proclamations declared that the combatants were fighting for king, country, and religion, this amounted to saying that they were doing so for the decisive defense of society as it was, as history had shaped it. In the Peninsula, Jovellanos states: "Spain is fighting for its religion, its constitution, its laws, its customs, its uses: in a word, for its freedom."[827]

Two years later and in almost the same words, Miguel Hidalgo would justify his uprising against the Europeans, suspected of collaboration with the French invaders, in order to defend: "our religion, our law, our freedom, our customs, and all that is most sacred and precious for us to protect."[828]

Both are obviously referring to a historical constitution of the kingdom, with its "laws," its "customs," its "uses," and not a constitution in

---

826 See "The Political Frame of Reference: Pactism Reborn," in chapter V.

827 Letter by Melchor Gaspar de Jovellanos, published by the *Gazeta de México*, July 8, 1809, 608.

828 "Proclama de Miguel Hidalgo, 1810," in De la Torre Villar 1964, 203.

the modern sense of the term, namely, as an expression of national sovereignty.

Most often, traditional references are used to justify resistance to the invader and the new dynasty.[829] As previously mentioned, there is an appeal to the "oath sworn" to the captive monarch as the expression of a relationship agreed upon between the king and the kingdom. As an argument of authority, the historical constitution is implicitly invoked by widely citing old medieval laws, and in particular *Las Partidas*, on the guardianship for a minor or disabled king:[830] from these premises follows the need for society to consent both to the change in dynasty and to the authorities who must govern in the name of Ferdinand VII.

Although what is denoted is clear, the vocabulary of the time is extremely confused. This society that claims an essential role in legitimizing the political authorities at times presents itself as "the people" in general—in the classic sense of society as a whole—through whom the power emanating from God passes *per populum*; at other times as the "people" of such and such a province, city or realm—that is to say the "peoples"—at others, as "realms," based on a plural notion of the monarchy; and finally, at still other times, as the "realm," that is, a unitary entity, equivalent to a nation, which at the time was massively bursting into the political vocabulary of the Hispanic world in order to designate the entire monarchy, all the Spaniards of both hemispheres.

In America, the frame of reference was the same and perhaps even more traditional than in the Peninsula. In the summer of 1808, the debates in the cabildo of Mexico City centered on quotations and commentaries of the old laws: *Partidas*, *Fuero Juzgo*, *Leyes de Indias*,

---

829 While we find few distinctly modern references, some examples are those of the Junta de Asturias, although the rites of government continued to be very traditional, even here: the secretary of the Junta del Principado opened the session by placing on his head and later kissing the document received from the city prior to reading it. See Martínez de Velasco 1972, 81.

830 See the arguments used by Jovellanos, based on the laws of the *Partidas*, in Jovellanos 1811.

privileges granted by the kings.[831] Everyone always mentioned the rights of the realm, even though, as in the Peninsula, some used the word "nation" and others, "people" or "peoples." Without a doubt, all these words referred to a political community of the old kind, made up of a group of bodies. As the cabildo of Mexico City stated in 1808 in its petition for a general Congress of the kingdom: "the final will and resolution of the realm interpreted through its capital metropolis, until such time as the other cities and ecclesiastic and noble estates, in conjunction with the capital, may carry it out themselves or through their *procuradores*."[832]

This is quite evidently the petition of a traditional Cortes composed of the union of the three branches: clergy, nobility, and cities, as expressed through privilege by the capital city of New Spain.[833]

The clearest pactist stances in the rejection of the king's abdication and the new dynasty were expressed with unparalleled clarity in the Peninsula:

> That disastrous abdication is involuntary, forced [...] and of no effect against the most respectable rights of the Nation. It strips it of the most precious royalty it possesses. No one can designate him Sovereign without his consent and the universal consent of all his peoples.[834]

The pact concluded between the king and the nation, considered as the integration of the realm into the crown, harkens back to the first years of the Conquest, and is renewed with each new coronation in the mutual pledge by the king to uphold the fundamental laws, and by the realm to be faithful to the king. The abdication is:

---

831 The majority of these debates can be found in the compilation by Hernández Davalos 1877, vol. I, and also in Tena Ramírez 1967.

832 Proceedings of the cabildo of Mexico of July 19, 1808, in Tena Ramírez 1967, 7–14.

833 Privilege granted by Charles V. See R.L.R.I., vol. II, book III, title VIII, law II.

834 Ibid., 12–13.

> contrary to the oath sworn by Lord Charles IV at the time of his coronation not to alienate all or part of the dominions that pledged obedience to him; and it is also contrary to the most solemn pact of fidelity established by Lord Charles the First with this Most Noble City as a Metropolis of the Kingdom not to alienate it nor deprive it of what it holds by privilege.[835]

The mutual bond is expressed in the most traditional language—oath, pact of fidelity—and to express the indivisibility of the nation, understood here as the entirety of the monarchy, and the non-transferable nature of the king's sovereignty, the texts even draw on the analogy, taken from private law, of property entailed by primogeniture, which also makes it possible to insist on the nation, the primordial origin of royal power: "The Spanish Monarchy is the estate entailed upon its Sovereigns, founded by the Nation itself, which established the order of succession within the lines of descent of the Royal Family."[836]

We thus find ourselves in a fully pactist mental universe, although this convenient term refers more to what it rejects—absolutism—than to the reasons for the rejection and the goals it wishes to achieve. Indeed, beyond this rejection, considerable differences emerged regarding how to understand this human community which many described with the word "nation." The differences were such that they would be among the most important factors in the definition of the political groups and in their disputes. But conceptualizing these differences and these groups is not easy, not only because the political language of the time was not yet very precise, but also because the differing conceptions of the nation were the result of specific combinations in which diverse variables came into play. The first referred to its basic components: the bodies and estates or the individuals; the second to its political structure: a unitary or a plural nation.

There is, however, a first definition that these groups all shared, aside from their differences: the nation meant the monarchy as a whole.

835 Ibid., 13.

836 Ibid.

As the unanimous reaction of its inhabitants on both continents clearly demonstrated, the Spanish nation was a community of men who felt united by the same sentiments, values, religion, customs, and above all, a common allegiance to the king. In this respect, the unity of the nation was an experiential fact that brooked no opposition; but it was a moral unity displayed primarily in relation to the outside.

As soon as one ceases to speak of this moral unity, the differences appear. As we mentioned, the first conception pitched those who believed the nation was shaped by the entirety of the bodies and estates of ancien régime society against those who thought it should be composed of autonomous individuals. These two positions had divergent implications not only for representation, but also for the relationship between the nation and history, the present and the future.

For the first group, the nation was above all a complex entity, born of a long history during which its values, laws, and customs—in other words, its identity—had been forged. From that history it inherited its "constitution"—we might almost say its nature—that is, the laws that governed it, its very structure. From it were derived the bodies and estates that shaped it and also its *fueros,* understood simultaneously as customs and as freedoms. All of this does not mean that this "constitution" could not be modified, but its reform must take into account and respect, as far as possible, all these fundamental laws, preeminent among which were those that governed relations with the king and those that concerned the representation of the most important bodies shaped by history.

Butthe definition of those bodies upon which history had conferred such a significance that it required their representation divided this approach into two additional tendencies. Should the estates—nobility, clergy, and cities—or the kingdoms—represent the peoples that still made up the monarchy? Most of the so-called historical constitutionalists of the Peninsula, such as Jovellanos, continued to align with absolutism with respect to the unity of the nation. Spain was a unitary nation in which representation of the kingdoms had no place, as in the Bourbon Cortes. What they did demand now was representation by estates, and they invoked the fundamental laws that absolutism had violated; but, in fact, they did so to imitate the much-admired English model and to avoid the dangers of a French-style national assembly.

Nearly alone among the peninsulars and deeply original in his position, Martínez Marina rejects the representation of the privileged estates:

> the hereditary nobility, this class that is always an enemy of the people, this scourge of the social order, formed another nation, another state within the nation [...] The clergy anxiously aspired to worldly rule [...] These powerful bodies rarely came together to promote the common good but rather to multiply evil.[837]

The rejection is made in the name of the people, in a tone which recalls Sieyès: "the people, which really is the nation itself and in whom sovereign authority resides."[838]

And yet, contrary to what might be expected, although it was consistent with his fundamentally historical view of the "Spanish constitution," for Martínez Marina this people should be represented in Cortes by the "*procuradores* of the commons, councils and *ayuntamientos*, the sole representatives of the realm according to law and custom:"[839] in other words, by the representatives of the "peoples," the monarchy's basic political communities.

Martínez Marina agreed on this with the Americans, who made up the bulk of this subcurrent. The vast majority of them continued to have a very traditional, plural view of the monarchy, as a set of "peoples," with their own rights, united in the person of the king. That defining these "peoples" according to the American conception is not easy either is another problem, which we will address later.

Finally, there is a last conception of the nation that was profoundly modern and very dependent on the one developed by the French Revolution: Quintana and the other members of his tertulia were its most eloquent spokespersons. To them, the nation was formed by a voluntary

---

837 Martínez Marina 1813, 1988, 130.

838 Ibid., 132.

839 Ibid., 150. This proposition was made in 1813, after the adoption of the 1812 Constitution, something which called into question the representativeness of the Cádiz Cortes.

union of autonomous and equal individuals. Therefore, the nation was a free construction requiring the union of wills. This construction might be inspired by history as a source of experiences, but in essence it did not depend on history, even less so at the time, since the "constitution" inherited from the past bore the hallmark of despotism and contradicted the most basic principles of natural law: equality among men, their freedom, the radical sovereignty of the nation. Although they did not explicitly say so, the nation had yet to be built. Like their French models, they inherited the unitary conception of sovereignty from the era of absolutism, and for them, this new nation was one and indivisible; hence, there could be no representation of the peoples, realms, or cities.[840] This was a logical corollary of their culture and peninsular origin, which the more modern among the Americans would not share. Among the latter, the modern conception of the nation, individualistic and voluntary, often went hand in hand with a plural conception of the monarchy. An original mixture, which would soon be embodied in American federalism, it is one more example of the multiple combinations that the same variables can produce.

These divergent conceptions of the nation would appear clearly throughout the political debates of these years, and would take center stage in the battle that the minority modern group would wage to impose the new understanding of the nation upon a society in which the traditional conceptions predominated.

## Victory of the Modern Nation

The battle for the modern nation was waged on several fronts. The first had an immediate objective: the convocation, modalities, and powers of the Cortes,[841] but it aimed at a more fundamental objective: the rad-

840 See chapter VII for this modern conception of the nation.

841 Suárez's 1982 book follows in its official dimension—within the Junta Central—the major phases of this debate, which at the time was called la grande affaire.

ical transformation of the social imaginary. Through the debates on how to elect the deputies—whether by estates or without class distinction—on how to assemble and vote in the Cortes—whether by branches or indiscriminately—on its powers—whether to reform abuses in the existing laws or to draft a new constitution—what was at stake was in fact the vision of a nation formed either by diverse bodies—kingdoms, cities, estates—or by a whole made up of equal individuals.

Although the traditionalist reaction of the early days did not seem to favor the modern minority, a series of factors provided the basis for carrying out the radical mutation to which this minority aspired. Though the diversity of the social actors in the uprising—provinces, cities, classes, and estates—was obvious, the very unanimity of this uprising and the homogeneity of its traditional references paved the way for conceiving a modern-style unitary nation.

Describing the three days of enthusiastic ceremonies with which Madrid celebrated, in August 1808, the oath of allegiance to Ferdinand VII, Quintana's *Semanario Patriótico*, the organ of the most radical modern group, made evident the process of transmutation of language that would be constantly practiced. The oath-taking ceremony was not only traditional it was even more archaic than usual: under pressure from the people, the cabildo attended dressed in the discarded traditional Spanish garb.[842] But it was precisely the presence and action of this very real "people"—the urban populace in all its diversity, including the "plebs"—that led the writer to imperceptibly shift to the *People*, capitalized and now identified with the modern nation:

> the People had the glory of being the soul, the stimulus and organizer of such an august ceremony. It was the People that inspired in its municipal body the happy idea of attending such an august act *dressed in the ancient and majestic garments which recalled the*

842 This was payback for the measures that led to the Esquilache Riots in 1766. [The Marquis of Esquilache, prime minister of Charles III in 1766, became impopular for various measures, among them forbidding certain traditional Spanish garments.—Trans.]

> *glory, perseverance and valor of our magnanimous grandfathers* [emphasis ours].[843]

This is followed by a description of the decoration, lamps, banners, and inscriptions adorning "all the buildings, from the palaces to the most humble abode," with the presence everywhere of "portraits of our august Monarch," which attract "the gazes of the lover of his Homeland and of the faithful vassal." At last, the great moment arrived for the oath-taking rites of the loyalty:

> Then the banner was raised for King Ferdinand and the oath of loyalty that the Spanish Nation made to its king, using the sacred rights it reclaimed, and by virtue of which it freely and spontaneously ratified the obedience already promised to a Prince, whom it had adored from his cradle, rang out across all of Europe [...].[844]

The people has become the nation, which, having recovered its rights, now concludes a new pact with the king, "freely and spontaneously." But the shift in the meaning of words continues. A few lines later, what could be interpreted in the classic terminology as the pact between king and kingdom becomes the constituent act of a new nation–the mutual and egalitarian pact among Spaniards, with no distinction of belonging to realms or provinces:

> On this august day the Spaniards, too, mutually pledged eternal and close union, seeing themselves from now on as a people of brothers guided by a single, same interest: on this august day the different designations of Realms and Provinces have ceased to exist, and only Spain remains.[845]

---

843 Semanario Patriótico I, no. 5, September 29, 1808, 78–79.

844 Ibid., 80.

845 Ibid., 81.

The inspiration provided by the celebration of the French federation on July 14, 1790, is evident, as is the portrayal of the nation as fraternal, "a people of brothers," which appears so often in the imaginary of the French Revolution as an expression of the modern nation.[846]

The equality—and hostility toward privileges—among the various bodies, based on criteria of social utility and the personal nature of merits, had many precedents in the era of Enlightenment. To this would now be added the equality arising from battle, forged by patriotic enthusiasm and demonstrated by the unitary action of the massive uprising, the *levée en masse* of the French Revolution.[847] How could legal inequality between Spaniards be justified when they were shedding their blood together, when it was, above all, the people that opposed the invader with the greatest energy?

In short, the very crisis that had made the invasion possible, and later even the defeats of the Spanish patriots—whose heroism is never questioned—would be used, after the autumn of 1808, as arguments by the supporters of a complete renovation of the principles and constitution of the monarchy. If the ills were so deeply entrenched, how could merely restoring a historical constitution that had proven incapable of preventing them suffice to eradicate them?

A further element that benefited the supporters of a reconstitution of the nation *a radice*—a refounding—was the very uncertainty of the notion of a historical constitution. It was exciting to talk about winning back the "ancient freedoms" and restoring the "fundamental laws" of the realm, but aside from the rhetorical aspect of these references, what were these laws? Keeping in mind that the old Spain was a plural Spain—the Spains, the different kingdoms—which one should be adopted as a model? Castile before Villalar? The former realms of the Crown of Aragon? The founding of Navarre? The Basque *fueros*?

In fact, the restoration of the old constitution was, like the one the radicals were proposing, a political invention that was equally

846 See Chris Southcott, "Au-délà de la conception politique de la nation," Communications, no. 45 (Paris: Le Seuil, 1987).

847 See Georges Gusdorf, "Le cri de Valmy," in ibid.

dependent on the ongoing debates and the state of opinion. The better informed knew perfectly well that the most ardent defenders of the historical constitution—Jovellanos, for example—were inspired at least as much by the British system as by the old "fundamental laws." So it should be no surprise that the Junta Central, when in May 1809, thanks to a coalition between those who drew on the French model and the historical constitutionalists, announced its intention to convene Cortes, it should also have launched a general consultation in the country so that the enlightened could give their opinion on the modes and role of the future Cortes. As Tocqueville remarked about the identical consultation that Lomenie de Brienne had conducted in France in 1788, to make the constitution a subject of debate meant a shift from the restoration of fundamental laws to modern politics, to the realm of opinion.[848]

The modern elites carried the day thanks to their skill in this battle of nascent "opinion:" thanks to the proliferation of patriotic literature, the discussions in the tertulias, and the deliberations of the provisional government bodies—the provincial juntas and the Junta Central. Over the two years between the summer of 1808 and September 1810, with the meeting of the Cortes, the modern language and imaginary would triumph in peninsular Spain. New words replaced the old ones: "kingdom" became "nation" ; "vassals" and "subjects" became "citizens" and "individuals"; the law in the sense of the general law replaced the freedoms, *fueros*, and privileges; the constitution replaced the fundamental laws. New terms now prevailed and with them new values. "Opinion," seen at first as necessary in an almost "arbitrista[849]" sense, as a means of resolving the problems of the monarchy, began to be seen, first, as an essential manifestation of individual rights, and, a little later, as the true basis of legitimacy—in other words, as the expression of the general will. The rights of man now appeared as primordial, preceding all positive law.

---

848 Suárez 1982, 507–8.

849 The "arbitrista" was a figure of sixteenth- and seventeenth-century Spain, who formulated proposals (called arbitrios) to the King for measures intended to solve the various problems of the kingdom (mostly economic problems).—Trans.

Little by little the "uses" and "customs," the old laws, so revered in the early days of the uprising, became old and tattered privileges that opposed the regeneration of the nation.

> Laws! Yes, Spain has laws; but its citizens are unaware of them: it has laws, but they are submerged in thousands of volumes, buried as if under piles of rubble; it has laws, but many are due to ancient ignorance; thousands to modern whim.[850]

By the autumn of 1809, in the debates over the future Cortes, the laws of the *Partidas*, formerly invoked with veneration, were now discarded as an authority. The division of powers became a basic tenet of the new organization of power; the sole dominion of the monarch, even tempered by the representation of the realm, was being replaced by that of a renovated Cortes. The dualistic vocabulary, so characteristic of the French Revolution and its modernity of rupture, gradually dominated political discourse. We find now the categorical oppositions between the old and the new, darkness and light, despotism and freedom, ignorance and enlightenment...

This evolution is evident in the patriotic and civic catechisms that began to appear. In 1808, the *Catecismo católico-político*, which gave a very classic view of "the social body, in the likeness of the human body" and therefore subject to "certain illnesses," later referred to "the universality of the citizens, or what is the same thing, the nation;" finally, from a pactist perspective, it evoked "the fundamental laws of our wise constitution, to whose observance our Kings pledge themselves in their exaltation to the throne and whose practice has been implemented over many centuries in the convocation of the Cortes."[851]

Two years later, the *Catecismo de doctrina civil*, published in Cádiz in 1810, prior to the Cortes, and bearing the epigraph *Salus populi*

---

850 Semanario Patriótico, Seville, XXIV, July 6, 1809.

851 Catecismo católico-político que con motivo de las actuales novedades de la España: Dirige y dedica a sus Conciudadanos, un Sacerdote amante de la Religión, afecto a su patria, y amigo de los hombres (Madrid: Imprenta de Repullés, 1808), in Catecismos políticos españoles..., 1989, 29 and 33.

*suprema lex esto*, might be said to have crossed the threshold of modernity.[852] Its judgment on the old laws is biting: "Spain has been, for many centuries, the prey of conquerors; and of the feudalists their helpers, so that its history presents nothing but repeated examples of more or less moderate despotism [...]."[853]

The situation now has radically changed, and a new era is dawning on the ruins of "Gothic" oppression:

> the people has recovered its freedom—held captive by so many selfish villains—and has placed itself in the state of anarchy by dissolution, unceasingly demanding order and its rights to form a new society, whose edifice begins with the solid foundations of natural law, and concludes with the most perfect harmony of civil law, while destroying the Gothic fortress built at the expense of the suffering and ignorance of our ancestors.[854]

The old constitutional structure has disappeared, and the people has returned to a state of "anarchy", that is, pre-social, without authorities, prior to the pact that founds society. It is starting from this state that the social pact must be reconstructed in order to form "a new society" founded on the principles of natural law. Quite logically, and as the end result of this evolution, the sovereign nation made its triumphant appearance on the very day of the meeting of the Cortes, on September 24, 1810, with the declaration that was voted late that night: "The deputies who make up this Congress, and who represent the Spanish Nation, declare

---

852 Logically enough, the rest of the catechism, clearly inspired by its French counterparts, devotes a chapter to the "Natural rights of man" and another to "The Estates General and the Constitution," in which the law now appears as the "expression of the general will." Ibid., 57.

853 Catecismo de Doctrina civil por Don Andrés de Moya Luzuriaga (Cádiz: Imprenta de la Junta Superior de Gobierno, 1810), in ibid., 51.

854 Ibid., 51–52.

themselves legitimately constituted in general and extraordinary Cortes, and declare that in these Cortes resides the national Sovereignty."[855]

From this moment on, and despite the resistance of the traditionalists, the Cortes would act as a sovereign assembly and even as a Convention, and one that was indeed very jealous of its sovereignty, as two of the regents called upon to swear fidelity to the Cortes would discover. The bishop of Orense, president of the Regency Council, was dismissed from office and had to go into exile. The marquis del Palacio, who took the oath "without detriment to the vows that I have made to King Ferdinand VII" was also removed, and there was an attempt to prosecute him.[856] The logical conclusion to this full sovereignty would be the drafting of a completely new Constitution, promulgated on March 19, 1812: it would be the key text of Spanish and Hispano-American constitutionalism. It would include a reprinting of the September 1810 declaration, with the same words as the passage that inspired it, taken from the Declaration of the Rights of Man and of the Citizen in the French Constitution of 1791: "Sovereignty resides essentially in the Nation."[857]

Thus, we see that this revolution has altered the very basis of legitimacy: the sovereignty of the nation replaces that of the king; the nation is "constituted", in the strongest sense of the term, that of a radical beginning. However, not everything was so radical nor so clear in this revolution. Indeed, we find many twilight zones both in the texts and in the debates of the period. This primitive ambiguity would influence the entire contemporary history of Spain. The sovereignty of the nation did not completely eliminate the sovereignty of the king, since the Spanish revolutionaries were not fighting against a physically present king, but

---

855 Decree of the Cortes on September 24, 1810, in Colección de todas las órdenes, Decretos y providencias emanadas de las Cortes generales y extraordinarias de los dominios de España e Indias instaladas en la Real Isla de León, 24 de septiembre del año (Tarragona: Brusi, 1810), 16.

856 See Memoria del Obispo de Orense a la Nación Española (a causa de la dimisión que juró de la Presidencia de la Regencia y de la Diputación de Cortes), La Coruña, in the office of the Exacto Correo, 1813, and Castro 1913, 337 and the following pages.

857 Constitución política de la Monarquía española (Cádiz 1812).

in the name of an absent one. In the decree that we just cited, the Cortes proclaimed, on the one hand, the sovereignty of the nation, while on the other: "in complete conformity with the general will, expressed in the strongest and clearest manner, we do recognize, proclaim and again swear fidelity, as to our sole and legitimate king, to Lord Don Ferdinand VII."[858]

Even if we take the reference to the general will literally and make the sovereignty of the king depend upon it, we will see that this sovereignty has not been explicitly discussed. This is because the insurrection was carried out in the name of the captive king's rights, and because the idea of the sovereignty of the monarch was deeply rooted. Whatever the intimate thoughts of the Spanish liberals in this respect, they were forced to act covertly when attempting to introduce their conceptions into a profoundly traditional society. As a result, the political imaginary of the contemporary history of Spain would be marked by the ambiguous continuity of a double sovereignty: that of the king and that of the nation, represented by the Cortes.[859] This attests to the inertia of the social and mental structures that harkened back to the old pactist theory, in which the popular origin of monarchical power went hand in hand with the reciprocal pact between the king and his kingdom.

This persistence of ancient elements explains the predominant use of the term "nation" in relation to the word "people" in official documents. In every ancien régime or traditional society, in which the existence of the individual in society can only be understood through his or her belonging to a group, the term "nation" refers, in a fairly unproblematic way, to a political community of the old type, whose unity was immediately understood and accepted by all. As we have mentioned before, during this period, comparisons of society to the human body, formed by various limbs all governed by a single head, and of social ills to organic phenomena—weakness, corruption, decay—were very widespread. All the more so because the political situation was such as to

---

858 "Decreto de las Cortes del 24 de septiembre de 1810," in Colección....

859 On this issue see the very relevant observations of Sánchez Agesta 1978, 71–101.

inspire fears that the social bonds would be dissolved.[860] The supreme danger, in this view was of course acephaly: after 1808, the formation of juntas would endeavor to remedy this danger in both Spain and America. As stated in a report from Barinas, in Venezuela, upon receiving the news of the formation of the Junta Central:

> the exhilaration and other displays of joy that overwhelmed the whole people when the pealing of bells brought the news are indescribable: men, women, and children speak of nothing else, they say: we are happy, we were born Spaniards, *we have a Head* [emphasis ours], we need not fear.[861]

The constant use of the word "nation" in all official documents is not the result of chance. Although the term "people" frequently appears in debates, newspaper articles, leaflets, and political catechisms, it is practically absent in official texts.[862] For example, in the "Preliminary discourse" which was read by the Constitutional Commission in 1811 in the Cortes and which stands as one of the most important documents of the revolutionary process, the "nation" is continually mentioned. The term "people," on the other hand, does not appear even once in its modern definition, in the singular, but rather always in the plural, alluding to the cities or provinces—in other words, to the old type of political

---

860 Demélas and Saint-Geours 1989 offer a very acute semantic study on the image of the political body, its premises, and consequences.

861 Report by Antonio Moreno to the Count of Floridablanca, in AHN, Estado, papers of the Junta Central, file 54, B, document 47.

862 The revolutionary press of Cádiz is much more radical and the "people," sometimes employed in the Jacobin sense, completely substitutes the "nation" and its ambiguities. See, for example, the article "Rights of Man," published in Cádiz by El Redactor general, in 1811, and reproduced in Mexico in the Correo semanario político y mercantil de México III (1811): 307–9. This is a barely modified translation from the French of 1793. The same thing occurs with the political catechisms written after the installation of the Cortes. For the political catechisms and their French models, see Alfonso Capitán Díaz, Los Catecismos Políticos en España: Un intento de educación cívica del pueblo, Granada, 1978, 135.

communities. The word "nation," which evokes a whole and does not allude to the constitutive components of this whole, made it possible to preserve the ambiguity as to this nation's internal structure, facilitating the introduction of new ideas. Nevertheless, the Constitution itself already illustrated the changes that had taken place: "The Spanish nation is the gathering of all the Spaniards of both hemispheres."[863]

A bit further on, the text specifies this nation's composition, speaking of the rights of "all the individuals that comprise it," with no distinction by estates.[864] The "nation" is made up of equal individuals and is, in turn, sovereign. But even so, this sovereignty of the nation made up of individuals can be interpreted as an intermediate sovereignty: that of the political community, whose ultimate origin is the one true sovereign, God. The solemn preamble of the 1812 Constitution refers us directly to this traditional universe, with which a great many of the Cortes' members, as well as most of the brand-new "citizens", no doubt identified:

> In the name of Almighty God, Father, Son and Holy Spirit, Author and supreme lawgiver of society.
> The general and extraordinary Cortes of the Spanish nation, convinced [...] that the ancient fundamental laws of this Monarchy [...] can duly fulfill the great objective of promoting the glory, prosperity and welfare of the entire nation, decrees the following political constitution for the good governance and proper administration of the state.[865]

The traditionalism of the words is evident: "ancient fundamental laws," "good governance," God... . And yet, some members considered the phrase mentioning God to be insufficient, going to far as to demand a full profession of faith, as was the custom in the Councils of Toledo in the Visigoth era. They also disputed over the precision of the Trinitarian

---

863 Constitución política, 1812, article 12.

864 Ibid., article 4.

865 Ibid., preamble.

formula employed and the possible inclusion of an invocation to the Virgin. Neither the debates nor the petition seemed at all out of place to the deputies, and the commission had to argue that the other articles of faith would be studied in the schools and therefore did not need to be included in the Constitution.[866] The "nation" that deliberates and speaks is also inseparably the Christian "people."

It is no surprise, therefore, that one of the liberal deputies should have published a book on the Cortes entitled *Un Tomista en las Cortes* (*A Thomist in the Cortes*),[867] since the theoretical foundations of the new Constitution might seem to some to be a direct continuation of classic political doctrine. Undoubtedly, the circle that led the revolutionary group was not of that opinion. To them it was a true revolution, although they avoided calling it that, considering how bad revolutionary France's image was at the time. It was a revolution in the most radical sense of the word, since it had to do with the very basis of legitimacy: what the "nation" and its powers were, and what it should be henceforth. The nation was "constituting" itself, beginning to exist in a new fashion; in the strongest sense of the word, it was a new foundation.

In any event, and with the exception of a few radicals, this sovereignty of the "nation" was to be exercised by its representatives. The memory of the French Revolution was still fresh in everyone's mind, as were its deviations: first, the Terror, and later, Napoleonic despotism. The means to avoid these dangers while preserving the same objectives was a well-balanced representative regime that would steer clear both of individual despotism and of "plebeian" anarchy and the tyranny of the demagogues. Very much in tune with French thinking under the Directorate and with Benjamin Constant, and inspired by the British example, the constituent members of the Cortes in1812 believed that being liberals was above all to be "constitutionalists": that meant separating powers, setting limits to the executive, and guaranteeing the rights of the citizen.

---

866 DSCGE, session of August 25, 1811.

867 Joaquín Lorenzo de Villanueva, Las Angélicas Fuentes o el Tomista en las Cortes, Cádiz, 1813. Oddly enough, it was this same Villanueva who in 1793 had published a Catecismo del Estado, inspired by Bossuet, and expressing the most rigorous absolutism.

## American Pactism

So far we have said very little about Spanish America. This is because both the imaginary and the theoretical bases of American political thought at the end of the ancien régime are merely one modality of that vaster whole, the Hispanic monarchy. It is also because, in the early years of the great crisis, the main driving center of the revolution, from which the new ideas and imaginaries were disseminated, was peninsular Spain. With the exception of a tiny minority which had been in direct contact with revolutionary France or had read French or North American works, the new ideas were only massively disseminated in America, after 1808, via the patriotic leaflets and newspapers of the Peninsula, the official decrees of the provisional governments, and, finally, the minutes of the debates in the Cortes.[868]

From 1808 to the formation of the American juntas in 1810, the vocabulary and doctrinal references would be the same as in the Peninsula, although with greater emphasis on the plural nature of the monarchy. The word "nation" applies above all to the monarchy as a whole, but also, in a very classic way, to each one of the realms that comprise it, at times called "peoples"—that is, the total political communities of the ancien régime: kingdoms and city-provinces. And naturally, if we ask ourselves who the depositary of the representation of that old political community was, we are immediately referred to its principal constituent elements: the cities represented by their municipal bodies:

> There is another body in every Spanish kingdoms that immediately represents it [the people] and must be the faithful interpreter of its will. It is called the Municipal Council, *Ayuntamiento*, which is the same as *junta* or assembly, *Cabildo*, from the Latin word *capitulum* [...], and it is simply called the city or villa according to the place that it represents and they are still given the name that is proper to them."[869]

---

868 See "Center and Periphery," in Chapter VIII.

869 Mier 1813, 1990, prologue, 31.

This traditional view of the nation and the people servedat the beginning as the basis for the formation of the autonomous American juntas. Once the unquestionable authority of the king had disappeared, the Americans once again, and with new energy, brought up their old demand, dating back to the sixteenth century, not only to enjoy rights equal to those of the Spaniards of Spain, but even to have precedence over them in their "Kingdoms of the Indies." On what basis should the insurrectional powers of the Peninsula claim to represent the entirety of the Spanish nation "of both hemispheres?" Should not Juntas Generales—also called Cortes or Congresses—be convened in each kingdom in order to provide a new legitimacy to the authorities by including them in the original sovereignty of the "people," of the political community?

This phenomenon, which began in Mexico and Montevideo in 1808, continued in Quito and in Upper Peru in 1809, gathered speed and grew more radical in 1810, when America received the simultaneous news of the advance of French troops in Andalucía, the revolt in Cádiz that toppled the Junta Central—until then recognized throughout America—, and its replacement by a Regency Council. Faced with what seemed to be a governing body born of the insurrection and doomed, perhaps, to an ephemeral existence, first Caracas, then Buenos Aires and, later, various cities of South America proceeded to establish juntas that did not recognize the new provisional government of the Peninsula. The principles invoked to justify the formation of these bodies rested on the same pactist foundations as those which the peninsular juntas had employed two years earlier.

With the demise of the legitimate government of the monarchy—now the Junta Central—power returned to the "peoples," the different political communities that composed the realm.

The Caracas Junta explained this clearly in its first proclamation:

> The Governing Central Junta of the Kingdom, which united the votes of the nation under its supreme authority, has been dissolved and dispersed in that turbulence and haste, and that Sovereignty legally constituted for the preservation of the state has finally been destroyed [...]. In this conflict the inhabitants of Cádiz have organized a new system of Government under the title of Regency [...] [which does not] bring together the general vote of the nation, and

> much less that of these inhabitants, who, as integral parts of the Spanish monarchy, have the legitimate right to take measures for their preservation and safety [...].[870]

The nation continues to be one, the entirety of the monarchy, but the disappearance of the titular head of sovereignty returns it to the "peoples" that make up the nation. This does not imply renouncing either their loyalty to the king, in whose name they will govern, or a general conception of the Spanish nation: "The people of Caracas [...] has debated establishing a provisional Sovereignty in this capital, for itself and the other Peoples of this Province, that they may unite with us, in their customary loyalty to Lord Don Ferdinand VII."[871]

The justification is perfectly coherent and understandable within the frame of reference of a plural monarchy governed by pactist principles. Since the legitimate power of the king has disappeared, political power returns to the nation, that is, to the whole of the monarchy. The provisional power of the Spanish Junta Central, composed of the representatives of the peninsular insurrectional juntas who at the time were the interim representatives of the "peoples" of Spain, was legitimate, especially now that it had finally been recognized by all the American kingdoms and provinces. The latter had sworn loyalty to it as a legitimate government, thereby establishing a new—and voluntary—mutual bond with the authority that was provisionally replacing the king, and which, for this reason, claimed the title of "Majesty."

Peninsular Spain had now broken this new bond without any consultation or consent by the American provinces. Consequently, each political community assumed a portion of that primordial sovereignty. For the time being, the Spanish nation continued to be one, but each "people"— that of Caracas, in this case, followed later by the others—, each principal city with its territory and its dependent cities, constituted

---

870 "Proclama de la Junta de Caracas," April 20, 1810, Gazeta de Caracas II, no. 95, April 27, 1810.

871 Ibid.

a provisional sovereignty while it awaited the reconstitution of a sole and irrefutable sovereignty.

Whether or not this declaration of intent was sincere—no doubt it still was in most cases—the process that would lead to independence had taken a fundamental step. For now, the phenomenon of the formation of government juntas in America was still in line with the formation of juntas in the Peninsula in 1808, and what is actually surprising is that they should not have been established earlier. But this normal reaction came after a series of American disappointments regarding respect for the equality of their rights by the peninsulars, something that had appeared clearly between 1808 and 1810 in the dispute over America's political representation, first in the Junta Central and later in the preparation of the Cortes.[872]

The Regency Council's rejection of these new juntas, seen as preambles to a separatist movement and a sign of disloyalty, would very soon lead to war: fear of independence contributed to hastening it. This war was inevitably a civil war, between the Americans who accepted the new provisional Spanish government and those who rejected it. In the course of this war, the differences, due to geographical origin, existing among the inhabitants of the monarchy—peninsulars and Creoles—would be exacerbated, and the word "nation," which until then had meant the whole of a monarchy sustained by two pillars, the European and the American one, would begin to be used in America to designate the "peoples" that comprised it.

## The Failure of the Plural Monarchy

While in America the process that would lead to independence was underway, in peninsular Spain, the work of the Cortes of Cádiz, by making the Spanish nation a unitary state, was putting a definitive end to the possibility of keeping the realms of the Indies within the monarchy.

872 See chapters IV and VI.

During the first phase of the revolution, in the struggle against absolutism, when it came to contrasting two types of legitimacy, the term "nation" was sufficient without any other qualifier to oppose the absolute power of the king. This was not the case when it came to representing the nation in a congress or in a Cortes of the modern type: then the problem of representation immediately evoked the nation's internal structure. In 1808, for the majority of the population and a large part of the elites, "nation" was still understood in the old manner, as a whole composed of "peoples"-communities, made up in their turn of various groups, estate-based or corporate.

In the peninsular debate on representation, the issue of the representation of the kingdoms and provinces was not central, since the majority of the constitutionalists—both historical and revolutionary—shared a unitary conception of the state and the nation. The debate centered on the representation of only one type of the old groups, that is, the estates: clerics, nobility, and "Estado llano", or commons (also called the Third Estate). No one defended the representation of other bodies for reasons that were both old and modern. Old, because it was felt that the "people," as a human group distinct from the privileged classes, was included in the representation of the principal cities, and these, as district capitals, represented in their turn the villas and towns of their districts.[873] Modern, because those who were debating the convening of the Cortes—the historical constitutionalists and the future liberals—actually shared, except with respect to the estates, the same imaginary of a society formed by individuals. The historical constitutionalists themselves were not opposed to the election of most of the peninsular deputies by all householders and in a number proportional to the total population.

Nor did anyone in the Peninsula defend a representation of the kingdoms and provinces as collective entities independent of their population. In the Cortes of Cádiz this problem did not cause major differences among the deputies, although it could well have done so,

873 Besides, the election of some of the deputies by the old cities with a vote in Cortes and by the cabildos of the American capitals contributed to avoiding a premature clash with traditional mentalities.

considering how deeply rooted communitarian reflexes were. This deep-rootedness was still evident in 1808 in the Peninsula in the formation of the insurrectional juntas and in the very structure of the Junta Central, which was composed of deputies from the provincial juntas; these, in turn, represented in fact the old kingdoms and provinces.

In this area, as in others, the Constitutional Commission relied on traditional references in order to then propose very modern solutions. In its view, its constitutional project contained "Nothing [...] that is not established in the most authentic and solemn manner in the various volumes of the Spanish legislation [...]."[874]

Follows a piece of enthusiastic praise for the old representative institutions of the kingdoms, heirs of the well-worn Germanic liberties dear to the European historical constitutionalists: "The national congresses of the Goths were reborn in the general Cortes of Aragon, Navarre, and Castile [...]."[875]

Then we have a statement, several pages long, completely aligned with historical constitutionalism, which seems more like a lesson in legal history than a parliamentary speech, in which homage is paid, kingdom by kingdom, to the old representative institutions of the realms. One might have expected, though a full restoration of these laws was not proposed, that the kingdoms and provinces that had enjoyed these freedoms would survive, all the more so since in some of them, such as Navarre and the Basque provinces, these institutions remained in force. Nothing of the sort happened, because the principle of the oneness of the nation had already radically prevailed. As we have already pointed out, the oneness resulting from the transformation of the social imaginary during the eighteenth century, especially following the French Revolution, is now presented, on the one hand, as an empirical given, and, on the other, as an undeniable historical fact. The empirical given: the unanimity of the uprisings and the identity of their cultural references.[876] The fact presented as historical is, actually, an intellectual

---

874 Discurso preliminar..., Cádiz, December 24, 1811.

875 Ibid., 71.

876 See "The Monarchy and the Nation," in chapter V.

construct that asserts the existence of a single unitary Spanish nation in the days of the Goths, later broken up into different states:

> The Spaniards at the time of the Goths were a free and independent nation forming a single empire; after the restoration [the reconquest], although still free, they were divided into different states which were more or less independent, depending on the circumstances in which they found themselves when the separate kingdoms were created [...].[877]

The preliminary sentences of the project presented it as a compilation of the ancient laws, "ordered and classified so as to form a system of fundamental and constituent law which might contain, in a connected, harmonious and concordant way, everything that is provided for in the fundamental laws of Aragon, Navarre and Castile;"[878] but very soon, the text affirms that the task is impossible, and declares that only the "spirit" of these laws will be preserved: "How can one possibly hope that, however well-ordered and closely followed, they might offer the nation the brief, clear, and simple tables of the political law of a moderate monarchy?"[879]

Consistently with these proposals, the Constitutional Commission not only does not grant individual status to any of the kingdoms within the single Spanish nation, but even regrets not having been able to carry out a totally new division of the territory, which obviously, as occurred in the revolutionary division of France into departments, would have completely erased the old kingdoms and provinces:

> Since another of the purposes of the Constitution is to preserve the integrity of Spain's territory, we have specified the realms and provinces comprising its empire in both hemispheres, *preserving for the time being* [emphasis ours] the same nomenclature and division

---

877 Discurso preliminar.... Cádiz, December 24, 1811, 76.

878 Ibid., 67–68.

879 Ibid., 76.

> that has existed until now. The Commission would have wished to make a more convenient and proportionate distribution of all the Spanish territory in both worlds [...].[880]

The absolutist reduction of the various peninsular kingdoms to a single homogeneous political unit, as reflected in the eighteenth-century Cortes, had already been fully internalized by all the enlightened elites of the Peninsula.

What was acceptable at the time in the Peninsula was much less so in America, where the plural conception of the monarchy, considered as a whole made up of "peoples"-communities, was still very much alive.[881] This understanding had led to the formation of the autonomous American juntas, and the rejection of these juntas by the Regency Council had led to war. But even those Americans who complied with the Regency Council did not at the time raise this fundamental problem in decisive terms. Some were physically far from the debates and mostly busy at the time with the war against the insurgents. Others, those who were members of the Cortes, found themselves in a rather peculiar situation, which explains their complicated attitude.

The most active segment of the American deputies—the alternates elected in Cádiz in September 1810—were as modern and radical as the peninsular revolutionaries. For them, too, the first objectives to be achieved were the affirmation, against the king, of the nation's sovereignty, the establishment of freedom of the press, the drafting of a new constitution, the destruction of the ancien régime, etc. In all these areas, their alliance with the peninsular liberals was steady and fundamental for the success of these liberals. It was thanks to their votes that freedom of the press was adopted in September 1810, and the same thing would occur later with all the texts expressing the ideological modernity of the Cortes.

880 Ibid., 79–80.

881 On this view, held by the majority of the American deputies in the Cortes, see Varela Suanzes-Carpegna 1983.

Perhaps it was precisely their ideological modernity, which also made them regard the nation as composed of individuals, that explains the attitude they adopted in discussing American problems. Their fundamental objective in this case was to fight for equality of representation between Spain and America. This was their primary objective, which partly explains why, despite their plural conception of the monarchy, they should have accepted the ideas of the peninsular liberals. The demand for equality with the Peninsula, and for the large number of deputies that this equality implied, made them accept, at the time, a unitary conception of the monarchy that was at odds with their own very deeply rooted view of it as a whole made up of different political communities. Nevertheless, their awareness of American particularities continued to be very strong; this can be seen in the fact that the deputies elected in America acted in practice like the former *procuradores* in Cortes defending the instructions received from those they represented. This same view explains why the proposal to establish provincial *diputaciones* (governing councils) should have come precisely from the Mexican Ramos Arizpe, who believed that they should constitute genuine provincial representative governments. His proposal was adopted, but radically transformed, in order to make of these councils mere consultative bodies in charge of advising the political leaders.[882] The new constitution of the monarchy was profoundly unitary.

It would not be until the second Spanish liberal revolution and the advances of the independence movements that the American deputies to the Cortes of Madrid, in 1821, would propose their plan for a plural monarchy, with three American kingdoms endowed with their own representative institutions and an executive power that could be entrusted to three infantes[883]: one that would comprise Mexico and Guatemala, another New Granada and Tierra Firme, and the third, Peru, Buenos Aires, and Chile. As one of its advocates, the Mexican Lucas Alamán,

882 On these diputaciones, see Benson 1955, and Hamnet 1985, 134–36.

883 The infantes were younger sons of the Spanish monarch, or relatives in the line of succession.—Trans.

explained, the idea was to implement the Count of Aranda's old plan and restore the ancient structure of the monarchy in America:

> this system bore a great similarity to the one that was in force in America before the constitution, [...] each one of the large sections of that continent was like a separate monarchy, with all the necessary elements for its internal government, in the image of those established in Spain for the entire monarchy, and now what was being proposed was merely to reduce these elements to the representative order [...].[884]

A proposal which in 1810 or 1811 might have provided the American aspirations for equality and distinctiveness with a possible course of action came too late, and because of this lateness, it continued to clash with the unitary conception of the peninsulars. The Cortes refused even to read the proposal.

## Uncertainties of the Nation in America

The American pro-independence elites, as full participants in the great ideological mutation of the elites in the entire Hispanic world, would use the same conceptual tools as the peninsular liberals to identify the "people"–the old community— with the "nation", and to find in this nation's sovereignty the principle of its independence. As the viceroy of Mexico would say in 1813: the Mexican insurgents used means such as "presenting the liberal principles of the Congress [the Cortes of Cádiz] in a dislocated way, distorting their foundation and sense and considering

884 Alamán 1972, vol. V, 127, the following pages, and 351. The proposal was presented to the Cortes on June 25, 1821; the text of the proposal in ibid., appendixes, document 19.

themselves as a separate nation in applying the consequences of these principles [...]."[885]

However, in the case of America, the transmutation of the nation in the old sense of the word—the traditional political community—into a modern nation and the invocation of its sovereignty presented an unexpected problem: with which political community of the old type should the sovereign nation be identified?

In an early period, which varied from one country to another, all of America was considered as a nation:[886] an "American nation" struggling against the Spanish nation. Since every "nation" is always founded as much on the likeness of its inhabitants among each other as on the difference this community with others of the same order, the context of the war allowed the friend-enemy opposition to become the founding identity trait.

The Americans had in common the sense of belonging to a single political, cultural, and religious whole, elements that in the Europe of the time were all constitutive of nationality and served as a basis forclaiming nation-state status; as a result, it was possible to speak of the "American nation" without much difficulty. The problem arose from the fact that all these elements were also shared by the kingdoms of the Crown of Castile in peninsular Spain,so much so that the cultural differences among these realms of Catalonia, Valencia, or the Basque provinces were incomparably greater than their difference with the American realms. The origin of the American particularity cannot be found here, but rather in a different kind of singularity whose construction had been underway throughout the colonial era, especially in the last third of the eighteenth century, and whose basis could only be geographical.[887]

---

885 Letter of the viceroy of New Spain, Félix María Calleja, to the minister of justice, on June 20, 1813, in De la Torre Villar 1982, vol. III, 491.

886 On this issue, see Géneviève Verdo, "L'américanité: Un pôle structurant de l'indépendance hispanoaméricaine (1808–1830)" (graduate thesis, Université de París I, 1991).

887 On these topics, see Gerbi 1960, for example, 164 and the following pages.

This singularity was based on the distinction of the American continent vis-à-vis Europe and shared many of its arguments with the identity that the British colonies in North America had recently been constructing.[888] This imaginary of "Americanness," in which a strong influence of Thomas Paine can be detected, sought its constituent elements in multiple fields: geography—the distance between the two hemispheres—,nature—animate or inanimate—, myths—the New World considered as a new world—,even in religion, after the French Revolution, with the contrast between pious America and European impiety.[889] Nonetheless, even more important than these elements, which pertained to elite culture, was the lived and vital feeling for the place of birth. It was this difference—and sometimes competition—with the peninsulars that defined what was American; that is, something like an informal personal status within a whole whose human and cultural homogeneity was extraordinary. American identity was real and unitary only in relation to peninsular Spain, and in this sense it was very operational during the War of Independence.

That said, this identity, which defined itself essentially in relation to things Spanish, was too tenuous to provide a solid and lasting basis for the modern nation. At the very moment when the "American nation" was invoked in the battle against the metropolis, the real actors in the struggle and the subjects of the proclaimed sovereignty also appeared: the "peoples," that is to say, all the political communities of the old kind as they existed in America: the realms and the cities.

We have already mentioned that the principal city, with its territory and dependent cities, was the basic political unit in all of Hispanic America and that the realm—the higher political unit—had only achieved a real and indisputable existence in Mexico and Chile.[890] In these last two cases, the assimilation of the realm into the nation was rapid. In the other insurgent regions, the definition of the nation was much more laborious and contentious. When the breaking of the bonds that tied

---

888 For the United States, see Marienstrass 1976 and 1988.

889 For some of these issues, see Gerbi 1960 and Demélas and Saint-Geours 1989.

890 See "The American City as the Basic Political Unit", in chapter 2.

the American realms to the supreme authority of the monarchy led to the proclamation of the sovereignty of the "peoples," it was the principal cities, acting as true city-states, that reassumed sovereignty, issued constitutions,[891] proclaimed independence, went to battle (including with each other): they were the real political actors, the true political communities who fought for independence and ultimately obtained it.

Admittedly, not all of these cities had the same dignity and preeminence; hence the efforst made by the capital cities of the viceroyalties or the independent governorates to recover—even by war—all the jurisdictional space corresponding to the old administrative divisions, of which they had been the capitals. Hence also the long civil struggles among provinces—indeed among cities—of which Venezuela, New Granada, and the Río de la Plata provide so many examples: if the capital cities were demanding their rights against the distant metropolis, if each "people" was recovering its sovereignty, why should the other principal cities accept the domination of the capital cities, acting as new metropolises?

Institutional tradition and old imaginary of the monarchy—or of a realm—composed of "peoples" made possible the breakup of vaster political units. The contradiction between a modern nation which did not yet exist but which was nevertheless invoked as the subject of sovereignty, on the one hand, and on the other, the reality of diverse communities of the older type with their pactist imaginaries explains a large part of the political problems that arose after Independence. The existence of political communities on the old model was easy to administer in a plural and pactist monarchy. It was much less so in an absolute monarchy, and the operation could only be achieved thanks to the traditional elements that still persisted in this now modern system. It was even more difficult in a republic founded on the sole sovereignty of the "people," insofar as this people in fact referred to the "peoples." The Argentine Sarmiento gave a lucid portrayal of this phenomenon when, in 1845, after describing the differences between "the parties that divided all the cities," he attempted to explain "the loosening of

891 It is particularly instructive to consult the constitutions of the cities of New Granada in that first period. See Uribe Vargas 1977, vol. I.

every national tie produced by the revolution of independence": "When authority is removed from one center to establish it somewhere else, it is quite a while before it takes root."[892]

And he immediately related this phenomenon to the change in the type of legitimacy—to the shift from a traditional, historical type of sovereignty to another, modern and contractual one: "*El Republicano* said the other day that 'authority is nothing more than an agreement between the rulers and the ruled [...].'" In his view, it was the reverse:

> Authority is *based on the involuntary consent that a nation gives to a permanent fact.* Where there is deliberation and choice, there is no authority. That state of transition is called federalism; and after every revolution and subsequent change in authority, all nations have their days and attempts at *federation.*[893]

Aside from its doctrinal premises, Sarmiento's comment implicitly makes evident the inexistence of the modern nation—understood as an association of autonomous individuals, the citizens—and, instead, the persistence of that other type of communities, historical in their origins, which were demanding their rights—rights which the new frame of reference was ignoring.

It has sometimes been said that in Hispanic America the state preceded the nation. It would be better to say that the old political communities—realms and cities—preceded both the state and the nation, and that the great task of the nineteenth century for the victors of the Wars of Independence would be, first, to build the state, and then, on that foundation, the nation—the modern one.

---

892 Sarmiento 1845, 1957, 125

893 Ibid.

# X

# The Sovereign People: Uncertainties and Opportunities of the Nineteenth Century

The presence of the term "people" is extraordinarily ubiquitous in both the texts and the political life of the Hispanic countries of the contemporary age. Two apparently contradictory positions regarding this pervasive reference have coexisted for a long time. At first this term was understood to refer to a real actor, so that the "people" mentioned in nineteenth-century speeches and accounts actually "spoke," "desired," or "acted," and moreover, it did so unanimously. Only its enemies, by definition, were not part of it. These facts implied the existence of a single actor, whose feelings, desires, and aspirations were expressed, at times, through certain individuals and, at others, through certain collective actions. However, in most cases it was believed that this implicit actor was oppressed or prevented from expressing itself. The "masses"—the modern version of this single actor—frequently replaced the "people" or alternated with it in contemporary analyses in order to explain how the former, or the latter, remained silent or absent, or, conversely, burst brutally onto the stage of history to become its protagonists and often its martyrs.

A second stance, arising as a reaction to this romantic reading while still sharing several of its assumptions, has erased from the field of research words like "people," "nation," "representation," "citizen" — all of them terms belonging to the political vocabulary that fascinated the nineteenth century. It was said—or thought—that these were mere words, which only served to hide the real problems, namely, the economic and social ones. Hence, prominent historians embraced chronological divisions that downplayed the political dimension, as if economic circumstances sufficed to explain not only the political but also the economic and social rhythms of a given cultural area or country.

Certainly, we need knowledge of economic circumstances in order to comprehend a sequence of important events, but we may wonder to what extent this knowledge suffices for an understanding of historical processes in their entirety, especially the great periods of rupture, like the French Revolution, the Hispanic revolution and the Hispano-American independences, or, closer to our time, the Bolshevik and Mexican Revolutions, or the disintegration of the Soviet Empire.

Can the Hispanic and Independence revolutionsbe considered a mere ripple on the surface of a vaster and more essential movement, that of production, commercial exchanges, investments, etc.? In this type of interpretation, the political and cultural aspects disappear or are relegated to secondary status in a fundamentally different interpretive structure. How can we think that politics and the language that expresses it are insignificant realities or mere masks that hide other problems? On the contrary, all the sources from the period show us that the political dimension was the reason the battles were waged, so many sacrifices endured, and, in many cases, riches and self-interest, even prosperity itself,[894] sacrificed. On what grounds can we consider all of this an illusion and eliminate it from our analysis?

So let us return to the political, in the strongest sense of the word: to the relations among those who constitute society and its cultural codes, whether those of a group or those of a whole made up of social groups at a particular time, since every social relation has a basic cultural content. It is within this framework that we must place the reflection on the "sovereign people," that is, on the principle that legitimizes all the modern regimes and whose adoption represents the fundamental phase of the passage to political modernity. However, the apparent simplicity of this new principle embraced very diverse contents, determined by a variety of political imaginaries: although the word "people" was central to the vocabulary of all nineteenth-century social and political groups,

894 See on this subject the comments in Demélas and Saint-Geours 1989. Also Lucas Alamán's disappointed reflections regarding the Spanish politicians' obsession with constitutional issues while the Spanish Empire was going under; or Bolívar's profoundly pessimistic words, at the end of his life, about Independence as the supreme good to which everyone else had sacrificed themselves.

its significance was not the same for all of them, and its definition was one of the main issues in the political disputes.

First, some semantic explanations are necessary, since the term "people" has a great many meanings. As in French, the "people" can refer to society as a whole, to the entire population of a territory or state, regardless of age, sex or social condition. It can also refer to an actual part of that population, whose borders are hard to define: the set of persons or social groups who do not belong to the world of the powerful; the "people" as opposed to "those on top," the "patricians," the privileged groups. The term "popular party" refers precisely to this sense of the word. A gradual shift in this meaning leads us to the sense of "people" as the masses, the commoners, the rabble: a group that appears from time to time as subject to sporadic turmoil, unforeseeable and sometimes brutal riots and uprisings; this meaning is very similar to that of the *popolo minuto* of the medieval cities of Italy. It is, thus, a social definition—referring to society's lowest, basically urban classes—but above all a cultural one. The term implies manners that are out of tune with those of the elites, modes of judgment that give a greater place to emotion or passions than to reason, and behaviors that clash with what is considered "civilized" conduct. This "plebs," which appeared at times of tension or crisis, though typical of the ancien régime cities , lingered well into the nineteenth century. To this actor, who was potentially present in political life, the age opposed the *hombres de bien* (men of means and standing), whose sphere of action was the world of civilization, and who must confront this ill-defined world that the nineteenth century tended to identify with barbarism.[895]

Another meaning, common to all Latin languages, is the one that was used, especially in the plural, to denote the structured and complete political communities of the ancien régime. The "peoples of Spain," for

895 This terminology of the "men of means and standing" appears, for example, in Mexico in the early 1830s, to describe the administration of Bustamante and Alamán. See Costeloe 1975. The terminology of barbarism, taken from the *Revue des Deux Mondes*, is central to Sarmiento's work, *Facundo, Civilización y Barbarie*, Buenos Aires, 1845, and abounds in Alberdi, *Bases y puntos de partida para la organización de la República argentina*, Buenos Aires, 1858.

example, refers to the communities that formed the Hispanic monarchy: essentially the realms, but also the provinces or principal cities.[896] The international terminology also resorted to this sense, though in a broader form: "civilized peoples," "before the peoples," etc.

And finally, there is another meaning in Spanish that refers to the rural communities, in particular to a kind of municipal corporation of the ancien régime, to which, on another level, the "villas" and "cities" also belonged: that is, those localities that were legal entities recognized by law, having their own authorities, communal property, and spaces and forms of sociability. This is the meaning that inspired the peasant uprisings of the nineteenth and even the twentieth century: these expressions were closely linked to the defense against the attacks of the liberals on the part of these traditional actors, of whom Zapata is the best example.[897]

The force and prestige of these old bodies dating back to the ancien régime were such that it is often difficult to know whether the texts that use the word "peoples" are referring to municipal corporations, broader political communities—provinces or realms—or to the population as a whole. This semantic ambiguity, however, is very significant. In the imaginary of the Hispanic countries, which resembled in this respect other European political imaginaries of the ancien régime, society appears as made up of manifold human communities that inserted themselves into others, forming subsets included in wider groupings, whose lowest level was composed of the towns and cities.

To conclude, we have the meaning that was most frequently used in nineteenth-century political life: the "people" as a principle of legitimacy, the title holder of sovereignty. In contrast to the other meanings, this was an abstract term, referring above all to a principle whose equivalence with the concrete meanings presented above was neither

896 See "The American City as the Basic Political Unit," in chapter II.

897 In the revolutionary plan par excellence of the Zapatistas, the Plan of Ayala, we can see these collective actors very clearly: "the fields, forests, and waters which the landlords, scientists, or caciques shall have usurped [...] the peoples or cities that hold the titles to them will of course enter into immediate possession of this property." Plan of Ayala, November 25, 1911, article 6.

immediate, nor definitive, nor innocent. This sense of the word is the beginning of modern politics, as it emerged first in the French Revolution and later prevailed in the Hispanic revolutions. Thus, in order to understand a large part of the political problems of the nineteenth century, which were so similar in the various countries of the Hispanic world, we need to analyze how this last meaning, which encapsulates the essence of modern politics and many of its ambiguities, ultimately prevailed.

## Defining the People

In 1810, with the victory of the liberals in the Cortes, the concept of the nation as a body of individuals carried the day. The Cádiz Constitution would define the Spanish nation as "the union of all Spaniards of both hemispheres." As in the French revolutionary conception, no estate or corporation could be represented, for none of them was constitutive of the nation: "Just as the different branches have been abolished [...] for the same reason no deputies have been granted to the cities with a vote in Cortes; [...] they are now incorporated into the general population, which will be henceforth the only basis for representation."[898]

That said, this apparent simplicity concealed challenging problems of definition, including the question of which part of the people-population was called upon to effectively exercise sovereignty. As in many of the constitutions of the day, the condition of the citizen is not that of the Spaniard:

> the right of nature is very different from that of the citizen. The citizen, Sir, has very different and broader rights than he who is merely a Spaniard [...] someone who is not of legal age, has been convicted of a crime, is of African descent, or is in the paid service of another, etc., although he be a Spaniard, does not have the right to perform

898 Discurso preliminar..., 85.

> these acts of a citizen until after the time indicated in other [constitutional] articles has elapsed.[899]

The bases of legitimacy are to be found in an abstract entity, which, theoretically, should coincide with the "people"-population. However, this last cannot be the political people, because "citizen" implicitly refers less to the elementary component of the nation than to the individual's independence and dignity.

Social independence is the reason given for excluding minors, servants, and, without expressly stating it, women. In all of these cases, the social individualism of the new imaginary had not yet reached its ultimate consequences. Rather than a society formed by autonomous individuals, what was imagined was a society whose basic political component was the family group in the broad sense of the word: a coherent whole naturally represented by the head of each family. As one of the main pre-liberal newspapers clearly explained: "since the will of each family is included in that of its head by the natural and imprescriptible right of paternity,"[900] the representation of the heads of familieswas that of the entire nation.

The dignity of the citizen was the motive adduced for exclusing those who had been convicted of a crime and those born with the stigma of slavery, however remote. Logically enough, the indigenous population was not excluded: they had always been legally consideredvassals, equal to the others in rights, though members of "another republic."[901] Being a citizen was an honor, and that honor must be unblemished. As a Peruvian member of the Cortes would later state forcefully, with the pride of that urban aristocracy to which a large part of the elites in Spain and even more so in America belonged: "in the republic, citizenship is the

---

899 Address by Arguelles to the Cortes, November 3, 1811, in DSCGE, no. 336, 1754.

900 "Continúa la question IV sobre elecciones," El Espectador Sevillano, Seville, no. 70, December 10, 1809, 277.

901 See the royal decree of the Regency Council of August 20, 1810, which reaffirmed that indigenous people and mestizos must have full participation in the elections to the Cortes. Published by edict of Viceroy Venegas, on December 19, 1810, in AGN, Virreinato, Bandos, vol. 25, file 134.

most glorious and respectable attribute, and it is exclusively through it that one reaches the highest office [...]."[902]

Yet, despite the limitations that reflected the distinction between nobility and plebeians so typical of the ancien régime, or between the people and elites, so pronounced in the mental universe of the Enlightenment, what is curious is that the constitutional provisions led to an extremely broad definition of the political people.

Logically, the above-mentioned conception of the citizen should have led to the exclusion of much of the population from that honor and, thus, to the adoption of a restricted suffrage. But curiously, the Spanish constituent deputies of 1812 and their counterparts in the first American assemblies in fact instituted a nearly universal suffrage that identified the political people with the majority of the male population, with the exceptions cited above.

This does not mean that in the debate preceding the Cortes the opposite solution was not defended:

> in the opinion of the most renowned publicists, this right [to vote in the primary assemblies] should not pertain to the day laborer, whether he be a skilled worker or an artisan, who, lacking any property but that of his work, is indifferent to the country's ills and good fortune [...] [to give the right to vote] to the mass of laborers is to set the lesser interest over the greater, or, what comes to the same thing, to subordinate the classes most interested in the general welfare to the class that, due to its very indigence, must be indifferent to the nation's prosperity or ruin.[903]

The arguments used in Spain to defend a restricted conception of the political people already bear a modern character. "The day laborer should be a mere proletarian. *He should neither pay nor choose.* He must and cannot give anything more than children to defend the homeland:

---

902 José Fausto Carrión, introductory address to the project for a Peruvian Constitution, 1823.

903 "Continúa la questíon IV sobre elecciones," *El Espectador Sevillano*, Seville, no. 71, 281.

the homeland owes him nothing more than the protection of his freedom and property."[904]

Only the "interests"—the proprietors, or the learned men—can conceive the country's general interest. However, in spite of the knowledge that the elites had of the ideas of their time, the broader conception of the political people paradoxically prevailed by force of tradition.

Precisely due to its ambiguous nature—a modern constitution disguised as a restoration of the old fundamental laws—the 1812 Constitution embraced the old ideal of the medieval councils and returned in the legislative elections explicitly to the electoral system in effect since 1767 in the municipalities for the election of *diputados* and síndicos del común, in which all householders took part.[905] In presenting themselves as the restorers of the old freedoms, the liberal group could not easily restrict the extensive suffrage already existing in the municipalities during the absolutist period. They also had to take into account the weight of tradition, insofar as the elites of the time were very conscious of the corporate nature of society and of the strength of the social bonds that organized men as collective actors: family clans, the clienteles of the powerful, he manors and haciendas, peasant communities, indigenous ethnic groups, etc. Nor was there yet any fear that the "plebs", the "rabble" might permanently escapc their control, though it could make itself felt, as always, in urban riots.

---

904 Ibid., 282.

905 See NRLE, Book VII, title XVIII, laws I–IV; Colección de pragmáticas y reales cédulas de su Majestad y autos acordados incluyendo el auto de 5 de mayo de 1766 sobre instrucción y elección de diputados y personero del común, con un tratado de las facultades de los mismos (Girona: Joseph Bro, impresor del Rey, n.d. [undoubtedly after 1788]); and Francisco Javier Guillemon Álvarez, "Campomanes y las reformas en el régimen local: diputados y personeros del Común," Cuadernos de Investigación Histórica, Madrid, no. 1 (1977): 112–35. [The diputados and síndicos del común were positions created by Charles III's 1766 reforms in order to give the common people more participation in municipal affairs; these functionaries were primarily in charge of overseeing food supplies. This use of the term "diputados" should not be confused with the deputies elected to the Junta Central and later to the Cortes.—Trans.]

Nevertheless, their intention to make the right to citizenship dependent on property in the future is clear:

> Nothing anchors the citizen more and strengthens the ties binding him to his country as much as the ownership of land or of the industries connected to it. However, the [Constitutional] Commission [of the Cortes], seeing the present obstacles that prevent the free circulation of land ownership, has decided to suspend the effect of this article until, the hindrances to this kind of property being removed and all the chains that bind it loosed, the future courts may usefully set a time for its application.[906]

So it will not be until the creation of modern property and a system of taxation based on it that the citizen will be identified with the property owner, since in the meantime the weight of taxation fell essentially on the lower classes. And the same thing goes for culture, something that was certainly desirable for that part of the people that must hold citizenship. To explain why this condition was not required at the time, it would be necessary to argue, curiously enough, that the people was not responsible for its ignorance.

We should add, however, that since elections were held in the form of a three-stage indirect suffrage, this mechanism actually reserved the exercise of power to the elites by allowing a progressive selection of the elected candidates in function of their social influence.

The reality of the old structure of society explains what at first glance might seem a mystery: How is it possible that traditional societies like the Spanish one and, *a fortiori*, the American ones, should have been able suddenly to establish such modern political regimes? Regimes founded on freely associated individuals, while society continued to be structured essentially by bonds of the old type, that is, mostly non-contractual. The reasons can be found in the interconnections between the world of modern politics, that is, the world of the elites grouped in different forms of modern sociability and a society ruled by values and ties of the older kind, that is, corporate orcommunitarian.

906 Discurso preliminar..., 85.

The intellectual transformation of the elites in no way prevented society from continuing to see them as their traditional authorities and to ensure their modern election by means of a collective vote ruled by old bonds. In this area, the more universal the suffrage, the easier it was to elect traditional social authorities. Alexis de Tocqueville underscores this phenomenon in France when he recounts his election as a deputy in 1848. The population of Tocqueville quite naturally voted for him, and he tells us: "I have never been surrounded by more respect than since the moment when brutal equality was proclaimed to the four corners of the earth."[907]

With regard to the countries of Hispanic America, this relationship between the elites and society accounts for another perpetual paradox: the very "advanced" nature of the texts and ideological references of their political life. "Advanced," since, for example, all these new countries had experienced only republican regimes, with some short-lived exceptions,[908] whereas Europe continued to be largely monarchical during the greater part of the nineteenth century.

Insofar as the new states had broken with Spain, and, consequently, with the historical legitimacy of the king, no other principle of legitimacy remained to them but the sovereignty of the people. From the standpoint of principles, Hispanic America would always be modern, since it lacked the traditional pole represented in Europe—in Spain, for example—by the sovereignty of the king. Here we find ourselves faced with a demonstration ad absurdum of the importance and the

---

907 Alexis de Tocqueville, Œuvres complètes, vol. XIII, Souvenirs (Paris: Gallimard), 114. The loyalists' demands during the July Monarchy (see Ronsanvallon 1975, 138n4) seem to have been justified by the results of the election, by universal suffrage, to the constituent assembly of 1848 which included a much greater number of large landowners, noblemen, and clerics than any of the July Monarchy assemblies. See Jean-Claude Lamberti, "Tocqueville et la constitution de 1848," Commentaire, Paris, no. 25 (Spring 1984): 141. We might add that the electoral results of 1870 in France, which gave a majority to the monarchists, confirm this interpretation.

908 Both of the known exceptions are Mexican: Iturbide's empire, at the time of Independence, and, later, that of Maximiliano, established, it is true, by French military intervention.

autonomy of the political: the modern ideology of the elites coexisted with the archaism of a society which they governed resorting to values and norms that were different from their own.

It is this distance between the imaginary of the elites and that of the mass of society that accounts for the peculiar features of the vote in the Hispanic countries of the nineteenth century: control of elections by the elites, rigged elections, fraud,[909] and, as a result, the impossibility of bringing down a government in power by means of the vote, and the need for extralegal means toward this end, such as the coup. Several complementary explanations can serve to cast light on these phenomena. The first refers us to the contradiction between the autonomous vote of the modern individual, theoretically independent of the other votes, and a society made up of collective actors of the older type. The only citizens in the modern sense of the word were the members of the elites who had internalized their status as citizens, that is to say, modern democratic culture.

The second explanation undoubtedly has to do with the still partially traditional nature of these same elites. Hypothetically, it would have been possible to imagine a peaceful competition among these elites as heads of the collective actors that they controlled. But the long-standing persistence of the organic imaginary of the "political body" clearly shows that power continued to be understood as concentrated and unified. The ideal continued to be unanimity, and the "parties"—or rather, the political groups that competed for power—were conceived pejoratively as "factions" whose activities led to a "discord" that endangered social cohesion. This fear was indeed justified insofar as the conflict between the political groups led to the gradual exacerbation of the struggle, entailing exiles, confiscation of property, and even summary executions, with their inevitable consequences: a chain of retaliations and vengeance.

The reality of a society composed of collective actors and dominated by the great family clans with their clienteles gave Hispano-American

---

909 For the logic of these political systems, see F. X. Guerra, "Les avatars de la représentation au XIXe siècle," in Georges Couffignal, ed., Réinventer la démocratie. Le défi latino-américain (Paris: FNSP, 1992).

political life during much of the nineteenth century a strong resemblance to the faction struggles in the Spanish cities[910] or the Italian republics of the Middle Ages.[911] As in medieval Italy, the disappearance of an authority higher than that of the city-state and the fight over the distribution of public offices among the members of the family coalitions engendered endless conflicts, in which the rivalry between family clans went hand in hand with the ideological decisions made by the heads of the clans. In this type of dispute, the vote of a theoretically autonomous "citizen" came into contradiction with the system of collective actors to which this citizen belonged; the same thing occured with the free competition of these actors, which was incompatible with the unanimist imaginary of the city as a political body.

The sovereignty of the people, understood as a principle of legitimacy, inevitably led to a "democratic fiction" whose perverse effects would become ever more evident in nineteenth-century America. Elections did not constitute a means of appointing leaders: at best, they merely provided indicators of the influence of the various collective actors; at worst, their results were by the established authorities. Thus, the only road to power was to symbolically assume the representation of the "people." This was a twofold symbolism, that of actions and that of words: the "people" expressed itself through the coup, "acted" through the rebellious chief, and "spoke" through the intellectuals who authored the proclamations that always accompanied the revolt. This double symbolism reveals the two essential components of the political class of the time: the men of arms and those of the pen and the spoken word, the military and the lawyers.

This symbolic representation of the people started early on, from the very beginnings of the revolutionary crisis, and its goal was to legitimize the seizure of power by means not stipulated in the laws. This could be

---

910 See, for example, Bandos y querellas dinásticas en España al final de la Edad Media, proceedings of the colloquium held at the Bibliothèque Espagnole in Paris, May 15 and 16, 1987, Cuadernos de la Biblioteca Española, Paris (1991): 180.

911 See Jacques Heers, Les partis et la vie politique dans l'occident medieval (Paris: PUF, L'historien, 1981).

a revolt led by a small fraction of the elites, as was the case in Aranjuez in 1808 to topple Godoy and proclaim Ferdinand VII king; or an urban demonstration also led by a segment of the elites, like those that took place in 1810 for the establishment of the autonomist juntas in Buenos Aires and in Caracas—"the people of Caracas has resolved to create a provisional sovereignty."[912] It could be a rural uprising, like that of Hidalgo in Mexico in 1810, or a riot by the urban "plebs" combined with a military coup, like the one that allowed Iturbide to proclaim himself emperor of Mexico in 1822, forcing the Congress to proclaim him in its turn: "thus confirming the acclamation of the people and the army."[913]

Here, indeed, as Rocafuerte, one of Iturbide's liberal adversaries, says in an unsigned book, it was the physical pressure of the "most despicable rabble" and the "filthy mob" that forced the Congress to submit. But in the same book, the same author, after mentioning the seventy-two signatories of a proclamation (this time they were members of the elites), did not hesitate to affirm that "they sign in the name of the people."[914] How the status of the "people" was assigned to the real actors varied, but the system of symbolic transfer of the will of the people to one or several men was the same. The substitute representation of the "oppressed people," mentioned in the Constitution of Apatzingán, which was proclaimed by the Mexican insurgents in 1814,[915] would not cease to threaten the governments of the Hispanic countries throughout the nineteenth century, since none of them had arisen as expressions of the actual vote of the "sovereign people." All of them could and did indeed fall into the vicious cycle of those uprisings that were the consequence and cause of the democratic fiction.

912 Proclamation of the Junta of Caracas, April 20, 1801, Gazeta de Caracas, vol. II, no. 95, April 27, 1810.

913 Alamán, 1972, vol. V., 376 and the following pages.

914 See Rocafuerte 1822.

915 Constitution of Apatzingán, October 22, 1814, article 8, in De la Torre Villar 1964.

## Mobilizing the People

Up until now we have dealt with the first period of modern politics in the Hispanic world, taking into account its importance for understanding future evolutions and the structural constants that stem from it. Nevertheless, there is no doubt that the problems posed by the new legitimacy would change over time.

For the first Spanish liberals, the national sovereignty was supposed to lead to the establishment of a "free government." The English model and the influence of Benjamin Constant paradoxically went hand in hand with a contractual notion of society very similar to Rousseau's social contract. The radicalism of the principles ran parallel with the desire to draft a well-ordered constitution informed by the experience of the French Revolution while avoiding the dangers that the predominance of the general will could entail. For this reason, in order to avoid their adversaries' recriminations about their desire for a tabula rasa of the past, the Cádiz liberals took care not to reveal the full implications of their thinking on this point during the debate regarding the Constitution. In the discussion of Article 1, which states that "the Spanish nation is the union of the Spaniards of both hemispheres," they refused to debate the issue of whether the nation was already constituted—with a sovereign and laws—or yet to be constituted; in other words, whether it could be radically founded. Argüelles evaded the controversy by declaring that "this is not about technical or philosophical ideas on the primitive state of society."[916]

The same ambiguity comes to light in the first American constitutions. In the Mexican constitution of 1824, for example, the nation appears as "a human association." But in this new founding pact–the constitution—the goal was not only to reflect the will of the members, but also to build a legal edifice that would collect numerous experiences:

---

916 DSCGE, August 25, 1811. The general will appears explicitly in the Catecismo politico de la Monarquía española, Cádiz, 1812.

"to revive the old republics as well as possible, thanks to the invigorating inspirations of modern geniuses."[917]

In order to achieve this, it was necessary to apply the discoveries of "social science", which for the Mexican constituent delegates of the time were the ideas of Benjamin Constant and the French ideologues: "to search for the constitutive bases of human associations in the immortal works of these sublime geniuses, who have been able to find the lost rights of the human race [...] The time has come to apply these principles."[918]

The period in which these early constitutions were drafted—approximately between 1810 and 1830—allowed the Hispanic liberals to fully situate themselves in the field of European thinking about the conditions of free government. France serves as both an example and a counterexample, as a case study, in order to avoid mistakes that might have disastrous consequences. In the words of the Mexican constituent delegates in 1824, the European experience must allow them to avoid "the bloody and dangerous political revolutions" of Europe. They are obviously referring to France, where "the Marats and the Robespierres, proclaiming these principles, placed themselves above their fellow citizens, and these monsters flooded the most enlightened nation on earth with blood and tears,"[919] before moving on the the despotism of a Caesar and, ultimately, the restoration of the monarchy.

Yet, despite this experience, we might argue that their own evolution was inexorably governed by the logic of the French Revolution. At different moments, which depend on the particular traits of each country–among which cultural modernity and the density of modern forms of sociability take first place—the majority of the Hispanic countries, each in turn, experienced episodes of radicalization, which contemporaries would unhesitatingly describe as "Jacobinism."

The Morenista phase of the Argentine revolution had already been an early episode of this type, due more to its theoretical references than

917 Manifiesto del Congreso constituyente mexicano, 1824, in Tena Ramírez 1967, 161 and the following pages.

918 Ibid.

919 Ibid.

to the actual mobilization of the "plebeians." But it was Spain that truly began this movement with the 1820 liberal revolution, prepared in the numerous Masonic lodges and secret societies in which the persecuted liberals had taken refuge following the restoration of absolutism in 1814. The revolution was markedly radical, due as much to its ideology as to the proliferation of "patriotic societies,"[920] the instrument used by the liberal elite to mobilize the urban "people," and which the most radical wished to convert into a means to direct governance by the people.

Mexico's Lucas Alamán, then a deputy in the Cortes, analyzed the phenomenon with great precision, emphasizing these societies' kinship with the clubs of the French Revolution:

> The legal power of the Cortes was subject to another, more absolute and essentially revolutionary. So-called patriotic societies had been organized that were the public face of secret ones, just as the national guard was their armed forces, and these societies, with headquarters in several Madrid cafés and branches in the provincial capitals, were imitations of the Clubs that formed in France at the start of its revolution.[921]

The Spanish experience did not achieve its ultimate goal, which was the assumption of the people's sovereignty by these societies, for two reasons: on the one hand, the moderate liberal leaders managed to neutralize this attempt at a parallel power and, on the other, Restoration France intervened militarily to restore absolutism in 1823. During their new exile in France and England, the Spanish liberals gradually subscribed to the ideological tendencies prevailing at the time throughout the rest of Europe: the doctrinaire thought that they would introduce into Spain upon their return in 1833.

Mexico, in turn, went through an analogous evolution. The intense struggle that took place among the political groups of the new state led to the founding, in 1825, of the lodges governed by the York Rite,

---

920 See the study by Gil Novales 1975.

921 Alamán 1972, vol. V, 27

opposed to the hitherto dominant adherence to the Scottish Rite. From the start, the new Masonic network described itself as a "popular party." Lorenzo de Zavala, one of its founders, would later say:

> The founding of the York lodges was, it is true, a very important event. Now the popular party was organized and in a short time overcame the Scottish party [...]. The number of lodges reached a total of a hundred and thirty: they were created in every state, and this opened the door to the people, which was entering with zealotry.[922]

At first, the "people" he speaks of was in no way the urban "plebeians" who had proclaimed Iturbide emperor three years earlier. It is actually the urban middle class which was thus entering political life: "All sorts of issues were discussed in the great lodge where deputies, ministers, senators, generals, clerics, governors, merchants and every class of people who had any influence gathered."[923]

But with the political struggle becoming ever fiercer and the revolts growing continual, the Yorkers tried to rally the lower classes of the cities in their favor. At first, they exploited the strong anti-Spanish sentiment to launch a campaign with a markedly social tone, calling for the Spaniards' expulsion. Then, as they began to mobilize and incorporate into their movement the city mob, they took over the role of sole representatives of the nation: "What we call the York party is not this fraction of the nation that has come together in bodies under the York Rite: we call Yorkers all those who cooperate in supporting the essential interests of the nation."[924]

Using the same mechanism of symbolic transfer already used in the Jacobin period of the French Revolution, once they had identified themselves with the nation, the Yorkers gave themselves the name of

---

922 Zavala 1831, 1969, 251–53.

923 Ibid.

924 Correo de la Federación Mexicana, February 22, 1828, cited in Costeloe 1975, 157.

"patriots" and claimed the effective and direct exercise of sovereignty in the name of the people:

> The Mexican people, under the current institutions that fortunately govern it, must be sovereign; on these same principles, the majority of the people must govern; its will must move those who have a power delegated by them because, if not, the Government itself will be a faction that will oppose the general will of the nation.[925]

The political discourse was now approaching rejection of the representative regime and the demand for direct democracy in which, evidently, the "people" would be embodied by the York societies. However, late in 1828, the coup organized by the Yorkers in late 1828 with the support of the societies led to the revolt of the "plebs" of Mexico City and the looting—deliberate or unforeseen?—of the great Parián market, followed by summary executions.[926] This event marked a turning point, after which the York party, loathed and feared by the social elites and abandoned by its more moderate members, began to decline.[927] This type of mobilization of the "plebs" would not be seen again in Mexico. In 1830 General Bustamante came to power and designated Alamán as his chief minister. This marks the beginning of the process aiming to restrict the suffrage: it would lead to the Constitution of 1836, which would attempt to put an end to federalism—based on the sovereignty of the "peoples"-states—and define the political people according to criteria of wealth and culture.

---

925 Ibid., February 9, 1828, ibid., 161.

926 Alamán 1972, vol. V, 529, attributes the looting to Zavala's desire to "attract people of the lower classes to his party"; Costeloe 1975 downplays this episode, which was caused in any case by the popular mobilization initiated by the Yorkers.

927 See Costeloe 1975.

## Redefining the People

In Spain as well as in Mexico, the sovereignty of the people was understood as the exercise of this sovereignty by the people within the institutional framework received from the Cádiz Constitution. That is to say, the existence of an almost universal but indirect suffrage, designed to found a representative regime in which the government, logically, was in the hands of the elites. The system was acceptable and relatively free of risk for the elites, so long as society continued to be traditional. However, the situation became dangerous once the press, the societies, and education allowed a large part of the urban lower classes access to the world of modern politics, paving the way for a fraction of the elites to use the mobilization of this urban "people" as a weapon in the dispute with its adversaries.

Even so, the liberals, whatever their leanings, had to continue opposing the ancien régime and its legitimacy: they were well aware that their final victory depended on their success in transforming traditional society into a modern people. This transformation, to which they aspired without reservation, was described in the following terms by Vicente Rocafuerte, the same writer who had described the Mexican masses as "the indecent mob" and "the most despicable rabble":

> Taking advantage of that pliancy of the people and their ability to enlighten themselves, good patriots will possess the first elements for laying the foundations of the Republic. Let opinion be enlightened through freedom of the press, newspapers, patriotic societies, and republican primers [...].[928]

Hence, it was necessary to pursue two goals at once: on the one hand, remodeling traditional society and, on the other, preventing the logic of the people's sovereignty from endangering the social order. This order seemed to be threatened not only by the mobilization of the urban lower classes but also by the unconstitutional mechanisms used to change governing teams and additionally, in America, by the territorial breakup

928 Rocafuerte 1822, 168.

caused by the national fiction: the fact of attributing sovereignty to nations most of which continued to be fictitious entities.[929]

In order to avoid these dangers, it was necessary to redefine the people and to set some practical and, above all, theoretical limits to the sovereignty of an undifferentiated populace. For the theoretical limits, the liberals drew first on the thought of the French, and later, the Spanish Doctrinaires[930]. France, always a basic intellectual source for the modern political thought of the Hispanic countries, became once again, after 1830, a practical example that could also inspire constitutional solutions. Indeed, the France of the Restoration had been regarded with reserve by the Hispanic liberals, still mired in their struggle against the ancien régime and its historical legitimacy. That is why most countries were amazed to discover the ideas of the French Doctrinaires and their application in the July Monarchy, for these ideas seemed to provide an explanation for the ills they were suffering.

Was this eagerness to seek in Europe, and particularly in France, the solutions of the moment perhaps nothing more than an imitation or fashionable trend—a form of Frenchification or cultural dependency? Certainly, if we think of Latin American nations as countries conquered by Europe and liberated from its control by Independence. Certainly not, if we keep in mind that most of the conquistadors and settlers from Europe remained in America, and it was their descendants, the Creole elites, who carried out the independence process. We must therefore consider Latin America as an integral part of the European area, like the United States, but with different ethnic components and a Mediterranean-style society and culture.

This common belonging to a Latin area is what explains why the passage to modernity, which we have called a "modernity of rupture," was similar in France, Spain, and America. Hence, it is completely normal that the various cultural conjunctions should affect this entire area

---

929 See "Uncertainties of the Nation in America," in chapter IX.

930 The Doctrinaires were a group of French liberal royalists during the Bourbon Restoration and the July Monarchy (in the years 1814-1848, approximately), who favored a form of constitutional monarchy based on a strictly limited suffrage.—Trans.

equally, although with some time lags, and that the political problems and the solutions attempting to address them should have spread from the center to the periphery of this cultural area: from France to Spain and Hispanic America, with Spain often serving as a mediator between the two continents. It was not, therefore, a matter of fashionable trends or influence—although these also existed—but, fundamentally, of a single logic arising from a common birth into modern politics.[931]

In 1845 the Argentine Sarmiento squarely acknowledged the shared cultural belonging, America's peripheral character within the same area, and the reality of Europe's impact on America.

> What must inevitably happen when the foundations of government, the political faith that Europe had given it, were riddled with mistakes, absurd and deceptive theories, and bad principles; because its politicians [those of Argentina] were not expected to know more than the great men of Europe, who hitherto knew nothing about political organization? [...] Buenos Aires professed and believed everything that the learned world of Europe believed and professed.[932]

He also forcefully expressed the transformation caused by the arrival of Doctrinaire thinking:

> Only after the 1830 revolution in France and its incomplete results do the social sciences change course and illusions begin to fade [...] Tocqueville reveals the secret of North America to us for the first time; Sismondi uncovers for us the emptiness of constitutions; Thierry, Michelet, and Guizot, the spirit of history; the revolution of 1830, all the deceptions of Benjamin Constant's constitutionalism; the Spanish revolution, all that is incomplete and backward in our race.[933]

---

931 See chapter I.

932 Sarmiento 1845, 1957, 121–22.

933 Ibid.

We do not, of course, intend to embrace Sarmiento's conclusions, but rather to make evident the change that occurred in the complex of problems faced by the American elites when they came into contact with the French intellectual mutations. The process of territorial disintegration and the "democratic fiction," an expression coined at the time in Alamán's writings, are considered to be the consequences of a theoretical error having to do, above all, with the sovereignty of the people.

The members of the Argentine generation of 1837, who gathered in Marcos Sastre's reading room—Alberdi, Echevarría, and Gutiérrez, among others to whom we may add Sarmiento—were the authors of the Argentine national project and the Constitution of 1853.[934] They recovered the main ideas of the Doctrinaire critique and reformulated the doctrine of rational sovereignty, in terms at times very similar to those of Guizot:

> Collective reason is the only sovereign, and not the collective will [...] From this it follows that the sovereignty of the people can only reside in the people's reason, and only the sensible and rational part of the social community is called upon to exercise it.
> The ignorant portion of the people remains under the tutelage of the law which the consent of the rational people dictates.
> Democracy is not absolute despotism of the masses or of the majorities, but rather the government of reason.[935]

Rational sovereignty provided the theoretical bases for what the modern elites were practicing and knew without daring to express it clearly: that the cultural mutation called modernity was limited to themselves, that is, to a very small minority, while the people, in whose name they

934 For this generation and the development of the social imaginary of modern Argentina, see Pilar González Bernaldo, "Idéologie de la conquête du desert en Argentine" (Masters thesis, Université de Paris I, 1984), 206.

935 Esteban Echevarría, Dogma socialista: first published in 1839 by the newspaper El iniciado, in Uruguay, the work was reedited in 1846 under its current title. Quoted in Alain Rouquié, Pouvoir militaire et société politique en République argentine (Paris: FNSP, 1978), 51.

exercised power, belonged, by virtue of their imaginaries and systems of value, to a different universe: one that these elites, quite naturally, qualified as obscurantist, ignorant or barbaric.

Rational sovereignty and its corollary, "ability-based" suffrage[936]—that is, a suffrage reserved for those able to exercise by virtue of their wealth or culture—aimed to match the theoretical people of sovereignty with the real people of politics. These principles also took away any legal foundation from possible attempts at popular mobilization by elite factions or caudillos like Iturbide in Mexico or Rosas in Buenos Aires. In contrast to France, in Hispanic America it was not so much a matter of "administering a postrevolutionary society" as it was of putting an end to the breakup initiated by the revolution, in order to "save society," construct the nation, and carry out the true revolution by creating the modern people.

During the 1830s, one after another, the main Hispanic countries drafted new constitutions instituting a restricted suffrage inspired by that of the French July Monarchy. The almost universal suffrage of the Cádiz Constitution was everywhere discarded. After facing similar problems, the Hispanic countries aligned themselves with France.

In Chile, a new Constitution inspired by Portales was promulgated in 1833. The longest-lasting one in the country's history, it included specific conditions for exercising the vote: profession, greater age, and literacy.

In Spain, the great French Doctrinaires enjoyed considerable and acknowledged influence. Their ideas set the standard for an entire era and had the support of politicians of the purest liberal affiliation, such as Martínez de la Rosa, Javier de Burgos, or Alcalá Galiano, and also of conservative intellectuals such as Donoso Cortés and Balmes.[937] Drawing on these French theories, they would strive to restrict the principle of national sovereignty by limiting its exercise: "[to] the property-owning, business, and industrial classes [...] belongs the exercise of sovereignty,

936 For the mental universe of the French Doctrinaires, see Ronsanvallon 1975, in particular part III.

937 See Díaz del Corral 1947, and Sánchez Agesta 1978, 144 and the following pages.

because only these classes are intelligent, to these classes alone do political rights belong."[938]

Restricting the suffrage continued to be the most visible application of the sovereignty of intelligence. After 1834, elections to the Cortes of the "Estatuto Real"[939] took place indirectly, as always, but now, additionally, the suffrage was tax-based. In 1836, the vote became direct but restricted: it was limited to those who paid the highest taxes and possessed the greatest professional and intellectual abilities. In 1846, the vote was further restricted by the return to indirect suffrage and very strict limitations based on taxation and "abilities."[940]

In Mexico, after 1830, Alamán and Bustamante —who had pushed the Yorkers out of power—, tried to stabilize the political system, on two fronts in particular. They worked to eliminate, first, the centrifugal tendencies of extreme federalism, and then the deeply rooted practice of vote-buying. The underlying idea was to form a government based on the opinion of those called "hombres de bien" ("men of means and standing") or "upright citizens," and not on the —nonexistent—opinion of the masses:

> The opinion of the masses of the peoples [of the cities and villages? of the states of the federation?] is not corrupted, for it has not been possible to corrupt it; but supposing it to be bad, opinion has only a precarious existence in the indigent masses; and a fleeting one in the town squares and taverns; what, in the long run, determines the fate of the peoples is the opinion of the statesmen, the men of letters, the industrious and upright merchant, of the judge and the jurist, of the military men who have distinguished themselves by

---

938 Juan Donoso Cortés, La ley electoral, cited in Sánchez Agesta 1978.

939 The "Estatuto Real" was a charter promulgated in 1834, after Ferdinand VII's death, by the Queen Regent María Cristina Borbón. It provided for the creation of new Cortes which were a compromise between the old estate-based Cortes and the modern ones. This amounted to an attempt to backtrack from Spanish liberal constitutionalism, in favor of a regime more congenial to the absolutist tradition.—Trans.

940 See Sánchez Agesta 1978, appendix II, 568 and the following pages.

> their feats and of all upright citizens, who are so many sentinels of the social order.[941]

These ideas did not belong exclusively to those who would later be called conservatives: the idea of the "upright citizen" was shared by many of those who would subsequently be considered liberals, such as José María Luis Mora who, in his newspaper *El Observador*, was campaigning at the time to reserve the right to vote to property owners.[942]

The 1830 electoral reforms did not modify in practice the electoral provisions inherited from Cádiz, though they did make fraud difficult. It would not be until the return to power of the centralistas in 1835 that the new Constitution of 1835–36 would establish a radically tax-based suffrage, which meant that even intellectual "abilities" alone did not guarantee the right to citizenship.[943] However, this did not actually resolve anything, because it continued to be impossible to overcome the deep divisions of the political elite, or to eradicate either the power of the provincial oligarchies or the unconstitutional methods of access to power.

Faced with the persistence of these problems, the dispute over the political principles that had served to build the new country became ever more radical, always following the example of France and Spain. In 1840, José María Gutiérrez de Estrada wrote his famous letter to the president of the republic, Bustamante, in which he went one step further and proposed the establishment of a constitutional monarchy in order to adapt the political regime to the social state since, in his view, "in Mexico everything is monarchical." He pointed to the cases of Spain and especially of France during the July Monarchy: this country

---

941 Registro Oficial, March 26, 1830, in Costeloe 1975, 277–78.

942 See Hale 1972, 107 and the following pages, and the article by Mora, "Discurso sobre la necesidad de fijar el derecho de ciudadanía en la República, y hacerlo esencialmente afecto a la propiedad," in Mora 1837, 1963, 630–39.

943 Bases constitucionales, October 23, 1835, and Leyes constitucionales, December 1835–April 1836, in Tena Ramírez 1967.

he considered much more advanced than Mexico, but also pacified by constitutional monarchy.[944]

In 1846, Lucas Alamán's *El Tiempo* took up the monarchical project again, stressing the stability that the monarchy had given to New Spain.[945] He went even further and proposed granting the military, the aristocracy of merit and of wealth, and the clergy a role in the political system that evoked estate-based representation. The controversy over the sovereignty of the people in this first period thus ended in the impossible attempt to restore an ancien régime political structure. The precedents of Maximilian's ill-fated Mexican experiment in empire can already be found in this era of radical debates.

## The Return of the People

In any case, whether in Mexico or anywhere else, there was no stopping the logic of the people's sovereignty when it came to defining the qualities that would make a man a citizen. Every definition of the citizen—whether based on property, profession, culture, etc.—was in continual contradiction with the founding principle of the concept of citizen: a man without attributes or determinations; a logical notion of maximum extension and minimum comprehension, that is, what remains after all particular differences have been eliminated through the exercise of reason. Sooner or later, and as new members of traditional society gradually entered the world of modern political culture, thanks to the press, education, and above all the new forms of sociability, the basic equation of political modernity ($people = individual_1 + individual_2 + \ldots + individual_n$) regained all of its ability to mobilize.

---

944 José María Gutiérrez Estrada, Carta dirigida al Excmo. Sr. Presidente de la República, sobre la necesidad de buscar en una convención el posible remedio de los males que aquejan a la República y opiniones del autor acerca del mismo asunto (Mexico: Cumplido, 1840), 96. See also Hale 1972, 29 and the following pages.

945 Ibid., 32 and the following pages.

Leaving the strictly political field, we might add that in the Hispanic countries, where Catholicism had long been one of the constituent elements of national identity, the sovereignty of the people had hitherto been subordinated to God, "author and supreme lawgiver of society," in the words of the Cádiz Constitution itself. From a logical point of view, the social truth specific to the modern forms of sociability presented an immanent character in contradiction with that ultimate foundation of human society that stood outside of it.[946]

During the 1820s and 1830s, ever-larger groups of liberals began to attribute the failures of the new regimes not to constitutional problems but to the "backward" nature of a society structured by religious values. Constitutional or political problems would soon cease to be the main points of contention in the political debate, leaving the struggles to focus on a much deeper issue: that of the church. Aside from the problems posed by the relations between church and state, the essential debate opposed, on the one hand, the advocates of religion as the ultimate reference of social values, to those who, on the other, adopting more or less radical positions, sought to diminish or eliminate the influence of the church as the keystone of traditional society's system of values.

The theories of Auguste Comte provide a good interpretive key to understanding the contrast between liberals and conservatives from the 1830s–40s onward: precisely around this time, Comte, in the realm of values, was distinguishing between an age governed by divine sovereignty and another ruled by the sovereignty of the people, with its individual values (he added, as a future ideal, a third age, in which the sovereignty of Humanity would reign).[947] This opposition focuses, certainly, on the status of the church, but also on its role in society and, above all, on education, which constitutes the privileged means for the massive creation of the modern people.

In Mexico the confrontation began very early, in 1833, with the educational policy of Gómez Farias. Men who, like Mora, had been

---

946 See Guerra 1985, vol. I, 146 and the following pages.

947 "The supremacy of Humanity replaces henceforth both the sovereignty of God and that of the People [...]." Letter from Comte to Barbès, 1852, in Pierre Arnaud, Politique d'Auguste Comte (Paris: Armand Colin, 1965), 281.

moderate liberals until then, from now on would give priority to the struggle against the church. The same thing occurred during the 1840s in New Granada, where this aspect would be one of the most important elements in the creation of the liberal party.[948]

It is no surprise that in this field, that of values, there should be a very close though not total correlation between the advocates of the individual, as the master of values, and the supporters of the people's radical sovereignty in politics.

The French revolution of 1848, which destroyed the explanatory model of the French Doctrinaires,[949] once again had a catalyzing effect on the Hispanic world, giving new impetus to the mechanisms of opposition to liberal regimes founded on a restricted conception of the people. From now on, the sovereignty of the people would be seen as intimately tied to democracy and universal suffrage.

In 1849, the Colombian liberal youth, most of them students, would in their turn mobilize the urban populace against the conservatives by means of the "democratic societies." Having carried the day with President José H. López, they then set their supporters to spreading this new form of sociability throughout the country. What had been primarily a weapon in the fight against the conservatives them became a social protest movement. In 1854, the liberal party, alarmed at this development, would divide and put an end to this experience.

As in Chile, which had just gone through the same experience with the society "La Igualdad", or in Mexico, during the Yorker period, the Colombian liberal elite would be careful never again to mobilize the urban masses in this way.[950]

In Argentina, the project of the intellectuals of the generation of 1837 was finally implemented in the 1853 Constitution after the fall of Rosas. Even though his main ideas, with their "ability-based" rationale, persisted unchanged throughout this period, the return to universal

---

948 See Fabio Zambrano, "La formation des partis politiques en Colombie, 1830–1858," in Cahiers des Amériques Latines 1 (1985): 37–45.

949 For France, see Ronsanvallon 1975, IX: "1848 comme rupture d'intelligibilité."

950 See Zambrano, loc. cit.

suffrage appeared as such an obvious necessity at this time that the Constitution had to adopt it—though its actual implementation would be based on fraud, thus nullifying in practice the effects of the new dispositions and maintaining de facto the logic of national sovereignty.[951]

In 1849, we also see in Spain the birth of the Democratic Party, some of whose members would be future actors in the Spanish revolution of 1868. This radical or pure liberalism now began to acquire certain features of utopian socialism, but its fundamental characteristic was still the exaltation of the citizen: that is, national sovereignty seen as absolute, individual rights not subordinate to the social order and universal suffrage, understood as democracy.[952]

Following a short-lived victory in 1854, the revolution that the new ideas had been incubating finally erupted in 1868 with a political and religious radicalism all the more intense for being so long in preparation. The removal of the Bourbons led, after the Amadeo de Saboya interlude, to the proclamation of the republic in 1873. This republican endeavor would be constantly threatened, just as it had been in many American countries half a century earlier, both by the instability at the summit of the state—four presidents in three years—and by territorial disintegration at the base. The federalism of the Constitution, inspired by Proudhon's ideas, would give rise to the cantonalista movement: insurrectional juntas multiplied in towns and cities and even went so far as to proclaim the independence of each canton. Sarmiento's reflection in 1845 that "after every revolution and subsequent change of authority, all nations have their days and attempts at *federation*"[953] seemed to be literally fulfilled verbatim with the disappearance of the king's traditional legitimacy. The sovereignty of the "people-nation," once again, was dissolving into the "peoples-communities."

The restoration of the Bourbons in 1876 again, for a time, established a new period of "democratic fiction" for a time. After the revolutionary

---

951 See Rouquie, op. cit., 48 and the following pages.

952 Sánchez Agesta 1978, 267 and the following pages, and A. Eiras Roel, El partido democrático español (1849–1868), Madrid, 1961.

953 Sarmiento 1845, 1957, 125.

phase, Cánovas again brought the key ideas of the doctrinaires to power. Limited suffrage came back into effect, and—an even more important phenomenon—the automatic alternation in power of the "dynastic parties" precluded divisions among the elites and the recourse to armed uprisings, since the opposition party knew that it would return to power thanks to rigged elections. When universal suffrage returned in 1890, this alternation continued thanks to the electoral fraud organized by the most perfect and most brazen caciquista apparatus that Spain has ever known.

Mexico experienced a very similar evolution. A new liberal generation carried out, in 1854, the Ayutla revolution, explicitly modeled on the French revolution of 1848.[954] They, too, wished to recover the full sovereignty of the people, restoring universal suffrage, and seeking to "constitute the nation in the form of a democratic, representative, and popular republic."[955]

Democracy appears here as one of the objectives of the revolution, but this democracy cannot be understood as aiming to adopt a popular government. The constitutional debates certainly established universal suffrage, but the Congress rejected a proposal from the Constitutional Commission to make it direct. According to the constituent delegates, the people still lacked preparation. Did this express fear of a slide into Jacobinism? No doubt this explanation was partly true, since we see appearing, at the time, a spate of revolutionary clubs which aspired to be the people itself, "worthy to govern itself on its own, to elect and judge its leaders, and to enter into the full exercise of its sovereignty."[956]

Actually, after their cautionary experience of the 1820s with the Yorkers, the liberal elite would block the development of this tendency

---

954 The constituent delegates of 1856–57 were certainly influenced by the United States Constitution with regard to federalism, but they mainly draw their ideas from 1848 France: Odilon Barrot, Blanqui, Béranger, Lamartine, etc. See Covo 1982, 105–6.

955 "Preámbulo de la Constitución de 1857," in Tena Ramirez 1967, 606.

956 Zarco, Siglo XIX, August 14, 1855, cited by Jacqueline Covo, "Los clubs en la Revolución de Ayutla," Historia mexicana, no. 103 (January–March 1977): 438 and the following pages.

and would keep these clubs under its control. But the fear that direct universal suffrage, in particular, inspired was essentially based on this elite's awareness of the strength of traditional society and its deep attachment to religious values. Indeed, the anticlerical position, which continued to be a dominant feature of radical liberalism, would cause many riots, and the liberals themselves recognized that it triggered rejection among a vast majority of the population.[957]

To resolve this contradiction between the ideals of the constituent delegates and those of the majority of the people-population, one of the delegates' spokespersons, Zarco, proposed a distinction between the "mob," the "rabble," and the true "people." How to identify this people, to whom sovereignty should belong? By its progressive ideas, especially in the field of religion. Until the population should become the people, democracy consisted of government by a minority bearing the representation of the future people, and which that we could describe as germinal: "the minority of the future marches on and gains proselytes. If the minority speaks the truth, it will soon become the majority, and their idea will prevail."[958]

This future was still very distant. Once the Constitution had been promulgated, the civil wars broke out—the Three Years War, the war against the French intervention—accompanied and followed by agrarian and religious revolts, which would ultimately contribute to usher in the dictatorship of Porfirio Díaz in 1876. With Díaz we see a new commitment to traditional society, but also a new "democratic fiction" entailing, as in Spain, rigged elections. The difference, in this case, was that instead of an automatic alternation, it was the entire liberal elite that exercised power thanks to their personal ties to the caudillo; and this is now an elite unified by the memory of the disintegration caused by the radicals' political project.[959]

---

957 For more extensive details, see Covo 1982, 150 and the following pages.

958 Ponciano Arriaga to the Constituent Congress, cited in ibid., 180.

959 For a more detailed presentation of the democratic fiction during the Porfirista era, see Guerra 1985, vol. I, chapters III and IV.

Over the century's final quarter, various forms of "democratic fiction" would emerge in other areas. Some, as in Venezuela or Guatemala, resembled that of Mexico, with an elite unified by a caudillo; others, as in Argentina, Peru, and later Colombia, would entail, as in Spain, a periodic alternation in power of the different sectors of the elite.

In all of these cases, a new theoretical wave coming out of France—positivism—captured the Hispanic world by providing the modern elites with a new justification for governing society without society's intervention, and with a revolutionary project: that of creating, via economic progress and modern education, a people worthy to exercise its sovereignty.

This was also a temporary solution, of course, pending the new wave of demands that would call these "democratic fiction" regimes into question, starting in the early twentieth century, as the traditional society began its transformation into the modern people by means of the modern economy and education. This would be a new embodiment of the fundamental problem familiar to all the Latin countries in the nineteenth century and which explains the similarity of their political circumstances: the abrupt introduction, in traditional societies, of the imaginary, the institutions, and the practices of modern politics.

# About the Author

François-Xavier Guerra (1942–2002) was a distinguished historian and a leading authority on the political and cultural history of the Hispanic world. A professor at the Université de Paris I Panthéon-Sorbonne and director of the Centre de Recherches d'Histoire de l'Amérique Latine et du Monde Ibérique (CRALMI), Guerra was instrumental in redefining the study of the nineteenth-century Spanish Atlantic.

He is widely recognized as the main creator of the "New Political History" within Hispanic American studies. His methodology went beyond traditional institutional accounts to explore the evolution of political imaginaries, worldviews, and the shift from "corporate" to "individualistic" sociability. By treating the Spanish monarchy and its American territories as a single, interconnected Atlantic cultural space, Guerra's scholarship dismantled nationalist divisions and established a new, transcontinental framework for understanding the birth of modern politics in the nineteenth century.

# Bibliography

The diversity of the topics and the broad scope of the period discussed in these essays make it impossible to give detailed comments on a bibliography that would really need to be enormous. I indicate the most important historiographical interpretations in the introduction and in each chapter. For a recent bibliographical resource, see Christian Hermann, coord., *Les révolutions dans le monde ibérique (1766–1834), Soulèvement national et revolution libérale: état des questions*, vol. I, *La Péninsule* (Bordeaux: Maison des Pays Ibériques, 1989), 260; vol. II, *L'Amérique* (1991), 458. Here I merely provide a list of the main books that I have cited.


Alamán, Lucas. *Historia de México, 1849–52*. Vol. 5. 6th ed. Mexico City: Jus, 1972.

Alcalá Galiano, Antonio. "Recuerdos de un anciano." In *Obras escogidas de D. Antonio Alcalá Galiano*. Vol. 1. Madrid: Biblioteca de Autores Españoles, 1955.

Andrés-Gallego, José, coord. *La crisis de la hegemonía española: Siglo XVII*. Vol. 8, *Historia general de España y América*. Madrid: Rialp, 1986.

Anes Álvarez, Gonzalo. *Economía e "Ilustración" en la España del siglo XVIII*. Barcelona: Ariel, 1969.

Amunátegui, Miguel Luis. *La Crónica de 1810*. Vol. 2. Santiago de Chile: Imprenta de la República 1911.

Anna, Timothy. *España y la Independencia de América*. Mexico City: Fondo de Cultura Económica, 1986 [in English, 1983].

Argüelles, Agustín de. *Examen histórico de la reforma constitucional que hicieron las Cortes Generales y extraordinarias desde que se instalaron en la Isla de León el día 24 de septiembre de 1810, hasta que cerraron en Cádiz sus sesiones el 14 del propio mes de 1813*. Vol. 2. London: Charles Wood and Son, 1835.

Artola, Miguel. *Los afrancesados*. Madrid: Turner, 1976.

Artola, Miguel. *Antiguo régimen y revolución liberal*. Madrid: Ariel, 1979.

Artola, Miguel. *La España de Fernando VII*. Vol. 26, *Historia de España*. 3rd ed. Madrid: Espasa-Calpe, 1983.

Artola, Miguel. *Los orígenes de la España contemporánea*. Vol. 2. Madrid: Instituto de Estudios Políticos, 1959.

Aymes, Jean René. *La guerre d'Indépendance espagnole (1808–1814)*. Paris: Bordas, 1973.

Aymes, Jean René, ed. *España y la Revolución Francesa*. Barcelona: Crítica, 1989.

Baczko, Bronislaw. *Comment sortir de la Terreur? Thermidor et la Révolution*. Paris: Gallimard, 1989.

Beaune, Colette. *Histoire de la Nation France*. Paris: Gallimard, 1985.

Benson, Nettie Lee. *La diputación provincial y el federalismo mexicano*. Mexico City: El Colegio de México, 1955.

Berruezo, María Teresa. *La participación americana en las Cortes de Cádiz (1810–1814)*. Madrid: Centro de Estudios Constitucionales, 1986.

Bolívar, Simón. *Escritos políticos*. Introduction by Graciela Soriano. Madrid: Alianza Editorial, 1975.

Bossuet, Jacques-Bénigne. *Politique tirée des propres paroles de L'Ecriture Sainte*. Critical edition by Jacques Le Brun. Geneva: Librairie Droz, 1967.

Brading, David. *Los orígenes del nacionalismo mexicano*. Mexico City: Era, 1988.

Bravo Ugarte, José. *Periodistas y periódicos mexicanos (hasta 1935, selección)*. Mexico City: Editorial Jus, 1966.

Brenot, Anne-Marie. *Pouvoir et profits au Pérou colonial au XVIIIe siècle : Gouverneurs, clientèles et ventes forcées*. Paris: L'Harmattan, 1989.

Burkholder, Mark, and David Chandler. *From Impotence to Authority: The Spanish Crown and the American Audiencias, 1687–1808*. Columbia, MO: University of Missouri Press, 1977.

Carmagnani, Marcello. *El regreso de los dioses: El proceso de reconstitución de la identidad étnica en Oaxaca. Siglos XVII y XVIII*. Mexico City: Fondo de Cultura Económica, 1988.

Castro, Adolfo de. *Cortes de Cádiz: Complementos de las sesiones verificadas en la isla de Léon y en Cádiz: Extractos de las discusiones, datos, noticias, documentos y discursos publicados en periódicos y folletos de la época*. Vol. 1. Madrid: Prudencio Pérez de Velasco, 1913.

*Catecismos políticos españoles arreglados a las Constituciones del Siglo XIX*. Madrid: Comunidad de Madrid, 1989.

Chavarri Sidera, Pilar. *Las elecciones de diputados a las Cortes generales y extraordinarias (1810–1813)*. Madrid: Centro de Estudios Constitucionales, 1988.

Clément, Jean-Pierre. "Bourgeoisie créole et Lumières: Le cas du *Mercurio Peruano* (1790–1795)." PhD diss., Université de Paris III, 1983.

Cochin, Augustin. *Les sociétés de pensée et la révolution en Bretagne (1788–1789)*. Vol. 2. Paris: Champion, 1925.

Cochin, Augustin. *Les sociétés de pensée et la démocratie moderne : Études d'histoire révolutionnaire*. Paris: Copernic, 1978.

Cochin, Augustin. *L'esprit du jacobinisme*. Paris: Presses Universitaires de France, 1979.

Collier, Simon. *Ideas y política de la Independencia chilena: 1808–1833*. Santiago de Chile: Editorial Andrés Bello, 1977.

Constant, Benjamin. *Ecrits et discours politiques*. Vol. 1, *Des réactions politiques: An V (1796–97)*. Coll. Champs. Preface and notes by Philippe Raynaud. Paris: Flammarion, 1988.

Constant, Benjamin. *De la liberté chez les Modernes: Ecrits politiques*. Coll. Pluriel. Selection, introduction, and notes by Marcel Gauchet. Paris: Le Livre de Poche, 1980.

Corona, Carlos. *Revolución y reacción en el reinado de Carlos IV*. Madrid: Ediciones Rialp, 1957.

Costeloe, Michael. *La primera república federal en México, 1824–1836*. Mexico City: FCE, 1975.

Covo, Jacqueline. "Les idées de la 'Reforma,' au Méxique (1855–1861)." PhD diss., Université Lille III, 1982.

De la Torre Villar, Ernesto. *La Constitución de Apatzingán y los creadores del Estado mexicano*. Mexico City: UNAM, 1964.

De la Torre Villar, Ernesto. *La independencia mexicana*. Vol. 3. Mexico City: Fondo de Cultura Económica, 1982.

Demélas, Marie-Danielle. "L'invention politique: Les cas de la Bolivie, de l'Equateur et du Pérou au XIXe siècle." PhD diss., Université de Toulouse-Le Mirail, 1990.

Demélas, Marie-Danielle, and Yves Saint-Geours. *Jerusalén y Babilonia. Religión y política en el Ecuador: 1780–1880*. Quito: Corporación Editora Nacional, 1988. In French: *Jérusalem et Babylone: Politique et religion en Amérique du Sud. L'Equateur XVIIIe–XIXe siècles*. Paris: Editions Recherche sur les Civilisations, 1989.

Díez del Corral, Luis. *El liberalismo doctrinario*. Madrid: Instituto de Estudios Políticos, 1945.

Dérozier, Albert. *Manuel Joseph Quintana et la naissance du libéralisme en Espagne*. 2 vols. Paris: Annales littéraires de l'Université de Besançon, 1968–70.

Díaz Lois, María Cristina. *Actas de la Comisión de Constitución (1811–1813)*. Madrid: Instituto de Estudios Políticos, 1976.

*Discurso preliminar a la Constitución de 1812*. Cádiz, December 24, 1811. Madrid: Centro de Estudios Constitucionales, 1989.

Domergue, Lucienne. *Le livre en Espagne au temps de la Révolution française*. Lyon: Presses Universitaires de Lyon, 1984.

Domínguez, Jorge. *Insurrección o lealtad. La desintegración del Imperio español en América*. Mexico City: Fondo de Cultura Económica, 1985 [in English, 1980].

Domínguez Ortiz, Antonio. *Sociedad y Estado en el siglo XVIII español*. Barcelona: Ariel, 1976.

Domínguez Ortiz, Antonio. *Instituciones y sociedad en la España de los Austrias*. Barcelona: Ariel, 1985.

Dumont, Louis. *Homo hierarchicus: Essai sur le système de castes?* Paris: Gallimard, 1966.

Dumont, Louis. *Homo æqualis: Genèse et épanouissement de l'idéologie économique*. Paris: Gallimard, 1977.

Dumont, Louis. *Essais sur l'individualisme: Une perspective anthropologique sur l'idéologie moderne*. Paris: Seuil, 1983.

Dupront, Alphonse, and François Furet. *Livre et société dans la France du XVIII siècle*. Vol. 2. Paris and The Hague: Mouton, 1965 and 1970.

Elorza, Antonio. *La ideología liberal en la Ilustración española*. Madrid: Editorial Tecnos, 1970.

Enciso, Luis Miguel, Agustín González Enciso, Teófanes Egido, Maximiliano Barrio, and Rafael Torres Sánchez. *Historia de España*. Vol. 10, *Los Borbones en el siglo XVIII (1700–1808)*. Madrid: Gredos, 1991.

Eyzaguirre, Jaime. *Ideario de la emancipación chilena*. Col. América nuestra. Santiago de Chile: Editorial Universitaria, 1957.

Fernández Martín, Manuel. *Derecho parlamentario español, Colección de Constituciones, disposiciones de carácter constitucional, leyes y decretos electorales para diputados y senadores, y reglamento de las Cortes que han regido en España en el presente siglo*. Vol. 2. Madrid: Impr. De los hijos de J. A. García, 1885.

Ferrer Benimelli, José Antonio. *La masonería española en el siglo XVIII*. Madrid: Siglo XXI, 1974.

Ferrer Benimelli, José Antonio. *Masonería española contemporánea*. Vol. 1, *1808–1868*; vol. 2, *Desde 1868 hasta nuestros días*. Madrid: Siglo XXI, 1980.

Flores Estrada, Álvaro. *Examen imparcial de las disensiones de la América con España, de los medios de su reconciliación y de la prosperidad de todas las naciones*. Cádiz: D. Manuel Ximenez Carreño, 1812.

Florescano, Enrique. *Memoria Mexicana*. Mexico City: Contrapuntos, 1987.

Fuentes, Juan Francisco. *José Marchena, biografía política e intelectual*. Barcelona: Editorial Crítica, 1989.

Furet, François. *Penser la Révolution française*. Paris: Gallimard, 1978.

Furet, François. *La Révolution (1770–1880)*. Vol. 4, *Histoire de France*. Paris: Hachette,1988.

Furet, François, and Jacques Ozouf. *Lire et écrire: L'alphabétisation de Calvin à Jules Ferry*. 2 vols. Paris: Éditions de Minuit, 1977.

Furet, François and Mona Ozouf, eds. *Dictionnaire critique de la Révolution Française*. Paris: Flammarion, 1988.

Furlong, Guillermo. "La Imprenta en Buenos Aires: 1808–1810." In *Historia y bibliografía de las primeras imprentas rioplatenses: 1700–1950*. Vol. 3. Buenos Aires: Librería del Plata, 1959.

Furlong, Guillermo. "La imprenta en Montevideo. 1807–1810." In *Historia y bibliografía de las primeras imprentas rioplatenses: 1700–1950*. Vol. 3. Buenos Aires: Librería del Plata, 1959.

García, Genaro. *Documentos inéditos para la Historia de México*. Vol. 9, *El clero de México y la guerra de la Independencia*. Mexico City: Librería de la vda. de ch. Büvrex, 1910.

Gauchet, Marcel. *La Révolution des Droits de l'Homme*. Paris: Gallimard, 1989.

Gerbi, Antonello. *La disputa del Nuevo Mundo*. Mexico City: FCE, 1960.

Gil Novales, Alberto. *Las sociedades patrióticas (1820–1823)*. 2 vols. Madrid: Tecnos, 1975.

Girardet, Raoul. *Mythes et mythologies politiques*. Paris: Seuil, 1986.

Gisbert, Teresa. *Iconografía y mitos indígenas en el arte*. La Paz: Editorial Gisbert y Cia., 1980.

Gómez Imaz, Manuel. *Guerra de la Independencia: 1808–1814*. Colección de papeles patrióticos. Madrid: Biblioteca Nacional de Madrid, 1868.

Gómez Imaz, Manuel. *Los periódicos durante la guerra de la Independencia (1808–1814)*. Madrid: Tipografía de la Revista de Arch. Bibl. y Museos, 1910.

González, Julio Víctor. *Filiación histórica del gobierno representativo argentino*. Vol. 2. Buenos Aires: Editorial La Vanguardia, 1937.

Grases, Pedro. *La conspiración de Gual y España y el ideario de la Independencia*. 2nd ed. Caracas: Ministerio de Educación, 1978.

Guerra, François-Xavier, ed. *L'Amérique latine face à la Révolution Française: Actes du Colloque de l'AFSSAL. Caravelle: Cahiers du Monde hispanique et luso-brésilien*, no. 54 (1990); *Cahiers des Amériques Latines*, no. 8 (1991).

Guerra, François-Xavier. *Le Mexique de l'Ancien Régime à la Révolution*. 2 vols. Paris: L'Harmattan and Publications de la Sorbonne, 1985. Spanish translation: *México del Antiguo Régimen a la Revolución*. Vol. 2. 2nd ed. Mexico City: Fondo de Cultura Económica, 1990.

Habermas, Jürgen. *L'espace public: Archéologie de la publicité comme dimension constitutive de la société bourgeoise*. French translation. Paris: Payot, 1978.

Hale, Charles Adams. *El liberalismo mexicano en la época de Mora, 1821–1853*. Spanish translation. Mexico City: Siglo XXI, 1972.

Halevy, Ran. *Aux origines de la sociabilité démocratique, les loges maçonniques au XVIIIe siècle*. Paris: Armand Colin, 1980.

Halperin Donghi, Tulio. *Tradición política española e ideología revolucionaria de Mayo*. Colección Biblioteca de América. Buenos Aires: Editorial Universitaria de Buenos Aires, 1961.

Halperin Donghi, Tulio. *Reforma y disolución de los imperios ibéricos, 1750–1850*. Vol. 3, *Historia de América Latina*. Madrid: Alianza Editorial, 1985.

Halperin Donghi, Tulio. *Histoire contemporaine de l'Amérique Latine.* French translation. Paris: Payot, 1972.

Halperin Donghi, Tulio. *La política española en una época revolucionaria, 1790–1820.* Mexico City: Fondo de Cultura Económica, 1985.

Hamnett, Brian R. *Revolución y contrarrevolución en México y el Perú (Liberalismo, realeza y separatismo, 1800–1824).* Spanish translation. Mexico City: Fondo de Cultura Económica, 1978.

Hermann, Christian, coord. *Le premier âge de l'Etat en Espagne (1450–1700).* Paris: Editions du CNRS, 1989.

Hernández y Dávalos, Juan Evaristo. *Colección de documentos para la historia de la Guerra de Independencia de México de 1808 a 1821.* 6 vols. Mexico City: José María Sandoval Printer, 1877–82.

Herr, Richard. *España y la revolución del siglo XVIII.* 2nd ed. Madrid: Aguilar, 1973.

Izard, Miguel. *El miedo a la revolución: La lucha por la libertad en Venezuela, 1777–1830.* Madrid: Tecnos, 1979.

Jovellanos, Gaspar de. *Memoria en que se rebaten las calumnias divulgadas contra los individuos de la junta central y se da razón de la conducta y opiniones del autor desde que recobró su libertad, con nota y apéndices.* Coruña: Office of D. Francisco Cándido Pérez Prieto, 1811.

*La América española en la Época de las Luces.* French-Spanish colloquium, Bordeaux, September 1986. Madrid: Cultura Hispánica, 1988.

"La Constitución de 1812." *Revista de Estudios Políticos* (Madrid) no. 126, commemorative issue (November–December 1962).

*La Constitución de 1812 en la Nueva España.* Vol. 2. Mexico City: Publicaciones del Archivo General de la Nación, 1812.

"La Revolución Francesa: Una de las causas externas del movimiento insurgente." *La masonería en México, siglo XVIII.* Vol. 21. Mexico City: Secretaría de Gobernación y Talleres Gráficos de la Nación, 1929–32.

"La vida colonial: Los precursores ideológicos de la Guerra de Independencia." *Publicaciones del Archivo General de la Nación* I, no. XIII (1789–94).

Langue, Frédérique. "Mines, terre et société à Zacatecas (Mexique) de la fin du XVIIe siècle à l'Indépendance." PhD diss., Université de Paris, 1987.

Leal Curiel, Carole. *El discurso de la fidelidad: Construcción social del espacio como símbolo del poder regio (Venezuela, siglo XVIII)*. Caracas: Biblioteca de la Academia Nacional de la Historia, 1990.

Lefebvre, Georges. *La Grande Peur de 1789*. Paris: Librairie A. Colin, 1932

López, François. *Juan Forner et la crise de la conscience espagnole au XVIIIe siècle*. Bordeaux: École des Hautes Études Hispaniques, 1976.

Lovett, Gabriel H. *La Guerra de la Independencia y el nacimiento de la España contemporánea*. Vol. 1, *El desafío al Viejo Orden*; vol. 2, *La lucha. Dentro y fuera del país*. Barcelona: Ediciones Península, 1975

Maravall, José Antonio. *Estado moderno y mentalidad social, s. XVI–XVII*. Madrid: Ediciones de la Revista de Occidente, 1972.

Marienstras, Elise. *Les mythes fondateurs de la nation américaine*. Paris: Maspero, 1976.

Marienstras, Elise. *Nous le peuple: Les origines du nationalisme américain*. Bibliothèque des Histoires. Paris: Gallimard, 1988.

Martínez de Velasco, Ángel. *La formación de la Junta Central*. Pamplona: Eunsa, 1972.

Martínez Marina, Francisco. *Discurso sobre el origen de la Monarquía y sobre la naturaleza del Gobierno español*. Preliminary study by J. A. Maravall, 1808–1813. Madrid: Centro de Estudios Constitucionales, 1988.

Martínez Marina, Francisco. *Teoría de las Cortes o grandes Juntas nacionales de los Reinos de León y Castilla: Monumento de su constitución política y de la soberanía del pueblo*. Vol. 3. Madrid: Fermín Villalpando, 1813.

Martínez Quinteiro, María Esther. *Los grupos liberales antes de las Cortes de Cádiz*. Madrid: Narcea, 1977.

Medina, José Toribio. *Historia de la imprenta en los antiguos dominios españoles de América y Oceanía*. Vol. 1. Santiago de Chile: Fondo histórico y bibliográfico J. T. Medina, 1958.

Medina, José Toribio. *La imprenta en México*. Vol. 8. Santiago de Chile, 1911; reprinted Amsterdam: N. Israel, 1965.

Mier, Fray Servando Teresa de. *Historia de la revolución de Nueva España (1813)*. Critical edition by André Saint Lu, coord. Marie-Cécile Bénassy. Paris: Publications of the Sorbonne, 1990.

Miquel y Vergés, José María. *La independencia mexicana y la prensa insurrecta*. Mexico City: El Colegio de México, 1941.

Miranda, José. *Las ideas y las instituciones políticas mexicanas*. Mexico City: Universidad Nacional Autónoma de México, 1952.

Mora, José María Luis. *Obras sueltas*. Paris: Librería de Rosa, 1837; 2nd ed. Mexico City: Porrúa, 1963.

Moral Sandoval, Enrique, coord. *España y la Revolución francesa*. Madrid: Editorial Pablo Iglesias, 1989.

Moreno Alonso, Manuel. *La generación española de 1808*. Madrid: Alianza Editorial, 1989.

Nora, Pierre. *Les lieux de la mémoire*. Vol. 1, *La République*. Bibliothèque des Histoires. Paris: Gallimard, 1984.

*Novísima Recopilación de las Leyes de España, mandada formar por el Señor Don Carlos IV.* 6 vols. Madrid: 1807.

O'Phelan Godoy, Scarlett. *Un siglo de rebeliones anticoloniales: Perú y Bolivia. 1700–1783*. Cuzco: Centro Bartolomé de las Casas, 1988.

Ozouf, Mona. *La fête révolutionnaire: 1789–1799*. Paris: Gallimard, 1976.

Parra Pérez, Caracciolo. *Miranda et la Révolution française*. Paris: Pierre Roger, 1927; reedited Caracas: 1989.

Pérez Gilhou, Dardo. *La opinión pública española y las cortes de Cádiz frente a la emancipación hispanoamericana: 1808–1814*. Buenos Aires: Academia Nacional de la Historia, 1981.

Phelan, John Leddy. *The People and the King: The Comunero Revolution in Colombia, 1781*. Madison: University of Wisconsin Press, 1978.

Pons, André. "Blanco White et la crise du Monde hispanique: 1808–1814." PhD diss., Université de Paris III, 1990.

*Problemas de la formación del Estado y de la Nación en Hispanoamérica.* Cologne: Böhlau Verlag Köln Wien, 1984.

*Recopilación de Leyes de los Reynos de las Indias: Mandadas imprimir y publicar por la magestad catholica del rey Don Carlos II nuesstro señor.* Madrid: Julián Paredes, 1681; and vol. 4, facsimile edition. Madrid: Cultura Hispánica, 1973.

Restrepo, José Manuel. *Historia de la Revolución de la República de Colombia (1827)*. Vol. 1. Medellín: Bedout, 1969.

Rieu-Millan, Marie-Laure. *Los diputados americanos en las Cortes de Cádiz*. Biblioteca de Historia de América. Madrid: Consejo Superior de Investigaciones Científicas, 1990.

Rocafuerte, Vicente. *Bosquejo ligerísimo de la Revolución de México, desde el grito de Iguala hasta la proclamación imperial de Iturbide, por un verdadero americano.* Philadelphia: Teracronef and Naroajeb Printers, 1822.

Rodríguez, Mario. *El experimento de Cádiz en Centroamérica: 1808–1826.* Mexico City: Fondo de Cultura Económica, 1984 [in English, 1978].

Roche, Daniel. *Les républicains des lettres, Gens de culture et Lumières au dix-huitième siècle.* Paris: Fayard, 1988.

Ronsanvallon, Pierre. *Le moment Guizot.* Paris: Gallimard, 1975.

Ronsanvallon, Pierre. *L'Etat en France.* L'Univers historique. Paris: Seuil, 1990.

Salvá, Miguel, and Pedro Sainz de Baranda. *Colección de documentos inéditos para la Historia de España.* Vol. 17. Madrid: Imprenta de la viuda de Galero, 1850.

Sánchez Agesta, Luis. *Historia del constitucionalismo español (1808–1936).* 4th ed. Madrid: Instituto de Estudios Políticos, 1978.

Sánchez Agesta, Luis. *El pensamiento político del despotismo ilustrado.* Madrid: Instituto de Estudios Políticos, 1953.

Sanz Cid, Carlos. *La constitución de Bayona.* Madrid: Reus, 1922.

Sarmiento, Domingo Faustino. 1845. *Facundo.* Col. Nuestros clásicos. Mexico City: Universidad Nacional Autónoma de México, 1957.

Seco Serrano, Carlos. *Godoy: El hombre y el político.* Madrid: Espasa-Calpe, 1978.

Silva, Renán. *Prensa y revolución a finales del Siglo XVIII.* Bogotá: Banco de la República, 1988.

Solís, Ramón. *El Cádiz de las Cortes.* Illustrated edition in commemoration of the 175th anniversary of the 1812 Constitution. Madrid: Silex, 1987.

Stoetzer, Otto Carlos. *El pensamiento político en América española durante el período de emancipación (1789–1825).* 2 vols. Madrid: IEP, 1966.

Stoetzer, Otto Carlos. *Las raíces escolásticas de la emancipación de la América española.* Col. de Estudios Políticos. Madrid: Centro de Estudios Constitucionales, 1982.

*Structures et cultures des sociétés ibéro-américaines: Au delà du modèle socio-économique.* Proceedings of the International Colloquium in honor of Professor François Chevalier. Paris: Editions du CNRS, 1990.

Suárez, Federico, ed. *Cortes de Cádiz, 1: Informes oficiales sobre las Cortes.* Vol. 2. Pamplona: Eunsa, 1967–68.

Suárez, Federico. *El proceso de convocatoria de las Cortes, 1808–1810.* Pamplona: Eunsa, 1982.

Tanck de Estrada, Dorothy. *La educación ilustrada (1786–1836).* Mexico City: El Colegio de México, 1977.

Tena Ramírez, Felipe. *Leyes fundamentales de México.* 3rd ed. Mexico City: Porrúa, 1967.

Torres, Camilo. *Memorial de agravios: Representación del cabildo de Santa Fe a la Suprema Junta Central de España..., 1809.* Facsimile of the 1st edition, 1832. Bogotá: Librería Voluntad, 1960.

Varela Suanzes-Carpegna, Joaquín. *La teoría del Estado en los orígenes del constitucionalismo hispánico (Las Cortes de Cádiz).* Madrid: Centro de Estudios Políticos y Constitucionales, 1983.

Uribe Vargas, Diego. *Las constituciones de Colombia.* Vol. 2. Madrid: Cultura Hispánica, 1977.

Verdevoye, Paul. *Domingo Faustino Sarmiento educador y publicista.* Paris: Institut des Hautes Études de l'Amérique Latine, 1963.

Vovelle, Michel, ed. *L'Image de la Révolution française.* 3 vols. Proceedings of the World Congress for the Bicentennial of the French Revolution. Paris and Oxford: Pergamon Press, 1989.

Zavala, Lorenzo de. *Ensayo histórico de las revoluciones de México desde 1808 hasta 1830.* Paris: P. Dupont et G.-Laguionie, 1831. Reedited in *Obras, Historiador y representante popular.* Mexico City: Porrúa, 1969.

# Index

## A

## D

## E

## F

## H

## K



## L

**M**

## N

## Q



## R

## S

## T

**W**



**Y**



**Z**

# About LASA Press

LASA Press is the open access publishing house of the Latin American Studies Association (LASA), dedicated to academic research related to Latin America. It seeks to contribute to the dissemination of knowledge through the publication of new research and translations of fundamental works on Latin America from a variety of disciplinary perspectives. It gives priority to proposals that are relevant to the region as a whole, contribute to defining the public agenda, and serve as a bridge between cultures, languages, and academic traditions, thereby extending the impact of Latin American knowledge throughout the world.

www.ingramcontent.com/pod-product-compliance
Lightning Source LLC
LaVergne TN
LVHW041055080826
845145LV00007B/1579

* 9 7 8 1 9 5 1 6 3 4 6 2 9 *